SACHIN
TENDULKAR

Playing It My Way

Playing it My Way

My Autobiography

Sachin Tendulkar

with Boria Majumdar

HODDER

First published in Great Britain in 2014 by Hodder & Stoughton
An Hachette UK company

First published in paperback in 2015

1

A CIP catalogue record for this title is available from the British Library

Paperback ISBN 978 1 473 60517 6
Ebook ISBN 978 1 473 60519 0

Typeset in Swift-Light by Palimpsest Book Production Ltd, Falkirk, Stirlingshire

Printed and bound by Clays Ltd, St Ives plc

Hodder & Stoughton policy is to use papers that are natural, renewable
and recyclable products and made from wood grown in sustainable forests. The
logging and manufacturing processes are expected to conform
to the environmental regulations of the country of origin.

Hodder & Stoughton Ltd
Carmelite House
50 Victoria Embankment
London EC4Y 0DZ

www.hodder.co.uk

To all my fellow Indians.

The author's proceeds from this book
will be used to support two charitable causes:
the alleviation of malnutrition in children
and the provision of clean water
to the underprivileged.

Contents

ACKNOWLEDGEMENTS

Who do I acknowledge first and how do I acknowledge the millions of cricket supporters who have stood by me throughout my career? My simple answer is to dedicate this book to those fans for their unwavering support and encouragement.

The others who need to be thanked profoundly must quite obviously start with Anjali, my devoted wife and partner in everything, who felt I could and should tell my story for posterity. My readers will know if I have managed to do so well enough.

Sincere thanks must also go to the following:

Ajit, who grew up with me and made me the cricketer I was, and who shared my passion for telling my story. Thanks to him for reading and commenting on the drafts.

Arjun and Sara, who when they read this book will know how much I have always loved them and how I felt at not being with them more as they were growing up.

Aparna Santhanam, family friend and much more, who was a real inspiration at the writing stage. She read each chapter and her suggestions proved invaluable.

Vinod Naidu, my manager and good friend, for putting the idea of an autobiography to me in the first place and more importantly for being someone I have always been able to depend on for guidance in commercial matters over the past decade.

Amit Bhangar, for constantly but gently reminding me of the deadlines and pushing me to complete the book in the time frame we were given.

Roddy Bloomfield, my publisher, who has worked closely with me on the book from start to finish and who is a man whose judgement I have been able to trust; Fiona Rose, his able and helpful editorial assistant at Hodder; Tim Waller, the external editor, who has helped to shape and refine the manuscript.

Finally, to Boria Majumdar, friend and co-writer. By sheer persistence he managed to persuade me over the last three years to spend endless sessions reflecting on every aspect of my life. His infectious enthusiasm and intelligent questions got me fully involved in animated, thoughtful and enjoyable discussion. Through his commitment and focus he has been able to convey the whole story in my own words, impressively expressing my thoughts.

PHOTOGRAPHIC ACKNOWLEDGEMENTS

The author and publisher would like to thank the following for permission to reproduce photographs:

Arif Ali/AFP/Getty Images, Tony Ashby/AFP/Getty Images, Barry Batchelor/Press Association, Ted Blackbrow/Daily Mail/Rex Features, Hamish Blair/Getty Images, Philip Brown, Suman Chattopadhyay/Aajkaal & Sangbad Pratidin, Victor Crawshaw/Mirrorpix, Arko Datta/Reuters/Action Images, Patrick Eagar/Getty Images, John Giles/Press Association, David Gray/Reuters/Action Images, Rob Griffith/AP/Press Association, Fiona Hansen/Press Association, Julian Herbert/Getty Images, Sajjad Hussain/AFP/Getty Images, Matthew Impey/Patrick Eagar Photography, Kamal Julka, Atul Kasbekar, Kamal Kishore/Reuters/Action Images, Narender Kumar, Sunil Malhotra/Reuters/Action Images, Rafiq Maqbool/AP/Press Association, Clive Mason/Getty Images, Graham Morris/Cricketpix, Indranil Mukherjee/AFP/Getty Images, David Munden/Popperfoto/Getty Images, Rebecca Naden/Press Association, Prakash Parsekar/AFP/Getty Images, Bipin Patel, Pal Pillai/AFP/Getty Images, Ben Radford/Getty Images, Tom Shaw/Getty Images, Milind Shelte/India Today Group/Getty Images, Prakash Singh/AFP/Getty Images, Prakash Singh/AP/Press Association, Sky Tower Official Photographer, Divyakant Solanki/EPA/Corbis, Darren Staples/Reuters/Action Images, Michael Steele/Getty Images, Manan Vatsyayana/AFP/Getty Images, William West/AFP/Getty Images.

Other photographs are from private collections.

PROLOGUE

On 16 November 2013, my cricketing journey finally came to an end at the Wankhede Stadium. After somehow managing to complete my farewell speech, I was having a conversation with my family, trying to soak in every moment, when my team-mate Virat Kohli walked up to me. He said, '*Paaji aapne kaha thha aap ko yaad dilaane ke liye ki aapko pitch pe jaana hai.*' (You asked me to remind you that you had to go to the pitch one final time.) To be honest, I hadn't forgotten; I was just trying to put the moment off for a little longer. It was to be my final visit to the 22 yards that had nurtured and cared for me for so long.

As I walked across the outfield I knew so well, my mind was a complete blank. A lump was forming in my throat as I reached the pitch to pay my final regards. I was there for barely fifteen seconds and all I said was, 'Thank you for taking care of me.' As I headed back to the pavilion for the last time, my mind was suddenly a muddle of memories. In a matter of seconds I had traversed the entire twenty-four-year journey of my career – from my first net session with my coach Ramakant Achrekar, to getting out for 74 in my final Test innings against the West Indies.

It seems to me that no autobiography can claim to document every detail of the author's life. That's impossible. There are bound to be issues that can't be written about for one reason or another, events that are too personal or perhaps too sensitive. Yet I have set out to make this account of my career as close to the full story as I can. Many of the events I describe are, of course, well-known to cricket fans, but I have also tried to talk about a number of things I have not addressed in public before, some of them a little embarrassing, and I hope that readers will find plenty to interest them.

Before starting this book, I had to think long and hard about whether it was the right thing to do. It wasn't an easy decision. I am not in the habit of being sensational for the sake of it or saying things to ruffle feathers. That's just not me. However, I knew that if I agreed to write my story, I would have to be completely honest, as that's the way I have always played the game.

So here I am, at the end of my final innings, having taken that last walk back to the pavilion, ready to recount as many incidents as I can remember from a career in which I was lucky enough to be able to spend my time Playing It My Way.

hallmarks and I owe a lot of my personality to my upbringing. Despite all my unreasonableness and all the embarrassments I caused them, my parents never gave up on me. In fact, I have often wondered just how they managed to cope with such a naughty child. Though he must have been pushed to the limits sometimes, my father would never shout at me and was always patient when dealing with my mischief. This added to my respect for my father as I grew older. Losing him during the 1999 World Cup in England remains one of the most traumatic moments of my life and I will forever remain indebted to him for helping me become the human being that I am.

My mother, the best cook in the world for me, will do anything to see a smile on my face. She used to make the most delicious fish and prawn curry, *baigan bharta* (smoked brinjal/aubergine dish) and *varan bhaat* (lentils and rice) for us at home, and I owe my appetite and love of food to her. I fondly remember lying on her lap after eating delicious home-cooked meals, as she sang the most beautiful songs while trying to get me off to sleep. Listening to her while dozing off at the end of the day instilled in me a love for music that has remained with me to this day.

My brothers, Nitin and Ajit, have always backed me in my endeav-ours and, on the cricket side, I owe a lot to Ajit, who is ten years older than me and was a good club cricketer himself but decided to sacrifice his own career to help me achieve my potential. As I said in my farewell speech after my final Test, Ajit and I lived the dream together and he was always my most trusted critic and sounding board. I may have scored the runs, but Ajit was always there with me in spirit, trying to put me right whenever I made a mistake. Even after my last Test innings, we had a discussion about how I had got out and what I had done wrong, despite knowing I'd never play for India again. Ajit is not just my brother, but my closest friend as well. He was always available when I needed him and always put my cricket before his own work.

My eldest brother, Nitin, easily the most creative of the siblings, was the strict disciplinarian in the Tendulkar household and helped rein in my exuberance when my mother had almost given up on me. He not only sketches really well, but is also an accomplished writer and poet and has recently written songs for a movie. Nitin, initially a chemistry teacher, subsequently worked for Air India and I remember on one occasion, when I was ten, his flight was delayed and he had to wait at the Centaur (now Sahara Star) hotel in Mumbai. Ajit and I went to have dinner in his room and for the first time in my life I tasted tandoori chicken, which subsequently became one of my favourite dishes.

Savita, my sister, gave me my first cricket bat. She travelled to Kashmir for a holiday when I was five and brought me back a Kashmir willow bat. She is easily the calmest of the siblings and has a very reserved and composed demeanour. She stays unruffled in difficult situations and we often consulted her on critical matters while growing up. When she got married, I, not knowing much about rituals and customs, tried to insist that my brother-in-law should come and stay with us rather than Savita having to go away. I did not want to let her go and I must say I missed her terribly when she left home.

Never sitting still

Undoubtedly I had a fascinating childhood. My early years were never boring; in fact, quite the opposite. I can trace a lot of the stamina and inner strength that sustained me during my cricket career to those early years, which were full of fun.

We had moved to Sahitya Sahawas in 1971. In my early years, there was a great deal of construction work taking place there. This gave me and my friends the opportunity to play quite a few pranks on our neighbours. While we were never violent and never caused bodily harm to others, I'm ashamed to admit we sometimes enjoyed having a laugh at the expense of other members of the colony. For us it was fun, plain and simple, but looking back now at some of the mischief we got up to is rather embarrassing.

One of our regular tricks was to dig a deep hole in the sand left behind by the contractors and cover it with newspapers before disguising it with sand. Then we'd deliberately lure people to walk over it. As they sank into the crater, we'd be in fits of laughter. Another was to pour water on unsuspecting passers-by from our apartment on the fourth floor, and I remember that feasting on mangoes picked from trees we weren't supposed to touch was also a favourite pastime. The forbidden nature of the act made it even more compelling and the complaints that would follow did little to put us off. Finally – and this is very embarrassing, looking back now – my friends and I would take pride in locking people in their flats. It wasn't dangerous, but the resulting delay, which must have caused them immense frustration, seemed very funny at the time.

As a child I was first enrolled at the Indian Education Society's New English School in Bandra. I was a reasonable student and though I was never a class-topper, I did not languish at the bottom either. While school wasn't altogether boring, the best time of the year was the two-month-long summer break. During the holiday period, I'd hurry down from our apartment at 9 a.m. and would be out in the sun playing for the rest of the day. The domestic help, Lakshmibai, (a common phenomenon in households where both parents were working) would have to bring down my glass of milk and sometimes she would also have to bring out my lunch, because I'd refuse to go up to our apartment.

The sweltering heat was never a distraction and I'd be out playing till late in the evening. In fact, even after most of my friends had disappeared to their apartments, I would be out alone trying to amuse myself. There were seven or eight blocks in the colony and sometimes I'd just run around them to expend energy. I'd run seven or eight laps on the trot and do so barefoot. Only when my brother Nitin instructed me to go up would I rush back. I was a little scared of him. He generally didn't say much to me but when he did it was always the final word. If my mother grew tired of trying to persuade me to come in, she would ask Nitin to perform the task.

In our two-bedroom apartment, the four children would all sleep together in one of the bedrooms. I was always the last one to drop off and would keep tossing and turning as the others drifted off. Often, while they'd be lying north–south, I'd end up stretched out east–west, and I'd receive a mouthful when they woke up to find me lying across them. The reprimands were part of the bonding and I never took them to heart. The whole experience brought us closer together.

A first taste of Chinese food

As a child I loved food. I grew up eating my mother's wonderful Maharashtrian home cooking and it wasn't till I was nine years old that I first tried Chinese food. In the early 1980s Chinese cuisine was becoming popular in Mumbai and, having heard so much about it, my colony friends made a plan to go out for a meal together. We each contributed ten rupees – which was a lot of money for me at the time – and I was excited about trying something new. The evening, however, turned out to be a disaster as I paid the price for being one of the youngest in the group.

In the restaurant we ordered chicken and sweetcorn soup as a starter. We were sitting at a long table and by the time the soup travelled to me at the far end, there was hardly anything left. The older members of the gang had finished off most of it, leaving very little for us younger ones. The same thing happened with the fried rice and chow mein and I barely managed to get two spoonfuls of each. The older boys had a great evening at our expense but I returned home hungry and thirsty.

Dreaming of a bicycle

As a kid I could also be quite obstinate. While most of my friends had their own bicycles, I did not and I was determined to have one. My father didn't really like saying no to me and tried to placate me by saying he'd buy me one in a few weeks. From a financial point of view, it wasn't easy to bring up four children in Mumbai, but our parents never let us feel any pressure. Not knowing what they had to go through, I remained determined to have my bicycle and refused to go outside and play till I had a new one to show off. It seems a little ridiculous now, but the truth is I didn't go out to play for a whole week. I just stood on the balcony and sulked and tried to guilt-trip my parents into buying me a bicycle.

It was on one of these days that I gave them a real scare. Ours was a fourth-floor apartment with a small balcony with a grille. As a small child, I couldn't see over the top and, with curiosity often getting the better of me, I would try to get my head through the grille. On this occasion it resulted in disaster. While I succeeded in pushing my head through, I couldn't get it back in and was stuck there for more than thirty minutes. My parents were flustered to start with, but quickly regained composure. After plenty of oil was squirted on my head, my mother finally pulled me out.

Seeing my desperation and worried about what I might get up to next, my father rearranged his finances to buy me a brand-new bicycle. I still don't know what adjustments he had to make to do so. Nor was I concerned at the time. All I cared about was the bicycle and I immediately showed it off to all my friends. However, my joy was short-lived as I met with a serious accident within hours of getting my precious new bicycle. A fruit and vegetable seller pushing a cart had come to the colony. As we came face to face, I was riding too fast and couldn't slow down in time. New to the bicycle, I applied the wrong brake and, bang, I hit the cart head on, lost control and was tossed into the air. As I looked down on the world, my only concern was what would happen to my new bicycle. When I came crashing back down, one of the spokes went through the skin just above my right eye. The cut was deep and blood was gushing out of the wound. Far more importantly, my bicycle was badly damaged.

News soon reached home that I had hurt myself and my parents were very concerned. I tried to be brave and made out that it was only a minor wound. It wasn't, and my father had to take me to a plastic surgeon friend of his, who put eight stitches just above the right eye. He gave me a couple of injections and I returned home feeling sorry for myself and frustrated. My mangled bicycle was parked close to our apartment, but my father told me that I wasn't allowed near it until the wound had healed and that he'd get it repaired in the interim. This time I had to give in, knowing it was the only way I'd get it back.

As soon as I'd recovered, I resumed cycling, and within a few months had become an accomplished biker. I could slow-cycle better than most kids and even went on to win a race organized in the colony. I rode with passion and within a few months had developed the ability to skid on one wheel, which took all my friends by surprise. In areas of the colony where there was sand on the concrete, I could get the wheels to skid for ten to fifteen feet, with my body bent at forty-five degrees. I wasn't bothered about what this was doing to the tyres, of course, as the larger the distance covered, the better I felt. Showing off my skills used to give me a thrill and what added to the fun was that I had learnt these tricks in quick time.

Nevertheless, things went wrong sometimes, causing me plenty of embarrassment and pain. In fact, I think I can trace my ability to withstand pain to my exploits as a child. I'd often get cut or hurt but rarely mentioned these minor accidents to anyone at home. So much so that my father got into the habit of examining my body when I was sleeping to check whether I'd injured myself. If he saw me wince in pain, he'd know I'd done something to myself again and he would take me to the doctor the next day.

No matter what I'd done, though, my father would never shout or scream at me. More often than not, he'd try to set out the reasons why I should or shouldn't do certain things, and his explanations left behind a lasting impact. My father's sense of reason was his biggest virtue and I try to act in the same way with my children.

In the wars again

I had a lot of adventures as a child, but one that stands out is when I was cut under my eye while playing at Shivaji Park, the breeding ground of cricketers in Mumbai, and had to return home covered in blood. I was captaining my team in a match at Shivaji Park when I was twelve and after our wicketkeeper got injured I asked my team-mates if anyone could keep wicket. No one volunteered and somewhat reluctantly I stepped up to the challenge, even though I'd never tried it before. I was uncomfortable standing in the unfamiliar position behind the stumps and soon missed a nick. The ball came at me fast and, even before I could react, it hit me smack in the face, just missing my eye. The cut was deep and there was a lot of blood.

I didn't have the money to pay for a taxi home and was embarrassed at the thought of getting on a bus with a bloodied face. I asked a friend of mine to give me a lift on his bicycle, and anyone who knows Mumbai will realize what a difficult task that is, especially with heavy cricket kitbags in tow. There was a busy flyover between East and West Bandra, which my friend found too steep with such a heavy load. As a result, I had to get off and walk, with commuters gaping at me in shock. A young kid with a bloodied face and bloodstained shirt lugging his cricket kit over a flyover wasn't an everyday sight.

When I got home, I was relieved to find my parents out at work. My grandmother was in the apartment, but I asked her not to panic and told her it was a minor injury. She said she knew how to handle it and put warm turmeric over the cut, an age-old Indian Ayurvedic treatment for cuts and bruises. I did not bother telling anyone else and the injury healed faster than I expected.

Suffice to say, that wasn't the only time I got hurt while playing cricket as a kid. Injuries were frequent because we played on half-baked and overused pitches and our coach insisted we should bat without helmets and learn to leave balls by swaying out of the way. On such wickets, injuries were a certainty, but they hardened us for the grind in the future and as a result I was never scared of getting hurt. It was all part of being a professional sportsman. However, the ability to withstand pain didn't mean I didn't take due precautions and exposed myself to injuries unnecessarily – something I was once surprised to be questioned about as a fourteen-year-old during a match at the Wankhede Stadium.

The match, which involved Mumbai's Ranji Trophy Probables, started early in the morning and the plan was for a pair of fast bowlers to bowl at the batsmen for five or six overs before they were rested and a new pair were asked to bowl with a new ball. The aim was to give batsmen practice against a fast swinging ball. To make things even more difficult, a lot of grass had been left on the track. I went out to bat early in our innings and was wearing my Under-15 cap. I didn't have a helmet at the time and the Under-15 cap was the only headgear I possessed. Raju Kulkarni, who was by then an accomplished Test bowler for India, was livid when he saw me taking guard in just a cap. All the senior batsmen had helmets, so how dare I, a fourteen-year-old, wander out without proper head protection? At first, I couldn't work out why he was so upset. He bowled a barrage of bouncers – though in hindsight I realize they were intended to teach me a lesson rather than to hurt me – but I managed to stay calm enough to sway out of the way. When I finally understood the reason behind his anger, I did not know how to explain to him that Achrekar Sir had not allowed me to wear a helmet in school cricket – I wasn't attempting to be brave at all. It was only later, when I was selected in the Mumbai team and came to know Raju well, that I finally told him the real reason for not wearing a helmet.

Music: my second love

Music was a constant presence in the Tendulkar household. All my siblings would regularly listen to the radio and always followed the weekly Hindi film music programme *Binaca Geet Mala* (a garland of songs), anchored by the well-known radio personality Ameen Sayani. As a result, while I was too young to understand much, I was exposed to music from a very early age. The exposure increased when my father bought a cassette player, which miraculously allowed everyone to listen to the music of their choice. Both my brothers were fans of the famous ghazal singer Pankaj Udhas. I couldn't really appreciate his songs then, but I was always in the room when they were played and was privy to discussions on the nuances and finer points of his music. On one occasion Nitin went to Dubai and brought back Pankaj Udhas's newly released album. Even though he didn't get home till midnight, we all waited up to listen to the cassette as soon as he got back, with our grandmother making us tea well past one in the morning.

It was natural that music should soon become my second love after cricket and it has remained that way ever since. I enjoy listening to all kinds of Indian music, ranging from film songs to the more classical variety, and I always feel relaxed with my headphones on. Later, during tours abroad, I began to pick up on Western music and I now love listening to Pink Floyd, U2, Dire Straits and a host of others. I passed that taste for Western music on to Ajit, and it is now an important feature of the Tendulkar household.

Turning to cricket

Besides cricket and music, I was also a big fan of tennis as a child. John McEnroe, the legendary American player, was my favourite. As a ten-year-old I would mimic McEnroe's look and antics, to the extent that I grew my hair into a curly mop and walked around wearing a headband. I was fascinated by the battles between Björn Borg and McEnroe and for a while I even contemplated choosing tennis over cricket.

Ajit knew about my obsession with tennis but had also seen me play cricket with my colony friends. He had observed my natural bat swing and that's what led him to believe that I might turn out to be a good batsman if groomed properly – though he never imposed anything on me.

What he would do is give me both a tennis racket and a cricket bat and take me up to the terrace to have a hit. He threw tennis balls to me while I took turns at tennis and cricket. We didn't have too many balls then and if they bounced over the walls of the terrace, I would quickly run down four floors and fetch them (there were no elevators then, something that explains the secret behind my strong legs!). It was clear to Ajit that I enjoyed myself far more while playing cricket. However, the episode that led him to take the next step and bring me along to Ramakant Achrekar's summer cricket camp in 1984, at the age of eleven, had nothing to do with cricket.

The turn to cricket was prompted by a group of friends – myself, Sunil Harshe and Avinash Gowariker – getting into a spot of trouble. At the time in India Doordarshan, the national broadcaster, would show a classic film every Sunday, and on this fateful day it was *Guide*, starring Dev Anand, one of India's legendary actors. Most of the residents of our colony were engrossed in the film, allowing us three the opportunity to climb up one of the trees and take some mangoes. Sunil, who was on the heavy side, and I were on a branch together, but it broke and we fell with a crash from quite a height. As we got up and tried to run away, we were caught and brought to book. It was evident that something needed to be done to channel my energies, especially during the school summer holidays. Ramakant Achrekar's coaching camp, where a lot of Mumbai's top cricketers had learnt their game, was Ajit's answer.

2

LEARNING THE GAME

From a very early age I played tennis-ball cricket with my colony friends. I loved watching cricket on television and in our games I often tried to emulate the mannerisms of my favourite players, Sunil Gavaskar and the West Indian legend Viv Richards. But it wasn't just the batsmen that I studied. I also loved bowling and tried my hand at different kinds of deliveries – medium pace, off-spin and leg-spin – all with a tennis ball, of course. I even experimented with tactics like the slower ball and bowling from wide of the stump. Throughout my career I have actually bowled a lot in the nets. As soon as I'd finished with my batting I'd pick up a ball and start bowling to whichever batsmen were around at the time.

The transition from playing with a tennis ball to playing with a cricket ball happened under the watchful eyes of Ramakant Achrekar, then cricket coach at Shardashram Vidyamandir school. Achrekar Sir, as I refer to him, started playing cricket at the age of eleven in 1943, which is the age I was when I went to him for the first time. He played for a number of Mumbai clubs, including the Gul Mohar Mills and Mumbai Port, and played a first-class match for the State Bank of India against Hyderabad in 1963. When I was growing up he was undoubtedly one of the most accomplished coaches in Mumbai.

From his own schooldays at Balmohan Vidyamandir, my brother Ajit knew that compared to other schools in Mumbai, Shardashram was by far the best organized in its approach to cricket, and that's why he took me along to Achrekar Sir's nets in Shivaji Park to try my luck at being a part of his summer camp.

Anyone could come for a trial at the camp but then it was up to Sir to decide who to accept. There were nets for players from all age groups, starting with the sub-junior (Under-15) and junior (Under-17) levels. I was eleven years old and trialled at the sub-junior nets to start with. The Mumbai Cricket Association had an Under-15 team and most candidates from the sub-junior section eventually vied for a position in that team.

I had never batted in nets before and felt somewhat overawed with so many people around. When I was asked to bat, I was not at all comfortable. With Sir watching me so closely, I failed to make an impact. After I had finished batting, Sir called Ajit aside and informed him that I was perhaps too young to make the camp and suggested that he should bring me back when I was a little older. I wasn't party to this conversation and had no idea what was discussed at the time. My induction into the Mumbai cricket circuit could have ended in failure – but for Ajit's insistence.

Having seen me play in the colony, Ajit knew I was capable of performing far better than I had in front of Achrekar Sir. He explained that I was nervous and asked Sir to give me one more opportunity. However, he suggested that while doing so Sir should pretend to go away and then watch from a distance. Sir agreed. Before long I was asked to bat again and, without Sir's trained eyes scrutinizing me – or so I thought – I felt more at ease and soon started to hit the ball well. This time, Sir agreed to let me join the camp. I was delighted and I must say it was an opportunity that transformed my life.

Participants in the summer camp had to pay an admission fee of 65 rupees (less than a pound) and a monthly fee of 10 rupees. In my case I don't remember having to pay the monthly fee after the first few months. The camp involved a session every morning and evening at Shivaji Park. I would practise between 7.30 a.m. and 10.30 a.m. before making my way home for lunch, then I'd come back in the afternoon and train till late evening. The schedule was rigorous and I would be exhausted by the end of the day. Travelling to Shivaji Park took forty minutes from my house in Bandra and I had to catch an early-morning bus to make it on time.

For the first few days Ajit accompanied me, to get me used to the routine, but once I was familiar with the journey, I'd travel to the camp on my own. During the bus journeys he would talk to me about the nuances of batting, and I always enjoyed these conversations a lot. In fact, the one thing that I have kept with me all my career is a note that Ajit gave me containing some thoughts about batting. It served as a very personal coaching manual.

As a child I had only one set of cricket clothes and the routine was to wash them as soon as I'd returned from the morning session. While I had my lunch, the clothes would dry out in the sun and I would wear them again in the afternoon. The pattern was repeated in the evening, so that I could use the same set of clothes the following morning. The system worked well – apart from my pockets. There was never quite enough time for the pockets to dry out completely and for the entire duration of the camp I played with wet pockets.

Changing schools

By the middle of the summer camp, Sir had started taking an active interest in my batting and at the end of the two months informed Ajit that I had the potential to be a good cricketer if I practised all year round. He had made a few changes to the way I batted and the impact was immediate. I was now practising with the older boys from the junior section. However, my school – the New English School in Bandra – did not have cricket facilities and Sir was keen for me to change schools if I wanted to pursue cricket seriously.

One evening Sir called my father and asked if he would speak to me about changing schools. Ajit was in the room with my father at the time and they both accepted that it was necessary, if cricket was to be my priority. However, neither of them ever forced anything on me and when I got home they asked me what I thought of the suggestion. By that time I had started enjoying my batting and was keen to play throughout the year. Without any hesitation I agreed to the move. My father sat me down and explained that while he did not have any objections to me changing schools, I should do so only if I was really serious about playing cricket. I assured him I was, and so it was agreed that I should move to Shardashram Vidyamandir, where Achrekar Sir was a cricket coach.

The move meant I lost contact with a lot of my New English School friends, but I soon made new ones at Shardashram, mostly through cricket. All the cricketers in the school were friends with each other and even though we were in different divisions and sections, such things hardly mattered. We played together during lunch breaks and discussed cricket all the time, and Achrekar Sir would coach us after school. Cricket was fast becoming my first love. All my excess energies were getting channelled into cricket, which acted as a kind of safety valve. Everyone at home was very supportive, but my father always said that all he wanted me to do was give it my best effort without worrying about the results.

Joining Shardashram undoubtedly helped my cricket a great deal. It allowed me the opportunity to play competitive matches regularly and my game rapidly improved as a result. There's nothing like playing matches to get better, because only in competitive situations are you forced to out-think the opposition and improvise. Net practice can never be a substitute for match-play and Achrekar Sir was an ardent believer in this principle.

I did not excel in my first ever match for my club, the Kamath Memorial Club, run by Achrekar Sir, which a host of my colony friends came to watch, I was out for a golden duck. I was the star batsman in the colony and it was natural that my friends would come to see me play. It was embarrassing to be bowled first ball and I had to make a series of excuses, saying the ball had kept low and the pitch wasn't good enough for batting. In the second match I got out for another duck and it was only in our third game that I managed to score my first run, having survived seven deliveries. I was seriously relieved to get off the mark. I used to keep a diary at the time that contained all the information from these games, but unfortunately I don't have them any more.

My debut for the school wasn't quite as bad and I managed to score 24 runs in the match, which we won comfortably. However, I will always remember the game for other reasons, because I learnt a very important personal lesson. It taught me never to resort to unethical ways and to play the sport with honesty and integrity at all times. The incident in question involved my first appearance in a newspaper, which should have been a happy occurrence. The rule in Mumbai at the time was that a player's name only appeared in print if he had scored 30 runs. I had made 24, but there were a lot of extras in the team's innings and the scorer decided to credit six extras to me, increasing my score to 30. The scorer's logic was that it didn't matter because the overall score did not change. I had consented to this without appreciating what I was getting into. The next morning, when my name duly appeared in a Mumbai paper, Achrekar Sir was seriously unhappy with what I had done and told me off for consenting to have runs added to my personal tally when I hadn't scored them. I acknowledged my mistake and promised never to allow such a thing to happen again.

The first-match jinx continued in my first season for the Mumbai Under-15 team in Pune in 1985. I was only twelve then and travelled to Pune with just 95 rupees in my pocket. This was to be supplemented with the little allowance we were given during the tour, which lasted more than a week. In my only match for Mumbai I was run out. I was batting with someone from my school who was older than me and because he was a faster runner he completed the runs quicker and pushed for a third run that was not on. As a result I was run out and I returned to the pavilion with tears in my eyes. Thoughtfully, two veteran Mumbai cricketers, Milind Rege and Vasu Paranjpe, consoled me, saying the run just wasn't there and I shouldn't have been called to go for it.

It rained a lot in Pune over the next few days and as it turned out this was my only innings. As a result I was not picked for the West Zone Under-15 team and was upset because a few of my team-mates who had not played a single ball had been chosen ahead of me. To add to my distress, I ran out of money because I spent it all on snacks and fast food – and arrived at Dadar station with no fare for the bus home. I had to walk back to Shivaji Park to my uncle's carrying two big bags and crying all the way. My aunt was very concerned when she saw me and asked what the matter was. I did not tell her that I hadn't been selected for the West Zone team and all I said was I was not feeling too well.

My first earnings from cricket

Playing for my school regularly helped me learn the art of scoring big runs and batting for a long time. During school holidays I played practice matches for my club almost every day. In fact, in my first year at Shardashram I played fifty-five practice matches during the summer break of sixty days. My summer sessions used to start at 7.30 a.m. and I'd bat for two hours, split into five net sessions. All of these sessions were rigorous and required intense concentration. After the morning session, I would go straight into the practice match, which would end at 4.30 p.m., then my evening session would start at 5 p.m., after only a thirty-minute break. During the break Sir would often give me some money to go and have a *vada pav* (a popular Mumbai fast food) or a soft drink as a treat.

Between 5 p.m. and 7 p.m. I'd have five more net sessions, before a final session of fifteen minutes, when Sir would place a one-rupee coin on top of the stumps and if I managed to avoid getting out, the coin was mine. In this session every bowler in the camp would come and have a go at me, with some sixty to seventy boys fielding. Even if the ball was caught 90 yards away, which was a distance bigger than the boundary length at any school ground in India, I was out. It meant I had to hit every ball along the ground to survive those intense fifteen minutes. It was a serious challenge but with time I started enjoying this session the most. Winning the one-rupee coin used to give me immense satisfaction and taught me how to concentrate even when physically drained.

At the end of it all, Sir would tell me to run two full circuits of Shivaji Park with my pads and gloves on. That was the last part of my training and I'd be completely exhausted by the end of it all. It was a routine I would repeat right through my summer holidays and it helped me to build up physical and mental stamina.

Occasionally my father came to take me home and I would always ask him to treat me to a special fruit cocktail at a juice centre near the club. While this regular demand was a little unreasonable, because at the time I did not realize that my parents also had to take care of the needs of my brothers and sister, my father would invariably end up giving me what I wanted, just to see me happy.

On other days, when I made my way home from Shivaji Park on my own, I'd often fall asleep on the bus – if I managed to sit down, that is. Anyone who has been on a Mumbai bus at peak hours will know just how difficult it is to get a seat. On days when I wasn't so lucky, it was still a challenge just to stand with the kitbag, because the bus conductors would inevitably complain about me taking up the space of another passenger. It could be embarrassing because the conductors were often rude and would sometimes ask me to buy two tickets. I didn't have the money for a second ticket and I had to learn to take these remarks in my stride. Dirty clothes often added to the embarrassment. After I'd played in them all day, the clothes were usually in quite a smelly state and this was the cause of a lot of discomfort and guilt on the way home. With time I evolved a way of wrapping the kitbag around me. Just as the helmet and pads became a part of me while batting, so the kitbag became an extension of me on the bus.

So when people ask me these days if I have ever been on public transport, I tell them I used to travel on crowded buses and trains four times a day during my first year at Shardashram. And from a very young age I used to do it alone. I'd often take the bus or train from Bandra to Churchgate, and it was all a great learning experience. Within a few months I had made a lot of friends and we had great fun travelling together to matches.

Moving to Shivaji Park

After a year of commuting between Bandra and school, my family realized that the daily travel was getting too much. I had to catch a connecting bus midway into the journey and if I missed the connection I'd be late for school. Also, the one-and-a-half-hour journey would end up exhausting me and it had started to have an impact on my training time. More worryingly, I had twice fallen sick in the first year of my daily commute to Shardashram and had also contracted jaundice.

It was decided that I should move in with my uncle and aunt, Suresh and Mangala, because they lived at Indravadan Society, an apartment block close to Shivaji Park. I ended up staying with them for four years and they were hugely supportive of my endeavours and had a formative influence on me as I grew up. In fact, there were times when I even made my aunt throw balls to me in our living room. I had bought a couple of golf balls and transformed them into an oval shape with the help of a blade. I had done this intentionally, so that when my aunt threw one to me, the ball would change direction after pitching, either coming in or going away. The whole idea behind this was that, while killing time at home, I would learn to play with soft hands without damaging things in our living room. Throughout the drill, my aunt would sit on her chair, and after playing the ball I would collect it and hand it back to her. When my aunt wasn't around, I would hang up the ball in a sock and hit it with the edge of my bat. Hitting it with the bat's full face was much too easy and when I hit it with the edge I would try to middle it as many times as possible. When it did not hit the middle, it would come back from different directions (it became an inswinger or an outswinger) and it was fun to negotiate the challenge. These drills helped my hand–eye coordination and also my awareness of which direction the bat should come from to meet the ball.

My uncle and aunt's house was a thirty-minute walk from school. It meant I could get more rest in the morning and could come home for lunch around 1 p.m. and go back to play a practice game at my club by early afternoon. Sir would invariably schedule three practice games a week for me and would ensure that I batted at number four in each one of them. He could do that because it was his club. I would bat in my favourite position in all the matches I played and if I got out I'd have to change quickly and go out and field. This was a good incentive to keep batting and not get out at all, as I didn't enjoy fielding as much as I did batting. After the match I'd resume my own training in the evening before calling it a day at 7.30.

On days when there was a school match, we'd try our best to stretch it to a second day. For example, if we were set to chase 300 we'd score 260–270 runs on the first day and keep the remaining runs for the next morning. This would allow us to miss school on the second day, and after quickly wrapping up the match in the first half an hour, the team would head off to the beach to play cricket. Playing beach cricket was always a lot of fun and we would all have a great time.

Both my parents would visit me at my uncle and aunt's almost every day after they finished work. For my mother in particular it was an arduous journey, since getting there from her office in Santa Cruz in peak-hour traffic on public transport was a real challenge back then. The fact that both of them would happily put in the time after a full day's work, just so I would not feel neglected, was remarkable.

In the 1986–87 season I started to make runs consistently and also scored my first hundred. We were playing Don Bosco School at Shivaji Park and I was not out on 94 at the end of the first day. A few days before this match I had invited Sir to my house for dinner. Sir, however, said he would come only when I had scored my first hundred in school cricket. Feeling excited and anxious, I decided to sleep next to my father that night and kept tossing and turning till late. My father tried to comfort me, saying I should go to sleep and that my body needed rest after batting all day. I couldn't and only managed to get a couple of hours' sleep before waking up very early the next morning.

Sensing my anxiety, my father took me to a Ganapati temple in Bandra to seek the blessings of Lord Ganesha and only then did I leave for Shivaji Park. On my way I visited another Ganapati temple, the one I regularly visited before games. There was a water tap inside the temple premises and I regularly used to drink from it before I went to the ground. I did the same that day and in the very first over hit two boundaries to reach my hundred. True to his word, Sir came for dinner that night and it was a deeply satisfying moment.

One of my best early seasons was at Shardashram in 1987–88, when I played in both the Giles Shield and the Harris Shield. For those unfamiliar with the intricacies of Mumbai cricket, the Giles Shield is meant for boys under the age of fourteen and Harris Shield for those under sixteen. Looking back, it seems remarkable that I played in both, but I didn't think much of it at the time. These tournaments are acknowledged as breeding grounds for young talent in Mumbai and good performances tend to get noticed in the city's cricket circles.

In the Harris Shield that season I scored a record 1,025 runs in five matches and was out only once. It now seems extraordinary, but my scores in the quarter-final, semi-final and final read 207 not out, 326 not out and 346 not out. What's more, after scoring 326 not out in the semi-final of the Harris Shield, I walked right across the Azad Maidan (a sports and recreation ground in South Mumbai) to play in a Giles Shield match, in which I made 178 not out, winning us the game.

I started out with a hundred in the first match of the season, scoring 125 before getting out, and it was a dismissal I have never forgotten. I was out stumped to an off-spinner who was hearing-impaired and I vividly remember the expression on his face when I was beaten by a beautifully flighted delivery. But the ball went on to elude the keeper and within a fraction of a second the bowler's expression turned from euphoria to despair as he saw the missed stumping opportunity. Yet I did not go back to the crease and instead started walking back to the pavilion, allowing the wicketkeeper to complete the stumping. It was the only time I was out in that season's competition. While I didn't consciously mean to show sympathy to the bowler, it was one of those moments that are difficult to explain. It was not an act of charity exactly. Rather, it was a good ball and I knew I had been comprehensively beaten. The keeper fumbled the take and the bowler looked distraught at the missed opportunity. He had done everything for the wicket and deserved the dismissal.

In the semi-final of the Harris Shield against St Xavier's in February 1988, a three-day game, we were 84–2 when I went in to bat at number four, with Vinod Kambli, an extremely talented young-ster in Mumbai's cricket circles at the time, already at the crease, having gone in at number three. We immediately plundered the St Xavier's attack and never let up all the way through what would become a record-breaking partnership. With the Azad Maidan being an open ground and a very big one, the opposition had to run long distances to retrieve the ball after a hard-hit boundary and we found ourselves singing songs and enjoying ourselves in the middle of the pitch. It was our way of switching off while batting together for long periods. At the end of the day we were both not out, with Vinod on 182 and me on 192, and, needless to say, Shardashram were in a commanding position in the game.

The following morning, we both made our double centuries and then just kept on batting – despite Achrekar Sir wanting us to declare the innings. At one point he sent our assistant coach to the boundary to instruct us to declare. We could hear him scream our names and shout instructions, but we pretended not to hear and tried not to look in his direction. He kept at it for ten minutes before he realized that it was a futile attempt and returned to the dressing room. We just wanted to carry on batting and enjoy ourselves in the middle.

At lunch we had reached 748–2, of which I had contributed 326. As soon as we left the field I was informed by the assistant coach that I was in serious trouble. When I asked why, he told me that Achrekar Sir had wanted us to declare in the morning and I had disobeyed him by carrying on. Sir was of the opinion that we had more than enough runs to declare, and if we weren't able to bowl the opposition out for less we did not deserve to be in the final. I decided to declare right away to save myself from Sir's ire that evening. Vinod asked me not to, however, because he was not out on 349. He pleaded with me to give him one more ball so that he'd reach 350. I said that it wasn't my call and we needed Sir's permission to continue. So I rang Sir from a public phone next to the ground and the first question he asked was how many wickets we had managed to take before lunch. That was Sir's style. He was well aware that we hadn't declared and hadn't taken any wickets, but he wouldn't say so. I informed him that we had batted till lunch and that I was about to declare. With Vinod pleading beside me, I quickly mentioned to Sir that Vinod wanted to speak to him and handed over the phone. But Vinod was scared of Sir and ended up not saying a word about batting on for another over.

I duly declared the innings and, despite having batted for a day and a half, went on to open the bowling with the new ball and bowled a lot of overs in the innings. I did not feel the least bit tired; all the hard work in the summer camps had started to pay off. I started out bowling medium pace, then changed to off-spin when the ball was semi-old and leg-spin when the ball had lost all of its shine. Vinod too bowled very well and picked up six wickets as we dismissed St Xavier's for 154 to make the final.

That partnership of 664 was the highest in any form of cricket in the world at the time. Coming in the semi-final of the Harris Shield made it all the more significant in the local cricket community. It gained us both a lot of recognition. We had become quite a pair and what made batting with Vinod fun was that I never knew what he'd get up to next. In one match in the same season he actually started flying a kite while we were batting together. Suddenly I couldn't see Vinod, because he had walked 20 metres away from the pitch and was holding the string of a kite – right in the middle of the innings! It was his way of enjoying himself and I knew he'd get a severe reprimand from Sir for doing so.

Sir wasn't to be seen on that day, however, and Vinod was confident of getting away with it. I wasn't so sure. I had a feeling that Sir was watching us from somewhere and would surely pick up the issue at the end of the day's play, as was his style. Sir was known to hide behind a tree on occasions to watch us play, and in fact it rarely happened that he'd miss a game of ours. At the end of the day, he would then give us a 'demonstration' session, so called because Sir would demonstrate what we had done wrong in terms of footwork, stance or stroke selection. Sure enough, at the demonstration session at the end of that day, I was given a chit to read aloud and the first item was 'Vinod kite'! Sir, upset at what Vinod had done, asked him what he thought he was doing flying a kite while batting and warned him never to do so again. He promised, but with Vinod nothing could be taken for granted.

Having defeated St Xavier's comprehensively, we were runaway favourites in the final against Anjuman-i-Islam, which was to be played at the Cricket Club of India, which is India's equivalent of the MCC, established in 1933. It was my first competitive game at CCI and a number of Mumbai cricket luminaries were present to see us bat in the final. They had heard about the world-record partnership and wanted to see if we were good enough to have a career in cricket. Dilip Vengsarkar, Sunil Gavaskar and CCI president Raj Singh Dungarpur were in attendance and I did not want to disappoint them.

On the eve of the final I was given a superb gift by Hemant Kenkre, Sunil Gavaskar's nephew, which served as an added incentive to perform well. At the time I did not have good pads to play with and Sir had a word with Hemant about it. Hemant had with him a set of pads used by Sunil Gavaskar, the really light ones with blue padding inside, and decided to give them to me. I was delighted and humbled and went with Ajit to his house to collect my gift.

I felt very proud to wear pads once used by Sunil Gavaskar. I went in to bat thirty minutes before lunch on the first day of the final and kept batting for close to two days. I was eventually unbeaten on 346 when we were bowled out before tea on the third day. It was a very significant innings in the context of my career, for shortly afterwards I was included in the list of Probables for the Mumbai Ranji Trophy team.

In my early days as a cricketer another person who helped me considerably was Hemant Waingankar. Hemant, a student of my father's, knew me as a child and followed my career from start to finish. It was at Hemant's initiative that Anil Joshi, Vijay Shirke and Sanju Khamkar of Sungrace Mafatlal, a well-known Indian company, came forward to support both Vinod and me with cricket equipment. I am glad that our friendship, which was close to three decades old, continued.

My Sir

Looking back at these years of cricket, I must say I owe a lot to my coach Ramakant Achrekar – as well as his assistants, Das Shivalkar and Laxman Chavan. Had it not been for Sir, I would not be the cricketer I turned out to be. He was a strict disciplinarian and did everything he could for me.

On certain days he would even drive me all the way across Mumbai on his scooter to get me to matches on time. Even though I loved cricket, there were still occasional days when playing with my friends at home was such fun that I would conveniently forget I was supposed to go to the nets. If I didn't turn up, Achrekar Sir would jump on his scooter and come to find me at Sahitya Sahawas. Inevitably, I would be outside, engrossed in some game or other with my chums. Sir would spot me in the melee and virtually drag me to our apartment. I would come up with excuses but he would have none of it. He would get me to change and put on my shoes and then I'd ride pillion with him as we headed off to Shivaji Park. On the drive he would tell me, 'Don't waste your time playing inane games with these kids. Cricket is waiting for you at the nets. Practise hard and see what magic can transpire.' At the time, I hated being dragged off but as I look back I feel sheepish about my actions and can only admire Achrekar Sir's farsightedness.

Sir also punished me on one occasion when trying to teach me a very important lesson. Shardashram English and Shardashram Marathi schools had made it to the finals of the Harris Shield and the match was to be played at the Wankhede Stadium. I was at that stage a Giles Shield player and had nothing to do with the Harris Shield. Knowing that I'd want to go and watch the game, Sir had arranged a practice match for me and warned me not to miss my own match and go off to the Wankhede. However, I disobeyed and went along to the final, not anticipating that Sir would be there. He was as angry as I'd ever seen him and he said it wasn't for me to come and watch other people play, for if I practised hard enough, one day people from across the world would come and watch me play.

Achrekar Sir has undoubtedly made a significant contribution to cricket in Mumbai and India. I am by no means the only pupil of his to go on to represent India; others include Lalchand Rajput, Vinod Kambli, Pravin Amre, Ajit Agarkar, Sanjay Bangar, Balwinder Sandhu, Chandrakant Pandit, Paras Mhambrey, Sameer Dighe and Ramesh Powar. Not for one moment has he been interested in financial gain, however. Quite the opposite, in fact – there were many occasions when he would help out those who were so poor they could not even afford the few rupees normally charged for his summer school.

Throughout my career, before each tour and each series for India, I would make four visits that were very important to me: to two temples in Mumbai, the Ganesh temple in Shivaji Park and the Siddhivinayak temple in Prabhadevi; to my aunt and uncle; and to Achrekar Sir.

My short career as a fast bowler

My first good season for Shardashram earned me a trial place at the MRF Pace Foundation in Chennai in 1987 under the legendary Australian fast bowler Dennis Lillee, who was head coach there. The MRF Pace Foundation had been set up with the explicit aim of grooming local fast-bowling talent, something that we have always lacked in India. Coaches from across India had been asked to name talented youngsters and my name was suggested by Vasu Paranjpe, veteran Mumbai cricketer and one of India's best coaches. Vasu Sir has always been extremely supportive of my efforts and has been a kind of mentor to me. Though the camp was primarily meant to identify talented fast bowlers, Ajit advised me to take my full kit to Chennai. The thought was that if I wasn't selected as a bowler I could benefit from batting in the nets there. Perhaps unsurprisingly, given my build and height,

I didn't stand out as a potential international pace bowler and Dennis Lillee jokingly advised me to focus on my batting instead. As it turned out, I remained a batsman who wanted to learn the art of fast bowling.

The first break

All the hard work under the watchful supervision of Sir finally paid off when I was picked in the squad to represent Mumbai in the Ranji Trophy on 14 November 1987. The Ranji Trophy, the premier domestic competition in India, was started in 1933–34 and named after the famous KS Ranjitsinhji, Indian cricket's first global figure, who played for England against Australia in 1896. It is an important platform and consistent performances in the Ranji Trophy can earn a player a national call-up. In the 1980s it was played on a zonal basis. First-class teams from each zone, West, North, South, East and Central, played each other before the top teams advanced to the knock-out stage.

Despite making the Mumbai squad, I did not make it to the final XI in any of the matches. This meant I narrowly missed out on playing alongside Sunil Gavaskar, who retired from all forms of cricket after the 1987 Cricket World Cup, a few months before I made the Ranji squad. When I was growing up, Mr Gavaskar's thirty-four centuries for India had always served as a huge inspiration. It was the ultimate benchmark for a batsman, and not to have played alongside him remains a regret. However, that season I did get a little taste of the Ranji Trophy, as a substitute fielder – and also of international cricket, while fielding at the Brabourne Stadium for a Pakistan team against India!

It was a festival match and two Pakistan cricketers, Javed Miandad and leg-spinner Abdul Qadir, had gone off the field at lunchtime. I was asked to substitute and was deployed at wide long on by skipper Imran Khan. Within minutes Kapil Dev hit a skier and, despite running in 15 metres, I wasn't able to reach the ball. I remember complaining to my friend Marcus Couto that evening on the train home that I could have taken the catch if I had been positioned at mid on instead of long on. I don't know whether Imran Khan remembers the occasion or has any idea that I once fielded for his Pakistan team.

One incident I remember from my Ranji Trophy debut season took place when we played in Baroda in one of the West Zone encounters. I was just fourteen then and was sharing a room with Suru Nayak, a former India international. The team had reached Baroda a few days in advance and on one of the days we had dinner a little earlier than normal. Afterwards Suru Nayak asked me to go to bed, suggesting that I should get some rest while the other players went out to offer *pooja* at the local temple. I had no reason to disbelieve him and went off to sleep in my room. Only later did I find out that the other players had gone out partying that night and because I was only fourteen I had been conveniently left out.

I wasn't always so well behaved, of course. In 1987 I remember playing for the Mumbai Under-15 team at Cuttack in the eastern Indian State of Odisha. We were staying in a college dormitory and there were fifteen beds aligned in a row. Next to the dorm was a balcony and beyond it lay the college sports field. Two of my friends in the team were Jatin Paranjpe (who went on to play one-day international cricket for India) and Vinod Kambli, and together we had planned that after lights-out we would sneak around and gather up all the other players' shoes, including their spikes. With the dorm pitch-dark, we started throwing them at Kedar Godbole, one of our hapless team-mates. Other players were also in our line of fire and before they could figure out what was going on they were hit by a barrage of shoe missiles. When they started throwing them back at us, we ducked and their shoes flew over our heads and over the balcony into the adjoining field. At two in the morning, the whole team was down on the ground looking for their shoes and chappals!

Ranji Trophy debut

The following year, I was watched closely by Mumbai captain Dilip Vengsarkar in the Cricket Club of India nets when the Indian team came to play a match against the touring New Zealand team. Vengsarkar was impressed with the way I played against Kapil Dev and sometime later, on 10 December 1988, when I was fifteen, he told the selectors that I was ready to play for Mumbai against Gujarat, giving me my first big break. Vengsarkar himself was busy with national duty and I filled in for him. In my debut match I scored 100 not out and in the process became the youngest Indian to score a century on his first-class debut. I finished the 1988–89 season as Mumbai's highest run-scorer and made half-centuries in six of the seven matches I played. Mumbai lost a hard-fought semi-final against Delhi and I ended my debut season with a respectable batting average of 64.77. In the semi-final, Madan Lal, former India fast bowler and coach, was playing for Delhi and I remember playing a straight drive to a fine ball from him that was much talked about that evening. It was a shot that got me noticed, adding to my stock at the time. Everything about the shot was perfect – balance, head position, timing – and the ball raced to the boundary.

My performances for Mumbai got me selected for the season-opening Irani Trophy match at the beginning of November 1989. The Irani Trophy, between the Ranji Trophy champions and the Rest of India, is a key component of the Indian domestic cricket calendar and is a major opportunity to get noticed. Playing for the Rest of India, I scored a hundred against Ranji champions Delhi in my first Irani Trophy game and it was during this match that the Indian squad for the much-awaited tour to Pakistan in November–December 1989 was announced.

Before I knew it, at sixteen years of age, I had been picked to play for India.

3

MY FIRST TOUR

I had always dreamed of playing cricket for India. Getting an opportunity to fulfil my dream at such an early age was indeed very special. What made it even more significant was that we were playing Pakistan in Pakistan and their bowling attack included fast bowlers of the quality of Imran Khan, Wasim Akram, Waqar Younis and Aaqib Javed, not to mention the leg-spinners Mushtaq Ahmed and Abdul Qadir – quite a test for any debutant.

It was baptism by fire. So much so that after my very first innings in Test cricket, during which I was all at sea against Wasim and Waqar, I began to doubt my ability to bat and questioned whether I was ever going to be good enough to play at international level.

Before describing my debut series, I want to go back to that first Irani Trophy game for the Rest of India against Delhi. I had scored 39 in the first innings before I was bowled by Maninder Singh, India's ace left-arm spinner at the time. The disappointment did not last long, however, because it was that evening when I learned I had been named in the Indian squad for the Pakistan tour. Ecstatic at my inclusion, I was determined to make a mark in the second innings.

The occasion was particularly special because my brother had come to see me play. In fact, since I was a minor and could not sign the tour contract, Ajit had to sign it on my behalf. Vasu Paranjpe had also mentioned to my father that morning that I would surely get a hundred and said that he should come and watch me bat. My father did just that and, to his satisfaction, what Vasu Sir had predicted came true. However, the century would not have happened but for the contribution of Gursharan Singh, the Punjab batsman who later played a Test match for India against New Zealand in 1990.

Gursharan had fractured his finger while batting against the bowling of Atul Wassan, a Delhi fast bowler who also made his debut for India against New Zealand in 1990. He was sitting in the dressing room injured and there seemed to be no way he could play a further part in the match. I was batting well and was unbeaten on 86 when our ninth wicket fell. Knowing that Gursharan couldn't bat, I started walking back to the dressing room, assuming it was the end of our innings. Just then I saw Gursharan walking towards me, ready to bat one-handed.

It was later revealed to me that Raj Singh Dungarpur, then chairman of the national selection committee, had asked if he would go out and help me get to my hundred. In an exemplary show of courage, Gursharan had agreed. In fact, when we met at the wicket I felt distinctly embarrassed seeing him there in such severe pain. I told him that it would be perfectly under-standable if we called off the innings. Showing tremendous grit, he told me, '*Ab to tera hundred kar ke hi jayenge.*' (I will get back to the pavilion only after you get your hundred.) He doggedly stuck to his task, and I'm glad to say that his bravery was respected by the opposition bowlers, who did not resort to bowling bouncers.

It was a favour I would never forget. It was a show of remark-able resilience by Gursharan and I tried to repay the debt by doing what I could at the time of his benefit match in Delhi in April 2005. I had promised him that as long as he gave me a few days' notice, I'd turn up to play, no matter where I was. I am glad I was able to keep my promise.

India in Pakistan, November–December 1989

Encouraged at having got a hundred against India's domestic champions, I headed to Pakistan soon after feeling reasonably confident. Maybe because I was still a teenager, I didn't feel any extra pressure about playing against Pakistan. The whole political baggage of India–Pakistan cricket meant nothing to me. I was simply treating it as my first tour, which was challenge enough. In any case, no one really expected me to be a part of the playing XI at such a young age, certainly not in any of the Tests. Some thought I might get a chance in one of the one-day games, depending on the team's performance in the series, while others believed I was there only to get a feel of international cricket.

To be honest, all the talk passed me by. I just wanted to do well for India and score a lot of runs. Other than that, everything else seemed unimportant. That was natural enough, because everything had happened rather quickly in my life. Just five years after I took to playing competitive cricket, I had become a part of the Indian squad – it was a pretty quick move from school to international cricket.

On arrival in Pakistan I didn't sense any tension and went out for regular meals in the evening with some of the other cricketers. Their friendly approach helped put me at ease and it was not until we reached Lahore that a curfew was imposed on going out in the evenings. On my travels around India I had always bought gifts such as sarees for my mother and aunt and shirts for my father and uncle, and so in the first few days in Pakistan I did the same. This time I bought them some local shoes and slippers.

There was tension within the squad, however, as a result of a dispute that had blown up before the tour between the Board of Control for Cricket in India (BCCI) and the players over the issue of players' involvement in a few unsanctioned matches in the United States on the way back from the West Indies tour in 1989. The matter had gone right up to the Indian Supreme Court and was eventually settled when the court lifted a ban imposed on the players by the BCCI. The other controversy that arose on the eve of the tour was over the issue of match fees. It had escalated into a serious dispute, with the players opting to give up their match fees altogether as a mark of protest. Fortunately for the junior players in the team, skipper Krishnamachari Srikkanth instructed us to stay away from the problems and concentrate on the job at hand, which was to evolve a strategy to tackle Imran, Wasim, Waqar and Abdul Qadir.

I had a good start to the tour and in one of the two games before the first Test, against the Pakistan Board Patron's XI in Rawalpindi, scored 47 before getting out to Iqbal Qasim, a left-arm spinner who played for Pakistan in fifty Tests. It was a decent innings and I received a standing ovation from the crowd. I began to feel I had a slim chance of getting into the Test team and dared to dream of my first Test cap. I finally heard the news of my inclusion in the playing XI from skipper Srikkanth on the night before the first Test in Karachi.

It is very difficult to describe the feeling. I was part of a band of eleven fortunate men who had been given the duty of repre-senting close to a billion Indians. It was an honour every aspiring cricketer lives for, to play for his country against the best of world cricket. And with the honour came responsibility. I was going to be accountable to the cricket fans back home and was expected to give my best for them. In fact, I could imagine nothing more significant than doing something worthy for the national team and the passionate Indian cricket fans.

I was sharing a room with Salil Ankola, the fast bowler who has now gone on to become an actor. Salil was bowling well at the time and was also making his Test debut. Neither of us could sleep the night before the match. We were both about to start a new chapter and were aware that it was an opportunity that could change our lives for ever.

First Test, Karachi, 15–20 November 1989

Pakistan won the toss and opted to bat first on a greenish wicket so I didn't have long to wait to walk onto the field for the first time as an India player. My life had taken a giant leap and it is a moment I will always remember. It also happened to be Kapil Dev's 100th Test match and we were all excited for him. Only Sunil Gavaskar and Dilip Vengsarkar had achieved the distinction before.

My first day of international cricket wasn't without drama and one incident in particular left an unpleasant feeling. In the post-lunch session a bearded man clad in salwar kameez entered the field and went straight up to Kapil Dev, abusing him for being in Pakistan. Kapil, who was preparing to bowl at the time, later recounted to us that he asked the fellow to leave him alone and allow him to continue with the game. After his exchange with Kapil, the intruder then went over to mid off, where Manoj Prabhakar, our top fast bowler on the tour, was fielding. He abused Prabhakar before moving on to skipper Srikkanth – and with Srikkanth he got physical. In those days, with the sport far less commercialized, players could choose what kit to wear. Most of our team preferred T-shirts, but Srikkanth liked to wear a buttoned shirt and this was torn open in the scuffle.

I was fielding at point and I was scared I would be next and was ready to run to the safe confines of the dressing room if the intruder came towards me. Up to this point, no security personnel had done anything to stop the intruder from disrupting things in the middle. It was only when the Indian captain was being manhandled that security finally came onto the ground to drag the spectator off. It was a serious security lapse, yet the organizers seemed hardly perturbed. The truth is that it was much more than a cricket match that was being played between the two teams. The political history of partition has always cast a pall over India–Pakistan cricket and it was my first taste of this unfortunate reality. The next day we were even more astonished to find the Pakistan press suggesting that the intruder had actually been trying to congratulate Kapil Dev on playing his 100th Test match. The issue of Srikkanth's torn shirt didn't merit a mention by the local media.

All at sea

On the second day of the match, Pakistan were all out for 409, with skipper Imran Khan scoring 109 not out. Finally, it was our turn to bat. The pitch was lively and we didn't get off to a good start. We were soon reduced to 41–4, with Srikkanth, Navjot Sidhu, Sanjay Manjrekar and Manoj Prabhakar out cheaply. Wasim and Waqar were bowling really fast and it was a trying time for every Indian batsman. I hadn't quite anticipated what awaited me out in the middle when I went out to bat at number six. There's no harm in admitting that I was all at sea against Wasim and Waqar in my first innings in Test cricket. I was trying to be aggressive to almost every ball, as that was how I had always played the game. I was trying to get on top of the bowlers, but more often than not I was comprehensively beaten. The pace was far greater than I had ever faced and the skill on display was of the very highest standard. The guile of both bowlers left me thoroughly confused.

An account of one Wasim over will give an idea of my plight in the middle. I was on strike to him for the third ball of the over, which turned out to be a vicious bouncer. Having studied Wasim's bowling, I was convinced the next ball would be a yorker and was mentally prepared for it. It turned out to be another bouncer, which I left. While I kept expecting a fiery yorker, balls five and six also turned out to be bouncers, and at the end of the over I said to myself, 'Welcome to Test cricket.' Not without reason is it acknowledged as the most challenging format of the game.

My stay at the crease was short but not so sweet. I had lasted only twenty-four balls, at least half of which I had missed. I had hit two boundaries but not for a moment had I felt comfortable. It was only a matter of time before I was dismissed. I was finally bowled for a rather lucky 15 by another debutant, Waqar Younis, and on my way back to the pavilion my mind was riddled with self-doubt.

It was a very important moment in my career. I had come to the international stage after blazing my way through domestic cricket. I had managed to score a hundred on debut in the Ranji and Irani trophies, but here I was on the international stage unable to put bat on ball. I was struggling, plain and simple. The difference in standard between domestic and international cricket was colossal.

I batted only once in that first Test match, which ended in a draw, and in the following days I approached our coach, Chandu Borde, and a number of senior team-mates to discuss what I needed to do to improve. I had a long chat with Ravi Shastri, already an established star at the time, who advised me to be patient for the first fifteen or twenty minutes, which were bound to be uncomfortable. Ravi was of the opinion that once I had played out the initial burst from the Pakistani bowlers, things would turn easier. The key was to spend time in the middle. But would I be given another opportunity to do so? I could easily have missed out on the second Test, not only because of my low score in the first but also because of the *way* I had batted.

It came as a huge relief to see my name in the playing XI for the second Test at Faisalabad.

Second Test, Faisalabad, 23–28 November 1989

I knew it was a chance I could not afford to squander; it would be a big test of my ability and temperament. What made the task considerably more difficult was that Pakistan won the toss on a green-top and put India in to bat. The stage was set. All through my career I have relished these moments of adversity. It is no good just performing on a docile track against weak opposition. A cricketer gets true satisfaction only if he is able to perform in difficult conditions against the best bowlers.

Once again we lost early wickets and I went in to bat with four top-order wickets down for 101. This time around, although it really wasn't my style then, I forced myself to stay at the wicket for the first fifteen minutes to get used to the conditions. I have no qualms about confessing that it was difficult. The bowlers were definitely on top at the start of my innings, but with time things turned easier. I was able to adjust to the pace and bounce of the wicket, and my confidence was gradually coming back.

I managed to play 172 balls en route to my first half-century in Test cricket and was finally dismissed by Imran for 59. I was involved in a 143-run partnership with Sanjay Manjrekar and though I hit only four boundaries, the innings gave me a lot of satisfaction. It also taught me a good lesson: there was no point in trying to blaze my way through every innings. Most importantly, this knock convinced me that I could actually cope with international cricket, though I knew I still had a lot to learn. In the second innings I ran myself out for eight, sacrificing my wicket for Mohammad Azharuddin, who was nearing a well-deserved hundred. In the end, we managed to thwart a Pakistan victory. After two Tests the series was still drawn and it was evident that Pakistan were feeling the pressure. Many had predicted a 4–0 scoreline in their favour and it was starting to play on their minds.

Third Test, Lahore, 1–6 December 1989

From Faisalabad we moved to Lahore for the third Test. Unable to venture out of the hotel in the evenings, the players and the touring Indian media were feeling a little restless and this called for some original thinking. For the first and only time in my career the media and the players got together for what was decreed a 'Sunday Club'. It was to be an evening of stories, music, food and fun and everyone had to wear something fancy. It turned out to be a very successful experiment, but sadly it hasn't been repeated since. It definitely helped to create a bond between the team and the media, so necessary during an arduous away tour.

I wore a blue pullover to the Sunday Club and that's where

the often-published picture of me with a thick moustache, Aussie fast bowler Merv Hughes-style, was taken. The food served that evening was unbelievable. Lahore is a foodie's delight and I wolfed down all the delectable kebabs on offer and I loved the *haleem* (a stew of meat and lentils). In fact, I had a voracious appetite throughout the tour. My body was still growing and I ate huge amounts. On non-match days I used to eat *keema parathas* (Indian flatbread stuffed with mincemeat) and *lassi* (yogurt drink) for breakfast and by the time I went back to India I had put on a few kilos and had also grown much stronger.

The Lahore Test was local hero Javed Miandad's 100th and in a change from the first two Test matches in Karachi and Faisalabad, we were faced with the flattest of batting decks, which had obviously been prepared to help Javed score a hundred, which he duly did. Even after five days, the first innings of both teams had still not been completed.

At the start of my innings in Lahore I misjudged the bounce of a straight delivery from Imran, which hit me on my biceps. I was furious at allowing myself to be hit on a flat pitch. The point of impact instantly turned numb and my first instinct was to step out and dispatch the very next ball over the boundary. However, the lesson learnt at Faisalabad came to my rescue and I reined myself in.

I had worked my way to 41 off ninety balls when I tried to play an on drive to Abdul Qadir and was bowled. I had been batting well and I regret not going on to play a long innings. It was an opportunity missed. It has to be said, though, that the match, a tame draw, was not the best advertisement for Test cricket.

Sweet dreams

The fourth and final Test of the series was at Sialkot and we knew that we'd be given a green-top, which offered Pakistan the best chance to take the series. By now they were desperate to win; a draw would have been considered tantamount a series defeat for Imran and his team. When we arrived at Sialkot, I was invited to the MB Malik bat-manufacturing company. Sialkot has quite a tradition of bat-making in Pakistan and at the time I didn't have a contract for my bats and could pick up any bat and play. I went to the factory with a few of the other players and chose two or three bats for myself.

I was so excited about my new bats that I even dreamed about them one night. Apparently, it was around midnight and I walked straight out of my room asking for my bats. Maninder Singh and Raman Lamba saw me advancing down the corridor and said to me, *'Tere bats to tere pass hi hai.'* (Your bats must be with you.) When I didn't respond, they realized that I was sleepwalking. They helped me back into the room and put me back to bed. By that stage of the tour, Raman and I had struck up a good friendship and spent many hours together discussing the nuances of batting. He was fun to be with and it was absolutely tragic that he died after being struck on his head by a ball while fielding during a first-class match in Dhaka in 1998.

Fourth Test, Sialkot, 9–14 December 1989

What made the Sialkot Test special was that my brother Ajit had travelled to see me play. It was an added incentive to do well and both Ajit and I still remember the kindness the locals bestowed on him the moment they became aware that he was from India and had come to watch cricket.

As expected, the wicket was green, but the December weather was also heavy, resulting in a lot of early-morning fog. So much so that play never started on time and it ended early each afternoon. This meant the four Pakistani fast bowlers could come at us all day, hoping to roll us over and secure the upper hand. In the first innings I played pretty well for my 35 and was feeling good before falling lbw to Wasim. I wasn't so uncomfortable at the start of my innings and the initial apprehension was no longer an issue. I hit some pleasing shots and scored at a good clip in the course of my 51-ball stay at the wicket.

India managed a 74-run first-innings lead, with Vivek Razdan, a fast bowler who played two Tests for India, picking up 5–79 in the Pakistan first innings. We had bowled them out for 250 and understandably Pakistan came back at us hard at the start of our second innings. We lost a cluster of early wickets and I went in to bat at 38–4, with a day and a half still to go in the match.

Waqar was bowling from one end and it was absolutely essential to survive the initial burst. I had just scored my first run when Waqar bowled a short delivery, which I thought would rise chin-high. I misjudged the bounce of the ball. It rose six inches higher than expected, hitting me on the flap of my helmet before deflecting onto my nose. At the time I was the only batsman besides Srikkanth not to wear a grille. It wasn't an act of bravado; I just wasn't used to playing with one. Ajit, who was sitting right in front of the Indian dressing room, later said to me that he had clearly heard the sound of the ball hitting my helmet and deflecting on to my nose.

My vision was blurred and my head felt heavy. After impact, the ball went towards the slips and my natural movement was to see where the ball had gone. It was then that I noticed all the blood spattered on my shirt. As I was trying to recover from the blow, I was amused by Javed Miandad's comments. In an attempt to psych me out, he was saying things like '*Arre tujhe to ab* hospital *jaana padega; teri naak toot gayi hai.*' (You may have to go to the hospital; your nose is broken.) To add to my discomfort, a banner in the stands read, '*Bachche, ghar jaake doodh peeke aa.*' (Hey kid go back home and drink your milk.)

I ignored all this while our team doctor, Vishwas Raut, inspected the injury. He put some ice on my nose and asked if I wanted to go off. I did not, for I considered it a moment of reckoning. Going off would suggest I was scared. And truly I wasn't. It wasn't the first time I had been hit, though the impact was much more severe than anything I had suffered before. I decided to carry on and said, 'Main khelega.' (I will play.) It was important for my own self-esteem, and by staying in I felt I had made a statement to the opposition.

Seeing me continue, Imran asked Javed to move away and all the Pakistani players went back to their respective field positions. Soon after the resumption, I got a full ball from Waqar on my legs and flicked it to the boundary. I followed it up with a drive on the off side and felt genuinely good about myself. I had treated the balls on merit and wasn't just being aggressive to avenge being hit. Soon it was time for tea and I had an opportunity to regroup. After the break I started to bat really well. I was feeling confident and was determined not to give my wicket away. Importantly for the team, I managed to play out the day and we were on course to force a draw.

Shortly after going back to the hotel, however, I felt heavy in the head. We had a team function in the evening but with the permission of our manager, Chandu Borde, I went to bed early with a few painkillers and having dinner with Ajit and Navjot Sidhu, which helped me calm down. When I got up the next morning after a good night's sleep, I was feeling ready for the challenge of the final day. We were on 102–4 overnight and needed to spend at least two more hours at the crease to deny Pakistan any opportunity of winning the Test.

Navjot Sidhu and I held out until I was dismissed by Imran for 57. It was my second half-century in Test cricket. Denying Pakistan a win on home turf was a big achievement for India, especially with the kind of bowling attack they had, and it served as a major confidence boost for the team. We were all elated at the performance.

The Abdul Qadir over

After the Tests, we played a five-match one-day series in which none of the matches was played for the scheduled fifty overs. While some of them were affected by rain, the third match was abandoned because of crowd trouble after Pakistan had been reduced to 29–3 by some good swing bowling from Manoj Prabhakar. The first match was due to be played in Peshawar on 16 December 1989 and had to be called off at the last moment because of rain. However, a large crowd had braved the inclement weather and it was finally agreed between both teams that a twenty-over-a-side exhibition game, perhaps the first ever Twenty20 game, would be played for the sake of the crowd. It was a good call, as the fans deserved to be given their money's worth. They are the ones who make the game what it is, after all, and they are pivotal to its health around the world.

Most people will agree that even an exhibition game between India and Pakistan can't help being a serious cricket match. At Peshawar Pakistan had scored 157 in their innings, and when I went in to bat with three wickets down, the asking rate had climbed to well past 11 runs an over. Srikkanth was batting with me and suggested we should dig in and get some practice for the following games. I was determined to go for the bowling and felt we still had a chance to make a match of it if we played our shots. That's what I suggested to Srikkanth and while he was a tad surprised, he told me to play the way I was comfortable with.

Mushtaq Ahmed, an up-and-coming Pakistani leg-spinner at that stage, was bowling and I hit him for a couple of sixes and a boundary in the first over I faced. While both sixes were hit over long on, the second went a fair distance and hit the dressing-room window, breaking the glass. The Pakistanis hadn't expected me to hit so far and Abdul Qadir, an old hand at the time, walked up to me and said, 'Bachhe ko kyoon maar rahe ho?

Dum hai to mujhe maar ke dikhao.' (What's the point of hitting sixes off a newcomer? If you have what it takes, try and hit me for a six.) I said to him that he was a great bowler and that I was sure he wouldn't allow me to hit him.

With just two overs left we needed more than 40 runs and Qadir was to bowl the penultimate over. Our only chance was to attack. I had made up my mind that if the ball was in my zone I'd go for my shots. As it happened, most of the balls were in my hitting arc and I took 28 off the over. I hit the first ball for six over long on and followed it up with a four off the third ball. The fourth ball resulted in a second six, which I hit straight over the bowler's head. Seeing me hit straight, Qadir bowled the fifth ball wide outside off stump in an attempt to get me stumped. I had anticipated the move and hit the ball over long off for the third six of the over. For the last ball he went even further outside off stump and I stretched out to hit the ball wide over long off, to make it four sixes in the over.

The crowd, which had been confident of a Pakistan victory till an over earlier, was roused by this unexpected turn of events and started making a lot of noise. There was a sudden increase in energy levels at the ground. The match was now being played in full seriousness and no one really knew which team would win. We needed 14 runs off the last over, bowled by Wasim Akram. Eventually we fell short by three runs. Straight after the match, Abdul Qadir walked up to me, and like a true sportsman, said to me '*Bahut aala* batting.' (Superior quality of batting.)

That innings of 53 off eighteen balls at Peshawar had a defining impact on my career. In the eyes of the public, it had overshadowed my effort at Sialkot, which was far more difficult and far more significant as far as I was concerned. The Sialkot innings had allowed us to save the Test match and also the series. But for people at home the innings at Peshawar was the real talking point. It had given me instant recognition and made me a household name. For the first time I was asked for autographs, which was a strange feeling. Before we went to Pakistan I had been able to go out with my friends and have *bhel* (a type of fast food loved all over Mumbai) and do all those normal things. Afterwards, when I went out with my friends, people would come up and ask if I was Sachin Tendulkar. And it was all down to that one innings at Peshawar. While it would have been premature to suggest I had established myself at international level, it had certainly given me a toehold.

When I got home, I could tell that my parents were proud of my achievements, but there has never been any over-the-top celebration in my house. While I knew that my father was extremely happy and satisfied, he wouldn't ever show off his emotions in an extravagant manner. When I did well, my mother would always light a *diya* (a kind of candle) and offer sweets to God, but that's as far as it went. Sometimes people are kind enough to compliment me on my off-the-field behaviour more than my on-field performance. They say that I seem to have managed to keep my feet grounded. If that's true, then I have no hesitation in saying that all the credit goes to my family.

Ajit's presence in Pakistan was a great help and we talked every evening about my game and how I could improve. While there were many senior team-mates who I could go to, I was most comfortable discussing things with Ajit, as he knew my game better than anyone. He had watched me grow up as a cricketer and it was natural that his observations would always be pertinent.

After coming back from Pakistan, I felt much more positive about myself as a cricketer and was looking forward to India's next away tour, to New Zealand at the start of 1990. I was pretty confident of getting picked but was still delighted to see myself in the squad when the touring side was announced.

India in Pakistan 1989

1st Test. Karachi. 15–20 November 1989
Pakistan 409 (Imran Khan 109*, J Miandad 78, S Mohammad 67;
    M Prabhakar 5–104, Kapil Dev 4–69) and 305–5 dec (S Malik 102*,
    S Mohammad 95; Kapil Dev 3–82)
India 262 (KS More 58*, Kapil Dev 55. **SR Tendulkar 15**; W Akram 4–83,
    W Younis 4–80) and 303–3 (SV Manjrekar 113*, NS Sidhu 85)
Match drawn

2nd Test. Faisalabad. 23–28 November 1989
India 288 (SV Manjrekar 76, **SR Tendulkar 59**; Imran Khan 4–45) and 398–7
    (M Azharuddin 109, SV Manjrekar 83, NS Sidhu 51, **SR Tendulkar 8**)
Pakistan 423–9 dec (A Malik 117, S Malik 63, R Raja 58; M Prabhakar 6–132)
Match drawn

3rd Test. Lahore. 1–6 December 1989
India 509 (SV Manjrekar 218, M Azharuddin 77, RJ Shastri 61, **SR Tendulkar
    41**; A Qadir 3–97)
Pakistan 699–5 (S Mohammad 203*, J Miandad 145, A Malik 113)
Match drawn

4th Test. Sialkot. 9–14 December 1989
India 324 (SV Manjrekar 72, M Azharuddin 52, **SR Tendulkar 35**; W Akram
    5–101) and 234–7 (NS Sidhu 97, **SR Tendulkar 57**; Imran Khan 3–68)
Pakistan 250 (R Raja 56; V Razdan 5–79)
Match drawn

Series drawn 0–0

4

FOREIGN CONDITIONS

New Zealand has always been a very difficult tour for an Indian cricketer. It's often windy and chilly and that, coupled with the short boundaries in most of the grounds, makes it very different from conditions back home in India. In 1990 the challenge was doubly difficult, with Richard Hadlee, one of the finest ever exponents of swing bowling, close to his best. As a seventeen-year-old on his first tour away from the subcontinent, I was excited about the opportunity.

India in New Zealand, February–March 1990

The first few days in New Zealand were not easy. The accent of the locals there was very strange to our ears and the food took some getting used to. The accent problem resulted in an incident involving Manoj Prabhakar very early in the tour. Prabhakar needed an adapter to charge his gadgets and for some reason decided to put on what he thought was a New Zealand accent while speaking to the housekeeping staff in the hotel. When asking for the adapter on the intercom he was almost chewing up the first 'a', as a result of which the word was sounding like 'dapter' and the staff were having difficulty understanding what he was asking for. Prabhakar got angry after a point and said he needed the 'dapter' immediately. In a few minutes there was a knock on his door and he opened it to find a doctor standing there. The staff had heard 'doctor' for 'dapter' (partly because they pronounced 'doctor' as 'dactor') and had sent the resident physician to Prabhakar's room.

The first game of the tour was in New Plymouth and the

ground was surrounded by hills. It was as if a stadium had been planted in the middle of mountains and Bishan Singh Bedi, our manager, decided to make the most of the conditions. Bedi, one of the best left-arm spinners of all time, was a really hard task-master and liked to make us run huge distances to improve our fitness. At New Plymouth our fitness drills involved running in the mountains and by the end of the training sessions we had absolutely no energy left.

As in Pakistan, I did not start particularly well and in the first Test at Christchurch, which started on 2 February, I was dismissed by Danny Morrison for a golden duck. It was a good delivery but the send-off was interesting, to say the least. I could hear most of the New Zealand players calling me a schoolboy, with plenty of F-words thrown in. They kindly advised me to go back to playing cricket with my school chums, suggesting that I wasn't fit to compete at international level. I kept my mouth shut.

The second innings was an improvement in that I managed to stay at the wicket for close to an hour, playing forty-four balls. My 24 runs were enough to give me confidence that I was capable of holding my own in strange conditions. Although I had fallen to John Bracewell, trying to cut a ball close to my body, I had successfully negotiated Richard Hadlee, which I counted as an achievement. Hadlee's first two deliveries to me were bouncers, but each was profoundly different from the other. The first was an outswinging bouncer that went away after pitching; the second came in from the same spot and I had to keep my eye on the ball till the last moment to get my head out of the way. Such was the ability of the man that you had to be at your best at all times to keep him at bay.

New Zealand won the first Test by ten wickets and the second Test match at Napier started only a few days later, on 9 February. We decided to bat first after winning the toss but the first day was completely washed out by rain. The match finally started on the second day and I was unbeaten on 80 by the end of the third day's play. The ball was doing a little and batting wasn't particularly easy, but not once did I try to dominate the bowling the way I had in domestic cricket.

When I went in to bat on the fourth morning the possibility of a hundred was on my mind. I was just 20 runs short and was determined to take my opportunity. I started well and hit the very first Danny Morrison delivery for four. For the rest of the over he bowled short and I was content to leave everything. In his next over, I again hit a boundary off the first ball. The next was pitched up and I had already made up my mind to go for a big drive but the drive was uppish and I was caught by the New Zealand captain John Wright at mid off for 88.

I was heartbroken. As I walked back to the pavilion I couldn't control my tears. Why on earth did I play that shot when I was just twelve runs short? By the time I reached the boundary rope, tears were flowing down my cheeks. I'm glad there weren't too many cameras then, as these days a cameraman would definitely have picked up an embarrassing shot of me in tears. On reaching the dressing room, I went straight to the bathroom and cried for a good few minutes. Missing out on what should have been my first Test hundred was just too painful. It was only later that I was told I would have been the youngest Test centurion ever. It was a missed opportunity and I remember telling John Wright, after he took over as coach of India in 2000, that he really shouldn't have taken that catch!

We eventually lost the three-Test match series 0–1 and then played the Rothmans Cup one-day tri-series, with Australia as the third team. As in the first Test, I was out for a duck in the first ODI against New Zealand at Dunedin on 1 March, caught and bowled by Shane Thomson, who was bowling medium pace. The only difference was that this time I had lasted one more ball. In the end, we lost the game by 108 runs.

I made a better fist of it in my next match, on 6 March 1990, an important one in the context of the tournament. We had lost

to Australia in the second game and now needed to beat New
Zealand to stay in contention for the final. I made 36 runs off
thirty-nine balls, in the process attacking their seam bowlers for
the first time and hitting them for quite a few boundaries. We
won the game by one run, with Martin Snedden run out and
Richard Hadlee bowled in the final over by Kapil Dev, who was
declared Man of the Match for his all-round performance. For
the first time my innings had been of use to the team in an
official ODI. I couldn't do much celebrating, though, because I
had damaged my right quadriceps during the game and had to
be carried off the field. I couldn't walk at all by the evening and
was on crutches for the next few days. It was the first serious
injury of my career and my tournament was over.

While we were in New Zealand, Asha Bhosle, one of the all-time
great Indian singers, happened to be performing in Wellington
and the team decided to go to her concert. It was the first time I
had seen her live and I just loved the experience. Asha Bhosle and
Lata Mangeshkar, another of India's finest singers, are still two of
my favourites and to see them perform is always very special.

On my return to India, my father told me that I had to hone
my God-given cricketing ability. He was right. It was time for more
hard work to master the skills needed to face the fast swinging
ball and I was determined to put in the hours in the nets.

India in England, July–August 1990

After the New Zealand series, India travelled to England for what
was our most important assignment of the year. India had won
a Test series in England in 1986 and we were all looking forward
to repeating the feat. We had a training camp in Bangalore just
before the series and Bishan Bedi continued with his policy of
making us run miles every day. We had to jog in a line at Cubbon
Park, opposite the Chinnaswamy Stadium, and the last man in
the line had to sprint to the front. The same drill was followed

for all the players and the exhausting routine finally resulted in Manoj Prabhakar jokingly suggesting that he was so fast now he would reach the batsman before his delivery did.

I had been to England twice before, in 1987–88 and 1988–89, as part of the Star Cricket Club, the team of Kailash Gattani (a former fast bowler who played first-class cricket for Rajasthan in Indian domestic cricket). In the first instance, I was sponsored by the Kolkata-based Young Cricketers Organization, who contributed my airfare. Among other things, I remember the tour for the food we ate. We stayed in school and college dormitories and had breakfast in their dining halls. For the first time in my life I was served cold meat for breakfast. That meat could be eaten cold was a revelation to me!

I was also amazed to see so many different types of cars. I have always had an interest in cars, though we didn't own one at the time. Kailash Gattani had hired a luxury sedan for us, and I was amazed at the many different types of cars I came across during that tour. I have always had a keen interest in cars and still find the engineering of these machines truly fascinating. Besides playing cricket, these were things that kept me occupied and I thoroughly enjoyed the opportunity of exploring a foreign country. Visiting Lord's, the mecca of world cricket, was a dream come true, and it all added to my ambition to play at such venues as a member of the Indian cricket team.

In 1990, the tour started with a few first-class fixtures, which were followed by two one-day internationals. While I was in good form at the start of the tour and scored runs in the first-class games, I didn't do so well in the first ODI at Leeds on 18 July, making only 19. Happily, it didn't matter because the team won – thanks to the batting of Manjrekar and Azharuddin – and we had a chance of victory in the series if we won the next game at Nottingham on the 20th.

In the second match England produced a better performance, batting first, with Robin Smith, the South African-born middle-order batsman, contributing 103 to their total of 281. We needed to bat really well to close out the series. When I went in to bat at number six we needed a further 145 off twenty overs. In those days, that was considered a stiff target. I scored a quick 31 off twenty-six balls and was dismissed with the score on 249, with 33 still needed to win, but we won the match and the series 2-0, with Azhar seeing us home with an unbeaten 63. It was a perfect start to the tour, giving us some welcome confidence going into the Test series.

First Test, Lord's, 26-31 July 1990

The first Test at Lord's will always be remembered for Graham Gooch's heroics with the bat. After being dropped on 33, he went on to make a triple hundred. He was eventually out for 333 and then produced another century in the second innings. For India, the highlights were Azhar's hundred and Kapil Dev hitting four successive sixes off Eddie Hemmings, the off-spinner, to save the follow-on.

My only significant contribution in the match was a catch off leg-spinner Narendra Hirwani's bowling to dismiss England's batting mainstay Allan Lamb in the second innings. It remains the most memorable catch of my career. Hirwani had beaten Lamb in the flight as he stepped out to hit straight down the ground. Despite failing to get to the pitch of the ball, Lamb went through with the shot and the ball went high into the air, looking as if it was going to land some 25 yards behind the bowler.

As soon as Lamb hit the shot, I started sprinting from my position at long off. There was very little chance that I would make it, because I had been positioned a few yards wide of the conventional long-off position. It was only during the last few steps that I realized I had an outside chance. I had covered a distance of more than 25 yards and was still short. I could dive forward, but I knew I would not have enough control to catch the ball. The other option was to carry on sprinting and try somehow to get a hand to the ball, which was dying on me. I chose the second option and to my surprise felt the ball land squarely in my fully outstretched right hand at knee height.

Having completed the catch, I threw the ball up in the air in sheer ecstasy. My team-mates were naturally delighted. Hirwani rushed to congratulate me and I felt thrilled at having pulled it off. The crowd appreciated the athletic effort and I vividly remember the warm applause as I walked back to my fielding position. The key to taking catches like these, it seems to me, is not to be afraid of taking the initiative and deciding quickly, while always keeping an eye on the trajectory of the ball.

We lost the Lord's Test by the huge margin of 247 runs and needed to tighten our game before the second Test at Old Trafford a week later to remain alive in the series.

Second Test, Old Trafford, 9–14 August 1990

In the first innings at Old Trafford, England once again put together a total of more than 500, with centuries from Gooch and Mike Atherton, and we simply had to get as close to their score as possible in our reply. We were due to bat fourth in the match and any total in excess of 250 would be difficult to chase down on a wearing pitch. Azhar made another hundred and almost everyone in the top order contributed to our first-innings effort. Had the lower middle order scored runs, we may have got closer to the English total and even managed a first-innings lead. It might also have given me an opportunity to go for my maiden hundred. But they got out in quick succession and I ran out of partners. I went in to bat at number six with the team score on 246 and was last man out for 68, trying to play a big shot off Eddie Hemmings. As Hirwani would I am sure agree, he was not the best number eleven in the world. I felt I had to go for my shots sooner rather than later and I holed out to Chris Lewis at deep midwicket as a result.

Hirwani was always fun to bat with and when he came in he said to me at the wicket that he would be fine as long as the balls were pitched up. He said he had a problem facing bouncers and I assured him that the English bowlers would not bowl bouncers at him because he wasn't a recognized batsman. He managed to bat on for a while and gradually gained in confidence. So much so that he suddenly charged out to Chris Lewis to give the ball a real whack. Chris's expression said it all. He did not take kindly to a number-eleven batsman giving him the charge. He was fuming as he walked back to his bowling mark and a bouncer was now inevitable. However, in charging out Hirwani had somehow broken his bat and it took a bit of time to get a replacement from the dressing room. Luckily, the few minutes that were lost in the bat change had a calming effect on Chris Lewis and Hirwani survived his innings unscathed.

We were finally all out for 432, conceding an 87-run first-innings lead. It was evident that England would want to score quickly and set us a target. Allan Lamb made a hundred in the England second innings and on the final day they declared on 320–4, leaving us ninety-two overs to bat out. The English attack, consisting of Angus Fraser, Chris Lewis, Devon Malcolm and Eddie Hemmings, had some variety, and while the fast bowlers used the cloud cover to good effect, Hemmings extracted considerable purchase from the fifth-day track. With all the bowlers performing at their best, we were soon reduced to 109–4. Then Azhar fell with the score on 127 and Kapil Dev was yorked by Eddie Hemmings, leaving us at a perilous 183–6.

My first Test hundred

When Manoj Prabhakar joined me in the middle we badly needed a partnership to save the game. I had been lucky at the start of my innings, with Eddie Hemmings dropping me when I had tried to play an on drive. The ball had hit the outside part of my bat and spooned back to Hemmings, who failed to hold on to it. I learnt my lesson and decided not to play any more uppish strokes. At the same time I was determined to play some shots and not go into my shell. Getting ultra-defensive would allow the English bowlers to put more and more fielders round the bat, and by trying to score I would be able to keep the field spread out. Every time I got a chance to score runs, I did so. Most of my scoring strokes were in the nature of punches played with minimum risk. The balance between aggression and caution was crucial and I was trying to focus on each and every ball. My fifty came up but it did not excite me. The match was far from saved and that was the goal.

At the other end, Manoj Prabhakar was playing well and after a while it was clear we had succeeded in frustrating the English bowlers. The first task had been accomplished. When trying to save a match, the important thing is to set small targets. These can be as little as batting the next five overs, or the next hour, or even a session. If a wicket doesn't fall for close to a session, the opposition, however much they are in control, are bound to feel pressure. Time was gradually running out for England and restlessness was creeping in.

When I passed 90 runs, it was obvious that the thought of scoring a hundred would start to affect me. After all, it would be my first international century and the crowd had already started expecting it from me. I reminded myself of what had happened in New Zealand and was conscious not to repeat the same mistake. There was still some time left in the day's play and England could press for victory if I got out.

In the mid-nineties I got a lucky reprieve against Angus Fraser. He bowled me a bouncer and I ducked under it with my bat held above my head like a periscope. The ball hit the back of the bat and went along the ground to fine leg. It could have gone straight into the hands of any of the close-in fielders or to the wicketkeeper. But it didn't. I was glad and thanked God for the reprieve.

At Old Trafford luck seemed to be with me. I batted patiently until I finally played a punch off Angus Fraser through mid off when on 98. Chris Lewis chased down the ball but by the time he threw it back to the bowler I had run three, completing my first Test hundred. The crowd stood to applaud but I was extremely uncomfortable about acknowledging them. I had never been in that position before and was acutely embarrassed about raising my bat to the stadium.

Every time I look back at the footage of my first century, I realize that celebrating was not something that came naturally to me. It was only with time that I became more confident of my presence in the middle. 'Presence' is actually very important in international sport. It is one thing just being there in the middle, but it is another making people aware of your 'presence'. It is about body language and radiating confidence, something that the West Indian batting legend Viv Richards would personify. With me it happened after I had scored a few hundreds and felt more established in international cricket. As I grew more assured of my presence, I came up with my own signature style of celebrating an achievement by showing the bat to the dressing room. Most cricketers develop their own style of celebrating. For example, the way Glenn McGrath and Shane Warne showed the ball to the crowd after picking up five wickets in an innings was something they evolved over the course of their careers.

At Old Trafford I continued to bat on after reaching my hundred and with every passing over it was becoming apparent that the match would end in a draw. When the match was finally called off with two of the twenty mandatory overs still to be bowled, we had reached 343 for no further losses. Prabhakar and I had put together an unbeaten 160-run stand.

I remember walking back to the pavilion to a standing ovation.

Both umpires, John Hampshire and John Holder, congratulated me on my hundred and all the England players walked up to me to offer some kind words. In the dressing room my team-mates congratulated me – not just on my maiden Test hundred but also for batting through the day and saving the game for the team, meaning that it was all to play for in the third Test. It was the second occasion I had done so. This one was more satisfying, though, because this time I played a central part in the effort, unlike in the fourth Test in Pakistan, where I had a supporting role.

Just when I was about to relax after a good day's work, I was informed that I had to face the media. It was going to be the first time I addressed a press conference. I asked our manager Madhav Mantri, a former Test cricketer who toured England with India in the 1950s, if it was compulsory or if I could just skip it. He assured me it was a routine matter and said that the journalists would only ask me questions about my performance and about the match. My team-mates, however, started pulling my leg, saying they'd ask me questions I couldn't answer and that it was going to be a really difficult session. Looking back, I must admit that I quite enjoyed the experience. I was uncomfortable to start with, but it was quite straightforward really. I just needed to share my thoughts and it wasn't such a daunting task after all. Most of the questions were pleasant and it felt good to receive compliments from well-known cricket writers.

I was declared Player of the Match – my first such award – and once again felt awkward at the ceremony. I was handed the bottle of champagne but, not being eighteen, I didn't drink at the time. I just wanted the presentation to be over and to hurry back to the dressing room with the award as soon as possible. In the end I brought the bottle home with me to Mumbai and finally opened it on the occasion of my daughter Sara's first birthday in 1998.

England v India

(2nd Test)

Played at Old Trafford, Manchester, on 9, 10, 11, 13, 14 August 1990

Umpires: JH Hampshire & JW Holder
Toss: England

ENGLAND

GA Gooch*	c More b Prabhakar	116		c More b Prabhakar	7
MA Atherton	c More b Hirwani	131		lbw b Kapil Dev	74
DI Gower	c Tendulkar b Kapil Dev	38		b Hirwani	16
AJ Lamb	c Manjrekar b Kumble	38		b Kapil Dev	109
RC Russell†	c More b Hirwani	8	(7)	not out	16
RA Smith	not out	121	(5)	not out	61
JE Morris	b Kumble	13	(6)	retired hurt	15
CC Lewis	b Hirwani	3			
EE Hemmings	lbw b Hirwani	19			
ARC Fraser	c Tendulkar b Kumble	1			
DE Malcolm	b Shastri	13			
Extras	(b 2, lb 9, w 1, nb 6)	18		(lb 15, nb 7)	22
Total	(160.5 overs)	**519**		(for 4 wkts dec) (81 overs)	**320**

INDIA

RJ Shastri	c Gooch b Fraser	25		b Malcolm	12
NS Sidhu	c Gooch b Fraser	13		c sub (CJ Adams) b Fraser	0
SV Manjrekar	c Smith b Hemmings	93		c sub (CJ Adams) b Hemmings	50
DB Vengsarkar	c Russell b Fraser	6		b Lewis	32
M Azharuddin*	c Atherton b Fraser	179		c Lewis b Hemmings	11
SR Tendulkar	c Lewis b Hemmings	68		not out	119
M Prabhakar	c Russell b Malcolm	4	(8)	not out	67
Kapil Dev	lbw b Lewis	0	(7)	b Hemmings	26
KS More†	b Fraser	6			
A Kumble	run out (Morris)	2			
ND Hirwani	not out	15			
Extras	(b 5, lb 4, nb 12)	21		(b 17, lb 3, nb 6)	26
Total	(119.2 overs)	**432**		(for 6 wkts) (90 overs)	**343**

INDIA	O	M	R	W		O	M	R	W	Fall of wickets:				
											Eng	Ind	Eng	Ind
Kapil Dev	13	2	67	1		22	4	69	2	1st	225	26	15	4
Prabhakar	25	2	112	1		18	1	80	1	2nd	292	48	46	35
Kumble	43	7	105	3	(4)	17	3	65	0	3rd	312	57	180	109
Hirwani	62	10	174	4	(3)	15	0	52	1	4th	324	246	248	109
Shastri	17.5	2	50	1		9	0	39	0	5th	366	358	–	127
										6th	392	364	–	183
ENGLAND	O	M	R	W		O	M	R	W	7th	404	365	–	–
Malcolm	26	3	96	1		14	5	59	1	8th	434	396	–	–
Fraser	35	5	124	5		21	3	81	1	9th	459	401	–	–
Hemmings	29.2	8	74	2		31	10	75	3	10th	519	432	–	–
Lewis	13	1	61	1	(5)	20	3	86	1					
Atherton	16	3	68	0	(4)	4	0	22	0					

Close of play: Day 1:   Eng (1) 322–3 (Lamb 20*, Russell 7*, 92 overs)
                 Day 2:   Ind (1) 77–3 (Manjrekar 21*, Azharuddin 4*, 27 overs)
                 Day 3:   Ind (1) 432
                 Day 4:   Eng (2) 290–4 (Smith 40*, Morris 15*, 76 overs)

Man of the Match: SR Tendulkar
Result: **Match drawn**

On returning to the hotel after the match I got a call from home and remember speaking to what must have been thirty or forty people on the phone. It was a spontaneous gathering of all my friends at our neighbour's apartment to celebrate the hundred and it was really touching to know that people in the colony were so thrilled at the accomplishment. Some of them jokingly mentioned to me that as I wasn't old enough to drink, they were enjoying a drink on my behalf. My parents were extremely happy with my performance and my brother too felt vindicated.

The third Test match, at The Oval at the end of August, was another draw, which meant that we lost the series 0–1, but I was still reasonably satisfied with my performances in England and felt I had taken a few important strides. I returned to India a better Test cricketer and far more confident of myself as a performer, ready for the next big challenges: a tour of Australia at the end of the following year, followed by the World Cup jointly organized by Australia and New Zealand.

India in Australia, November 1991–February 1992

We began the tour with a couple of one-day practice matches in Perth in November 1991, the first at Lilac Hill and the second at the WACA, one of the fastest cricket wickets in the world. At the WACA we were bowled out for just 64 and it was clear we had to adjust to Australian conditions as soon as possible if we were going to be competitive in the series.

Our first three-day tour game was against a full-strength New South Wales team at Lismore between 23 and 25 November and it was in that game that I got my first taste of real Australian competitiveness. It was a fast, lively wicket and Geoff Lawson, the NSW captain, had no hesitation in putting us in after winning the toss. In addition to Lawson, their bowling attack included Mike Whitney, Steve and Mark Waugh, Greg Matthews and Wayne

Holdsworth, and it was a tough test for us. The team also included Mark Taylor and five players – Whitney, Lawson, Steve Waugh, Mark Taylor and Matthews – had already played Test cricket for Australia.

I was looking to be aggressive from the very beginning and played a number of horizontal-bat shots over point and gully. It was in this match that I had my first exchange with Steve Waugh, who didn't seem keen on the idea of an eighteen-year-old attacking the bowling like that. A lot of things were said to me and they were the first of many over the years.

It was in the course of this match that the Australian Test team for the first Test at Brisbane was announced. Steve Waugh was not included in the side, so I said to him that if he wanted to fight with me, he first needed to get into the Australian team. It was all done in good spirit and throughout our careers we had great mutual respect; in fact, the banter, it must be said, was a result of this. We knew how important it was to get Steve Waugh out early and tried all we could to unsettle him. There were occasions when we even resorted to observing total silence when Waugh batted as we came to believe that saying things to him actually strengthened his resolve to do better.

A tough start

In the first Test at Brisbane, starting on 29 November 1991, the Australians beat us convincingly, thanks in large part to superb bowling from Craig McDermott and Merv Hughes. Like most of our team, I didn't do much with the bat and we knew we had to bounce back in Melbourne in the Boxing Day Test. At the MCG we remained competitive till the middle of the third day, with Kiran More coming to the rescue with 67 in our first innings and Kapil Dev and Prabhakar both bowling well, before a batting collapse in our second innings dampened our hopes. I managed to stay in for a reasonable time and scored 40 off 107 balls, but

I was disgusted with myself for trying to hit a big shot and getting out caught by Allan Border against the off-spinner Peter Taylor after doing all the hard work and playing myself in. I was so fed up that I didn't eat lunch in the dressing room and was on edge for the whole day!

Something else happened in Melbourne that has never happened again in my life, I'm pleased to say. When I went back to the dressing room I realized that my abdominal protector had been broken into three pieces when I was hit by a Bruce Reid delivery. Reid, the tall left-arm fast bowler, got a lot of wickets in the series and I was lucky that no major damage was caused by the accident!

Fighting back

Down 0–2, we went to Sydney for the next Test on 2 January 1992 knowing it was our last chance to get back in the series. It was a typical SCG wicket, helpful to the batsmen to start with, and I thought our bowlers did very well to bowl Australia out for 313 in the first innings. It was essential for us to take a substantial lead and give our bowlers a chance to bowl Australia out again in the second innings. I didn't sleep much the night before batting. I was sharing a room with Sourav Ganguly, who later captained India and is a very good friend. I remember a startled Sourav waking up in the middle of the night and seeing me shadow-practise. Sourav wasn't playing in that game and was surprised to see me up so late. I told him I was planning how to play McDermott and the other bowlers.

Unsurprisingly, the next day I was feeling rather tired. India were batting and I was batting at number six, so I decided to take a nap on the dining table inside the SCG dressing room – asking Sourav to wake me up at the fall of the next wicket. He did so when Azhar got out. By then I was feeling refreshed and was ready to go out and bat.

For the first time in the series our top order had fired and by the time I went in, the score was a healthy 201–4, with Vengsarkar having contributed a half-century. We needed another good partnership to push on for a lead and, with the opener Ravi Shastri playing extremely well at the other end, that's what we managed to do. The second innings at Melbourne had definitely helped me and I was now able to middle the ball from the very start. There was a phase halfway through when I began to lose concentration and feel edgy, but I forced myself to exercise restraint and it soon passed.

After reaching my half-century, I began to play a lot more shots and was soon close to my second Test hundred. I vividly remember the glance to fine leg that brought up my century. I ran two and the second run was the fastest I have ever run. Ravi went on to score an excellent double hundred, the first by an Indian in Australia, as we put on 196 runs for the fifth wicket. Sydney continues to be my favourite ground outside India and to score my first hundred in Australia at the SCG was special. I had grown up watching cricket in Australia on the TV and used to wake up early to watch the World Championship of Cricket in 1985. Now I was playing at the actual venues and scoring runs.

The SCG Test is also remembered for the debut of a plump Australian leg-spinner with a mop of blond hair. Though Shane Warne took only one wicket in the match, it was evident to us all that he could give the ball a fair rip. While no one could have predicted the 708 Test wickets he would take in his career, the fact that he had talent was obvious from the very first day he took to the field in January 1992.

Knowing that we could bat only once – because of valuable time lost to rain and bad light on the third and fourth days – we batted for close to an hour on the final day and declared with a lead of 170 runs. With the track doing a fair bit and the bounce turning variable, we had a good chance of closing out the game in the time remaining. A win still seemed on the cards when Shastri's bowling helped reduce Australia to 114–6 and it was only some dogged rearguard action from Allan Border and Merv Hughes that saved Australia.

In the one over I bowled I picked up the wicket of Hughes and it was a big moment for me because it was my first wicket in Test cricket. He was caught by Prabhakar in the slips for 21 after playing seventy-three balls, and if we had got his wicket a little earlier, we might have been able to close out the game.

Learning some lessons

The fourth Test of the series started at Adelaide on 25 January 1992 and for the first time I was going to bat at the home ground of the legendary Sir Donald Bradman, the greatest batsman to have played the game. While I did not do much at the Adelaide Oval, the team played some good cricket. We lost the match by 38 runs in the end, but we remained competitive throughout and dominated the first two days of the match. Kapil Dev had a good match with both bat and ball and in our second innings Azhar played a wonderful captain's innings, scoring 106. He and Prabhakar, who made 64, had brought us to the brink of victory, but we were eventually all out for 333 chasing 371. With a bit of luck, the series could have been 2–2 at Adelaide. Instead we went to Perth for the final Test 0–3 down.

I scored my second hundred of the series in the fifth Test, which started on 1 February, and I count it as one of the very best I have scored. It was a quick wicket and for the first time since my debut I was going in at number four in a Test. I relished the opportunity from the outset and hit sixteen boundaries in my 114. By that stage of the tour I had mastered a back-foot punch. While most batsmen favoured the cut shot at Perth because of the extra bounce, I used the back-foot punch at every opportunity and because I was able to do so against good-length balls, it was making the bowlers' job that much more difficult. It would usually bring me at least a couple of runs and when

I timed the ball really well it would even go all the way to the boundary.

Earlier, the Australian media had talked up the fast, bouncy WACA wicket and how difficult it would make it for us to cope with the Australian quick bowlers. But I never had a problem batting at the WACA. This was because I managed to adjust to the bounce. Every time the ball got big on me, I stayed on the back foot and played the ball with soft hands at the last moment, standing up on my toes rather than playing a flat-footed defensive stroke.

One incident at the WACA brought home the intensity and competitiveness of the game in Australia. I had just played a ball defensively and had no chance of a run. In what I thought was the spirit of the game, I was about to pick the ball up and throw it to Allan Border, the Australian captain, who was fielding at gully. When AB spotted me bending down he screamed at me, saying, 'Don't you dare touch the ball.' After that I never tried to pick up the ball and throw it back to fielders. It was a lesson in how international cricket is played and I remembered it till the last day of my career.

Meeting a hero

It was on this tour of Australia that I first saw a batsman who had been my hero when I was growing up – though it wasn't on the cricket field. I was in a hotel lobby in Adelaide with Sanjay Manjrekar when a cab pulled up outside. A guy wearing a cap got out and I immediately said, 'I've seen him somewhere before.' As he got closer I said, 'I don't believe it – that's Viv Richards!'

When he walked past us and headed up to his room, I turned to Sanjay and told him that I just had to meet my hero. So we went to Reception and found out his room number and I made Sanjay call him – Sanjay had played a series against him in the West Indies in 1989 – and before long we were on our way to his room. That was my first meeting with Viv. I spent only three minutes with him, just to say hello, but it was a very exciting moment for me.

1992 World Cup in Australia and New Zealand

After the Test series we stayed in Australia, as the World Cup – my first – was just a few weeks away. The idea was to help us acclimatize to the conditions, not that this was necessary after being in Australia for close to three months. We had a few weeks to ourselves and with Vinod Kambli around there was never a dull moment. Vinod and I shared a room and one thing that always stood out about him was his dress sense. Vinod's clothes were as colourful as they could possibly get and on one occasion our manager Ranbir Singh Mahendra even said to him, '*Arre India ke liye khel rahe ho, aise clown jaise dress kyun pehente ho tum? Kuch dhang ka kapda pehna karo.*' (You are playing for India. Why do you dress like a clown? You should dress sensibly.) Not that it had any impact on Vinod, though!

Those few weeks were relatively stress-free and we spent a lot of time relaxing in each other's company. On one occasion the leg-spinner Narendra Hirwani and I were having tea in our physio Dr Ali Irani's room. Ali used to make special tea for us, with a particular kind of sugar. In the middle of our conversation Ali got a call from Ranbir Singh Mahendra, who was a vegetarian, asking if he could get him some garlic bread. After the call Ali turned all philosophical and said, 'There will come a time when you guys will be there and will think about old Ali Irani who used to take care of us and make us really nice tea.'

Hirwani and I found it funny that he had turned unnaturally thoughtful and Hirwani asked him to repeat what he had just said. Ali was reluctant to do so but when Hirwani insisted, he said it again. At this Hirwani jokingly said to Ali with reference to his efforts to keep Ranbir Singh Mahendra in good humour, '*Tu to har din 200 marta hai. India team mein tera naam pehle likha jaata hai. Uske baad hamara naam aata hai.'* (You score a double hundred every day by being in the good books of the manager. Your name always appears first on the team list and only then do our names feature on it.)

In the World Cup, India failed to make the semi-finals, despite being competitive in most of the matches. We lost to England and Australia by the narrow margin of nine runs and one run respectively and our second match against Sri Lanka at Mackay on 28 February was washed out because of rain.

The high point of the tournament for us was the match against eventual winners Pakistan on 4 March 1992 at Sydney. After two consecutive defeats, we were determined to turn things round against Pakistan. Batting first, we had to negotiate a hostile spell of fast bowling from Wasim Akram. At one stage he was bowling magnificently to Vinod Kambli and, batting at the other end, I just kept telling Vinod to nudge the ball and run. We put together an important partnership and I followed it up with another with Kapil Dev, who scored a valuable 35 off just twenty-six balls. I was unbeaten on 54 at the end of the innings.

Our total of 216 wasn't a big score to defend, but we started well and Kapil Dev and Prabakhar picked up two early wickets for very little on the board. Our bowlers and fielders were charged up and there was a lot of chat out in the middle. We were cheering each other on and giving the Pakistan batsmen a hard time.

This match is often remembered for the tussle between our wicketkeeper Kiran More and Javed Miandad. Javed, if I remember right, was having back spasms and could not play his strokes freely. He was finding it difficult to bat but was performing an uncharacteristic job for his team, trying to anchor the innings and hold up one end. Behind the stumps, Kiran was constantly up and down, shouting out instructions to our bowlers, saying Javed was in no position to play his shots. Infuriated at the continuous chatter, Javed imitated Kiran's actions by doing a frog jump. We were all stunned and amused at the same time and this tiff between Kiran and Javed made the eventual victory even sweeter.

I bowled my full quota of ten overs, conceding just 37 runs and picking up the vital wicket of opener Aamer Sohail. It was a satisfying win and by the end of the match I had completely lost my voice because of all the shouting. It was the first time India had played Pakistan in the World Cup since the inception of the tournament in 1975 and it was the start of a string of victories against them in World Cups. The 1992 victory was particularly pleasing because I was also Player of the Match.

When we returned to India at the end of March after four and a half months in Australia I was a transformed cricketer. The 1991–92 Australia tour undoubtedly had a fundamental impact on my career.

A brave man

The story of the Australia tour is incomplete without a story that has stayed with me over the years. It involves Venkatapathy Raju, our left-arm spinner, and Merv Hughes. They were great pals and on a flight to Perth, which is a little under four hours from Sydney, we dared Raju, one of the skinniest cricketers in the team, to go and grab Hughes's famous thick moustache. Merv, a huge man, was known for his volatile temper and most of us were convinced that Raju would chicken out in the end. To our surprise, he boldly went up to Merv and pulled his moustache, a feat of incredible bravery – or foolishness. Merv took it all very sportingly and the act was applauded by everyone on the flight, making Raju an instant hero.

India in New Zealand 1990

1st Test. Christchurch. 2–5 February 1990
New Zealand 459 (JG Wright 185, KR Rutherford 69, AH Jones 52) and 2–0
India 164 (NS Sidhu 51, M Azharuddin 48, **SR Tendulkar 0**; DK Morrison
    5–75) and 296 (f/o) (WV Raman 96, **SR Tendulkar 24**; RJ Hadlee 4–69)
New Zealand won by 10 wickets

2nd Test. Napier. 9–13 February 1990
India 358–9 dec (M Prabhakar 95, **SR Tendulkar 88**, KS More 73;
    DK Morrison 5–98)
New Zealand 178–1 (JG Wright 113*, TJ Franklin 50)
Match drawn

3rd Test. Auckland. 22–26 February 1990
New Zealand 391 (IDS Smith 173, RJ Hadlee 87; AS Wassan 4–108) and
    483–5 dec (AH Jones 170*, MD Crowe 113, JG Wright 74)
India 482 (M Azharuddin 192, AS Wassan 53, KS More 50, **SR Tendulkar
    5**; DK Morrison 5–145) and 149–0 (M Prabhakar 63*, WV Raman 72*)
Match drawn

New Zealand won the series 1–0

India in England 1990

1st Test. Lord's. 26–31 July 1990
England 653–4 dec (GA Gooch 333, AJ Lamb 139, RA Smith 100*) and
    272–4 dec (GA Gooch 123, MA Atherton 72)
India 454 (M Azharuddin 121, RJ Shastri 100, Kapil Dev 77, **SR Tendulkar
    10**; ARC Fraser 5–104) and 224 (SK Sharma 38, **SR Tendulkar 27**)
England won by 247 runs

2nd Test. Old Trafford, Manchester. 9–14 August 1990
England 519 (MA Atherton 131, RA Smith 121*, GA Gooch 116; ND
    Hirwani 4–174) and 320–4 dec (AJ Lamb 109, MA Atherton 74, RA
    Smith 61*)
India 432 (M Azharuddin 179, SV Manjrekar 93, **SR Tendulkar 68**; ARC Fraser
    5–124) and 343–6 (**SR Tendulkar 119***, M Prabhakar 67*, SV Manjrekar 50)
Match drawn

3rd Test. The Oval. 23–28 August 1990
India 606–9 dec (RJ Shastri 187, Kapil Dev 110, M Azharuddin 78, KS More
    61*, **SR Tendulkar 21**)
England 340 (GA Gooch 85, RA Smith 57, EE Hemmings 51;
    M Prabhakar 4–74) and 477–4 dec (f/o) (DI Gower 157*, GA Gooch 88,
    MA Atherton 86, AJ Lamb 52)
Match drawn

England won the series 1–0

India in Australia 1991-92

1st Test. Brisbane. 29 November-2 December 1991
India 239 (M Prabhakar 54*, **SR Tendulkar 16**; CJ McDermott 5-54) and
  156 (RJ Shastri 41, **SR Tendulkar 7**; CJ McDermott 4-47, MG Hughes
  4-50)
Australia 340 (MA Taylor 94, DC Boon 66; Kapil Dev 4-80) and 58-0
Australia won by 10 wickets

2nd Test. Melbourne. 26-29 December 1991
India 263 (KS More 67*, **SR Tendulkar 15**; BA Reid 6-66) and 213
  (DB Vengsarkar 54, **SR Tendulkar 40**; BA Reid 6-66)
Australia 349 (GR Marsh 86, IA Healy 60, DM Jones 59; Kapil Dev 5-97,
  M Prabhakar 4-84) and 128-2 (MA Taylor 60, DC Boon 44*)
Australia won by 8 wickets

3rd Test. Sydney. 2-6 January 1992
Australia 313 (DC Boon 129*, MA Taylor 56) and 173-8 (AR Border 53*;
  RJ Shastri 4-45, **SR Tendulkar 1-2**)
India 483 (RJ Shastri 206, **SR Tendulkar 148***, DB Vengsarkar 54;
  CJ McDermott 4-147)
Match drawn

4th Test. Adelaide. 25-29 January 1992
Australia 145 (DM Jones 41; SLV Raju 3-11, Kapil Dev 3-33, **SR Tendulkar
  2-10**) and 451 (DC Boon 135*, MA Taylor 100, AR Border 91*; Kapil Dev
  5-130)
India 225 (Kapil Dev 56, **SR Tendulkar 6**; CJ McDermott 5-76) and 333
  (M Azharuddin 106, M Prabhakar 64, **SR Tendulkar 17**; CJ McDermott
  5-92)
Australia won by 38 runs

5th Test. Perth. 1-5 February 1992
Australia 346 (DC Boon 107, AR Border 59, TM Moody 50; M Prabhakar
  5-101) and 367-6 dec (DM Jones 150*, TM Moody 101)
India 272 (**SR Tendulkar 114**, KS More 43; MR Whitney 4-68, MG Hughes
  4-82) and 141 (K Srikkanth 38, **SR Tendulkar 5**; MR Whitney 7-27)
Australia won by 300 runs

Australia won the series 4-0

India in the 1992 World Cup

2nd match. England v India at Perth. 22 February 1992
England 236-9 (50/50 ov); India 227 (49.2/50 ov)
England won by 9 runs

9th match. India v Sri Lanka at Mackay. 28 February 1992
India 1-0 (0.2/20 ov)
No result

12th match. Australia v India at Brisbane. 1 March 1992
Australia 237–9 (50/50 ov); India 234 (47/47 ov, target: 236)
Australia won by 1 run (revised target)

16th match. India v Pakistan at Sydney. 4 March 1992
India 216–7 (49/49 ov); Pakistan 173 (48.1/49 ov)
India won by 43 runs

19th match. India v Zimbabwe at Hamilton. 7 March 1992
India 203–7 (32/32 ov); Zimbabwe 104–1 (19.1/19 ov, target: 159)
India won by 55 runs (revised target)

24th match. India v West Indies at Wellington. 10 March 1992
India 197 (49.4/50 ov); West Indies 195–5 (40.2/46 ov, target: 195)
West Indies won by 5 wickets (with 34 balls remaining) (revised target)

27th match. New Zealand v India at Dunedin. 12 March 1992
India 230–6 (50/50 ov); New Zealand 231–6 (47.1/50 ov)
New Zealand won by 4 wickets (with 17 balls remaining)

32nd match. India v South Africa at Adelaide. 15 March 1992
India 180–6 (30/30 ov); South Africa 181–4 (29.1/30 ov)
South Africa won by 6 wickets (with 5 balls remaining)

Final. England v Pakistan at Melbourne. 25 March 1992
Pakistan 249–6 (50/50 ov); England 227 (49.2/50 ov)
Pakistan won by 22 runs

5

ANJALI

As I was trying to establish myself as an international cricketer, my personal life changed dramatically in August 1990 when I met Anjali, my future wife. It was the beginning of by far the best partnership of my life.

I had just landed in Mumbai on our return from the 1990 tour of England and was waiting to pick up my bags when I first saw an extremely attractive woman looking down from the viewing gallery in the airport. Little did I know then that I had just seen my life partner. She was standing with a friend of hers, Dr Aparna Santhanam, now a well-known dermatologist in Mumbai. We had fleeting eye contact and then she disappeared.

The next I saw of the two of them was when I was making my way out of the airport. I spotted Anjali, dressed in an orange T-shirt and blue jeans, running out of the gate, apparently chasing after me. That was not all, because she soon started yelling, 'He is sooooo cute!' I felt awkward and started to blush, as I knew both Ajit and Nitin were waiting outside to take me home. My childhood friend Sunil Harshe was with me and he murmured in my ear that a very good-looking girl was calling my name and seemed keen to meet up with me. I had of course seen her and found her particularly attractive, but I told him there was no way I could speak to her at the time, not with Ajit and Nitin around.

The years of courtship

Anjali and I courted each other for five years between 1990 and 1995, a commitment that led to engagement and finally marriage.

It has to be said that the two of us come from very different backgrounds. Anjali is half Gujarati, half English and is a South Mumbai girl from a very well-to-do family. She went to St Xavier's College and then studied medicine at JJ Hospital. She was well-spoken and had an upbringing fundamentally different from my own. In her family, wearing Western outfits was the norm. My situation was completely different. I had hardly ever been out of my colony and had always mingled with cricket friends. I had never gone out with a girl, let alone brought one home. Unlike most men of my age, who were able to meet girls at college, I had been playing for India from the age of sixteen and simply hadn't had the opportunity.

While I first saw Anjali at Mumbai airport, it turns out that she had actually seen me a few weeks earlier on 14 August, when I got my first Test hundred at Old Trafford. At the time she was in England with her parents, and her father, Anand Mehta, a former national bridge champion and a serious cricket fan, had called her to catch a glimpse of the innings on television. However, she had no interest in cricket and didn't watch at all. Soon afterwards she came back to India and it was when she went to the airport to receive her mother, Annabel, who is English but has worked in India tirelessly as a social worker for more than three decades, that we ran into each other for the first time.

The day after she saw me at the airport – and this is her version, by the way – she asked a friend of hers, Muffazal 'Mufi' Lakdawala (who played club cricket and is now a very well-known surgeon), if he could get her my phone number. After coming home from the airport, she apparently jokingly declared to her parents that she had seen the man she wanted to marry.

Mufi did get her my number but it was pure chance that I happened to pick up her call. There were no mobile phones then and I was hardly ever at home to pick up the land line. The stars, I can say in hindsight, must have been aligned. She said she was the girl from the airport and asked if we could meet. While not trying to sound too eager, I told her that I remembered her and could meet with her at the Cricket Club of India, where I was playing. At first she did not believe me and asked if I could remember what she was wearing on the day I had first seen her. When I mentioned the orange T-shirt and blue jeans, she was impressed.

She came along to the CCI, as we'd arranged, but we couldn't really meet up and talk properly with so many people around. Being discreet was the best thing under the circumstances. All we did was exchange numbers and after that we started talking on the phone fairly regularly. It wasn't long before my sister-in-law Meena began to suspect that something was cooking between the two of us. She often asked me about this girl who kept on calling me but I tried to avoid answering. I wasn't used to discussing private things with my family and felt distinctly uncomfortable.

Our first proper meeting finally happened at my house when we came up with the idea that Anjali should come over posing as a reporter wanting an interview. That was her first and last foray into journalism. A female reporter had never come to my home for an interview before and, in light of all the phone calls, my sister-in-law was particularly suspicious about who this special reporter was.

For that first visit, I was keen to offer Anjali something to eat and was disappointed to see that hardly any of the chocolates I had brought back from England remained. In fact, there were only two left and in my keenness to salvage the situation I carefully cut them up and set a plate of chocolate pieces in front of her. She couldn't stay for long, however, and our first meeting was much too brief for my liking.

Despite being brief, it left a lasting impression. I simply felt happy in her presence. I can't really pinpoint what I liked about her but what I can say is that I was able to relax and be myself with her from the very first day. I had intentionally spoken very little because I was worried about embarrassing myself by saying something stupid. She did most of the talking and that was fine with me. In any case, at the time I wasn't as fluent with my English, which was the language of conversation. It was perhaps a defensive act, but Anjali never made me feel self-conscious. She was just the most ideal soulmate I could have asked for.

While we continued to speak for long periods on the phone after our first meeting, we hardly ever got a chance to meet. On some occasions we did plan to meet at around 8.30 p.m. and go for a drive. However, it turned out that Anjali's parents, who were unaware of the relationship then, were watching television and so, despite wanting to meet, Anjali was unable to leave the house without arousing suspicion. For my part, I drove all the way from Bandra to Warden Road, a journey of about forty minutes, and waited in the car until I was finally forced to turn back. Because of the risk of people recognizing me, I couldn't even call her from the public phone close to her house (there were no mobiles then) and had to go all the way back to Bandra to find out what had gone wrong, then I'd ask her to try again and drive all the way back. Needless to say, I am now an ardent advocate of mobile technology!

The second time we met was when Anjali suggested I pick her up from her house and we go for a drive in her Maruti 800, India's most affordable small car in the early 1990s. She wanted to have coconut water along Marine Drive and it was the only time in our lives that we have sat on the bench opposite the Air India building in Mumbai drinking coconut water. In my eagerness to please her, I had agreed, despite knowing that there was a possibility of people spotting me and coming up to speak to me. The century in England had made me a household name and people had started to ask for autographs. I did not mention this to her in case she thought I was pompous. Because Anjali knew nothing about cricket, it had never occurred to her that people might recognize me. She simply wasn't aware of how public a cricketer's life in India can be. It is true that there is hardly any privacy, which means that we've never been able to do the things couples normally do – watch a film, stop at roadside eateries in the evening, take a walk along the beach and the like. It was an adjustment Anjali and I had to make very early on in our lives together. The one time we tried to defy the odds was when a few of us – Anjali, her father Anand and some of our friends – went to see the film *Roja* in Worli in South Mumbai in 1993. We planned the outing meticulously and I put on a wig, a false moustache and glasses in an attempt to hide my identity. Things went smoothly till the interval, when I dropped my glasses and broke one of the lenses. My friends asked me not to put the broken spectacles back on just in case something went into my eye, but in my panic the moustache came off too and soon people recognized me, causing us all a lot of embarrassment. There was such pandemonium that we had to flee from the cinema halfway through the film.

We had a similar experience in Switzerland just a few years ago, when we were holidaying as a family. I had suggested we stay in a chalet rather than in a hotel and do our own cooking. Things were going to plan till the day we decided to visit Interlaken, now famous for Indian tourists as the location of the hit Bollywood musical *Dilwale Dulhania Le Jayenge*. We had planned to leave early in the morning and walk to the site. A few of our friends had advised us not to do so in case people recognized me on the way, so instead we hired a horse and carriage. Just as we were setting out, a few of the other Indian tourists spotted me. Within minutes they started following us and even when I told the carriage driver to go faster, they kept running behind us, trying to catch up. It was only when they realized that they couldn't keep pace that they finally gave up.

Such intrusion meant that Anjali and I could hardly meet in public and after our second meeting we weren't in touch at all for a period of six months. I was away on tours, while Anjali was busy preparing for her medical finals. I knew how hard she had worked and was sure she'd do well in the exam. On the day of the exam I rang her from Australia very early in the morning to wish her luck. I must say I was delighted to hear her voice after so long. She was panicking and was worried that she'd fail the exam. Knowing that was impossible, I said to her that if *she* failed the examination, so would everyone else in Mumbai. She had always come top and there was no way it would be different this time round. I also said that the number of hours she studied in a day equalled the total number of hours I used to study in a whole month! It was only much later that she told me that my call made a big difference to her. She felt I must have really cared to have called from Australia after six months. It was far more than care, as far as I was concerned.

As expected, she topped the examination and wanted to go ahead with pursuing an MD in paediatrics. I was extremely proud of her achievement and encouraged her to do so, which resulted in her getting posted to a hospital at Palghar, on the outskirts of Mumbai, as an intern. Luckily for us both, her friend Mufi was also posted in the same hospital. Palghar was such a small town that Anjali had to take a train to Boisar, some twenty minutes away, to find a phone to call me, and Mufi was her partner during these trips.

It was while studying for the MD that she began to take more of an interest in cricket. We had started talking about the game on the phone and she even bought a book of rules. Often she'd come up with questions like: where's cow corner, or is the wicket-keeper right- or left-handed? But she picked up the game quickly and I would ask her questions from time to time to keep her interest going. The first tournament she watched on television was the 1992 World Cup and she was heartbroken to see me get out cheaply against the West Indies after I had edged a ball from Curtly Ambrose. So much so that Mufi had to console her, saying the ball was so good that others wouldn't have come near it and it was because of my exceptional batting prowess that I had managed to somehow get an edge. If only that were the truth!

In the absence of mobile phones and text messages at the time, Anjali and I wrote a series of letters to each other. Because I was not stationed in a particular city for more than a few days when on tour, Anjali would have to work out where I would be in two or three weeks' time and post the letters accordingly. These letters remain prized possessions and when I look at them again one thing that stands out is Anjali's handwriting. Compared to mine, hers was wonderful to look at. I also have to confess that writing did not come naturally to me. I would often take a very long time thinking through each word that I would write for my beloved.

After coming back from the World Cup in March 1992, I visited Anjali in her family's house for the first time. Once again Mufi played a crucial role. Anjali's parents were told that it was our first meeting and that Mufi had orchestrated the visit. It was carefully stage-managed and was quite a performance. In fact, it was only after we decided to get engaged that we told her parents the real story. I must say I was extremely thankful to Mufi for all the help.

We weren't comfortable with the fact that the relationship was still a secret and decided it was time we let our families know that we were serious about each other. So I asked my childhood friend Sunil Harshe to arrange for Ajit and Anjali to meet, and the three of them got together at the Willingdon Club in South Mumbai. Waiting at home, I was anxious the whole time the meeting was on. It wasn't that I was looking for approval as such from Ajit, but it meant a lot to me to see my friends and family like Anjali as much as I did. I remember waiting for what seemed like an age, but when I finally saw Sunil and Ajit coming back, Sunil, who was walking one step behind Ajit, gave me a quick thumbs up to indicate the meeting had gone well. I was delighted to know that Ajit too thought Anjali was the right person for me.

All this time Anjali's interest in cricket was growing and by the time I went to New Zealand in 1994 she had a grasp of the nuances of the game. It was the series in which I started opening the batting for India in one-day cricket. I was delighted with my new role and was happy to be able to share my sentiments with Anjali when I spoke to her from New Zealand.

By the end of the New Zealand tour we had been seeing each other for four years and it was time to move on to the next stage of the relationship. It was during one of our numerous phone conversations from New Zealand that Anjali broached the subject of engagement and I immediately took her up on the suggestion. I told her that I was ready to get engaged whenever she was but it would be better if she could speak to both of our parents on my behalf – talking was never my strong point. She was hesitant at first but it was a great relief to me when she reluctantly agreed to take on the responsibility, as I would not have felt comfortable discussing the engagement with my father. Not that my father would not have agreed – I was absolutely certain he would – it was just that I felt slightly embarrassed at the thought of discussing my future wife with him.

Anjali later told me that she too had initially felt self-conscious informing my parents that their son wanted to get engaged to her. But my parents knew me well enough to realize why she had ended up being the one to speak to them about it and all they wanted to know was if we both felt the same way about the engagement. They were in fact delighted with the decision. The same thing happened a year later, when it was Anjali who spoke to both families about our wedding plans. She has far better social skills than I do and I was once again relieved to see her take on the rather difficult task. I have no hesitation in acknowledging that she did a commendable job!

Engagement and marriage

We got engaged on 24 April 1994, which also happened to be my twenty-first birthday. The engagement party was a low-key affair with family and close friends and was held at Anjali's family's house at Warden Road, Breach Candy, in South Mumbai. It was an occasion of great significance in our lives and we will always remember the joy we felt. Our families were delighted at the union and it marked a whole new beginning for me. We finally tied the knot on 25 May 1995. Anjali Mehta had become Anjali Tendulkar and I entered a new phase in my life.

Even before we got engaged, Anjali had mentioned to me that she wanted me to pursue my dream and was willing to give up her career for the family. This was a huge sacrifice. We were aware that it was impossible for us both to continue with our respective careers and that one of us needed to be at home to take charge of the house and family. To my relief, Anjali took over the home front, allowing me to continue with my cricket, and I will always appreciate the sacrifice she made very early in our lives.

The wedding was a traditional affair and, as in most conventional Maharashtrian households, my mother gave Anjali the *mangalsutra* (a necklace worn by the wife to ensure her husband's good health), *sindoor* (vermilion, the red powder worn as an auspicious mark by Indian married women), green bangles, anklets and a toe ring, which are all considered part of the wedding ritual. In fact, I remember her asking me if I wanted her to wear all or any of the things that my mother had given her. All I said was I wanted her to wear the mangalsutra, and to this day she has never taken it off.

These adjustments, both in her professional and personal life, could not have been easy but she has never shown any resentment. This has not only added to my respect for Anjali but also meant I had actually found someone who I could love and depend on. I must confess it is not always in my nature to say what I feel, but there is no doubt how much I owe her. Funnily enough, I have never called her by her name. I haven't ever said 'Anjali' or 'Anja' or any such thing while calling her. In all these years

I have not been able to figure out how I should refer to her. Frankly, it doesn't really matter, for that is how I am and, despite all my shortcomings, my wife has been with me every step of the way.

At the beginning, marriage did have one unfortunate side-effect, however. Marital bliss led me to relax my routine and the outcome was weight gain. I enjoyed myself thoroughly during our honeymoon and indulged my palate to a nicety. We had a few of our friends with us in Goa, where I was also playing a double-wicket tournament, and that added to the fun. Almost every day during the honeymoon I feasted on deliciously decadent desserts and other delicacies I normally kept away from during the playing season. There were plenty of chocolates and ice creams and such indulgence came at a price.

When I returned to Mumbai I realized that I couldn't get into any of my clothes. I had put on a few inches around the waist and it was time for some strict control on the culinary front. We weren't playing a great deal of cricket in 1995 and that was another reason why I had let down my guard. So for twenty straight days after returning to Mumbai, I put myself on a diet of nothing but tea without sugar, boiled *chana* (chickpeas), oranges and sweet lime. I also started doing some rigorous exercise again to get back into shape. I used to run for an hour in the morning, followed by weight training, and played two hours of table-tennis every evening. And during the table-tennis sessions I'd go and fetch the ball from wherever it went. Even if I had played a smash and the ball had gone behind my opponent, I'd perform the chore myself, to get more exercise. The result was a weight loss of 10 kg in twenty days. But I had started to feel dizzy and weak and my trousers were now too loose, so I decided it was time to stop. The first meal I had after three weeks on the diet was boiled spinach and broccoli and after that I went back to eating normally.

The perfect partner

To come from such a different background and yet be able to integrate herself into the more traditional Tendulkar household speaks volumes for Anjali's character and commitment. Frankly, no credit can be enough for her. She was an exceptional student and could have had an exceptional career. But she decided to stand by me and has been with me every moment over the past two decades and more. There have been occasions when I have been away from home and haven't seen my kids, Sara and Arjun, for months. For example, soon after the 2011 World Cup I suddenly realized that I hadn't noticed that Arjun was almost my height. (He is in fact taller than me now.) There is no doubt I have missed out on some really precious moments with my family. Such separations are part of a professional sportsman's life, of course, but I was only able to get through them because I always knew Anjali was there.

At the same time, I knew Anjali appreciated why I was away and was proud of what I was doing. She is the one person I can turn to at all times, for whatever she says is always in my best interests. Not only has she given me critical feedback on key decisions; she has taken care of everything on the domestic front. Starting with the kids, my mother, extended family, finances and a host of other issues, with Anjali in control I could focus on playing cricket. She is also my emotional rock, someone I turn to at every moment of self-doubt. There has never been any pressure on me to return home early from my engagements, for Anjali has always insisted that I should get back home only after I have finished work to my satisfaction. Of course I regret that I couldn't spend more time with her and the kids during my cricket career, and I also appreciate more than I can say the understanding and support I have received from her and the children at all times. Finally, I have always cherished the advantages of having a doctor wife who has shielded me at times when I have been injured in the course of my career.

6

YEARS OF CONSOLIDATION

In March 1992, after returning from the gruelling Australian tour and the World Cup, I badly needed a few weeks of relaxation. Our next international assignment was a tour of South Africa towards the end of the year and we had several months off in the interim. Fortunately for me, I managed to spend the first few days at home. I played tennis-ball cricket with friends and it was terrific to be able to unwind in familiar surroundings.

I was playing downstairs with my friends one day when Ajit called down from our apartment balcony to say that there was a phone call from Yorkshire County Cricket Club and that they wanted me to play for them! I came up to take the call and was very excited at the offer. I did not bother asking about the contract and other details and was determined to make the most of this opportunity to play in the County Championship in England. That I would have to cook, do my laundry, drive and perform all the other household chores never occurred to me at the time. A few days after the conversation, the CEO of Yorkshire CCC, Chris Hassell, came over to India to complete the formalities. We met at Thane, a suburb of Mumbai, where I was playing a match. I signed the contract at the ground, proud to become Yorkshire's first overseas-born player in 128 years.

A Yorkshire lad

I left for England towards the end of April 1992, right after my nineteenth birthday, and stayed there for three and a half months. It was my first long stint away from home on my own and it wasn't easy coming from such a different cultural background, but the generosity and openness of my employers made the stay immensely enriching and it was a great learning experience, to put it mildly.

One of the first problems was that I had little idea of the roads and had to follow my team-mate Richard Blakey as he drove to the ground. I was not really used to driving in England and often opted for the fastest lane while driving to the ground. There were occasions when I missed an exit and also lost Richard in the process. It was difficult to turn back and I cursed myself for not staying in the slowest lane, where it would have been easier to see the exit. There were no mobile phones then and getting lost meant I would be late for practice, which I hated.

I had actually driven a little in England in 1991 when I was there to play a few games of league cricket. Back then I stayed with the former India fast bowler Atul Wassan and he was generous enough to give me his car to drive around. He asked me if I had driven before and I assured him that I had passed all the tests and had an international licence and was confident of my driving skills. He said the key to driving in the UK was not to use the brake much and just to follow the lanes. However, the very first day ended in disaster. I was in the fast lane when all of a sudden the car came to a halt. There was no power and the car would not restart, and I panicked when I saw a string of cars behind me. I told Atul, '*Gaadi start nahin ho rahi hai, yaar!*' (The car is not starting, my friend!) Atul initially thought I was joking and asked me to accelerate. Anxious, I said to him that I was trying to, but there was no power and nothing was working. Only then did we realize that we had run out of fuel. Atul immediately asked me to put on the hazard lights and in my state of nervousness it took me ages to find the switch in the unfamiliar car. Finally, Atul put on the hazard lights for me. Somehow we got the car onto the hard shoulder, then we called the AA and after a while a breakdown vehicle arrived.

Another problem was my complete lack of knowledge of English geography, which caused a number of blunders during my stay in Yorkshire. Some of these I now remember with fondness. One such was to commit myself to playing at opposite ends of the country on consecutive days. I had agreed to play in an India–Pakistan festival match in London but had also committed to playing for a Rest of the World XI versus England at Newcastle the following day. To add to my woes, the India–Pakistan match started at 6 p.m. and finished close to midnight. I had driven from Yorkshire to London for the early-evening start and by the time the match was over I was exhausted.

Afterwards the other players were heading back to the hotel in London to relax and they asked me to join them. When I said I had to leave for Newcastle because I was playing there the next day I could see the shock and bewilderment on their faces. I had wrongly believed that it was easy to get from any part of England to another in two or three hours. It was only when they told me that it would take a minimum of six or seven hours to drive there that I realized the seriousness of the situation. I was advised to leave for Newcastle straight away. I was stumped. I had left Yorkshire at one o'clock that afternoon to get down to London, and here I was at midnight getting ready to drive all the way to Newcastle.

Jatin Paranjpe was with me at the time and we set off on the long drive together. Unfortunately, we had little knowledge of the roads and were completely dependent on the signs. To add to our misery, we missed a turn and ended up going south for close to thirty-five minutes when we should have been driving north. It was just one of those nights.

After driving for a couple of hours, my eyes started to give way. I asked Jatin to drive while I napped to regain a bit of energy. Jatin did so and after a few minutes I took my turn in the driver's seat again. A coffee break helped and eventually we reached the hotel at 8.15 a.m., only to see the team bus about to leave for the ground. We were both pretty much out of it by then and

The best partnership of my life.

Left: Ready to enjoy the game at the age of four.

Below left: In my mother's arms at our apartment in Sahitya Sahawas.

Below right: I owe him everything – with my father, who taught me to be the person I am.

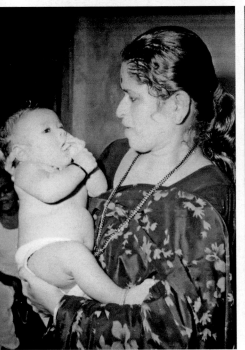

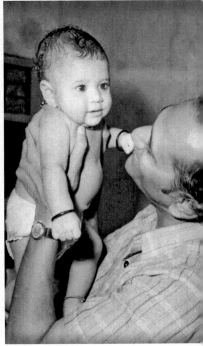

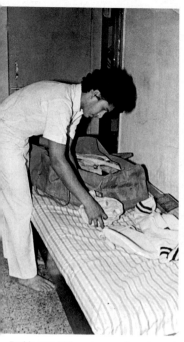

Packing my kitbag at my uncle and aunt's place in Shivaji Park as a 14-year-old. I owe them so much.

With my coach Achrekar Sir. A nod of appreciation from him would make my day.

Inspecting one of my beloved bats with my father, as my mother looks on.

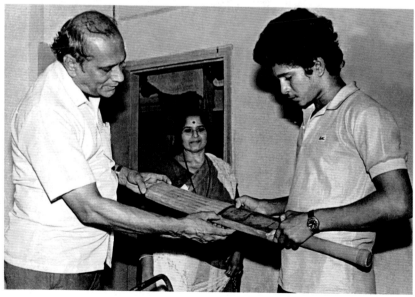

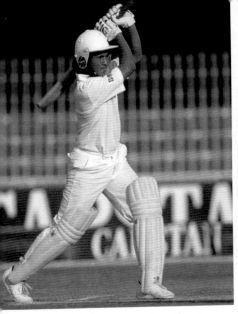

My first Test series, in Pakistan in 1989, was a baptism of fire.

During that series, Sanjay Manjrekar and I came across a court in Lahore and decided to try our hand at tennis.

After my first Test hundred, at Old Trafford in 1990. Little did I know that there were 99 to follow!

Left: At Heathrow in 1992 on my way to Yorkshire as their first ever overseas and non-Yorkshire player.

Above: Proud to wear the Yorkshire rose. Please don't mistake me for my son Arjun here!

Below left: One of the many wonderful moments in England in 1990. That tour taught me a lot.

Below right: Celebrating with my new team-mates after taking a wicket in my very first county match in 1992.

Opposite page:

Above: Meeting Nelson Mandela in Johannesburg in 1992. He also saw me play in Cape Town in 1997 and on both occasions I made a hundred!

Below: After beating England at Eden Gardens in Kolkata in 1993. Remarkably, 70,000 Indian fans had come to watch the little action that remained on the last day – such passion!

Right: At Chennai, one of my favourite grounds, on the way to my first hundred on home soil, against England in February 1993.

Below: Enjoying the victory lap after winning the five-nation Hero Cup at Eden Gardens in November 1993.

The day Anjali Mehta became Anjali Tendulkar.

desperately needed to close our eyes. I walked up to the team manager and explained to him my plight and asked if he could possibly let me have twenty-five minutes of sleep. I promised to join the team at the ground in an hour. He was most kind and I set the alarm at exactly twenty-five minutes.

When I woke up I didn't know where I was and felt like a complete zombie. I stumbled out of the hotel and made my way to the ground. I was sleepy and tired and was in no physical state to play a day's cricket. I still find it hard to believe, but somehow I managed to go out and make a hundred. After lunch, however, I could hardly stay awake and for the first time in my life I was taking ten-second naps between overs. I was actually sleeping while fielding and don't really know how I managed to get through the rest of the game.

As soon as the match was over Jatin and I rushed to the hotel. Our plan was to sleep for a couple of hours before joining the rest of the team for dinner. The next thing I remember is waking up in the early hours of the morning. My first thought was that I had missed dinner. We tried calling room service but no one picked up the call. We called Reception and were told that at that hour they couldn't serve us any food. With no hope of food, we drank three glasses of water each and went back to bed, setting the alarm for 7 a.m., in plenty of time for breakfast. We did manage to get up in time for breakfast and after eating a hearty meal of eggs and toast went to the ground to resume duty for the Rest of the World XI. For all the exhaustion, I still managed to score some runs and must say that, amidst all the chaos, the only thing that was going right was my batting.

After the match Jatin and I decided to drive back to Yorkshire in the evening, so that I could rejoin my county the following morning. This journey too was rather eventful. There were road-works everywhere as we got out of Newcastle and the speed limit had been brought down to 55 mph from the normal 70 mph. Given that it was fairly late, we decided to follow a police car that was in front of us, reckoning that as long as we followed a police car while maintaining a safe distance we would also be safe.

After a while I saw the police car making some sort of gesture to me. The driver had his hand out of the window and had all five fingers stretched out. He then closed his fist before spreading his fingers again. I thought he was asking me to put my lights on full beam and duly followed his instructions. A few minutes later the police car put on its hazard lights and signalled us to stop.

I was confused but did exactly as I was told. The policeman asked me if I had seen his earlier signal. I said yes and told him that I had followed his instruction and turned on my lights. He said that wasn't what he had meant and explained that the signal was for me to slow down because I was speeding. The police car was doing 65 mph while the speed limit had been set at 55 mph. As I'd been maintaining the same distance for the last hour and a half, I must have been speeding. He went on to say that the reason he stretched his five fingers twice was to indicate to me that the speed limit was 55 mph and I should slow down.

I was taken aback and immediately confessed to my mistake, saying it wasn't intentional and that I was blindly following the police car, believing it to be the safest option. In the interim the policeman had seen the white rose and Yorkshire CCC printed on my car and asked what it meant. I informed him that I played cricket for Yorkshire and it was a car given to me by the county. At this he asked my name and queried if I was indeed the first overseas professional to play for Yorkshire. I think it was my identity that earned me a reprieve and I was let off with a warning that I should always keep the speed limit in mind while driving.

Life lessons

At Yorkshire we often played back-to-back matches and it helped me improve my batting a great deal. The conditions were very different from those back home and I definitely matured as a batsman during my time in county cricket. The ball would swing a greal deal more than in India and it allowed me to improve my technique and ability to adjust to different conditions. Over the years, the lessons learnt from my stint at Yorkshire continued to help me whenever I toured England as part of the Indian team.

Socially too it was a good learning experience. The authorities, including the president Sir Lawrence Byford, were extremely sociable. The team had a great time and I particularly remember some extremely interesting Sunday club bonding sessions. In one it was decided that everybody had to wear towels and a tie without a shirt and meet in the hotel's convention centre. At first I thought my team-mates were pulling my leg and I wasn't prepared to dress up without seeing a few of the other players do so. I kept a close eye on the lobby and only when I saw a number of my team-mates sporting a towel and tie did I do the same. It turned out to be an eccentric but hilarious evening in the end.

Everyone at Yorkshire knew I was only nineteen and they were always eager to help. This was just as well, because things were not at all what I was used to in Mumbai. I had toured England in 1990, of course, but back then I had been with the Indian team and everything was arranged for us. This time I had to do everything on my own – from organizing my own food to doing the laundry.

Coping by myself sometimes caused me great embarrassment. One incident involved my first attempt to use a washing machine. I had no idea how much detergent was needed and must have emptied about half a packet into the machine before starting the washing cycle, then I went out. On my way back I could see something oozing beneath my front door. I was shocked at first until I remembered that I had left the washing machine on. All the detergent had made it overflow and there was foam everywhere.

That was the first and last time I did the laundry on my own. Every other time Solly bhai's family kindly came to my rescue. Solly Adams, who I fondly referred to as Solly bhai, was a resident of Dewsbury in West Yorkshire. I had first met Solly and his wife Mariam in 1990 in the company of Dilip Vengsarkar. Every Mumbai cricketer who had played league cricket in England had spoken to me about Solly bhai's hospitality and it was natural that I should get in touch with him. His house had become a refuge for all Indian cricketers in the area and we all looked forward to the delectable food we were served at Solly bhai's place, particularly the biryani, tandoori chicken, raita and mango lassi. It soon became a ritual for me to visit him three times a week when I was in Yorkshire.

Solly bhai's brother Younus and his wife Ruksana were also great hosts and it was from them that I learnt the art of filling the salad bowl. When a few of my friends – Jatin Paranjpe, Mufi and Vinod Kambli – came to stay with me in Yorkshire, we mostly survived on cheap fast food. As the only member of the quartet who was earning, I would pay the bills and, with limited resources, fast food was the most affordable option. We would eat out at KFC, Burger King and the like, but the all-you-can-eat buffet at Pizza Hut was our favourite. While we could eat as many pizzas as we wanted for a fixed price, we could only fill up our salad bowl once. And it was here that the training from Younus and Ruksana came in handy. They taught me to use lettuce leaves to construct a wall, so that the size of the bowl, which was ordinarily just two or three inches tall, increased to five or six inches. We could then fill it with as much salad as we wanted.

I finally left Yorkshire for India around mid-August, to get back in time for the Duleep Trophy, India's second most important domestic competition. It's named after Ranjitsinhji's nephew Duleepsinhji, who played for England in the early 1930s, and features teams representing the country's five zones: West, North, South, East and Central, It was suggested that I should play in it before we left for what would be a challenging tour of South Africa in October. The Yorkshire management was most considerate and allowed me to come back early, thus ending a really fruitful and productive time in county cricket.

India in South Africa, November 1992–January 1993

It was a historic tour because it was the first time the South Africans had played a Test series at home since returning to the international fold in 1991. They had toured India in November 1991 to end their international isolation after twenty-one years and in the three one-day internationals showed they were a very good side. In Allan Donald they had one of the best fast bowlers in the world and he was ably supported by Richard Snell, Brian McMillan, Craig Matthews, Meyrick Pringle, Brett Schultz and a host of other really good bowlers. In South African conditions the fast bowlers would pose a serious challenge.

The United Cricket Board of South Africa had made every effort to make the tour memorable. We landed in Durban and were immediately met by the hosts, who put us in open-top cars. There were two cricketers in each car and hordes of people lined the road as we made our way to the hotel. I was in a car with Pravin Amre, a middle-order bat and another of Ramakant Achrekar's students, and remember listening to Kishore Kumar songs all the way to the hotel. It was a fabulous experience.

We played our first tour game against Nicky Oppenheimer's XI at his private ground in Randjesfontein. It had rained heavily before the start of the game and it looked highly unlikely that we would get any cricket on the day. But I had underestimated our hosts and was totally taken aback to see what they were pouring onto the pitch to dry it out. They actually burnt petrol on the pitch to expedite the drying process, something I had never imagined could happen. That wasn't all. To our surprise, a couple of helicopters hovered over the ground to dry the pitch for a good forty-five minutes. As a result of all this effort, the pitch was finally playable and we managed to get a game. I made a hundred and we won the match easily, making a very good start to the tour. Afterwards, the talk in the dressing room was that we would beat the South Africans easily. We carried this sense of complacency into the next match, where we scored over 500 runs against a Combined Bowl XI after bowling them out for 230. The tour was turning out to be a walk in the park.

Things changed dramatically when we played the South African Board President's XI at Centurion on 6 November 1992. We bowled first and, standing at slip, I could see that the ball was not carrying through to the keeper. Manoj Prabhakar and Subroto Banerjee, a promising medium-fast swing bowler with a terrific sense of humour, opened the bowling for us and neither generated much pace off the wicket. Apart from Srinath, who could bowl fast, none of our bowlers could get the ball to carry to the keeper on that slowish track and we felt reasonably happy to get the opposition out for 268.

As our innings started we felt confident of batting the opposition out of the game again, but things didn't quite go according to plan. The second over was bowled by Brett Schultz and he generated serious pace in his very first over; in fact, it was one of the quickest first overs I had seen. This wasn't what we had expected and within minutes the atmosphere in the dressing room had become very subdued. The wicket had started to look lively and the batsmen were having all sorts of problems. It wasn't difficult to see that the Test series might not be so easy after all.

During the match it rained a little and the drizzle had made the outfield slippery. As a nineteen-year-old full of energy, I decided it would be a good idea to use the rain to practise sliding, at the opposite end of the ground from the pavilion. Chamundeshwarnath, a former South Zone first-class player who was playing club cricket there, helped the Indian team in fielding practice and also gave me throw-downs in the nets. He was with me and was helping me with my drills. If under normal circumstances I was able to slide for about three or four yards, the rain encouraged me, in my stupidity, to slide a few extra yards each time I chased a ball. In doing so I twisted my ankle and had to be carried off the ground. When I went to the hospital to get the injury checked, I was told it would take at least four to five weeks to recover.

With the first Test still a week away, I was desperate to play a part in the series and pushed myself to get fit as quickly as possible. After a few days, I started to walk but I was still finding it difficult to run. The team management was keen for me to play because I was batting well, but the only way I could do so was by standing in the slips, where I did not have to do much running about. It eventually turned out to be quite embarrassing because there I was, a youngster, standing in the slips while Kapil Dev, the senior member of the side, was running about in the deep.

In the first Test match at Durban, starting on 13 November 1992, we batted well and remained competitive throughout the game, which ended in a draw. Pravin Amre scored a fantastic hundred on debut and it was an innings full of character. I, unfortunately, wrote myself into the history books by becoming the first batsman to be given out by the third umpire – the use of TV replays had just been introduced. I had played the ball to point, where Jonty Rhodes was fielding. He was on it in a flash and returned it to the keeper in quick time. Still hampered by the ankle injury, I took a little extra time to turn back and, thanks to Jonty's brilliance, fell short by two or three inches. Just to be sure, umpire Cyril Mitchley went to the third umpire, Karl Liebenberg, who declared me run out.

It was my first taste of Jonty Rhodes's fielding prowess, something that caused us problems for the whole tour. Jonty was particularly effective in the ODI series and was undoubtedly the best fielder I played against. His anticipation and reactions were the quickest I have encountered and he managed to dry up all the singles around point, cover point and towards third man. On difficult pitches they can be crucial runs and all of a sudden they had been cut off, with Jonty manning the entire area on the off side with amazing speed. He ran a number of us out and saved a lot of runs every game, making a significant difference to the outcome of the series.

The other thing about Jonty was his running between the wickets. In the third match of the ODI series, which we won, Jonty had played a slog sweep off Ravi Shastri to deep square leg, where Kapil spilled the catch. In the interim Jonty had completed the first run really fast and had almost made it back to the striker's end, only to realize that his batting partner Andrew Hudson had not made any attempt to run a second. To our amazement, Jonty turned back and almost made it to the other end before the bails were dislodged to run him out. He had all but completed three runs in the time the non-striker had managed just one.

Coming back to the Test series, we followed the Durban draw with another good performance in the second Test at Johannesburg, which started on 26 November. I got a hundred in this game, my fourth in Test cricket. It is an innings I remember with great satisfaction. I was not out on 75 at the end of the second day and had to fight really hard on the third morning. Allan Donald was bowling a brilliant spell and patience was the key to survival. I kept leaving balls outside the off stump and knew I had to see Donald off before I was able to get on with scoring. I played just one cover drive before lunch, otherwise it was a battle of attrition and patience. That memorable contest against Allan Donald typefies what Test cricket is all about for me, making it the pinnacle of all formats of the sport. Here was a fast bowler propelling the ball at close to 150 kph. For a batsman there's nothing more challenging than really hostile fast bowling in bowler-friendly conditions. You don't get to play spells like that in domestic cricket and surviving is a true test of a batsman's calibre.

At Johannesburg, I finally got to my hundred after lunch, facing 270 balls in the innings, which lasted for six and a half hours. With Kumble taking six wickets in South Africa's second innings, we managed to draw the match and went into the third Test at Port Elizabeth with all to play for. The other bowler who bowled very well for South Africa was Craig Matthews. He was the most accurate of the lot and bowled a crafty line outside off stump, from where the ball would generally swing away. Occasionally he would get one to nip back and it was difficult to play this incoming ball. So much so that almost the whole team ended up with very similar black bruises on our thighs after being hit by Matthews. We even joked about it in the dressing room, saying, '*Aare, isko bhi medal mila hai, dekh!*' (Hey, look! He's got a medal, too!)

Unfortunately, we lost the third Test at Port Elizabeth to the pace and guile of Allan Donald, who picked up twelve wickets in the match. We were still in the game at the end of the first innings of both teams, but it was Donald's opening burst in the second innings that made all the difference. We lost our first six wickets for 31 and, despite a brilliant hundred from Kapil Dev, we never really had a chance. I got a bad umpiring call and was declared out to Brett Schultz, caught behind, when the ball had actually hit the inside of my thigh. The umpire met me at the end of the game and apologized for getting it wrong. It was understandable, for umpiring is one of the most difficult jobs in cricket and it is only human to get things wrong sometimes.

We were determined to level the series in the fourth and final Test match at Cape Town, which started on 2 January 1993. While we failed to achieve that, we didn't play badly. Javagal Srinath bowled particularly impressively, picking up six wickets. This time Allan Donald bowled a lot of overs to me from round the wicket, pitching it short of a length to make the most of the spongy bounce Cape Town is known for. I decided to try a new approach. He was bowling short and was getting the balls to come into my body. I realized that the best way to counter him would be to frustrate him. My thinking was simple: if taller guys can use their height to stand up on their toes and get on top of the bounce, why shouldn't the shorter guys use their height to go *under* the ball. So I decided to change my stance in this match. Normally I used to leave a gap of ten inches to a foot between my feet while batting, but in Cape Town I increased the gap to two and a half feet. This meant I was effectively even shorter than normal and could easily get under Donald's deliveries, forcing him to change the length he was bowling. It proved successful and I managed to bat for more than four and a half hours, facing 208 balls for my 73, which helped us draw the game.

In the ODI series, which for some reason was played between the second and third Tests and which for the first time was played with two new balls, one from each end, we gave a good account of ourselves, despite losing the seven-game contest 2–5. Most of the matches were low-scoring and 200 or thereabouts was considered a competitive score, which seems extraordinary these days.

We had lost to South Africa in both formats but I must say I had relished the challenge of playing against some of the best fast bowlers in the world. Every side faces difficulties away from home and at the end of the tough South Africa series we were looking forward to dishing out a few challenges to Graham Gooch's England when they toured India in February–March 1993. Remarkably, it would be my first ever Test series on home soil.

England in India, January–March 1993

There's nothing quite like playing in front of home crowds and in home conditions. When the first Test at Eden Gardens in Kolkata started on 29 January 1993, the enthusiasm among the spectators acted as huge motivation. Mohammad Azharuddin, our skipper, who always relished playing at Eden Gardens, set the tone with a brilliant 182, while I managed a half-century. By the fifth day we needed just 34 to win and to my complete amazement 70,000 people had come to the stadium to see us knock off the winning runs and take a 1–0 lead in the three-Test series. I remember hitting a short ball from Paul Jarvis, the England fast bowler, over square leg to the boundary to win the game.

Back in the dressing room there was no holding back. We really needed that win after the disappointment in South Africa and it felt particularly great to see the spinners come into play in conditions that suited their art. The English batsmen I had seen hitting through the line in England in 1990 were now struggling against the turning ball. The boot was on the other foot and we were enjoying every moment of it. Playing spin in the subcontinent is quite a challenge and England were finding it very difficult. We had a three-pronged spin attack in Anil Kumble, Rajesh Chauhan and Venkatapathy Raju – a lethal three-some. With the fast bowlers Kapil Dev and Manoj Prabhakar both very able with the bat, we had the flexibility to go in with five bowlers, making our attack look that much more potent.

The second match of the series started in Chennai on 11 February and it was in this match that I got my first home Test hundred. The surface, a very good track to bat on, was hard with a little bit of bounce. I scored 165 and could easily have gone on to score a double ton if I hadn't played a disappointingly loose shot to Ian Salisbury, the leg-spinner. I had set out to hit the ball over midwicket and ended up top-edging it back to the bowler.

Navjot Sidhu also made a century and we posted a sizable total of 560. Despite some resistance from Neil Fairbrother in their first innings, England were forced to follow on. Chris Lewis put up a good fight in the second innings, making his maiden century, but Kumble took six wickets and we ended up winning the match comfortably. We headed to Mumbai for the third Test four days later, having already taken an unassailable 2–0 lead in the series.

This was to be my first Test match at the Wankhede Stadium, where I had grown up playing a lot of my cricket, and hence it was a homecoming of sorts. It was the same for Vinod Kambli, who got a spectacular double hundred in this match. England must have been reasonably pleased to post their biggest total of the series in their first innings, 347, with Graeme Hick making his highest Test score of 178. Yet we posted an impressive 591 in reply, of which I contributed 78, and then Manoj Prabhakar took three quick wickets and the spinners did the rest, handing the English another innings defeat. It's fair to say that we had successfully put the disappointment of South Africa behind us.

Anil Kumble, who had bowled beautifully in all three Test matches, was declared Player of the Series. Anil was becoming the match-winner we had been looking for and discipline and rigour were the hallmarks of his craft. He did not turn the ball much but made up for it with great accuracy and tenacity. I never saw Anil let up in intensity and have nothing but the highest regard for him, one of the greatest players to have represented India.

The ODI series was more closely contested and we went into the last match at Gwalior on 5 March 1993 needing to win to level the series. Up till then, I had had a mediocre run batting at number five or six. However, at Gwalior I managed to score a quick 34 off thirty balls at a crucial time in the game and was involved in a key partnership with Azhar, who scored a brilliant 95 not out as he took us to victory.

The England series marked the beginning of a very successful phase in Indian cricket. We followed up by beating Zimbabwe in a one-off Test at home and were gradually getting into a healthy winning habit in home conditions. In ODIs we had started winning close contests and we went into the next major one-day tournament – the Hero Cup, also featuring South Africa, Sri Lanka, the West Indies and Zimbabwe – as one of the favourites.

Turning my arm over

Not long before the Hero Cup I played a festival match in Bangalore. When Kiran More, normally a wicketkeeper, bowled me a juicy full toss I tried to hit it for six but ended up twisting my wrist. It was a freakish injury and while I was able to continue batting, I was in serious pain. After a few days the injury had still not eased and it was decided that I needed to have an injection. This was my first cortisone injection and Dr Anant Joshi flew in from Mumbai to Delhi to administer the shot. I was to be injected on my wrist very close to the palm, and with the Hero Cup just days away, I was apprehensive about the recovery. The injection, which was pretty painful, was the first of a hundred or more cortisone injections over the course of my career.

The one match of the Hero Cup I will never forget is the semifinal against South Africa on 24 November 1993. We batted first, scoring a very modest 195 in our fifty overs. We knew we needed to bowl and field exceedingly well if we were to stop South Africa from making the final. Our bowlers, led by Anil, did a very good job and at the end of the forty-ninth over South Africa needed six runs to win. Having made a match of it despite scoring too few runs, we now had to decide who should be entrusted with the task of bowling the all-important final over.

I volunteered to take the responsibility. I had not bowled on the day and so I thought my bowling would have a surprise element to it. Also, the track had assisted the slower bowlers and Kapil's pace might have been easier for the South African batsmen to deal with. Then I realized that after fielding for forty-nine overs and in the slightly nippy evening, my body was stiff and my hands were frozen. I knew I had to warm up again quickly because there was no second chance. One wide could mean the match was over.

The first ball was a good-length delivery to Brian McMillan, one of the best all-rounders in the world at the time, who managed a single. But in the process South Africa lost Fanie de Villiers, who, in trying to get McMillan back on strike, was run out by a throw from Salil Ankola. Importantly, it meant that McMillan was at the non-striker's end and the new man was facing me. This was my opportunity. Allan Donald, the new batsman, wasn't great with the bat and if I managed to pin him down we definitely had a chance of winning the contest. The key was to keep the big-hitting Brian McMillan away from the strike.

As Donald walked to the wicket, I knew he was feeling the tension. I just had to hold my nerve and not try anything fancy. I deliberately bowled slower to him and even tossed one up, giving it a bit of spin. Donald was unable to cope with the lack of pace and ended up putting himself and his team under pressure by playing out three dot-balls. He didn't manage a single till the fifth ball of the over. South Africa now needed a boundary off the last ball to win. For our part, we just needed to stop the boundary and we were in the final.

The key to handling pressure situations like these is to keep yourself steady, follow your instincts and think clearly. I was aware that there had been occasions in the past when a batsman had got an inside edge attempting a huge heave and the ball had beaten the keeper standing up and sped to the boundary. In such circumstances there's little the bowling team can do. Remembering this, I asked Vijay Yadav, our keeper, to stand back, as if to a fast bowler.

It's difficult to believe, looking back, but McMillan did try a slog and he did get an inside edge. Yadav easily picked up the ball twenty yards back and South Africa could only sneak a single. In the most dramatic of finishes we had managed to win and were in the final. I had conceded only three runs in the over and we had won by two runs. The packed Eden Gardens crowd, which numbered close to 100,000, turned hysterical. Paper torches were lit all round the stands, creating an unbelievable atmosphere. I felt a sense of exhilaration and was soon engulfed by my team-mates. It was one of the best one-day internationals I had played in.

The other, rather unexpected, contributor to the Indian victory was a mongoose, which kept coming onto the ground during the second half of this day-night encounter at the Eden Gardens. It seemed that every time the mongoose came on the field the momentum shifted and the South Africans lost a wicket. While it was a coincidence, of course, it turned out to be a lucky charm for India!

After such a nerve-racking semi-final, the final was a relatively easy affair, with Anil running through the West Indies line-up to give us the title. He bowled brilliantly and finished off with career-best figures of 6–12 as we won the Hero Cup in front of a packed Eden Gardens. To make the victory even sweeter, I managed to get the wicket of Brian Lara. Getting Brian Lara out was interesting because Ajit, who had travelled to Kolkata with me to watch the semi-final and the final, had mentioned to me in the hotel that I should look to get Brian Lara out if I got a chance to bowl to him, and also suggested that I should bowl stump to stump to him. As it happened, I did get a chance to bowl to Brian, who had opened the batting for the West Indies. After he had hit me for a few runs, I bowled him a delivery slightly outside the off stump, which nipped back in a shade and bowled him. Delighted with the wicket, I immediately thought of the discussion I had had with Ajit.

My first year of cricket on home soil had gone really well. However, there were still things I desperately wanted to do. One was getting my first ODI hundred and another was opening the batting for India in one-dayers.

India in New Zealand, March–April 1994

It was the morning of 27 March 1994 and later that day we were playing New Zealand in the second game of a four-match

ODI series in Auckland. Navjot Sidhu, our first-choice opener, woke up with a stiff neck and was in no position to play. That's when I went up to Azhar and our manager Ajit Wadekar, a former Indian captain and a leading batsman of his time, and pleaded with them to give me an opportunity at the top of the order. Why did I think I should open? Well, I had the ability to attack bowlers and play shots from the word go, and in the one-day game, the key was to take advantage of the field restrictions in the first fifteen overs. I was sure that I just needed a chance to prove myself. I told Wadekar Sir that if I failed I'd never ask him again. In any case, there was no reserve opener in the team and they had no choice but to experiment with an irregular opener in place of Sidhu. If they put me at the top, they could still get a middle-order batsman to fill in for me at number four or five. After a lot of pleading, they finally agreed.

New Zealand scored just 142 batting first, but we still needed to make a good start. As I walked out to bat, I felt different in some way. I told myself that this was my big chance to open the batting for India. I did not want to let down the captain and the coach. Once I was at the wicket I cleared my mind and was just intent on hitting the ball hard, come what may. It was one of those days when everything fell into place and soon I couldn't wait for the next delivery. The quicker the better, as far as I was concerned. I managed to score 82 off forty-eight balls, finally holing out to the left-arm spinner Matthew Hart off a leading edge. I had hit fifteen fours and two sixes.

After that I no longer had to plead with Wadekar Sir to allow me to open and I continued to score runs in that position for the rest of the series, which ended up being tied 2–2. It was no surprise because New Zealand at home were always formidable opponents. In this series, I was able to dictate terms to the bowlers and all my plans were working out well. For example, against Gavin Larsen, known to be a bowler who bowled a stump-to-stump line, I came down the wicket a couple of times, forcing him to adjust his length. When he bowled short I was waiting for it and promptly dispatched the ball to the stands.

With one aim achieved, I was determined to accomplish the second as soon as possible. I had started to feel frustrated and a little embarrassed at not having scored a hundred in ODI cricket. Having already played seventy-odd games, it was about time. The moment finally came against Australia in Sri Lanka in the Singer World Series in September 1994 and it was more of a relief than anything else. So much of getting to a century is in the mind. Once you score one, you know you can score another and the doubts aren't there any more – getting the first one is the tricky bit. My first ODI hundred certainly soothed the nerves and it was an important milestone in my career.

Playing against Brian Lara

With five years of experience, I was now firmly established in the Indian team and people had started comparing me with other players on the international scene at the time. The press love to set up rivalries and with a home series against the West Indies coming up at the end of 1994, it was inevitable that the fans and the media would pit me against Brian Lara.

Without doubt, Brian Lara is one of the best players to have played this sport. I first met Brian in November 1990 during a festival match in Toronto between the West Indies and a World XI, which was played at the SkyDome, a stadium designed for Major League Baseball. We got along straight away and I enjoyed talking to him and listening to his insights. He was a clear thinker and had an excellent grasp of the nuances of the game. To add to his unrivalled flamboyance, he also had great hands and footwork, making him a champion batsman of our time. Brian was capable of playing a number of shots to the same delivery and his ability to adjust at the last moment set him apart. His technique wasn't orthodox but that had never mattered to him. He more than made up for it with skill and footwork.

By the time the West Indies came to India in November–December 1994, Brian was already the premier batsman of his team. We knew we had to stop Brian from scoring to have a chance in the Test series, but it was easier said than done, and Brian played a very important role for the West Indies in the third and final Test at Mohali. It was his innings of 91 that set the platform for a series-levelling West Indies win. For the visitors, Jimmy Adams too played a crucial part, with 252 runs in the match.

I had a pretty good series and in the first match at Mumbai I was pleased with my performance in the second innings, scoring 85 after coming in to bat at a precarious 11–3. We won the match by 96 runs, having managed to get Brian out early in both innings. In the second Test at the VCA stadium in Nagpur, I scored 179 in our first innings. I remember this innings for my wild celebrations after scoring the century, something I hardly ever did in my career. In fact, it was an aberration, caused by a combination of factors. I was not out on 81 overnight and started the second day against the second new ball. I hit Kenneth Benjamin for four fours in the first few overs and raced to 97 in no time. Courtney Walsh was bowling from the other end and I was trying to get into his mind, to understand what he was likely to do. I had a feeling he would bowl outside off stump or full if he wanted to get me out. On the other hand, he would probably bowl bouncers if he just wanted to keep me quiet. He bowled a short ball and that's when I realized that another one might be coming my way the very next delivery. I was ready. I played the hook to perfection and the ball sailed into the stands. It was an exhilarating way to get to a century and I just couldn't control my emotions. I pumped my fists and screamed in joy, though none of it was meant for Walsh. It was simply because my plan had come off.

Facing criticism

The story of this series against the West Indies remains incomplete if I don't talk about the five-match ODI series that preceded the Tests in October and November 1994. It was played in two parts. The first two ODIs were followed by a tri-series, with New Zealand joining India and the West Indies as the third team, before we went back to playing the last three games of the bilateral series.

In both of the first two ODIs against the West Indies, on 17 and 20 October, I was out without scoring. I didn't do much better in the first match of the tri-series, on 23 October, making only eight. After just three failures, a surprising number of people started to find flaws with my game. While they might have been well-intentioned, it seemed that every ex-cricketer I met during the tri-series had some advice for me. Everyone was trying to tell me what was wrong with my game, which I found a little strange.

Yes, I had scored two consecutive ducks, but this reaction was extraordinary. Every performer goes through lean patches. I was still at ease with myself and knew that with one good score, things would fall back into place. That's exactly what happened in the final of the tri-series, when I scored 66 at Eden Gardens. That was followed by three consecutive half-centuries in the bilateral series, culminating in a hundred in the final game at Jaipur on 11 November. I ended up as Player of the Series.

Having won the tri-series and also the five-match ODI series, we had given our fans a lot to cheer about. Coming on top of the Hero Cup win a year earlier, all these victories helped boost the popularity of ODI cricket in India ahead of the World Cup, which was being co-hosted by India, Pakistan and Sri Lanka in 1996. It was set to be a massive event.

India in South Africa 1992-93

1st Test. Durban. 13-17 November 1992
South Africa 254 (KC Wessels 118, JN Rhodes 41; Kapil Dev 3-43) and 176-3
   (AC Hudson 55)
India 277 (PK Amre 103, KS More 55, **SR Tendulkar 11**; BM McMillan
   3-52)
Match drawn

2nd Test. Johannesburg. 26-30 November 1992
South Africa 292 (BM McMillan 98, JN Rhodes 91; M Prabhakar 4-90) and
   252 (AC Hudson 53, DJ Richardson 50; A Kumble 6-53)
India 227 (**SR Tendulkar 111**; BM McMillan 4-74) and 141-4 (A Jadeja 43,
   SR Tendulkar 1; CR Matthews 2-23, AA Donald 2-43)
Match drawn

3rd Test. Port Elizabeth. 26-29 December 1992
India 212 (M Azharuddin 60, **SR Tendulkar 6**; AA Donald 5-55) and 215
   (Kapil Dev 129, **SR Tendulkar 0**; AA Donald 7-84, BN Schultz 2-37)
South Africa 275 (WJ Cronje 135, AC Hudson 52) and 155-1 (KC Wessels 95*;
   SR Tendulkar 1-9)
South Africa won by 9 wickets

4th Test. Cape Town. 2-6 January 1993
South Africa 360-9 dec (JN Rhodes 86, BM McMillan 52; A Kumble 3-101)
   and 130-6 dec (KC Wessels 34; J Srinath 4-33)
India 276 (**SR Tendulkar 73**, M Prabhakar 62; CR Matthews 3-32)
   and 29-1
Match drawn

South Africa won the series 1-0

England in India 1993

1st Test. Kolkata. 29 January-2 February 1993
India 371 (M Azharuddin 182, **SR Tendulkar 50**; GA Hick 3-19, DE Malcolm
   3-67) and 82-2 (NS Sidhu 37, **SR Tendulkar 9***; GA Hick 2-9)
England 163 (MW Gatting 33; RK Chauhan 3-30, SLV Raju 3-39, A Kumble
   3-50) and 286 (f/o) (MW Gatting 81, AJ Stewart 49; A Kumble 3-76,
   SLV Raju 3-80)
India won by 8 wickets

2nd Test. Chennai. 11-15 February 1993
India 560-6 dec (**SR Tendulkar 165**, NS Sidhu 106, PK Amre 78, Kapil Dev 66,
   VG Kambli 59)
England 286 (NH Fairbrother 83, AJ Stewart 74, GA Hick 64; SLV Raju 4-103)
   and 252 (f/o) (CC Lewis 117, RA Smith 56; A Kumble 6-64)
India won by an innings and 22 runs

3rd Test. Mumbai. 19–23 February 1993

England 347 (GA Hick 178, CC Lewis 49; Kapil Dev 3–35, A Kumble 3–95) and
    229 (RA Smith 62, MW Gatting 61, GA Hick 47; A Kumble 4–70)
India 591 (VG Kambli 224, NS Sidhu 79, **SR Tendulkar 78**, PK Amre 57;
    PCR Tufnell 4–142
India won by an innings and 15 runs

India won the series 3–0

West Indies in India 1994

1st Test. Mumbai. 18–22 November 1994

India 272 (NR Mongia 80, SV Manjrekar 51, **SR Tendulkar 34**; CA Walsh 6–79)
    and 333 (**SR Tendulkar 85**, SV Manjrekar 66, J Srinath 60; KCG Benjamin
    4–82)
West Indies 243 (SC Williams 49; SLV Raju 5–60) and 266 (JR Murray 85,
    JC Adams 81; J Srinath 4–48, SLV Raju 3–85)
India won by 96 runs

2nd Test. Nagpur. 1–5 December 1994

India 546–9 dec (**SR Tendulkar 179**, NS Sidhu 107, M Azharuddin 97,
    A Kumble 52*) and 208–7 dec (NS Sidhu 76, **SR Tendulkar 54**)
West Indies 428 (JC Adams 125*, CL Hooper 81, JR Murray 54, BC Lara 50,
    PV Simmons 50; SLV Raju 5–127) and 132–5 (CL Hooper 67; A Kumble
    3–45)
Match drawn

3rd Test. Mohali. 10–14 December 1994

West Indies 443 (JC Adams 174, AC Cummins 50; A Kumble 4–90, SLV Raju
    3–73) and 301–3 dec (BC Lara 91, JC Adams 78*, KLT Arthurton 70*)
India 387 (M Prabhakar 120, J Srinath 52*, **SR Tendulkar 40**) and 114
    (J Srinath 17*, S Manjrekar 17, **SR Tendulkar 10**; KCG Benjamin 5–65,
    CA Walsh 3–34)
West Indies won by 243 runs

Series drawn 1–1

7

WORLD CUP 1996

Our preparations for the World Cup began with a training camp in Bangalore in January 1996. For some reason, it had been decided by the management that it would be a good idea for the team to run from the hotel to the Chinnaswamy Stadium every morning, with the team bus and security cars trailing behind. I still don't understand the logic behind this bright idea or why somebody came up with it in the first place. None of us were used to road running and injuries were bound to happen. I ended up with a sore shin on the very first day, while a number of other guys had problems with their backs and hamstrings.

A joke started doing the rounds in the dressing room about whether we would be fielding on the road or on the cricket field. We were all prepared to run as much as they liked on grass, but there was no point risking injuries by running on hard roads just weeks before the World Cup. A few players suggested calculating the distance between the hotel and the ground and running the same distance inside the stadium instead. The management listened to what we had to say and road running was quickly abandoned. Our World Cup preparations started in earnest the following morning.

During the camp we would get to the ground by 7 a.m. and stay there till 2 p.m. The sessions were long and draining and I made sure to have a big breakfast to keep up my energy levels. I was only twenty-three in 1996 and could digest everything I ate. Every morning I would have four fried eggs sunny side up, with ketchup and tabasco sauce, making two sandwiches of the four eggs, which I just loved. The breakfast would keep me going for hours and I thoroughly enjoyed the long training sessions. In the evenings we spent time in the pool or in the gym and soon all the players were looking forward to the tournament. No team had won the cup on home soil and it was our chance to make history.

Group stages, February–March 1996

Our first match was against Kenya at Cuttack in Odisha in Eastern India on 18 February and we won the match comfortably. I scored a hundred and was Man of the Match. We then moved on to Gwalior in the west of the country to play the West Indies three days later, confident of sustaining the momentum. While February in the east of India can be nippy, in the west the temperatures can touch 30 degrees during the day. I had a fever the night before the West Indies game but still played and contributed 70 to our victory, which was set up by some fine bowling by Prabhakar and Kumble once again. Early on in my innings Courtney Browne, the West Indies wicketkeeper, dropped a skier at short square leg and I was able to make the most of my reprieve.

Having won our first two games, we played Australia in Mumbai on 27 February, determined to upstage the tournament favourites. Australia batted well and put up a competitive 258, riding on a brilliant innings from Mark Waugh, the younger of the Waugh twins, who scored 126. We did not begin the chase well and lost two early wickets to Damien Fleming, who bowled well throughout the tournament. That's when I tried to counter-attack, to get on top of Glenn McGrath and Fleming.

I managed to establish control and was going really well until the Australians gave the ball to Mark Waugh to have a go with his off-spin. I immediately picked up a couple of runs to square leg, followed by a sweep for four. As I'd hoped, the deep midwicket fielder was moved slightly towards square leg. Space at midwicket meant I could now go over the top for a boundary. Seeing me jump out, Mark Waugh bowled a wide ball. I couldn't reach it and was out stumped for 90. I have to admit I had been out-thought. It was a key moment in the game and we soon lost control amid a flurry of wickets. It was dispiriting to lose the match from a winning position.

Looking after my interests

An odd thing happened during the break between innings in that Australia game. At the time, I was perhaps the only Indian player who was playing without a bat sponsor. Most players had 'Four Square' or 'Wills' on their bats, but my determination not to endorse a tobacco brand meant I was playing without a bat sticker. A few months before the tournament started, a leading multinational, which had just entered India, had approached me but talks had not progressed much. I had quoted an amount to them to which they did not agree. I was therefore surprised when, in the middle of the game, the managing director of this company came over to meet me and suggested that if I put his company's sticker on my bat there and then, they would pay me any amount I wanted.

I turned down the offer. I was clear I wanted no distractions in the middle of a tournament. I did not want an alien element on my bat, something I had not come to terms with, to catch my eye while I was batting. It might have affected my rhythm. I said I would put a sticker on my bat when *I* wanted to and not when I was asked to do so. I had done well without a bat sticker up till then and, like most sportsmen (though not all care to acknowledge it), I was superstitious about such things. I did not want to risk making changes when I was batting well. The bat sticker could wait.

Towards the closing stages of the tournament, my friend and manager Mark Mascarenhas, head of the sports management company WorldTel, mentioned to me that he had lined up MRF, the well-known Indian car tyre brand, as a bat sponsor but the deal would only come into effect *after* the tournament. Mark, who was based in Connecticut and had made a name for himself by winning the television rights of the 1996 World Cup, knew my concerns well and never pushed me into doing anything against my wishes. His ability to understand and appreciate my issues made him a really special person. Mark was more a friend than a manager and I was able to trust him fully with all my needs. While he changed the nature of player endorsements in cricket by bringing a string of major corporates to the table, he did so without ever forcing a particular endorsement on me.

I first met Mark in Sri Lanka in 1995 and it was Ravi Shastri who introduced us. Ravi said to me that here was a man who could shake things up and had a very interesting proposition for me. As soon as I met him I was impressed by his professionalism and attention to detail. Mark never left anything to chance. We were really close and even went on a couple of family holidays together. On one of these holidays, to Coonoor in South India, we had a fantastic time eating all the local delicacies and playing golf. Mark was another foodie and I have fond memories of the many fantastic meals we had together in his house in Connecticut in 1998 when I spent a week there. I was totally shocked when I first heard about his fatal car accident at Kharbi, not far from Nagpur in central India in 2002, and must say I lost a very close friend and confidant. We worked wonderfully well together and it is impossible to fill the void created by his untimely death.

After Mark was gone a number of agents approached me and expressed an interest in managing my affairs. However, my relationship with Mark was such that it never occurred to me to leave WorldTel. And I am happy to say I have been proved right, with Vinod Naidu, my current manager and friend, taking care of my affairs for a decade and more, first on behalf of WorldTel and then on behalf of WSG (World Sport Group). I first met Vinod in Sharjah in 1998 and then in London over a delicious lunch at my favourite

Thai restaurant, Patara, when Mark introduced the two of us. It was after Mark's untimely demise that Vinod and I started working closely together. We spoke to each other regularly and, like Mark, Vinod soon came to understand and respect my concerns. It was always clear to him that my cricket was my top priority. Between Mark and Vinod, I have been lucky to have two great people to work with. In fact, it would perhaps not be wrong to say that I have spent more days with Vinod than anyone else in the professional realm over the last decade and I have enjoyed every bit of it. Vinod knows me inside out and has been a constant presence whenever I needed him. To spend so much time away from his family in order to manage my interests is evidence of his commitment to his profession, and his is another friendship I deeply cherish.

Pakistan again

The quarter-final against Pakistan on 9 March 1996 was by far the biggest match of the World Cup. There was tremendous security around the team hotel and we knew that the nation would be watching. That was not so unusual for an India–Pakistan match, but the World Cup had added a further dimension to this particular knock-out encounter. On the day of the match we reached the ground early and found the atmosphere at the Chinnaswamy Stadium to be truly unbelievable. The stadium was packed hours before the game and the crowd was loud and boisterous.

We batted first and I was the first to get out for 31 to Ata-ur-Rehman, the Pakistan fast bowler, trying to steer the ball to third man. Navjot Sidhu, who opened the batting with me, batted well for his 93 and Ajay Jadeja played a fantastic cameo towards the end, scoring 45 off twenty-five balls to get us to a very respectable 287 in our fifty overs.

Pakistan started brightly in response and raced to 80 in their first ten overs. We badly needed a wicket to keep the scoring in check and that's when a famous incident took place involving Aamer Sohail, the Pakistan opener, and Venkatesh Prasad, our fast-medium bowler. Sohail had hit Venky for a boundary towards point and suggested rather aggressively that that was where he wanted to keep Venky all day. He waved his bat towards the boundary and said a number of rather rude things. Venky, understandably angry, bowled him with his very next ball. It was sweet revenge. Having got his man, it was now his turn and he showed Aamer Sohail the way to the dressing room.

The team was pumped up after this incident and we soon took control of the match. Prasad picked up two more crucial wickets and Ajay Jadeja and I bowled ten reasonably tight overs between us in the middle, while Kumble chipped in with three wickets. In what turned out to be his final international innings, Javed Miandad was run out for 38, ending a glorious career for Pakistan. Despite some good late hitting by wicketkeeper Rashid Latif, which caused us a bit of a panic, we were on the ascendancy throughout and in the end won the match fairly comfortably, by 39 runs, prompting celebrations all over the country.

On our way back to the hotel we could see people lining the streets and they were throwing garlands and flowers at the team bus. In the hotel too we were being treated differently. We stayed on in Bangalore for one extra day and spent a relaxed few hours in the pool the next afternoon. We could sense that the staff were trying to please us and were looking at us differently. They were looking after our every need and when somebody ordered prawns, three different varieties were served, all on the house. We were being treated like royalty and it felt wonderful to see the country so happy and proud.

Things fall apart

We were due to play Sri Lanka in the semi-final at Eden Gardens on 13 March. We arrived in Kolkata two days before and the first thing that struck us on landing at the airport was the security. There were commandos everywhere and no fans were allowed near the hotel lobby. This was no ordinary match.

Someone had mentioned to us that the surface at Eden Gardens had been relaid with soil brought over from Australia. The first look at the surface seemed to support this statement, with the pitch apparently hard and firm. In fact, it did look like a typical Australian wicket. On that basis, it was unanimously decided that we should field first if we won the toss, particularly because Sri Lanka had chased very well throughout the tournament. Their openers, Sanath Jayasuriya and Romesh Kaluwitharana, had been going for the bowling in the first fifteen overs and had given them fantastic starts in most matches. They had beaten us in the pool stage of the competition and it was important to take early wickets and put them under pressure.

We won the toss and put the Sri Lankans in and got off to a great start, picking up Sanath for one and Kalu for zero. They both got out playing cut shots to third man, vindicating our belief that the wicket was hard and firm. It was only when I came on to bowl that I realized we had misread the wicket. The ball started to hold up and was stopping on the batsmen. The top layer might have been firm enough, but immediately below the surface it was loose. It would clearly not last the full hundred overs and it became even more important to keep Sri Lanka down to a manageable score. Though we managed to restrict Sri Lanka to 251 in their fifty overs, that proved far too many in the end.

When it was our turn to bat the wicket had started doing all sorts of things. The ball was turning and holding up and batting was extremely difficult. Opening, I scored 65 but got out rather strangely to a ball from Sanath Jayasuriya. He was bowling left-arm orthodox spin and the ball hit my pad and rolled off to the on side. I thought there was a quick single and stepped out of the crease. Too late, I saw that the ball had stopped very close to Kaluwitharana, the keeper, and there was no way I could finish the run, but by then it was too late. He dislodged the stumps in a flash and I didn't bother waiting for the third umpire's decision because I knew I was out. It was a long and frustrating walk back to the pavilion and I could sense it would not be easy for the batsmen who followed.

Sure enough, we soon lost wickets in a heap, handing Sri Lanka the game. The crowd, desperate for an Indian victory, grew increasingly restless and disrupted the game by throwing things onto the field. By then, however, the match was all over. Our World Cup dream lay shattered and there was a deathly silence in the dressing room.

This time the journey from the ground to the hotel was painful and when we reached the hotel we realized that everything had changed. We were made to feel as if we had done something seriously wrong. There was no doubt we had let our fans down, but we were hurting as much as anybody. It was a long and difficult night as we sat around picking over the way the match had played out.

We left Kolkata by the first available flight the following morning and I still found it difficult to accept that Sri Lanka and not India would be travelling to Pakistan to play in the World Cup final against Australia. We had done so well to win the quarter-final against Pakistan, the high point of our World Cup. Personally, I had had a good tournament and ended up with the most runs in the competition – 523, with two centuries and three half-centuries – but that was of little consolation. Our biggest mistake was misreading the Eden Gardens pitch. That is what cost us the game.

Indian cricket was not going through a good phase. With the World Cup dream over, team morale was low and we had little time to recover before a difficult tour of England, which we lost 1–0, though we did discover two superb talents in Rahul Dravid and Sourav Ganguly along the way. Though I scored a couple of centuries in this series, at Edgbaston and Trent Bridge, and Sourav scored two consecutive hundreds, on debut at Lord's and at Trent Bridge, we weren't able to make our way back after losing the first of the three Tests. The England bowlers, led by Chris Lewis, Dominic Cork and Alan Mullally, did well throughout the series and run-scoring was never easy. Nasser Hussain, the England skipper, also had a good series, leading from the front all the way.

Off the pitch, one incident from this tour is difficult to forget. Sourav Ganguly and Navjot Sidhu were travelling on the Tube in London when a few young guys, who'd probably had a bit too much to drink, boarded the train. For some reason they started making gestures at Sourav and Navjot and eventually one of them threw a beer can at Navjot, who promptly stood up to confront them. It turned ugly and a fight ensued, until the train reached the next station, where their attackers staggered off – but then one of them came back onto the train and started waving a gun at Navjot. At this, Sourav's first reaction was to drop to the ground and cover his face in fright, but then he started pleading with the boy and dragged Navjot away as quickly as he could. Looking back at the incident, it seems a funny scene in some ways, but it must have been pretty scary at the time!

Soon after returning to India after a generally disappointing tour of England on the field, I was made captain of India at the age of twenty-three, replacing Azhar, who had been captain since 1990. It was time for the team to make a fresh start and get back to winning ways as soon as possible.

India in the 1996 World Cup

6th match. India v Kenya at Cuttack. 18 February 1996
Kenya 199–6 (50/50 ov); India 203–3 (41.5/50 ov)
India won by 7 wickets (with 49 balls remaining)

10th match. India v West Indies at Gwalior. 21 February 1996
West Indies 173 (50/50 ov); India 174–5 (39.4/50 ov)
India won by 5 wickets (with 62 balls remaining)

19th match. India v Australia at Mumbai. 27 February 1996
Australia 258 (50/50 ov); India 242 (48/50 ov)
Australia won by 16 runs

24th match. India v Sri Lanka at Delhi. 2 March 1996
India 271–3 (50/50 ov); Sri Lanka 272–4 (48.4/50 ov)
Sri Lanka won by 6 wickets (with 8 balls remaining)

29th match. India v Zimbabwe at Kanpur. 6 March 1996
India 247–5 (50/50 ov); Zimbabwe 207 (49.4/50 ov)
India won by 40 runs

2nd quarter-final. India v Pakistan at Bangalore. 9 March 1996
India 287–8 (50/50 ov); Pakistan 248–9 (49/49 ov)
India won by 39 runs

1st semi-final. India v Sri Lanka at Kolkata. 13 March 1996
Sri Lanka 251–8 (50/50 ov); India 120–8 (34.1/50 ov)
Sri Lanka won by default

Final. Australia v Sri Lanka at Lahore. 17 March 1996
Australia 241–7 (50/50 ov); Sri Lanka 245–3 (46.2/50 ov)
Sri Lanka won by 7 wickets (with 22 balls remaining)

India in England 1996

1st Test. Birmingham. 6–9 June 1996
India 214 (J Srinath 52, **SR Tendulkar 24**; DG Cork 4–61) and 219
    (**SR Tendulkar 122**; CC Lewis 5–72)
England 313 (N Hussain 128; BKV Prasad 4–71, J Srinath 4–103) and 121–2
    (MA Atherton 53*)
England won by 8 wickets

2nd Test. Lord's. 20–24 June 1996
England 344 (RC Russell 124, GP Thorpe 89; BKV Prasad 5–76) and 278–9 dec
    (AJ Stewart 66; A Kumble 3–90)
India 429 (SC Ganguly 131, R Dravid 95, **SR Tendulkar 31**; AD Mullally
    3–71)
Match drawn

3rd Test. Nottingham. 4–9 July 1996

India 521 (**SR Tendulkar 177**, SC Ganguly 136, R Dravid 84; CC Lewis 3–89)
and 211 (**SR Tendulkar 74**, SC Ganguly 48, NR Mongia 45; MA Ealham
4–21)

England 564 (MA Atherton 160, N Hussain 107, MA Ealham 51, AJ Stewart
50; SC Ganguly 3–71)

Match drawn

England won the series 1–0

8

CAPTAINCY – THE FIRST STINT

Captaining India is undoubtedly a great honour, and it was a job I felt ready for at that point in my career. I had captained Mumbai and led them to victory in the Ranji Trophy in 1994–95. In all, I captained Mumbai in sixteen out of the thirty-eight Ranji Trophy matches I played in, and I continued to do well as a batsman in these games, scoring at an average of 99.53. I had also captained West Zone in the Duleep Trophy, so it wasn't an altogether new experience. Yet captaining India is fundamentally different, with its own particular challenges.

First, there is the need to cope with the demands of the non-stop media machine. The Indian captain's every move is headline news and it was no easy task to protect myself from the constant media glare. More important, perhaps, was learning how to deal with the selection committee and the practice of zonal representation associated with it.

In India the committee consists of five selectors, one from each zone: West, North, South, East and Central. The zonal representation system sometimes resulted in certain selectors pushing players from their particular zones and in my first stint as captain the team undoubtedly suffered as a consequence. There were occasions when I wasn't given the team of my choice and did not get particular players I asked for. For me, the priority was always the Indian team. For some of the selectors, however, things may have been different. I felt there were other factors dictating team selection and at times I felt disappointed after selection committee meetings.

A promising start

My first match as captain was against Australia at the Kotla in New Delhi in October 1996, and we were keen to bounce back after the series defeat in England in the summer. We also needed to win the Test to keep our amazing home Test record intact. We managed to do so, with Nayan Mongia, our wicketkeeper and stand-in opener, scoring a remarkable 152. It wasn't a bad start as skipper.

Unusually, Australia had travelled all the way to India just to play a single Test, which was intended to mark the inauguration of the Border–Gavaskar Trophy, named after two of world cricket's greatest icons. At least there was a good reason for that one-off game; at other times it was a little difficult to understand the thinking behind some of our shorter tours. A couple of years earlier, for example, we went all the way to New Zealand for one Test match and four ODIs, with no practice games, and that was considered a tour of New Zealand! We also played our fair share of two-Test series over the years and they are not altogether satisfactory either – you blink four times and a two-Test series is over!

Next on the horizon was a home Test series against South Africa, which was preceded by another one-day tournament, the Titan Cup, involving India, Australia and South Africa. It was no small achievement to beat Australia and South Africa, two of the best teams in the world at the time, on our way to the title. In the final at the Wankhede on 6 November, I scored 67 in our modest 220, with Jadeja adding 43, and then it was all down to Anil Kumble, who took four wickets as we bowled the South Africans out for 185, winning the match by 35 runs. It was a very welcome victory after our disappointing loss to Sri Lanka in the World Cup semi-final and it was particularly satisfying for me, because I had experimented with something radically different as captain.

After Srinath and Venkatesh Prasad had bowled good first spells and Anil had picked up a couple of wickets, I had to turn to Robin Singh, our all-rounder, for the fifth bowler's quota. Robin bowled medium pace and was extremely accurate. I decided to go with a four–five field. In an ODI, it is very unusual, with a medium-pacer operating, for there to be only four fielders on the off side and five on the on. I had no deep point and had fielders at third man, short point, cover and long off. On the on side I had fielders at fine leg, short square leg, short midwicket, deep square leg and long on. I asked Robin to bowl stump-to-stump and make sure not a single ball was pitched outside the off stump, otherwise the South Africans would pick off singles to third man. Three or four singles an over would really ease the pressure on them in a relatively low-scoring contest. I wasn't worried about Robin bowling a leg-stump wide, just as long as he didn't pitch the ball outside off stump. I was confident that the South Africans were not prepared for this strategy. Robin did his job well. He bowled his full quota of ten overs, giving away only 40 runs and also picking up the important wickets of Hansie Cronje and Daryll Cullinan.

The Test series that followed the Titan Cup was always going to be fiercely competitive. South Africa were one of the better teams at the time and had fast bowlers of the calibre of Allan Donald and Fanie de Villiers and batsmen of the class of Cronje, Gary Kirsten, Daryll Cullinan and Jonty Rhodes. The first match of the series at Ahmedabad started on 20 November 1996 and was a great contest, with multiple twists and turns. After we were bowled out for a modest 223 in the first innings, South Africa managed a handy 21-run lead. It was a good lead in the context of what seemed likely to be a low-scoring game and we had to bat well in the second innings to set them a reasonable target. We faltered and left South Africa needing just 170 to win in a little under two days.

The game wasn't lost yet, however. There was a lot of wear and tear on the pitch by the end of the third day and we knew that 170 might prove tricky on that surface. We were playing two leg-spinners, Anil Kumble and Narendra Hirwani, and a left-arm spinner, Sunil Joshi. The South Africans would undoubtedly expect me to attack them with spinners on a crumbling pitch.

Instead, I decided to use Javagal Srinath, because Sri, with his extra pace, could also get the ball to reverse-swing. Swing at a good pace is very difficult to deal with and in no time Srinath had given us a dream start, reducing the South Africans to 0–2.

After his successful short opening burst, I rested Srinath for a while before bringing him back for another long spell. I kept talking to him to check if he was feeling tired. He was bowling beautifully and had the batsmen in all sorts of trouble. I put Sunil Joshi on at the other end to keep the batsmen in check and not concede too many runs. I asked Sunil to pitch the ball in the rough outside the left-handers' off stump and keep them tied down to one end. This was to allow Srinath to bowl to the right-handers, as reverse swing was more effective against right-handed batsmen. This move paid real dividends. Sunil managed to stem the run flow while from the other end Srinath picked up wickets at regular intervals.

At no time during the chase were South Africa in with a chance. We kept up the pressure and managed to bowl them out for 105 in just thirty-nine overs, recording a famous victory. It was the high point of my captaincy; the plan to use Srinath from one end had worked really well. Hansie Cronje walked up to me after the game and confessed that he had been caught off-guard. He had expected me to employ spinners and had a strategy in place to negotiate the turning ball on a wearing pitch. He did not have a plan for Srinath, and by the time he had come to terms with our tactics the match was over.

The other thing I tried out in that Test match for the first time, something that served India well for a decade and a half, was to get Rahul Dravid to bat at number three and Sourav Ganguly at five, which was not an obvious decision at the time. Both had had great starts to their careers in England batting in other positions. Sourav had scored two consecutive hundreds batting at number three. In his third Test against Australia, which was the first of my captaincy, he once again batted in that position and scored 66 in the first innings and was unbeaten on 21 in the second. He was full of confidence and was keen to continue batting at three. Rahul too had scored consecutive fifties in England in his first two Tests and was looking good at number five. However, I felt that by changing the batting order I could get the best out of each of them in the long run.

Sourav was a boundary-hitter and liked playing his shots from the start of his innings. He was flamboyant and more attacking and I felt his style was more suited to number five. Rahul on the other hand played within himself at the start of his innings and was comfortable leaving a lot of deliveries outside the off stump. That's an important ability for a number-three batsman. The two had very different strengths and I knew that both were terrific players and had the talent to serve India for many years. With Rahul at three and Sourav at five, I felt the team would have a better balance, especially in overseas conditions. Though we reverted to Sourav at three and Rahul at five for the deciding third Test of this series and the first two Tests in South Africa shortly afterwards, we repeated the experiment in the third and final Test of that series at Johannesburg in January 1997. It worked very well and became a permanent fixture of India's batting for over a decade.

In the second Test of the home series at Eden Gardens at the end of November 1996, South Africa beat us comfortably, with Lance Klusener and Gary Kirsten playing well for the visitors. Klusener took eight wickets on debut and Gary scored hundreds in both innings. One of South Africa's most prolific opening batsmen, Gary had the remarkable ability to pick up singles at will with a nudge into the gap between midwicket and square leg. This made him an extremely difficult batsman to bowl to. A fierce competitor, he is someone I had the highest respect for as an opponent.

We went to Kanpur for the third Test with the series level. Azhar was in commanding form in the second innings, remaining undefeated on 163, and once we had managed to set South Africa a target of over 450 we knew we were in control. We bowled South Africa out for 180, winning the Test by 280 runs and the series 2–1. To beat Australia and South Africa in my first two series as captain was the best start I could have hoped for, and when we left for South Africa in December 1996 we were a team brimming with confidence.

India in South Africa, December 1996–February 1997

The planning for the return series was not the best. We landed in South Africa on 19 December and played just one practice game before the first Test match in Durban on Boxing Day. On a tour like that you really need at least two or three practice games and close to two weeks of acclimatization to be competitive. The conditions are so different from those in India that players have to have that time to get used to the seam movement and the bounce. Balls that hit the bottom half of the bat in India come at heights close to the bat handle in South Africa.

We lost the Durban Test miserably, bowled out by the South African fast bowlers for 66 in the second innings in just thirty-four overs. It was a demoralizing loss and I had never experienced anything like it before. South Africa proved superior to us in all aspects of the game and we were left with a huge amount of work to do ahead of the second Test at Cape Town.

To add to my problems, I had injured myself in Durban while bowling and the injury was taking a few days to heal. It happened when I decided to bowl to Andrew Hudson just before lunch on the first day. I thought I would run in slowly and bowl him an unexpected bouncer, hoping to induce a top edge. In doing so, I pulled a muscle in my side. The pain was surprisingly acute and I had to go to the hospital during the lunch break to have three cortisone injections. Even when I rejoined the team at the ground I was still extremely sore and found it difficult to run or bend.

The second Test started on 2 January 1997, so there were only a few days for the team to recover and regroup. It was never going to be enough to cope with a really good South African side. In Allan Donald and Shaun Pollock, the South Africans had two of the best fast bowlers in the world, and they complemented each other beautifully in home conditions. While Donald was fast, Pollock could swing the ball both ways and was a master of his craft. Nevertheless, we did manage to show some signs of competitiveness in Cape Town and both Azhar and I got hundreds in the first innings.

I went in to bat towards the end of the second day and was unbeaten on one at the end of play, with the team score on 29–3. The following morning I was practising against throw-downs ahead of the game and tried shuffling back and across to a few of the balls. It felt really good and I even timed the balls well. Something in me said that I should employ the back-and-across movement that day. I did so and found that, even when the bowlers were bowling at close to 150 kph, I still had plenty of time. Normally I would stand just outside my leg stump while taking guard, but at Cape Town I was standing a good few inches outside to accommodate the shuffle. I ended up making 169. I always felt that I needed to be comfortable in my head before I focused on technique. If I wasn't comfortable to start with, fretting about technique would not do much for my batting.

The other incident I remember from the Cape Town Test – and one I thoroughly enjoyed – involved Allan Donald and the Indian medium-fast bowler Dodda Ganesh. Donald, who was in top form in that series, had no patience with lower-order batsmen and was frustrated to see Ganesh hanging around. As Dodda faced his onslaught fearlessly, Allan started mouthing words at him. For three consecutive deliveries Dodda was all over the place but luckily for him did not lose his wicket. At the end of the over Allan went up to Dodda and told him what he thought of him in no uncertain terms. Dodda's face remained impassive.

I witnessed all this from the non-striker's end. When Allan came to fetch his cap from the umpire, I told him, 'Allan, Dodda only knows a local Indian language called Kannada. I find it difficult enough to communicate with him myself, so how can he understand your abuse in English? If you want to get to him, speak to him in Kannada.' This made Allan even more irritated. He almost snatched his cap from the umpire and, making wild gestures with his hands, stomped off to his fielding position.

By the end of the Cape Town match the players were much more used to the conditions and this augured well for us going to Johannesburg for the third Test. We were taking the game very seriously, even though it was a dead rubber. We played well from the start and Rahul Dravid, batting at number three for the first time in the series, scored a fantastic hundred. He played the fast bowlers late and helped us to a position of strength. Sourav too batted extremely well at number five and we scored 410 in our first innings, which put South Africa under pressure for the first time in the series. The bowlers followed up with a good effort to give us a handy first-innings lead.

In our second innings it was once again Rahul and Sourav who did the business. We could sense victory and were buoyed by the opportunity. Our bowlers prised out the South African top order fairly quickly. Even when there was a partnership between Daryll Cullinan and Lance Klusener for the eighth wicket, we knew we were within striking distance and just needed to keep plugging away.

We finally got our breakthrough, in the form of Klusener, and were just two wickets away from a hard-earned victory when the skies opened up. It was a torrential downpour and it soon became clear that we had lost a great opportunity to win a Test match in South Africa.

I was distraught. We had done everything we could to win the match and here we were being deprived by the rain. I felt cheated by the forces of nature. I went to the umpires as soon as the rain stopped and said we were ready to play even if the outfield was a little wet, but they were within their rights to say that they couldn't permit a restart unless the conditions were fit to play. The Test series ended 2–0 in favour of South Africa, but that scoreline didn't reveal just how close we had come to making it 2–1. It left me disconsolate and in my disappointment I locked myself in the bathroom and just cried.

The other disappointment in this match was that VVS Laxman, then a youngster, fractured his finger and was faced with having to go back to India. Distressed, Laxman was sitting in one corner of the dressing room in tears. I tried to console him, saying that injuries happen, but that he shouldn't worry too much about them as he had a long career ahead of him. In hindsight, it was a prophetic statement!

India in the West Indies, March–April 1997

India had not won a series in the Caribbean since 1971 and I looked on this tour as a major opportunity to leave the disappointment of South Africa behind. The conditions were different again from those in South Africa, and we needed to adjust quickly. However, our preparations suffered a serious jolt when Srinath, our leading fast bowler, was ruled out of the tour because he needed shoulder surgery. Abey Kuruvilla, a tall fast-medium bowler from Mumbai, performed admirably as his replacement, but the situation illustrates a very serious problem I faced in South Africa and subsequently in the Caribbean.

On tours like that, I believed we really needed three quality fast bowlers, but unfortunately I never had more than two. In South Africa, Abey Kuruvilla was not even part of the squad. Even when I was desperate to have him, the selectors refused to include him. After making his Ranji Trophy debut in 1991, Abey had played five seasons of first-class cricket by then and would have been a handy bowler in South Africa. As it was, after good opening spells from both Srinath and Prasad, we failed to sustain the momentum. In the West Indies, we would once again rue the absence of a quality third seamer.

Despite losing Srinath, we played well enough in the first two Tests in March 1997, at Sabina Park and Port-of-Spain. Both matches ended in hard-fought draws and for once it seemed that we had managed to adjust to the conditions, with our batting looking solid against the West Indian pace quartet of Curtly Ambrose, Mervyn Dillon, Ian Bishop and Franklyn Rose. By the time we went to Barbados for the third match of the five-Test series on 27 March, I was feeling confident that we could do something special.

We started well at the Kensington Oval and managed to bowl out the West Indians for under 300, thanks to some fine bowling from Venkatesh Prasad, with 5-82, and despite a Shivnarine Chanderpaul century. As I write this, Chanderpaul has now played more than 150 Test matches in his career. He has been one of the most consistent middle-order batsmen for the West Indies for close to two decades, which is remarkable. We followed up the bowling with a good batting effort and managed a small first-innings lead. I scored 92 and was wrongly given out to an Ian Bishop delivery by umpire Lloyd Barker. Replays showed that Bishop had overstepped by at least four inches, and it was a key moment in the match. As things turned out, Lloyd Barker wasn't able to officiate for much of the match after that because – as I was told by the stand-in umpire who replaced him – he had had to go to hospital with a serious headache and couldn't focus properly.

In the second innings our bowlers did well to dismiss the West Indies for 140 on the third day of the match. This time Abey Kuruvilla picked up 5-68 and we needed 120 runs to win, on a pitch that was increasingly uneven, with plenty of wear and tear for the West Indian fast bowlers to exploit. We picked up two of those runs without loss in the few overs we had to see out at the end of Sunday's play. On that track we knew that scoring would not be easy the next day, but we also felt that one good partnership should be enough to take us to victory.

A humiliating collapse

Monday, 31 March 1997 was a dark day in the history of Indian cricket and definitely the worst of my captaincy career. And yet it had promised so much. In fact, over dinner at a restaurant in St Lawrence Gap in Barbados the night before, I remember having a joke with the waiter, who was predicting a West Indian win. He was confident that Ambrose would bounce India out the next morning. Now, in the first innings of this match, Franklyn Rose had bowled me a bouncer and I had pulled him into the stands for six. So I reminded the waiter of the shot and jokingly said to him that if Ambrose tried to bowl me a bouncer, I would hit him all the way to Antigua. I was so confident of our chances that I pointed to the fridge and said he should immediately chill a bottle of champagne and I would come and open it the next day and pour him a glass to celebrate winning the match.

Instead, we collapsed for a miserable 81 all out, handing the West Indies a 38-run victory. Frankly, there can be no excuses for such a poor batting effort, even though it was a difficult track. I certainly don't want to point fingers at anyone for the defeat, as that's not my way. In any case, I was part of that team and as captain it was my responsibility to steer us to victory. I did not get the feeling that we were over-confident, yet none of the batsmen apart from Laxman even reached double figures in the second innings and it was one of the worst batting displays I have been part of.

I got out for just four. In my anxiety to get a feel for the ball I got a tentative edge. I should either have left the ball alone or tried to counter-attack. The defeat left me totally devastated and

I shut myself in my room for two whole days trying to come to terms with the loss. I still feel the pangs of that defeat when I look back at the series.

From bad to worse

After eventually losing the five-Test series 0–1, we went on to lose the ODI series as well. The good start to the tour had given way to a complete lack of application and that proved catastrophic in the end. The best example of this ineptitude was the third one-day game, at St Vincent, where we needed 47 runs to win off the last ten overs with six wickets in hand. Rahul and Sourav had set up the platform and we should have strolled to victory. Again and again I instructed the batsmen not to go for big shots and to play along the ground, saying there was no need for any risk-taking with the asking rate under five runs an over. However, all our middle- and lower-order batsmen kept playing the ball in the air. The loss of a few wickets resulted in panic, which in turn led to a number of suicidal run-outs. It was infuriating to see the team lose from a winning situation.

At the end of the match I called a team meeting and lost my cool with the boys in the dressing room. I spoke from my heart and said the performance was unacceptable. I said that losing matches in which the opposition play better cricket is one thing – I had no problem with such defeats – but losing a match that we had completely under control suggested there was something seriously wrong with the team.

I was extremely upset with the way we were playing and Anil came to my room in the evening to try and calm me down. Anil said that I should not blame myself for the defeats and that we would learn from the mistakes we had made in South Africa and the West Indies. However, things were really starting to get on top of me. I hated losing and as captain of the team I felt responsible for the string of miserable performances.

More worryingly, I did not know how I could turn it around, as I was already trying my absolute best.

Not long after the series was over, I confided in Anjali that I feared there was nothing more that I could do to stem the tide of defeats. Losing a string of very close matches had left me badly scarred. I had given it everything and was not sure if I could have given even one per cent more. The fact that we failed to chase down 120 had nothing to do with lack of talent. It was because we batted horribly on the day. It was hurting me badly and it took me a long time to come to terms with these failures. I even contemplated moving away from the sport completely, as it seemed nothing was going my way. Anjali, as usual, managed to put things in perspective and assured me that things would surely get better in the months to come. Looking back, it was just frustration getting the better of me.

The final few months

The string of defeats came to a temporary halt when we drew a two-Test series in Sri Lanka in August 1997 and then beat Pakistan 4–1 in the Sahara Cup, a one-day series in Toronto, in September. The tournament was memorable because Sahara had not only lent their name as sponsors but senior officials like Abhijit Sarkar were personally there to ensure that everything was in order and that players felt comfortable. This win was all the more gratifying because we won with a young bowling unit, without the experience of Srinath, Prasad and Anil Kumble. Sourav Ganguly was the star performer for us in the series, winning four Man of the Match awards on the trot.

There was one rather strange incident during the second match of this series involving Inzamam-ul-Haq. While it appears funny in hindsight, it wasn't at the time. During one of the drinks breaks when we were batting, having bowled Pakistan out for 116, one of the Pakistan players not playing in the match brought out a bat for Inzamam – to the great surprise of those of us watching from the dressing room. We initially thought he was taking the bat out to get it autographed; only later did we realize that Inzamam had wanted to charge, with bat in hand, towards a few fans in the crowd who were taunting him for his physique!

When we came back from Toronto to Delhi, there were more than 5000 fans to receive us at one thirty in the morning at Delhi airport. The police were finding it difficult to control the crowd but I insisted that the team should wave to the fans before we left the airport. It was a grand homecoming. However, the satisfaction of beating Pakistan was short-lived, because within weeks we had lost a three-match ODI series in Pakistan.

In the second game, which we won, I remember telling our off-spinner Rajesh Chauhan how to play Saqlain Mushtaq's doosra ball. I gave him a mini-lecture for five minutes or so and told him to give the strike to Robin Singh, who was batting well at the other end. To my surprise, Rajesh ended up hitting a six in the last over and won us the game! However, we didn't really celebrate, as there were armed guards outside our hotel rooms for security reasons, something that made us uncomfortable and put a dampener on things. The deciding match of the series belonged to Ijaz Ahmed, who smashed our bowlers to all parts of the park on his way to 139, winning the game for Pakistan comfortably.

When we got back to Delhi this time having lost the series 1–2, the fans who had queued up just weeks earlier were nowhere to be seen. To cap it all, I also remember that those of us who were flying on to Mumbai were asked to pay for excess baggage. I told my team-mates that we should just pay up and not argue.

The defeat in Pakistan added to the pressure that was building on me and an incident from the home Test series against Sri Lanka in November–December 1997 perhaps gives an indication of how I was feeling at the time. As captain, I was expected to deliver a winning performance in the three-Test contest. I had not done well as a batsman in the first two Tests, both of which ended in a draw. To add to my misery, the second Test at Nagpur was a washout. A section of the media was having a go at me before the third Test in Mumbai, which started on 3 December 1997, and a lot was written about my poor form. It was a crunch situation and I needed to deliver both as batsman and captain.

On the first day I went in to bat with an hour left and was unbeaten on eight at the end of play. I had not batted at my best but at least I had survived. As the overnight not-out batsman, I needed to rest but as has often been the case with me, I couldn't sleep. By 10.30 p.m. I had started to feel very agitated. To get out of the stifling environment of the hotel, I called my friend Atul Ranade and asked him over. When he arrived I told him that I wanted to go for a drive and to visit the temple at Shivaji Park.

It felt good praying at well past midnight. It gave me a sense of calm again and helped take my mind off the game. Then we went to the Siddhi Vinayak temple and finally, on our way back to the hotel, decided to have a milkshake at Haji Ali. Strange as it may sound, Atul and I sat on the roadside at 1 a.m. drinking milkshake and relaxing. We talked about anything but cricket and I was feeling much better when I went back to the hotel. I even managed to get some sleep and the following day I made 148.

Unfortunately it didn't bring the win I needed, even though at one point we were in a great position. At a crucial moment in the innings we dropped a catch which would have put the Sri Lankans under tremendous pressure. To add to our frustration, it also started drizzling and the game was stopped. I felt it was a combination of missed chances and bad luck that cost us the match.

The Sri Lanka series was followed by a four-nation tournament in Sharjah in December 1997. We played some very poor cricket against England, Pakistan and the West Indies, losing all our matches and failing to make the final. The match against Pakistan on 14 December highlights how things were just not going my way. I was batting at number four in this competition, at the selectors' request. Sourav and Navjot Sidhu had given us a good start against Pakistan, and when Sidhu got out at 143–2, I sent in Robin Singh, the all-rounder, to accelerate the innings. It was a strategy I had given considerable thought to. Manzoor Akhtar, the leg-spinner, was at one end bowling around the wicket to the right-handed batsmen. The theory was that Robin, a left-hander, would be able to negotiate his leg-spin better and also hit some big shots. However, Robin got out without scoring after just three balls from Azhar Mahmood, the medium-pacer, and the experiment proved a disaster.

In the press I was criticized for sending in Robin ahead of me and the move was blamed for our defeat. A month later, however, in January 1998, Azhar, back as captain, repeated the very same move in the final of the Silver Jubilee Independence Cup in Dhaka against Pakistan. Robin was sent in at three to keep up the momentum after Sourav and I had got off to a flier and this time Robin played a terrific hand, scoring 82 and setting up the run chase. This was arguably a bigger gamble, because he was pitted against the off-spinner Saqlain Mushtaq and it is no secret that left-handers find it more difficult against off-spinners. The same experiment was now hailed as a master stroke. Not without reason is it said that success has many fathers while defeat is an orphan.

The Sharjah losses were followed by a three-match ODI series against Sri Lanka at home. After we'd taken a 1–0 lead in the series, the second match was a washout and Sri Lanka played well to beat us in the third game in Goa. At the end of the series I was unceremoniously sacked as skipper. No one from the BCCI managed to call me or inform me of my removal as captain before someone from the media called to say I was no longer captain. I was actually with my friends in Sahitya Sahawas. I felt extremely humiliated to hear this, but the manner in which the whole thing was handled strengthened my resolve to be a better cricketer in the years to come. I told myself that the BCCI mandarins might be able to take the captaincy away from me, but no one could do the same as far as my own cricket was concerned.

The sense of ignominy and the pain were still there, however. During my tenure as captain some of the players used to call me 'skip', so when one of the players shouted out 'skipper' in our next engagement in Dhaka, I automatically turned around to answer the call. That's when it really hit me that I was no longer the captain of the Indian cricket team. Now I simply had to focus on my batting and win some matches for the team. So that's what I did. In fact, not long after this, I was so focused on doing well that I ended up shouting at someone who has since become a good friend. This incident, which has caused us both much embarrassment, took place in the second of the three finals of the Silver Jubilee Independence Cup in Dhaka in 1998. There was a lot of movement in front of and around the sightscreen and, despite my repeated complaints, things did not improve. I was distracted and lost my wicket soon after. On my way back to the pavilion I was livid and, when someone came across to apologize, I just screamed at him, saying Bangladesh did not deserve to host international cricket if the basic fundamentals were not in place. Only later did I realize that the man I had yelled at was Ashraful Haq, then president of the Bangladesh Cricket Board and currently chief executive of the Asian Cricket Council. Ever since, whenever we meet, we start by saying sorry to each other for what happened!

Australia in India 1996 - The Border-Gavaskar Trophy

One-off Test. Delhi. 10-13 October 1996
Australia 182 (MJ Slater 44; A Kumble 4-63, AR Kapoor 2-30, SB Joshi 2-36)
  and 234 (SR Waugh 67*; A Kumble 5-67, BKV Prasad 3-18)
India 361 (NR Mongia 152, SC Ganguly 66, **SR Tendulkar 10**; PR Reiffel 3-35)
  and 58-3 (SC Ganguly 21, M Azharuddin 21, **SR Tendulkar 0**)
India won by 7 wickets

India won the series 1-0

South Africa in India 1996

1st Test. Ahmedabad. 20–23 November 1996
India 223 (**SR Tendulkar 42**; AA Donald 4–37) and 190 (VVS Laxman 51,
    SR Tendulkar 7; AA Donald 3–32)
South Africa 244 (PS de Villiers 67*; SB Joshi 4–43) and 105 (WJ Cronje
    48*; J Srinath 6–21, A Kumble 3–34)
India won by 64 runs

2nd Test. Kolkata. 27 November–1 December 1996
South Africa 428 (AC Hudson 146, G Kirsten 102; BKV Prasad 6–104) and
    367–3 dec (DJ Cullinan 153*, G Kirsten 133)
India 329 (M Azharuddin 109, A Kumble 88, **SR Tendulkar 18**; AA Donald
    3–72) and 137 (M Azharuddin 52, **SR Tendulkar 2**; L Klusener 8–64)
South Africa won by 329 runs

3rd Test. Kanpur. 8–12 December 1996
India 237 (**SR Tendulkar 61**, WV Raman 57; PR Adams 6–55) and 400–7
    dec (M Azharuddin 163*, R Dravid 56, **SR Tendulkar 36**)
South Africa 177 (G Kirsten 43; A Kumble 4–71, J Srinath 3–42) and 180
    (WJ Cronje 50; J Srinath 3–38, SB Joshi 3–66)
India won by 280 runs

India won the series 2–1

India in South Africa 1996–97

1st Test. Durban. 26–28 December 1996
South Africa 235 (AC Hudson 80; BKV Prasad 5–60) and 259 (AM Bacher
    55, AC Hudson 52, BM McMillan 51*; BKV Prasad 5–93)
India 100 (SC Ganguly 16, **SR Tendulkar 15**; AA Donald 5–40, SM Pollock
    2–18, BM McMillan 2–27) and 66 (R Dravid 27*, **SR Tendulkar 4**;
    AA Donald 4–14, SM Pollock 3–25, L Klusener 2–16)
South Africa won by 328 runs

2nd Test. Cape Town. 2–6 January 1997
South Africa 529–7 dec (G Kirsten 103, BM McMillan 103*, L Klusener 102*,
    DJ Cullinan 77; BKV Prasad 3–114, J Srinath 3–130) and 256–6 dec
    (BM McMillan 59*, AC Hudson 55, DJ Cullinan 55; J Srinath 3–78)
India 359 (**SR Tendulkar 169**, M Azharuddin 115) and 144 (VVS Laxman 35*,
    SR Tendulkar 9; AA Donald 3–40)
South Africa won by 282 runs

3rd Test. Johannesburg. 16–20 January 1997
India 410 (R Dravid 148, SC Ganguly 73, **SR Tendulkar 35**; L Klusener
    3–75, AA Donald 3–88) and 266–8 dec (R Dravid 81, SC Ganguly 60,
    NR Mongia 50, **SR Tendulkar 9**; AA Donald 3–38, PR Adams 3–80)
South Africa 321 (SM Pollock 79, BM McMillan 47; J Srinath 5–104) and
    228–8 (DJ Cullinan 122*, L Klusener 49; A Kumble 3–40)
Match drawn

South Africa won the series 2–0

India in the West Indies 1997

1st Test. Kingston. 6–10 March 1997

West Indies 427 (CL Hooper 129, BC Lara 83, S Chanderpaul 52;
A Kumble 5–120) and 241–4 dec (BC Lara 78, S Chanderpaul 48;
A Kumble 3–76)
India 346 (NR Mongia 78, VVS Laxman 64, **SR Tendulkar 7**; FA Rose 6–100)
and 99–2 (R Dravid 51*, **SR Tendulkar 15***)
Match drawn

2nd Test. Port-of-Spain. 14–18 March 1997

West Indies 296 (RIC Holder 91, S Chanderpaul 42; A Kumble 5–104) and
299–6 (SC Williams 128, S Chanderpaul 79; SB Joshi 3–57)
India 436 (NS Sidhu 201, **SR Tendulkar 88**, R Dravid 57; CEL Ambrose 5–87)
Match drawn

3rd Test. Bridgetown. 27–31 March 1997

West Indies 298 (S Chanderpaul 137*, CEL Ambrose 37; BKV Prasad 5–82)
and 140 (BC Lara 45; A Kuruvilla 5–68, BKV Prasad 3–39)
India 319 (**SR Tendulkar 92**, R Dravid 78; FA Rose 4–77, IR Bishop 3–70)
and 81 (VVS Laxman 19, **SR Tendulkar 4**; IR Bishop 4–22, FA Rose
3–19, CEL Ambrose 3–36)
West Indies won by 38 runs

4th Test. St John's. 4–8 April 1997

West Indies 333 (BC Lara 103, RIC Holder 56; SB Joshi 3–76)
India 212–2 (A Jadeja 96, VVS Laxman 56)
Match drawn

5th Test. Georgetown. 17–21 April 1997

India 355 (R Dravid 92, **SR Tendulkar 83**; CL Hooper 3–34, FA Rose 3–90)
West Indies 145–3 (S Chanderpaul 58*, SC Williams 44)
Match drawn

West Indies won the series 1–0

India in Sri Lanka 1997

1st Test. Colombo (RPS). 2–6 August 1997

India 537–8 dec (**SR Tendulkar 143**, M Azharuddin 126, NS Sidhu 111,
R Dravid 69; ST Jayasuriya 3–45)
Sri Lanka 952–6 dec (ST Jayasuriya 340, RS Mahanama 225, PA de Silva
126, A Ranatunga 86, DPMD Jayawardene 66; SC Ganguly 2–53)
Match drawn

2nd Test. Colombo (SSC). 9–13 August 1997

Sri Lanka 332 (PA de Silva 146, M Muralitharan 39; DS Mohanty 4–78)
and 415–7 dec (ST Jayasuriya 199, PA de Silva 120; A Kumble 3–156,
A Kuruvilla 2–90)
India 375 (SC Ganguly 147, **SR Tendulkar 139**; M Muralitharan 4–99) and

281-5 (M Azharuddin 108*, SC Ganguly 45, **SR Tendulkar 8**;
  M Muralitharan 3-96)
Match drawn

Series drawn 0-0

Sri Lanka in India 1997

1st Test. Mohali. 19-23 November 1997
Sri Lanka 369 (MS Atapattu 108, ST Jayasuriya 53; A Kuruvilla 4-88,
  J Srinath 4-92) and 251-6 (PA de Silva 110*; J Srinath 3-75)
India 515-9 dec (NS Sidhu 131, SC Ganguly 109, M Azharuddin 53,
  SR Tendulkar 23; M Muralitharan 3-174, ST Jayasuriya 2-59)
Match drawn

2nd Test. Nagpur. 26-30 November 1997
India 485 (SC Ganguly 99, R Dravid 92, NS Sidhu 79, A Kumble 78,
  SR Tendulkar 15; KR Pushpakumara 5-122)
Match drawn

3rd Test. Mumbai. 3-7 December 1997
India 512 (SC Ganguly 173, **SR Tendulkar 148**, R Dravid 93; KR Pushpakumara
  3-108, HDPK Dharmasena 3-144) and 181-9 dec (R Dravid 85, NS Sidhu 43,
  SR Tendulkar 13; HDPK Dharmasena 5-57)
Sri Lanka 361 (MS Atapattu 98, PA de Silva 66, ST Jayasuriya 50; RK Chauhan
  4-48) and 166-7 (ST Jayasuriya 37, RS Mahanama 35; A Kumble 3-56,
  RK Chauhan 3-59)
Match drawn

Series drawn 0-0

9

A FOUR-MONTH HONEYMOON

The three-Test series in March 1998 was the first fully fledged home series against Australia of my career. It generated a lot of hype and much of it was being built up as a contest between myself and Shane Warne. It's inevitable that there are times when battles between two individuals hog most of the limelight. For example, Brian Lara versus Glenn McGrath, Ricky Ponting versus Courtney Walsh, or even Tendulkar versus Lara, as had been the case in 1994. I maintained that the series was a contest between two teams and not two individuals, though in my heart of hearts I knew it was a very important match-up against Warne. Shane was bowling beautifully and had just had a great series against South Africa in Australia, taking twenty wickets in three Tests.

Knowing that I would soon be facing him, I studied Warne's bowling in that series carefully. It appeared to me that his biggest strength was the drift he managed to get, which meant that the batsman was somewhat blinded by the delivery if he was batting with a traditional side-on stance. Because of the extra drift, the ball would tend to veer away from the line of vision of the batsman and it became that much more difficult to negotiate the extra spin. As a result, I decided to open up my stance a little to Warne and to stand slightly outside the leg stump. I also planned to play him more from the crease and as late as possible. I hardly stepped out to him all series and, more often than not, kept hitting him towards midwicket with a horizontal bat whenever he tried to extract extra spin from leg stump or slightly outside. By playing from the crease and by using the horizontal bat, I reckoned I had opened up the option of punishing him if he bowled short and could also play the cut shot on the off side.

While there was always the risk of a top edge, I was prepared to accept it to surprise Warne. After all, he was Australia's most potent weapon and I had to have a strategy against him.

Having worked on the theory, I now needed to practise against the kind of deliveries Warne would use when under pressure. I started training in late January, with still a month to go before the series, and asked for the best spinners available in Mumbai to bowl at me from round the wicket into the rough outside leg stump. I was certain that's what Warne would do if I succeeded in attacking him when he bowled from over the wicket. All that practice in Mumbai against Sairaj Bahutule and Nilesh Kulkarni, both of whom played for India against Australia in 2001, and subsequently in Chennai against Laxman Sivaramakrishnan, now a respected television commentator who played for India in the mid-1980s, proved immensely useful, and by the time the Australians arrived in India in February 1998 I felt ready to face Warne.

An early skirmish

The first game the Australians played was against Mumbai on 24 February. I was captaining Mumbai and knew it was crucial to establish a psychological advantage over the visitors at the start of the tour. The most important thing was to attack Warne. I had instructed all our batsmen to take Warne on whenever he came on to bowl. I did not care if we lost wickets, but there was no way we would allow Warne to settle into his groove and dictate terms.

When it was our turn to bat, Amit Pagnis, opening the batting for Mumbai, did exactly what we had planned. Though we lost an early wicket in Sulakshan Kulkarni, Pagnis and I attacked Warne from the start. While Pagnis hit Warne for four boundaries in two overs, I hit him for a six in his very first over and continued to attack him right through the innings. His sixteen overs cost him 111 runs and that was far more important than my own double hundred off 192 balls – though I was particularly pleased with my effort because I had made a conscious attempt to dominate the bowling and it was my first double in first-class cricket. Having conceded a lead of more than 100 in the first innings, the Australians collapsed to 135 all out in their second innings, with Nilesh Kulkarni, who had first played for India in 1996, running through half the side. We finished the match without losing a wicket in our second innings, handing the Australians a ten-wicket defeat.

A crushing loss in the first tour game was the worst possible start for the world's best team and was more than we could have hoped for. We now needed to carry the momentum forward into the first Test match in Chennai. Of course, I was well aware that the Australians had not played all their cards against Mumbai. Even when we were attacking Shane Warne, not once did he bowl from round the wicket into the rough outside leg stump. I was certain he would do so at the first available opportunity in Chennai, and I even said as much in the post-match press conference in Mumbai. The series was nicely set up.

First Test, Chennai, 6–10 March 1998

Having played a lot of cricket in Chennai, I knew that the physical preparation in the lead-up to a Chennai Test has to be different from normal. You have to prepare your body for the heat and humidity well in advance and I always did so at least thirty-six hours before the match by drinking a lot more water than normal. The extra water intake was particularly important, because you lose so much fluid during matches at the Chidambaram Stadium.

Nowadays, unlike in the late 1980s and 1990s, when there wasn't much research about players' diets and training schedules, cricket is much more sophisticated about such matters. There are specialized dieticians who draw up charts of what players can or can't eat. After long and arduous batting stints, players take ice baths and drink specially prepared shakes to rehydrate the body and replace lost energy. For example, I remember Paddy Upton, our high-performance trainer, asking me to drink two glasses of a shake made of crushed dry fruits after a particularly draining innings at Gwalior in 2010.

At Chennai, we won the toss and opted to bat first. It was an important toss to win, as the ball was expected to turn in the fourth innings and we were playing three spinners, in Anil Kumble, Rajesh Chauhan and Venkatapathy Raju. Despite a good start, with the top three of Mongia, Sidhu and Dravid all scoring fifties, we lost our way in the middle of the first innings and failed to push home the advantage, getting bowled out for a modest 257. Batting at number four, I managed just four runs and fell to Warne. I hit him for a boundary and then tried to repeat the shot, only to get an outside edge to Mark Taylor at slip. I was extremely disappointed with myself for not playing myself in and was determined to make amends in the second innings.

Our bowlers, in particular Kumble and Raju, did well to get the first eight Australian wickets for 201. It seemed we had a good chance of taking a first-innings lead, but we were frustrated when the Australian wicketkeeper Ian Healy and off-spinner Gavin Robertson, the debutant, put together a very good partnership. They added 96 runs between them, and Australia eventually gained a 71-run advantage. It seemed a crucial lead and at a dinner organized by former BCCI president AC Muthiah, Srinivas Venkataraghavan, a former India captain and leading off-spinner of the 1970s, said to me that it would be very difficult for us to get back into the match. He said that he thought there wasn't enough time left in the game to make up the deficit, set a target and finally bowl Australia out to win the match. I replied confidently that there was still plenty of time and that I was sure we would be able to turn things round.

Before the start of our second innings I remember saying in the dressing room that it was the responsibility of the batsmen to put their hands up and try to score 75 runs each for the team. You don't always need to set the bar really high and demand a hundred. I thought that scoring 75 in the second innings at Chennai would be good enough to set up the match.

When Sidhu was out for an important 64, I walked out to bat at 115–2, in effect 44–2 after deducting the deficit of 71 runs, and as on many occasions in my career I had Rahul Dravid for company in the middle. I started out watchfully and was soon into my groove. As expected, Shane Warne started to bowl round the wicket and I instantly took the attack to him and hit him over midwicket. From an individual perspective it was a defining moment in the game. We couldn't afford to lose another wicket, but we also couldn't go too much on the defensive.

Rahul and I added more than a hundred runs, to set up a strong platform. By the time Rahul was dismissed for another well-played half-century, I felt in control. I went on the attack and scored at a fair clip, hitting fours and sixes with regularity. Azhar gave me good support and we also added over a hundred runs, at almost five runs an over, a potentially match-winning partnership.

When we declared, I was not out on 155, the first-innings lead had been nullified and we were in with a great chance of winning the match, having set the Australians a target of 348 on a turning track. It was certainly one of my better hundreds and what made the sensation sweeter was that we proceeded to bowl the Australians out for 168, with Kumble taking four wickets, and we won the match by 179 runs. It was a tremendous start and, to add to my delight, I was Man of the Match. I had made up for getting out to Warne cheaply in the first innings of the match.

Importantly, we had performed as a unit and most of the senior members had played their parts to perfection. Anil had taken eight wickets in the game while Navjot Sidhu, opening the batting, had done a good job in both innings. He had attacked Warne from the start of our second innings and had set the game up for the other batsmen. Rahul too batted well in each innings and pocketed a couple of important catches at slip. We had shown good fighting spirit and that, more than anything, seemed to augur well for the team for the second Test match at Eden Gardens in Kolkata later that month.

Second Test, Kolkata, 18–21 March 1998

If Chennai was a rollercoaster, in Kolkata we were in control from the start. Australia won the toss at Eden Gardens but failed to press home an early advantage, losing four top-order wickets within the first hour of play. Srinath bowled a fine opening spell to take three wickets and Sourav too chipped in with the wicket of Mark Taylor. Despite a brief period of Australian resurgence under Steve Waugh and Ricky Ponting, we kept our nerve and bowled them out for 233 in the first innings.

Our batsmen followed up with some big runs and – a rare event in Test cricket – the first five batsmen passed 75, with Azhar going on to score a hundred at his favourite venue. I scored 79 and once again took the attack to Shane Warne, who went wicketless in his forty-two overs, conceding 147 runs. The plan against Warne was working and without his wickets the Australians were in trouble. I remember one particular shot against Warne on day two. In my determination to attack him, I hadn't noticed that it was the last over before tea and I hit him for a big six over long on, which I normally wouldn't have risked so close to a break. It just goes to show how hard you had to concentrate to cope with Warne.

We knew, of course, that the Australians were all excellent players, despite being at the receiving end for the time being, and we knew that it was important to keep them under pressure throughout the match. A champion team needs only a small window of opportunity to stage a fightback, something I had learnt over the years. If the Australians were on the back foot, you couldn't allow them the whiff of an opportunity to stage a recovery. We needed to be ruthless and we were. Having scored 633 in our first innings, we let Kumble and Srinath do the rest on a track that was offering variable bounce. Australia collapsed for 181 in their second innings, giving us one of our biggest Test wins. More importantly, we were 2–0 up in the three-Test series against the best team in the world and were justly proud of the achievement.

Third Test, Bangalore, 25–28 March 1998

In the final match of the series our team included a teenaged debutant in off-spinner Harbhajan Singh. I scored a big hundred in the first innings and once again we managed to put the Australian bowlers under pressure. Though Warne picked up three wickets, he also went for a lot of runs. To his credit, he was always in the game, despite being attacked. In fact, as I played out the last over of the first day against him, I had to keep telling myself to concentrate till the very last ball was bowled. A true great, Warne would not let you relax for a single delivery.

Mark Waugh batted brilliantly in the Australian first innings, scoring an unbeaten 153, and Michael Kasprowicz, the fast bowler, picked up a five-wicket haul in our second innings to set up the match. I was caught and bowled by Kasprowicz for 31, playing a ball early, and we collapsed for a paltry 169. There was no doubt about it: Australia had played better than us in Bangalore and had shown what they were made of. For our part, we were disappointed at not closing out the series on a winning note.

It was one of the most intense series I played in my career, and one of the most personally successful. I had scored close to 450 runs at an average of 111. Weeks of rigorous practice had paid off and it was a deeply satisfying feeling.

Pepsi triangular series, April 1998

The Test series was followed by a one-day tri-series, with Zimbabwe as the third team. Our first match was against Australia at Kochi on 1 April, and it remains a match I have extremely fond memories of. I was opening the batting again in one-day cricket by this stage but unfortunately got out early. Luckily it did not matter, with Ajay Jadeja batting well in the middle order for a hundred and taking us past 300.

Australia got off to a flier. Adam Gilchrist, the best wicketkeeper-batsman of our generation, went after the bowling and they cruised to 100 in just twelve overs. It was apparent that if they played out the full fifty overs they'd win the game. Midway through the innings, I was brought on to bowl and I started bowling off-spin to the left-handers and leg-spin to the right-handers.

It's one of those strange things, but for some reason sometimes a batsman just does not like the sight of a particular bowler. In my case, I was never comfortable facing Hansie Cronje, who got me out on a number of occasions with his medium pace. Even when I was in control against the likes of Allan Donald, Hansie would somehow get the better of me and I'd get out to him in the most unexpected ways. So you don't always need to be a front-line bowler to trouble a particular batsman – and that's what happened between me and Steve Waugh. Throughout my career I had a feeling Steve wasn't comfortable against my leg-spin. At Kochi, I bowled a perfect leg-spinner to him and he lobbed the ball straight back to me.

I was elated at the dismissal and it was a big moment in the game. It was the opening we needed to put the pressure back on the Australians. The other big wicket that gave me a lot of satisfaction was that of Michael Bevan, a very effective batsman in limited-overs cricket, who was constantly trying to come down the wicket to negate the turn. I had warned Nayan Mongia, our wicketkeeper, that I'd bowl a quick one down the leg side if I saw Bevan try that against me. The ploy worked and Bevan was stumped off a wide ball down the leg side.

This was one of those rare matches when every ball was coming out of the hand perfectly, and I even had a fielder at slip past the thirty-over mark. The odd thing is that over the course of my career I found that whenever I practised hard at bowling leg-spin, I could never land the ball properly. And yet sometimes when I hadn't practised for months it just landed on the spot at crucial times in a match. In the end I decided to bowl leg-spin in the nets as and when I felt like it, without thinking too much about the technical aspects. In any case, Anil Kumble once explained to me that to bowl leg-spin consistently, I needed to hold my shoulder while bowling. What he meant was that I needed to have my fingers, arm and shoulder position aligned for longer. It was something I could never get the hang of, so I just left it to my natural ability, and I rarely bowled more than three overs at a stretch in a match unless I was bowling really well. This gave me licence to experiment and I could give the ball a rip if I wished to. At Kochi it all worked beautifully. I finished with 5–32 and Australia were bowled out for 268 in the forty-sixth over. We had won the match by 41 runs.

We continued the good form against the Australians in the next ODI at the Green Park stadium in Kanpur on 7 April. It was a low-scoring encounter, with the Australians setting us 222 to chase. The pitch was keeping low and I had figured out that the best option was to be aggressive at the start. I got another hundred in this match and remember one particular shot against Tom Moody. Even before he had released the ball, I stepped out and he followed me. The ball was down the leg side and, having stepped out of my crease, I wasn't in the best position to meet the delivery. I connected on the full but played it slightly off-balance. To my surprise, the ball landed in the stands, way beyond the boundary. Later in the innings I came down the wicket to Warne and this time the ball hit the bottom of my bat. Warne immediately screamed 'Catch it!' – only to see the ball soar over the long-on fielder and land 10 yards behind him for another six. I hit seven in all and we won the game comfortably, to book a spot in the final, which we unfortunately lost to Australia. It was disappointing after winning all the group matches and it resulted in an imperfect end to the tour.

Coca-Cola Cup, April 1998

Soon after the series was over we went to Sharjah for yet another tri-series, with Australia and New Zealand. It is a tournament I remember well because I played some of my best cricket then, and because of an incident that took place on the flight out to Sharjah. The Indian team included two relative newcomers, Harbhajan Singh and Harvinder Singh, the medium-fast bowler. The flight attendant asked both of them if they wanted soup. Not very good with English at the time, Harvinder may not have understood the question. I overheard Harvinder tell Bhajji that it was prudent just to take what was being served. Then Harvinder, trying to figure out what to add to his soup, ended up adding sugar-free sweetener instead of salt. Bhajji, who always enjoyed a laugh, was aware of what Harvinder had done and kept asking him if he was enjoying his food! Harvinder was too embarrassed to admit his mistake and so he pretended to like it.

Sharjah, in April, was hot, very hot. The heat was oppressive and it was a real test of stamina. I could feel the heat through my shoes and it often caused a burning sensation, which was extremely discomforting. It was physically draining to bat for long hours and, with little recovery time between games, it was a stern test of a player's skill, both physical and mental.

The two matches everyone remembers were both against Australia, on 22 and 24 April 1998. The first one was our last round-robin game, which we needed to win, or score a certain number of runs in, to qualify for the final. Australia had already made it to the final by winning all three of their pool games.

In the first of the two games, Australia batted first and scored a very healthy 284, with 81 from Mark Waugh and a century from Bevan. We needed a good start to get our chase on track. Unfortunately, however, we had lost four wickets for just 138 runs in twenty-nine overs when the match was interrupted. I had never seen a sandstorm in my life. Waves of sand were blowing from one end of the ground to the other and the wind was so strong that I feared my five-foot-five-inch frame would get blown away. The wind was also making a strange sound and we could only see a few metres ahead of us. Players and umpires were understandably worried about getting sand in their eyes and instinctively dropped to the ground. I quickly went and lay down behind Adam Gilchrist, who I reckoned was strong enough to withstand the force of the wind. My plan was simple – if the wind ever got too strong, I would hold on to Gilchrist for support. While it appears funny in hindsight to have used an Australian wicketkeeper as a shield, the whole experience was rather bizarre to start with.

Because the match was interrupted for more than forty-five minutes, it was reduced to forty-six overs a side but the target was cut by only eight runs. To win the match, we now needed 138 off seventeen overs, which may appear eminently gettable in this age of Twenty20 cricket but was a really steep target in 1998. A deduction of eight runs for the loss of four overs didn't make sense to us, and we knew we were up against it. Effectively the target to win had become stiffer. On the other hand, to qualify, we only needed 100 runs.

Anshuman Gaekwad, a former India opening batsman and then our coach, was in charge of the calculations and I asked him the exact target before I went out to resume the innings. Several of my team-mates thought we should just concentrate on getting the 100 runs we needed for qualification and not risk our place in the final by going for the win. However, I was determined to win the match and go to the finals, because I was timing the ball well and felt good about my batting. And beating Australia would give us an edge over them in the final.

It was important not to let the Australian bowlers settle. I hit Tom Moody for a six as soon as the game resumed, making my intentions clear. I followed it up with another six off Warne and attacked the Australians in every over I faced. They were doing their best to keep me off strike, while my partner VVS Laxman was doing his best to make sure I faced the bulk of the bowling. Looking back, I feel I owe him an apology as at one point I lost my temper with him when he refused a second run, thinking I was in danger of getting run out. I just wanted to play every ball I could.

When we passed 200 I started to feel that the Australian score was within reach. I was determined to bat on and finish the game. I have to say that if I had not got out to a dubious decision by the umpire with three overs still left in the game, I think we would probably have chased down the Australian score. I was given out to Damien Fleming, caught by Gilchrist for 143, when the ball seemed to me to be above shoulder height and should have been declared a no-ball. But such things happen in cricket and in the end we lost the game but qualified for the final and still had a chance for revenge.

Thinking of this match reminds me of a story about Anshuman Gaekwad. I have very fond memories of Anshu bhai as our coach and he undoubtedly had a very positive influence and helped me in a number of ways, but I can also never forget his amazing capacity to eat the hottest of hot food. On one occasion in New Zealand in 1999 he asked the hotel chef to make a paste of green chillies for him. The chef took on the challenge and returned later with a fresh bowl of chilli paste, warning him that he should be careful only to have a little because it was extremely hot. To the chef's amazement, Anshu bhai gratefully took the bowl from him and polished off the lot without breaking sweat – and even asked for some more! Frankly, no one else could have eaten even half a spoonful.

A final to remember

When we returned to the hotel after the last pool game, I was very tired and yet I just couldn't get to sleep. I eventually dropped off well after 2 a.m. With just a day before the final, this didn't bode well. In the extreme heat I had lost a lot of fluid and I needed time to get myself rehydrated and allow my body and mind to recover.

When I got up in the morning my body was stiff. My back was tight and I was even finding it difficult to walk to the bathroom. The stiffness was partly a result of the dehydration and the first thing I did was drink a lot of water. There have been a few occasions in my career when I have had difficulties standing up straight in the mornings. Sometimes I have really had to push myself to get off the bed and in extreme situations the physio and the masseur have had to give me a helping hand. Of course, I didn't mind the stiffness so much if I had scored a hundred or played a match-winning knock the day before. In that case, it was a happy feeling and a reminder of the effort I had put in! However, if the stiffness was caused by fielding for two long days, I would resent it immensely. So at Sharjah I had no reason to complain about the pain – it was a very small price to pay.

At lunchtime, I met Mark Mascarenhas for a meal at his hotel. Ravi Shastri, Shane Warne and Richie Benaud, former Australian captain and one of the greatest cricketers to have played the game, were also present and I had a brief non-cricketing chat with them all before returning to the hotel. I wasn't particularly concerned about the physical aspect of the recovery, as I was confident of digging into my reserves. I was more concerned with the mental recovery after such a high-intensity encounter.

In the evening, I had an interesting conversation with Mark. It was the Coca-Cola Cup and I was informed that, as sponsors, Coca-Cola wanted to announce a reward for me for the innings I had played the night before. They wanted to give me £25,000, which was a substantial sum of money. When Mark asked me what I'd do with it, I said that I would share it with my team-mates. It was our practice to share rewards among all players and I'd do no different. After that the issue wasn't raised again and I had put it out of my mind by the time I went to bed.

In the final, Australia batted first and put 272 runs on the board. It was a very good score, considering it was the final. We couldn't afford to lose an early wicket and I knew I had to stay in to set up the game. People were expecting me to blast the Australian attack from ball one, but that was an impossible propo-sition. Perhaps in people's minds I could just pick up from where I had left off two nights before. The reality, of course, was different. It was a new match and I was starting a new innings. I had to play myself in all over again and it wasn't going to be easy.

To make matters more difficult, the Australians bowled a good line and I had to work very hard not to get out. In the first over I faced against Damien Fleming, I played five dot-balls and was trying to leave the sixth ball, which hit my inside edge and went for a streaky boundary, missing the stumps by two inches. It was a lucky escape and I told myself that I was obviously still fatigued and wasn't moving my feet properly. I would have to spend time in the middle for my body to get used to the conditions and for my timing to come back.

We managed to score just 12 in the first five overs and the Australians continued to apply pressure by bowling a very tight line around the off stump. There were no loose balls on offer and I wasn't happy. The pressure was mounting and it was time to try something different. I was forced to take a risk to push the run rate up and so I came down the wicket to Michael Kasprowicz in the sixth over of our innings. I managed to connect well and the ball soared over the boundary. The crowd was in raptures and the bowler was taken by surprise. I now anticipated that he'd bowl me a bouncer the very next ball. It is a fast bowler's natural response and I was more than prepared for it.

I stayed back in the crease and easily hit the short ball for another six. It definitely rattled Kasprowicz and the Australians. The risks I had taken had paid off and the touch had come back. There was no need for any further risk-taking and the run chase was back on track.

With Nayan Mongia, who had been promoted up the order, and Azhar giving me good support, I was able to pace my innings without allowing the Australian bowlers to dominate and gradually the match was turning our way. Shane Warne tried coming round the wicket and yet again I countered him by hitting him over midwicket and square leg. With Warne ineffective – he conceded more than six runs an over in his spell – the Australians were forced to turn to Tom Moody. We attacked him throughout his spell and also put pressure on Australia's irregular bowlers, Mark and Steve Waugh.

By the time I finally got out for 134, the result was a mere formality. We needed just 24 from six overs. As I was walking back to the pavilion I could see Mark Mascarenhas waiting for me next to the sightscreen. I was soaked in sweat and, seeing Mark was about to give me a hug, I remember warning him that he would spoil his smart clothes. Mark wasn't bothered and he lifted me up into the air with a broad grin.

The post-match presentation turned out to be really special. Steve Waugh said that they had lost to *me*, which was quite something coming from the Australian captain on a day which also happened to be my twenty-fifth birthday. There could have been no better birthday present.

During the presentation ceremony, it was announced that Coca-Cola had decided to present me with a Mercedes SL600. My interest in cars was as strong as ever, and the announcement took me back to my first trip to England with the Star Cricket Club in 1988, when I had first come across a whole range of fancy European cars.

Good to be back

On our return to Mumbai we were greeted by a sea of humanity and it was touching to see fans showering such warmth on the players. In the ultimate analysis, we play for our fans and to be able to make them happy has always been extremely important.

Sometimes things can get a little out of hand, however. After coming back from Sharjah I was invited to a double-wicket tournament at the Shivaji Park Gymkhana in Mumbai. Pravin Amre called me and said the organizers were keen for me to go along to encourage the players. Shivaji Park has always been special to me and I decided to take Anjali with me. When we arrived we found that a huge crowd had assembled to see me. My visit had caused a law-and-order situation and in the end it was difficult to get away from the chaos. We somehow managed to leave Shivaji Park Gymkhana for home and I felt humbled at the affection I had received. Fans asking for autographs always makes me feel special and I make it a point to oblige them whenever I can. The people who wait for hours are the ones who make the game what it is in India and we are lucky that we have such a passionate fanbase for the sport in the country.

Looking back at the four months between January and April 1998, I feel a sense of deep satisfaction. I had led the charge against the Australians and had enjoyed the personal contest against Shane Warne. But it didn't stop there. I went on to bat at close to my best throughout 1998 and in November played my part in winning us the Champions Trophy tri-series at Sharjah against Sri Lanka and Zimbabwe.

What I remember about that competition is that the Zimbabwe fast bowler Henry Olonga had taken me by surprise in the last match of the group stage with a short ball and the manner of my dismissal had kept me restless right up to the final. So much so that I decided I had to settle the score. It was like in boxing – either you go down or I go down. In the final I managed to score 124 off ninety-two balls, but I must confess that some of my shots were not what you might call orthodox cricketing shots, as all I was doing was smashing the ball. That's what happens when you are batting well – even slogs go for boundaries – whereas during a lean patch, you get out to bad balls.

Invitations I couldn't turn down

A few months before that Champions Trophy, in July and August 1998, two things happened that I will never forget. The first was an invitation to play in the Princess Diana Memorial Match at Lord's on 18 July. The opposition bowling line-up included Glenn McGrath, Javagal Srinath, Allan Donald and Anil Kumble, and I managed to score 125 against them while opening the batting. Though I didn't manage to make a hundred at Lord's in Test cricket, this was a ton I have fond memories of, especially because it came against a top-quality bowling attack.

The second memorable thing happened in August when Shane Warne and I had the great honour of being invited to visit Sir Don Bradman at his house in Adelaide on the occasion of his ninetieth birthday. We were both very nervous about meeting the great man and I remember debating with Shane in the taxi on the way about who should talk to him first. I said that it should be Shane, because he's a fellow Australian; he said that it should be me, because I'm a fellow batsman. In the end, Sir Don, who fondly referred to me as 'Bonzer', took control of proceedings as soon as we arrived and quickly made us feel at ease.

One of the things I remember asking him was how he thought he would have coped in the contemporary game. He said that he didn't think he would have scored quite so many runs because of the more defensive field settings that are used nowadays; when he was playing, the fields weren't changed much, even if a batsman was scoring a lot of runs, and fielding positions like deep point weren't in vogue back in the 1930s. He also said that the standard of fielding was much better in the contemporary game.

Finally, we asked what he thought his Test average would be if he played today. 'Around 70,' he said. We were slightly surprised and asked if he was sure it would be so much lower than his famous career average of 99.94. He said, 'Well, 70 isn't bad for a ninety-year-old!'

All in all, 1998 was a special year in my career.

Australia in India 1998 – The Border–Gavaskar Trophy

1st Test. Chennai. 6–10 March 1998
India 257 (NS Sidhu 62, NR Mongia 58, R Dravid 52, **SR Tendulkar 4**; GR Robertson 4–72, SK Warne 4–85) and 418–4 dec (**SR Tendulkar 155***, NS Sidhu 64, M Azharuddin 64, R Dravid 56)
Australia 328 (IA Healy 90, ME Waugh 66, GR Robertson 57; A Kumble 4–103, SLV Raju 3–54) and 168 (SK Warne 35, IA Healy 32*; A Kumble 4–46)
India won by 179 runs

2nd Test. Kolkata. 18–21 March 1998
Australia 233 (SR Waugh 80, RT Ponting 60; SC Ganguly 3–28, A Kumble 3–44, J Srinath 3–80) and 181 (MA Taylor 45; A Kumble 5–62, J Srinath 3–44)
India 633–5 dec (M Azharuddin 163*, NS Sidhu 97, VVS Laxman 95, R Dravid 86, **SR Tendulkar 79**, SC Ganguly 65)
India won by an innings and 219 runs

3rd Test. Bangalore. 25–28 March 1998
India 424 (**SR Tendulkar 177**, NS Sidhu 74, M Azharuddin 40; AC Dale 3–71, SK Warne 3–106) and 169 (NS Sidhu 44, **SR Tendulkar 31**; MS Kasprowicz 5–28, GR Robertson 3–28, SK Warne 2–80)
Australia 400 (ME Waugh 153*, MJ Slater 91, DS Lehmann 52; A Kumble 6–98) and 195–2 (MA Taylor 102*, MJ Slater 42; **SR Tendulkar 1–41**)
Australia won by 8 wickets

India won the series 2–1

10

TUMULTUOUS TIMES

While I was starting to play some of the best cricket of my career, at home my life had undergone a fundamental transformation. That is because on 12 October 1997 I had received my greatest ever gift, with Anjali giving birth to our first child. I had shared the news that I was expecting a child with my team-mates when we were touring Zimbabwe in February 1997 and organized an impromptu party in celebration. I was thrilled at the thought of becoming a father.

The night before the moment finally arrived I was with my friend Sunil Harshe on the terrace of Anjali's family house in Breach Candy. The house was just two minutes away from the hospital and I had been told by Anjali's paediatrician friend, Dr Ajit Gajendragadkar, that he would call me the moment they brought her out of the delivery room. My prolonged presence in the hospital would have caused difficulties for the authorities and it was best that I waited for the call. Restless and anxious, I was lying on the terrace, staring up at the sky, and I remember saying to Sunil that within hours I would be a father and turn a new page in my life. All I was praying for was that Anjali and the child would both be safe and healthy.

When Dr Gajendragadkar finally called me with the good news the following day, I arrived at the hospital within minutes, with video camera in hand. Seconds after reaching the maternity ward, I saw the doctor carrying my child in his arms and that's when I was told that God had blessed us with a baby girl. I recorded the whole thing and cherish the recording of the doctor bringing my daughter out to me. It's impossible to describe the over-whelming sensation of seeing my child for the first time. I went up to Anjali and said to her that we would call our daughter Sara. In fact, it was a name that Ajit had suggested and both Anjali and I loved it. When the doctor asked me to hold Sara, I was much too nervous to do so at first, though I was longing to take her in my arms. I had never held a newborn in my arms before.

On the day of Sara's birth, I asked permission from the hospital authorities to stay with Anjali in her room. I simply did not want to leave my wife and daughter alone. While I knew that they were in good hands, I wanted to be with them the whole time. The hospital staff were only too kind and suggested that, while there wasn't an extra bed for me, I could stay in the same room as Anjali and they were happy to provide a mattress, which was placed on the floor. That was fine with me and I will always be grateful for their help.

Sara, according to everyone who saw her, was a carbon copy of me and I loved the act of putting her to sleep in my arms. I would just rock her for a couple of minutes and she would go off to sleep. I had a beard then and once she was a few months old I would place her on my lap and brush her hair with my beard. It was a favourite father–daughter pastime and something both of us loved to do every day.

With a packed cricket calendar, which entailed me being away from home for long periods, it could not have been easy for Anjali to bring up young Sara alone, but not once did she appear to resent this or ask me to spend more time at home. For my part, I know I found it difficult to leave my newborn daughter. Every time I came back after a tour I could spot the changes in her and I was aware that I was missing out on something truly special.

The first international destination that young Sara travelled to was New Zealand in December 1998. We arrived in Napier to start with and the team were given comfortable serviced apartments to stay in. I was given a two-bedroom apartment and it was decided that Anjali and Sara would sleep in one bedroom while I used the other. Sara, who had just turned one, had serious trouble adjusting to the time difference. She would be awake all night and would expect Anjali to play with her the whole time. I would put her to sleep all right, but then she would wake up an hour later and start wandering all over the apartment. Because I had to train or play a match the next day, there was no way I could stay up with her. As a result the responsibility fell on Anjali.

At one stage we were both finding it extremely tough to adjust and Anjali suggested that she would much rather return to India. It was difficult managing a toddler alone, having to cook, clean and wash her clothes, and when it was time to sleep she would be wide awake and ready to play. But then we took her to the park to feed the ducks in the pond, which she loved, and that gave us so much joy that the thought of going back was buried.

There is another story about Sara in New Zealand that I will never forget. The door to my bedroom was always kept open so that Sara could come and go whenever she wanted. One morning Bhajji said to me that I ought to check if she had something in her mouth. I was surprised, because we had not given her anything. I had to persuade Sara to open her mouth for me and when she did I was shocked to see that she had four or five cherry stones in her mouth. She must have had them in there for at least a few minutes, and had it not been for Bhajji there could have been a serious problem.

The team spent Christmas and New Year in New Zealand in 1998–99 and we will always remain grateful to two expat Indians for bailing us out on Christmas Day. None of us had an idea that everything in Wellington, including restaurants, would remain shut from Christmas Eve to Boxing Day. In India all restaurants and hotels are open on Christmas Day, with people eating out to celebrate the occasion. In Wellington, even the team hotel would not serve food and the team was left to fend for themselves. That's when Mori Patel, Ilesh Patel and Nanu bhai came to our rescue.

Mori bhai, Ilesh bhai and Nanu bhai are residents of Wellington, and on Christmas Day they came over to our hotel with all sorts of amazing food. We all enjoyed feasting on the fantastic Indian food that had been specially prepared for us. Apart from not starving on Christmas Day, it meant we could also get a taste of fantastic home-cooked Indian food. Over the years, the Patels came to watch a lot of our games in New Zealand and sometimes even travelled to Australia to see us play. Each time they would bring food and tea for us. Ilesh bhai's *desi chai* (Indian tea) was a hit among the players and each time I saw him I would ask, '*Ilesh bhai chai nahi pilayenge kya?*' (Ilesh bhai, would you not get us to drink tea today?)

It was in New Zealand that Sara started to speak. She recited her first nursery rhyme during this tour and each word she said delighted Anjali and me, and made us feel fulfilled.

A painful series

While I was gradually adjusting to the responsibilities of fatherhood, I suffered my first serious injury, a back problem from which I took more than eight months to fully recover. The problem surfaced in Chennai at the end of January 1999 during the first Test against Pakistan.

Pakistan had come to India after a gap of thirteen years and the entire country was focused on the two-Test series and the Asian Test Championship involving India, Pakistan and Sri Lanka that was to follow. Pakistan had a versatile bowling attack, with Wasim Akram, Waqar Younis and the off-spinner Saqlain Mushtaq, leg-spinner Shahid Afridi and slow left-arm orthodox spinner Nadeem Khan all in good form, and there was no doubt it would be a keenly contested series.

The Chennai match lived up to the hype and after three days of gripping Test cricket, India were left with a target of 271 in the fourth innings. It was a difficult run chase, as Wasim and Waqar started out very well for Pakistan, reducing us to 6–2 on the third evening. I walked out with just under an hour left on the third day, with Wasim and Waqar still charging in and full of energy. Rahul was already out there and we knew we needed to see out the rest of the day and resume battle the following morning. These little sessions are always tricky because the bowling side know they can come back refreshed the next morning and so they throw everything at the batsmen, in the hope of getting a bonus wicket. For the batting team there's little to be gained and the priority is not to lose another wicket.

Waqar welcomed me to the crease with a couple of bouncers and even walked up to me on one occasion to say, '*Ball nazar aayi?*' (Did you see the ball?) I didn't say a thing, but my eye contact was enough to give him the message. I hardly moved and he was soon walking back to his bowling mark. I remember muttering to myself, 'You are not bowling that quick, my friend.' This exchange only helped to strengthen my resolve and I was unbeaten on 20 at the end of play, determined to win the Test match on the fourth day.

Rahul was not out at the other end and there are not many other players you would rather bat with in a situation like that. He has always been rock solid. The next morning, however, the usual script was torn up when Rahul was bowled by a beauty from Wasim. Azhar soon followed and when Sourav got out we were down to 82–5 and badly needed a partnership.

When Nayan Mongia came out to join me in the middle I asked him to be patient and just play himself in. With the cream of our batting back in the dressing room, I realized it was time for me to take charge. I was fully focused on the job at hand and had gone into a zone where I was praying before each ball was bowled. Even when Nayan was on strike I was rehearsing in my mind how I'd have played the balls bowled to him. In effect, I was trying to bat at both ends. As I concentrated really hard, everything else around me seemed a blur and all I knew was that I had to bat through to the end of the game.

And then the pain struck. It was forty-five minutes before tea when I felt a scorching pain in my back. By now Nayan and I had put together a good partnership and the game was starting to tilt ever so slightly towards India. But Pakistan had yet to take the new ball and I knew we still had a fair amount of work to do. Wasim and Waqar would give their best in one final burst. The hot and humid conditions in Chennai were harsh and I was starting to suffer from cramp. Playing each ball was turning out to be an ordeal and the pain in my back was becoming unbearable. The tea break came as a blessed relief. I remember lying flat on a towel in the dressing room with cold towels spread all over me to bring down my body temperature. My whole body was cramping up and I knew it was going to be really difficult to bat for two more hours.

After tea I had no choice but to attack the bowling, because I knew my back was about to give up. I informed Nayan of the change in strategy and hit a few boundaries in the next few overs. Soon the target was down to manageable proportions and we just needed to play out the second new ball. We had put on 136 runs for the sixth wicket and Pakistan were gradually losing their grip on the match. In fact, we were cruising along when Nayan got out to a bad shot. He tried a slog to a Wasim delivery and top-edged the ball in the process. There was no need to play that shot and it had once again given Pakistan a ray of hope. It was a sad end to a very good innings from Nayan.

Sunil Joshi, who came in next, settled well and even hit a six off Saqlain during his forty-minute stay at the wicket. We made 36 in the six overs after Nayan got out and the target was now just 17 runs away. In the meantime my back had all but given up on me and I was finding it difficult to stand up straight. Every movement was hurting and every shot increased the pain. I soon realized that all-out attack was my only option. Unable to bear the pain any longer, I tried to hit a Saqlain doosra – the off-spinner's delivery that goes the other way from normal after pitching, a ball that Saqlain was the first to master – over mid off for another boundary. The ball bounced more than expected and I ended up top-edging the ball. I could see Wasim getting under the ball at mid off and was praying for him to drop the catch. But I was out for 136 and was devastated.

It was a painful walk back to the pavilion. Even the standing ovation from the crowd did little to alleviate the pain at not having finished the match. However, I must say that I really did not expect us to lose the match from there, with just 17 runs to get and three wickets, including Srinath and Kumble, still left. In fact, I couldn't believe what was happening when we were bowled out for 258 and lost by 12 runs. My world seemed to collapse around me and I just couldn't hold back the tears in the dressing room. My back was in horrible shape and mentally I was at a serious low.

It was the only time in my life when I didn't go out to receive the Man of the Match award. Raj Singh Dungarpur tried to persuade me but I said to him that I was in no state, physically or mentally, to leave the dressing room. He understood and left me to myself. Even when we were leaving for Delhi the next morning, I couldn't even carry my hand luggage. It was as if someone was sticking needles into my back all the time and I couldn't sit in one position for more than two or three minutes.

In hindsight, I should not have played the Delhi and Kolkata Test matches that followed, but my urge to play against Pakistan drove me on. I had told the BCCI all about my physical condition and they had left it up to me whether to play or not and at the time I felt I would be able push myself.

The second Test, starting in Delhi on 4 February 1999, was very much Anil Kumble's match and it was his world-record spell of 10–74 in the second innings that helped us level the series. Anil has won many Test matches for India and he was unplayable at the Kotla in Delhi, as he became only the second bowler in the history of Test cricket, after Jim Laker in 1956, to pick up all ten wickets in an innings. In Pakistan's second innings I handed Anil's sweater and cap to umpire Arani Jayaprakash before every over he bowled. It worked well for us and there was no reason to change the pattern. It seems incredible to think that Anil singlehandedly won us a Test match against Pakistan, but he certainly did.

The two-Test series was followed by the Asian Test Championship and India played Pakistan in the inaugural match of this new competition at Eden Gardens in Kolkata, which started on 16 February. Many looked upon it as the third and deciding leg of the bilateral series. I remember the match for the way I was run out in the second innings. Chasing 279 for victory, we were well placed at 134–2 when I walked out to bat. I was in the process of playing myself in when I clipped a Wasim delivery past wide mid on. The ball was finally pulled up yards from the rope by the substitute fielder Nadeem Khan. I was jogging to the crease for an easy third run when the throw came in on the full to hit the stumps. Despite the direct hit, I would have been well in if I hadn't collided with Shoaib Akhtar. Shoaib, who was fielding at mid off, had come forward to back up the throw and was standing a few yards behind the stumps, right in my line of running. I could not comprehend why he was standing there rather than right behind the stumps. With my eyes on the ball, I collided with him moments after I had run my bat in. As a result of the collision, my bat was in the air when the ball hit the stumps.

While not imputing any motive to Shoaib, I must say I was shocked to see the Pakistanis appeal for the run-out. The crowd, sensing the injustice, turned violent and started throwing things onto the ground. After walking off, finding it difficult to come to terms with the incident, I went straight to the third umpire's room to check the replay and was dismayed to see what had really happened.

Because of the crowd disturbance, the match had to be stopped for a good twenty minutes, and finally Jagmohan Dalmiya, then president of the ICC and one of India's most distinguished administrators, came to our dressing room to ask if I would go out and pacify the crowd. I didn't really feel like it, because I felt wronged, but I changed my mind to ensure there was no further violence at Eden Gardens. It was only after Jagmohan Dalmiya and I appealed to the crowd that the match was finally allowed to resume.

The sense of outrage, however, was still there and the crowd turned violent again the following morning, resulting in unreal scenes towards the end of the match. In an unprecedented move, 65,000 people were forced to vacate the stadium and the match was completed without a single spectator inside the ground. Perhaps it could all have been avoided if Shoaib had not stood in my way or if Wasim had withdrawn the appeal.

India lost the Test match by 46 runs and the way the match ended left us all feeling rather bitter.

Losing my father

Continuing to play on with my back injury had unfortunately aggravated the problem. As a result, I played the World Cup in England in May and June 1999 in considerable physical discomfort. But the World Cup was not a tournament I could miss and I did all I could to get ready. Every time I trained, my back would get stiff and I would need a cooling-off period for it to settle down. The fickle English weather did not help matters and I was advised to sleep on the floor of the hotel room with a pillow below my knee, to make sure that my back was flat on the ground. In time, I learnt to sleep in the tiny gap between the bed and the cupboard in most hotel rooms, which ensured there wasn't much space for me to toss and turn.

Ajit, Anjali and Sara were all in England before the World Cup and that was a great comfort. We would go out for meals together and it was during one of these dinners at a Chinese restaurant that I ordered crispy aromatic duck. I just love to eat this dish served with thin pancakes and sliced cucumber and can finish a portion on my own. However, just as I placed my order, Ajit asked me to cancel it. He declared that he would not allow me to eat duck before the World Cup. While I found it amusing at first, I soon realized he was serious and felt obliged to do what he wanted. When I asked him his reasons, he said he had read an article which said that three English players had once gone out for a meal before a very important match and they had all had duck for dinner. Subsequently each one got out without scoring. Of course, in cricket a 'duck' is associated with a batsman scoring zero and on the Australian television coverage a duck is even shown accompanying a batsman back to the pavilion if he gets out without scoring. Ajit said to me I could have as much duck as I wanted once the World Cup was over!

Just before the tournament started Anjali decided to go back to London, leaving me to focus solely on my cricket. In the second trimester of her pregnancy and with one-and-a-half-year-old Sara with her, it must have been immensely difficult for her to negotiate things on her own. While I missed her badly and desperately wanted to be with her to help out, there was little I could do but appreciate what she was doing for me and the family.

It was in the middle of all this that I received the news of my father's passing. Ajit, who had gone back to India by then, called Anjali to tell her what had happened and asked her to break the news to me personally. Anjali in turn called two of my teammates, Robin Singh and Ajay Jadeja, and asked them to be outside my room as she drove back to the team hotel in Leicester very late at night on 18 May – the day before our second match of the tournament, against Zimbabwe. She also called the hotel manager and asked him not to transfer any calls to my room.

When I opened the door at well past midnight and saw her standing with Ajay and Robin I immediately sensed something serious had happened. Atul Ranade, one of my closest friends, was with me in my room and I asked Atul to go out as Anjali came in. I could not believe what she was saying. It was a cruel blow and not something I had expected at all. It left me numb for a few minutes. I could not say a thing. Father had always been there for me. My mind had stopped working and all I could do was hold Anjali and cry. I felt helpless and was unable to come to terms with the shock for a while.

My first thought was to go back to India at the earliest opportunity to be with my mother and see my father one final time. Mark Mascarenhas, as always, had already made all the arrangements for the following morning and drove the two of us to Heathrow just before dawn. All through the journey I kept thinking about my father, who had been in reasonable health when I had left India for the World Cup. In fact, I couldn't believe he was not alive and felt that if I went back to India he would open his eyes again. He had undergone angioplasty a few months earlier and had stayed with us, so that Anjali could take care of him. By the time I left for the World Cup, he seemed back to his normal self and had even started to climb three floors. The doctors had asked him to have a drink every evening and I made a point of coming home most evenings to share a drink with him. In my wildest dreams I had never imagined that I would be sharing a drink with my father, but medical advice had forced me to do so. The thought that I would never see him again was just too much to digest.

My brothers and friends had come to pick me up at Mumbai airport but this was a very different homecoming from normal. When I got home I could see that my mother had aged considerably in the past few days and was sitting facing the wall. She hardly said a word to anyone and was in a state of shock. I felt devastated to see my mother like that and what was more worrying was that she did not move from her position for close to two days. It became unbearable when I came face to face with my grandmother, who had lost her son. She said to me that she wanted to spend a few quiet minutes with him and I immediately asked all who were present to leave us alone for a while. I accompanied my grandmother to the room where my father's body was lying, then left her to mourn with her son in peace. I remember standing a good few yards away, giving her the space she needed.

I couldn't sleep for many nights having lost my biggest inspiration. And it was a deeply emotional moment for all of us when the watchmen, postmen and all the other people he had helped during his life came over for his funeral. I put a gold coin with my face on it in his pocket before the cremation, so that I could always be there with him.

Without my father, my life would never be the same again.

A very difficult tournament

After spending four days in India, I returned to England to rejoin the team on the eve of the match against Kenya. That, it seemed to me, was what my father would have wanted me to do, and that's what prompted the decision to return to London to play the remaining World Cup matches. Mentally, however, I was not at my best throughout the tournament. I had to wear dark glasses during the practice sessions, because at times I could not hold back my tears. Though I managed to score a hundred in the match against Kenya – which remains one of my most cherished centuries, one I dedicated to my father – my mind was not always on the game.

The back injury, which had not shown any signs of improvement, also continued to bother me throughout the rest of the World Cup, helping to make it one of the toughest tournaments I have played in. It wasn't India's best World Cup either and we were knocked out in the Super Six stage after winning a couple of memorable matches against Sri Lanka and England at the group stage.

Against Sri Lanka at Taunton on 26 May 1999, Sourav and Rahul played two of the finest innings I have seen in a World Cup. Sourav was at his elegant best on his way to a majestic 183 and Rahul played beautifully for his 145. In our next match against England on 29 May, Sourav yet again made a significant all-round contribution, to give us a much-needed win, and Rahul was consistent right through the tournament.

At the Super Six stage our only consolation was another win against Pakistan. The match had assumed great significance against the backdrop of strained political relations between the two countries – the war in Kargil in Kashmir was on at the time. India won the highly charged encounter by 47 runs, with Venkatesh Prasad picking up a five-wicket haul.

An unexpected appointment

The back pain continued to bother me after the World Cup and in fact turned worse in the twin tournaments in Sri Lanka and Singapore in August–September 1999, at the end of which I decided to go to Australia to get my back examined. I had already resorted to acupuncture and acupressure – and even had my tongue pricked by an expert in Singapore trying to identify the pressure points that might help in the recovery. They were the acts of an increasingly desperate man.

Dr Anant Joshi, one of India's leading doctors and one who has always been there for me right through my career, travelled with me to Adelaide in September 1999 to meet a number of specialists. A series of checks were conducted and I eventually received four injections for the injury. I was glad I could not see the injections at the time because afterwards I realized I had never seen bigger needles in my life. I actually carried one back to show my friends and family and nobody could believe the size of them. But they did the job, and soon after my return to India the back injury that had bothered me for eight months was finally sorted. It was certainly a relief to be pain-free.

My determination was even greater because in August 1999 I had been appointed captain of India again, despite having deep reservations about taking on the job for a second time. What happened was that Ajit Wadekar had come to my house to ask me if I was prepared to captain India again and I told him that I was reluctant to do so. The next I heard was that I had been appointed captain ahead of a tri-series in Sri Lanka in August. It appears that Wadekar Sir had come over to speak to me on behalf of the BCCI and it was after consultation with him that the selectors had decided to give me the responsibility, despite my unwillingness. Once the appointment was made public it was difficult for me to turn it down. I have never ducked a challenge and I went on to accept the job, determined to give it my best. We were due to tour Australia at the end of the year and I knew it was the toughest assignment in cricket at the time.

A new arrival

All of this coincided with the birth of our second child, when Anjali and I were blessed with a baby boy on 24 September 1999. I decided to name him Arjun and remember announcing my intention to Anjali soon after I had seen my son for the first time. She later mentioned to me that she had thought of a few other names herself but, seeing my enthusiasm for Arjun, went ahead with my choice. Once again I filmed the day and I cherish the recording of Arjun being brought out to me for the first time.

Watching the children grow up is a fantastic feeling and I must say I missed them every time I was away from them. With Arjun it was particularly hard. He would resent my going away and would refuse to speak to me on the phone. For the first six years of his life Arjun never talked to me when I was on tour. In my desperation to hear his voice I often requested Anjali to ask him to say hello, but he would always refuse. Then, on my return, he would cling to me for the first three days, trying to make up for lost time.

While Sara did not seem to resent my going in the same way as Arjun, she did find it difficult on occasions to bond with me on my return. Sara was just a few months old when I had to travel to Sri Lanka for a tour. It was extremely hot in Colombo and I returned home with quite a tan at the end of the assignment. I had turned really dark and she didn't recognize me. She thought someone else had walked in and she refused to go near me for the first few minutes!

When I had my kids at the turn of the century, technology was not as advanced as now and there was no option to use Skype or FaceTime. Had the technology been available, I'm sure I would have asked Anjali to bring Sara and Arjun in front of the webcam so that I could at least see my kids when I was off in some other part of the world. It would have meant not missing out on so many of the changes they went through.

New Zealand in India, October–November 1999

After a couple of weeks at home following Arjun's birth, I was back on the field at Mohali on 10 October captaining India against New Zealand in the first of three Tests. Just like the first time, the start to my captaincy was not too bad, as we beat New Zealand in the series, though we made it hard for ourselves in the very first innings at Mohali when we were bowled out for 83, with Dion Nash taking six wickets. It was just one of those days when nothing worked and we collapsed for one of our lowest ever scores on home soil. It seemed as if the ghost of Barbados was back to haunt me. This time, however, our bowlers did a good job restricting the Kiwis to 215 and we batted with a lot more discipline in the second innings. We scored 505, losing just three wickets, with both Rahul and me scoring hundreds, and the game ended in a draw.

The second innings, however, was not without incident. Chris Cairns, the New Zealand all-rounder, bowled a spell of excellent reverse swing. Part of the problem for Rahul and me was that he concealed the shiny side of the ball so well that there was no way for the batsman to work out which way the ball would swing. That's when I came up with a plan. I suggested to Rahul that while it was impossible for the striker, it was not so difficult for the non-striker to work it out as he was far closer to Cairns. It was decided that while standing at the non-striker's end, I would spot the shiny side and if it was on the outside of the ball, I would hold my bat in my left hand to indicate to Rahul that the ball would swing away from him. If the shiny side was on the inside, I would hold my bat in my right hand to indicate that the ball would be coming in to him. And if I was not able to figure out which way the ball would swing, I would hold my bat in the middle.

The plan worked surprisingly well and soon we were able to attack Cairns, who ended up going for 76 runs in his twenty-four overs without picking up a wicket. It took a while for Cairns to work out what we were doing. To catch us unawares, he decided to bowl a cross-seam delivery, so I held my bat in the middle to indicate to Rahul that I didn't know which way the ball would swing. Soon after delivering the ball, Cairns turned towards me to see what I was doing. He was angry and frustrated and wanted to know how I had reacted to him bowling a cross-seam delivery. Winning this battle against Chris Cairns definitely helped us save the match.

In the second Test match, at Kanpur, we beat New Zealand comprehensively, with Kumble picking up ten wickets in the game, and in the final Test at Ahmedabad I scored a double hundred in a drawn encounter. At Ahmedabad we scored a mammoth 583 runs in the first innings and, despite bowling the opposition out for 308, did not enforce the follow-on. This was a unanimous decision taken in consultation with the fast bowlers, who were tired after an exhausting first-innings effort and needed some rest before they bowled again. We won the series 1–0 and then went on to win the ODI series 3–2. It may not have been ideal preparation for the tour to Australia that started at the end of the month, but a series win never does any harm.

India in Australia, November 1999–January 2000

During my second stint as captain we had Kapil Dev as our coach. He is one of the finest cricketers to have played for India and one of the best all-rounders of all time, and I had great expectations of him in Australia. I have always maintained that the coach's job is an important one, for he is in a position to play a key role in formulating team strategy. Who better than Kapil to come up with options for me during a tough tour of Australia? However, his method of involvement and his thought process was limited to leaving the running of the team to the captain, and hence he did not involve himself in strategic discussions that would help us on the field.

Things did not start badly for us in Australia. Unlike in South Africa in 1996–97, we reached Australia a good two weeks before the series started and played three practice games before the first Test. All in all, we weren't underprepared when we walked onto the field at the Adelaide Oval on 10 December 1999, and if the first morning was anything to go by, we were in with a good chance against the best team in the world.

Javagal Srinath and Venkatesh Prasad bowled extremely well to reduce Australia to 52–4 before lunch and we needed just one more wicket to get into the Australian lower middle order. We almost had that wicket in the form of the always dangerous Ricky Ponting, but he was given not out to a very close lbw shout early in his innings. He escaped again when he clearly under-edged a ball from Ajit Agarkar to the wicketkeeper MSK Prasad when on 62 but was again adjudged not out. Australia were still not out of the woods at that stage and that could well have been the opening we were looking for. However, luck was with Ponting on the day and he and Steve Waugh both went on to make big hundreds.

When it was our turn to bat, I faced a probing spell from Glenn McGrath towards the end of the day's play, playing out five or six maiden overs in the process. Some people may have wondered why I allowed McGrath to bowl those maidens and why I was not playing my natural game, but Test cricket is all about getting into the mind of the opposition. After that passage of play, the Australians changed their tactics, and later Shane Warne told me that I had forced them to make the change. The Australian plan, I was told, was to make me leave 70 per cent of the deliveries in each innings. But with me playing out the maiden overs, they realized that attempts to frustrate me wouldn't work. The next morning, I changed my strategy and hit McGrath for two boundaries in the first over.

In this Test match we were at the receiving end of what seemed to us to be a howler from umpire Daryl Harper. Sourav and I had embarked on a good fightback and I had scored 61. The team score was at 215–4 and another hundred runs could have helped set up the match, but just as we were looking to consolidate, Daryl Harper gave me out bat-pad to Shane Warne, caught by Justin Langer at forward short leg. I was sure I hadn't hit the ball. Warne had pitched the delivery on my legs and the ball simply hit the pad before being caught by Langer. In the second innings I felt I was unlucky again. Glenn McGrath tried to bounce one at me but the ball actually stayed low. I instinctively ducked and it hit me on my shoulder. To everyone's surprise, umpire Harper declared me out lbw. It was a strange decision, because there was surely no way it would have gone on to hit the stumps.

While I'm not trying to excuse our under-par performance, there's no doubt that those decisions played a huge role in such a hard-fought Test match. To Australia's credit, they capitalized on the opportunities and went 1–0 up as a result. In the second and third Tests of the series, however, we were comprehensively outplayed. Even when VVS Laxman produced a magical 167 in Sydney in the third Test, something that prompted me to ask the selectors to keep him back for the ODI series that followed, the result was never in doubt. McGrath and Brett Lee, who made his debut in the series, were exceptional and had great back-up in Damien Fleming and Shane Warne. We were never allowed to take charge and there's no harm in conceding that Steve Waugh's Australian team in 1999 was one of the best teams I ever played against.

Personally I had a pretty good series and batted well for a hundred at the MCG in the Boxing Day Test. However, it counted for nothing because I was not able to change the fortunes of the team. A hundred in a losing cause is something of a bitter pill. Even in the second innings I scored 52 and while it was a personal milestone, it was not enough to save the game.

After the 3–0 defeat in the Test series we lost the ODI tri-series with Pakistan and Australia, failing even to make the final. The tour had gone from bad to worse and I was deeply frustrated. On my way back to India I was going through serious mental turmoil. I was finding it difficult to unwind. In the past I had been able to leave the disappointments of cricket behind and switch off. Not this time. Even when I was with my kids, my mind was still on the series. I was unable to figure out what I was doing wrong. I was failing to get the team to play to their potential and it was all starting to get to me.

As a batsman, I was accountable for my own mistakes and could do what was required to sort out my flaws and get back to form. As a captain it was not. As skipper, I was responsible for the actions of my team-mates, but I couldn't control everything they did. For example, sometimes I carefully put a plan in place but it was simply not implemented, which I found hard to cope with.

The ODI against Pakistan in Brisbane on 10 January 2000 is a case in point. It was a low-scoring game and we had made 195 batting first in our fifty overs. Pakistan, docked an over for a slow over rate, were reduced to 71–6 at one point in their innings. Clearly, we should have closed out the match from that position. Eventually, however, Pakistan won the match off the last ball, with Saqlain Mushtaq and Waqar Younis taking the team over the line with an unbeaten 43-run stand for the ninth wicket.

The defeat particularly hurt me because I had predicted what the Pakistani batsmen were planning in the final stages of the innings. While fielding at mid off, I had repeatedly spoken to my fast bowlers and had specifically asked them not to bowl a slower ball without informing me. Despite my repeated warnings, one of them bowled a slower ball without the proper field in place and the Pakistan batsman promptly dispatched it to the boundary. Such incidents caused me immense frustration and I was finding it increasingly difficult to get them out of my mind.

Over to Sourav

Even before the start of the Australia series, I had spoken to the selectors about appointing Sourav Ganguly as my deputy. I had always felt he had the ability to lead the team in my absence. If I got injured in Australia or had to leave the field temporarily, I wanted Sourav to be in charge of the side.

Within weeks of coming back from Australia I had communicated to BCCI president AC Muthiah and the selection committee that I did not want to continue as captain. It was in the best interests of the team to pass the baton to Sourav and focus on my batting. At the same time, we did not want to spring the Indian captaincy on him and leave him unsettled. He needed a little time to come to terms with the pressures and it was my responsibility to ensure that the transition was smooth. So I informed the selectors that I was happy to lead the side in the two home Tests against South Africa in February 2000. It was agreed that Sourav would take over after the Test series and before the start of the five-match ODI series.

I had discussed my decision with my family in Lonavla, where we had gone for a break. They were all in agreement that the frustration of not achieving what I wanted with the team was affecting me badly and that I was pushing myself too hard. Anjali knew how I was feeling and I also spoke to Ajit at length about what I was going through.

Never again

After giving up the captaincy at the start of 2000, I never captained India again. That is not to say I wasn't given the choice of captaining the team later in my career. I was actually offered the job quite a few times but was never tempted. One occasion was soon after Rahul Dravid stepped down after the tour of England in September 2007.

The final time I was offered the job was at the end of Anil's captaincy in late 2008. We were in the middle of a home series against Australia and Anil's retirement had left a huge void. This time I recommended MS Dhoni. Earlier I had recommended him as captain for the Twenty20 World Cup, and Test captaincy was a natural progression.

Dhoni had already captained the team with distinction in the Twenty20 format and had also done well in the fifty-over format. He was one of the few players who played all formats of the game and read the game well at critical times. Having discussed things with him when fielding in the slip cordon, I knew he was a good choice for the job and had little hesitation in putting his name forward. He had age on his side and would be able to guide Indian cricket into the future.

All of the people I recommended or played under after giving up the captaincy – Sourav Ganguly, Rahul Dravid, Anil Kumble or MS Dhoni – I had a good relationship with, and when I felt it necessary I would give them my opinion and then leave it to them to take the final call. As a senior player in the side, I felt it was my job to give the captain options, as he had way too much on his plate and it was sometimes easy to miss things. I loved being involved and they all seemed to welcome my contributions. The final decision was always the captain's, but I felt it was important for me to let them know what I thought was best for the team.

Every captain I played under had his respective strengths. Sourav was an excellent strategist and had a very good understanding of the game. He was an aggressive captain and wasn't afraid to experiment in difficult situations. It was under Sourav that we started winning overseas Test matches consistently.

Anil Kumble was an excellent communicator and clearly explained to the players what he wanted from each of them. He was aggressive and trusted his instincts. Sourav and Anil were both great players and equally capable leaders.

Rahul, on the other hand, was more conventional. He was more methodical and his mental toughness was an added strength. He was committed to the job but stayed away from experimenting too much. Dhoni, in contrast, was impulsive and loved to back his instincts. He has a really good grasp of the game and is not afraid to try something different. He is never flustered and handles pressure well. Under these men India won some big series and tournaments and I enjoyed playing with them all.

Among the captains I played against, I consider Nasser Hussain the best. He was an excellent strategist and even if some of his tactics occasionally bordered on the negative – using the left-arm spinner Ashley Giles to bowl to me outside my leg stump from over the wicket, for example – he was a very good thinker about the game and was proactive. Nasser would not place a fielder in a particular position *after* a shot was played. Rather, he had the ability to anticipate the shot and would place a fielder well in advance, making a real difference to his team.

Among the Australians, I rate Michael Clarke as the best captain I played against. While I was too young to judge Allan Border in 1992, the other Australian captains in Mark Taylor, Steve Waugh and Ricky Ponting benefited from having some of the greatest players of our generation in their teams. With so many match-winners, the role of the captain is automatically reduced. Clarke's case, however, was different. He had to rebuild the Australian team from scratch and to do so in such a short time speaks volumes for his ability as leader.

Graeme Smith of South Africa is yet another player I have great regard for as skipper. Taking over the reins of the side at the age of twenty-two in the most tumultuous of conditions, Smith did brilliantly to propel South Africa to the top of the world Test rankings.

Looking back at my own captaincy career, I feel I could have achieved better results during my first stint as captain had there been more cooperation. I never felt totally comfortable with the relationship with the selectors. This was reflected in the teams I was given, which were not always the ones I would have chosen. In my first stint as captain of India, it seemed that each series was a personal test and losing one series badly meant my position was immediately in question. Such pressure did not always send out the best signal and it was as if I was constantly being evaluated. Every captain sets out to win but it's not always possible to do so in international sport. The opposition were also playing to win and at times they simply played better cricket than we did. That was the case in Australia in December 1999.

There is no point lamenting what could have been. It was time to look beyond the captaincy and contribute to the team in the best way possible. I am glad I was able to do so for a good thirteen years after giving up the captaincy in February 2000.

The difficulty of being a Tendulkar

There is a common misconception that cricketers' families have an easy time of it. On the contrary, in my absence Anjali had to do most of the parenting, and bringing up two young kids almost on her own was anything but easy. For the children too it was hard at times. They were not always able to do the things normal kids enjoy and, with their father away for long periods, they missed out on fatherly affection and care.

When Arjun was just nine months old, for example, I was going to Germany to visit the Adidas factory and asked Anjali if she would like to come along. I was going for only five days and

Anjali hadn't left home for nine months – after Arjun's birth. We left Sara and Arjun with her parents in India. It was on the third night away that calamity struck. We had finished work in the Adidas factory and had retreated to a small village for the evening when Anjali got a call from Dr Ajit Gajendragadkar, who asked us to come back as soon as possible. We were informed that Anjali's mother had suffered a brain haemorrhage (from which she later recovered) and was in the hospital unconscious, while Arjun was seriously sick at home.

It was night-time in Germany and the earliest we could leave for India was the following morning. All through the journey the next day we kept worrying about who was taking care of nine-month-old Arjun. When we finally got home, the first sight of Arjun reduced us both to tears. He had lost weight and had a pained expression in his eyes. While there was a glint of happiness in seeing us both back at home, his expression was predominantly one of hurt, as if to ask why we had to leave him and go away. Since then, Anjali has never left the kids alone at home to travel abroad with me.

Another example occurred soon after we had been knocked out of the World Cup in the Caribbean in March 2007. We had played poorly in the tournament and it was a low for the country. My family were aware that the repercussions of the first-round exit might reach the kids. As a precautionary measure, Anjali tried to explain to Arjun, who was seven years old at the time, that if someone made a snide comment about his dad at school, he should ignore it; he should just say that it was disappointing and we would surely do better the next time. When a friend of his accosted him at school and said that India had lost because his dad had got out for zero, our advice went out of his head and Arjun punched the boy and told him not to say anything bad about his father again.

While Sara is interested in studying science, Arjun, who started with football, now wants to play cricket. I am perfectly happy with them doing whatever they want to do. In the last few years

Sara has changed perceptibly and has started taking far more responsibility. Anjali has allowed her the freedom to shape her timetable and she is showing signs of maturity. She went to Oxford in the summer of 2012 for her summer school and is happy pursuing her dream of becoming a doctor. I'd be delighted to see her do so and have always felt that the best thing for parents is to allow kids to chase their own dreams. That's what I did and it's what I want my daughter to do as well.

Arjun, on the other hand, is deeply passionate about cricket. Mind you, he and I hardly ever spoke about the game till he turned seven. I would chat with him about everything else but never talk cricket at home. This was an attempt to keep my professional world separate; I found it often helped to keep the two spheres distinct from each other. So much so that my wife and children have hardly ever come to the stadium to watch me play. Anjali has been to the stadium just a handful of times in her life. The first time she saw me bat was at Edgbaston in 1996 when I scored a hundred. She was with her father at the time. The second time was in Melbourne in 2004, when I was out for a first-ball duck. Thereafter, she didn't come to the stadium again till my 199th Test match at Eden Gardens in November 2013. Instead, she had a special seat at home for watching matches on TV and refused to speak to anyone or take phone calls when I was batting. That was her way of being with me the whole time.

Arjun has come to my games frequently, however, and has travelled with me to England, Australia and South Africa. Arjun got seriously attracted to cricket after watching India win the inaugural world Twenty20 in September 2007. We watched the matches together at home and he was hugely inspired to see the Indian triumph in South Africa.

Many have asked me if I feel added pressure at Arjun trying to become a cricketer. I really don't. I am happy that he is trying to do something he enjoys, for that in itself will make him really happy. Also there is nothing negative about playing a sport. While it is never possible to guarantee performance, one can guarantee the effort put in and there's no doubt that he is putting his best foot forward. I am not concerned with how far he goes with his game, but am happy that he is doing his best to excel in what he loves. I firmly believe that you take to playing cricket only if you are madly in love with it. And that's what has happened with Arjun over the last few years. There's no doubt there will be pressure on him every time he plays. But he has chosen what he wants to do and will have to deal with that pressure as best he can.

India in New Zealand 1998–99

1st Test. Dunedin. 18–22 December 1998
Match abandoned without a ball bowled

2nd Test. Wellington. 26–30 December 1998
India 208 (M Azharuddin 103, **SR Tendulkar 47**; SB Doull 7–65) and 356 (**SR Tendulkar 113**, SC Ganguly 48, M Azharuddin 48; DJ Nash 3–20, SB Doull 2–49)
New Zealand 352 (DJ Nash 89*, DL Vettori 57, NJ Astle 56; A Kumble 4–83 **SR Tendulkar 2–7**) and 215–6 (CD McMillan 74*, CL Cairns 61; J Srinath 3–82, A Kumble 2–70)
New Zealand won by 4 wickets

3rd Test. Hamilton. 2–6 January 1999
New Zealand 366 (CD McMillan 92, RG Twose 87, MJ Horne 63; J Srinath 5–95) and 464–8 dec (CL Cairns 126, CD McMillan 84, DJ Nash 63, AC Parore 50; **SR Tendulkar 2–30**)
India 416 (R Dravid 190, J Srinath 76, **SR Tendulkar 67**; CL Cairns 4–107, SB Doull 3–64) and 249–2 (R Dravid 103*, SC Ganguly 101*; CL Cairns 2–30)
Match drawn

New Zealand won the series 1–0

Pakistan in India 1999

1st Test. Chennai. 28–31 January 1999
Pakistan 238 (M Khan 60, Y Youhana 53; A Kumble 6–70, J Srinath 3–63, **SR Tendulkar 1–10**) and 286 (S Afridi 141, Inzamam-ul-Haq 51; BKV Prasad 6–33, **SR Tendulkar 2–35**)
India 254 (SC Ganguly 54, R Dravid 53, **SR Tendulkar 0**; S Mushtaq 5–94, S Afridi 3–31) and 258 (**SR Tendulkar 136**, NR Mongia 52; S Mushtaq 5–93, W Akram 3–80)
Pakistan won by 12 runs

'Please don't spoil your shirt, I am all sweaty!' Mark Mascarenhas wasn't bothered and embraced me after a hundred against Australia in Sharjah in 1998.

With the Border-Gavaskar Trophy in Delhi after beating Australia in October 1996 in my first Test as captain.

At Lord's in the famous Long Room. Captains of the world unite for an ICC meeting in 1997. From the left: Hansie Cronje, myself, Wasim Akram, Mark Taylor, Alistair Campbell, Michael Atherton, Courtney Walsh, Arjuna Ranatunga and Stephen Fleming.

'I hope you are seeing it from heaven.' – This hundred against Kenya in the 1999 World Cup will always remain special. It was for my father, who I had lost a week earlier.

With the Queen during the 1999 World Cup in England. Also pictured are Zimbabwe's Heath Streak and Pakistan's Moin Khan.

Celebrations after winning the one-day series against New Zealand in November 1999, during my second stint as captain.

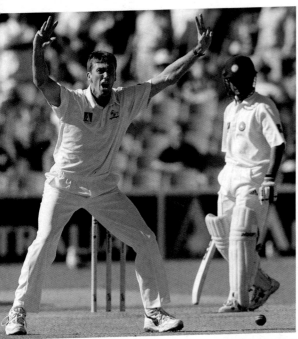

Left: After being hit on the shoulder ducking a Glenn McGrath bouncer, I was surprised to be given out lbw by umpire Daryl Harper in Adelaide in 1999.

Below left: With Shane Warne in Mumbai on the eve of the first Test against Australia in the 2001 series.

Below right: Harbhajan Singh takes India's first ever Test hat-trick at Eden Gardens in 2001.

Opposite page:

Above: What a partnership – 335 runs on the fourth day at Eden Gardens and still unbeaten! In the end, VVS Laxman scored 281 and Rahul Dravid 180, turning the 2001 series on its head.

Below: I played my part with the ball, bowling leg-spin and taking three wickets in a five-over spell. Here Adam Gilchrist is out lbw.

Left: Evading a bouncer during a hostile spell from Andrew Flintoff in the third Test at Headingley in 2002.

Below left: On the attack at Headingley. A famous victory and we went on to draw the series 1–1.

Below right: Bowling at The Oval in 2002 in what was a very exciting Test series.

Opposite page:

Above: The whole team went for a ride in New Zealand in 2002. They kept driving us straight at a cliff and then turning at the very last minute – it was great fun.

Below left: With Sunil Joshi and Ashish Nehra – enjoying ourselves in the Caribbean in 2002.

Below right: Battlefield Centurion: on my way to 98 in the much-anticipated clash with Pakistan in the 2003 World Cup.

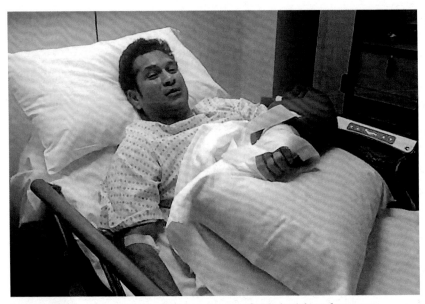

Recuperating after elbow surgery in 2005. It was the most frustrating injury of my career.

Listening to the children at a home for the underprivileged in Bangalore in 2003.

2nd Test. Delhi. 4–7 February 1999
India 252 (M Azharuddin 67, S Ramesh 60, **SR Tendulkar 6**; S Mushtaq
    5–94) and 339 (S Ramesh 96, SC Ganguly 62*, **SR Tendulkar 29**; S
    Mushtaq 5–122, W Akram 3–43)
Pakistan 172 (S Afridi 32, S Malik 31; A Kumble 4–75, H Singh 3–30) and
    207 (S Anwar 69, S Afridi 41; A Kumble 10–74)
India won by 212 runs

Series drawn 1–1

Asian Test Championship 1999

1st Match. India v Pakistan. Kolkata. 16–20 February 1999
Pakistan 185 (M Khan 70; J Srinath 5–46, BKV Prasad 2–27, **SR Tendulkar
    1–8**) and 316 (S Anwar 188, Y Youhana 56; J Srinath 8–86)
India 223 (S Ramesh 79, **SR Tendulkar 0**; S Akhtar 4–71, W Akram 3–65)
    and 232 (VVS Laxman 67, S Ramesh 40, **SR Tendulkar 9**; S Akhtar
    4–47, S Mushtaq 3–69)
Pakistan won by 46 runs

2nd Match. Sri Lanka v India. Colombo (SSC). 24–28 February 1999
India 518–7 dec (S Ramesh 143, R Dravid 107, M Azharuddin 87,
    SC Ganguly 56, **SR Tendulkar 53**) and 306–5 (**SR Tendulkar 124***,
    SC Ganguly 78; KEA Upashantha 2–41, PA de Silva 2–59)
Sri Lanka 485 (DPMD Jayawardene 242, A Ranatunga 66; A Kumble 4–134,
    H Singh 3–127)
Match drawn

Pakistan beat Sri Lanka in the final

India in the 1999 World Cup

2nd match. India v South Africa at Hove. 15 May 1999
India 253–5 (50/50 ov); South Africa 254–6 (47.2/50 ov)
South Africa won by 4 wickets (with 16 balls remaining)

8th match. India v Zimbabwe at Leicester. 19 May 1999
Zimbabwe 252–9 (50/50 ov); India 249 (45/46 ov)
Zimbabwe won by 3 runs

15th match. India v Kenya at Bristol. 23 May 1999
India 329–2 (50/50 ov); Kenya 235–7 (50/50 ov)
India won by 94 runs

21st match. India v Sri Lanka at Taunton. 26 May 1999
India 373–6 (50/50 ov); Sri Lanka 216 (42.3/50 ov)
India won by 157 runs

25th match. England v India at Birmingham. 29–30 May 1999
India 232–8 (50/50 ov); England 169 (45.2/50 ov)
India won by 63 runs

1st super. Australia v India at The Oval. 4 June 1999
Australia 282-6 (50/50 ov); India 205 (48.2/50 ov)
Australia won by 77 runs

4th super. India v Pakistan at Manchester. 8 June 1999
India 227-6 (50/50 ov); Pakistan 180 (45.3/50 ov)
India won by 47 runs

8th super. India v New Zealand at Nottingham. 12 June 1999
India 251-6 (50/50 ov); New Zealand 253-5 (48.2/50 ov)
New Zealand won by 5 wickets (with 10 balls remaining)

Final. Australia v Pakistan at Lord's. 20 June 1999
Pakistan 132 (39/50 ov); Australia 133-2 (20.1/50 ov)
Australia won by 8 wickets (with 179 balls remaining)

New Zealand in India 1999

1st Test. Mohali. 10-14 October 1999
India 83 (J Srinath 20, **SR Tendulkar 18**, MSK Prasad 16*; DJ Nash 6-27,
    CL Cairns 2-23, SB O'Connor 2-20) and 505-3 dec (R Dravid 144,
    SR Tendulkar 126*, DJ Gandhi 75, S Ramesh 73, SC Ganguly 64*)
New Zealand 215 (CM Spearman 51, NJ Astle 45, SP Fleming 43; J Srinath
    6-45) and 251-7 (SP Fleming 73; A Kumble 3-42, SB Joshi 2-38)
Match drawn

2nd Test. Kanpur. 22-25 October 1999
New Zealand 256 (CL Cairns 53, DJ Nash 41*; A Kumble 4-67, J Srinath 3-62)
    and 155 (AC Parore 48; A Kumble 6-67, H Singh 3-33)
India 330 (DJ Gandhi 88, S Ramesh 83, R Dravid 48, **SR Tendulkar 15**;
    DL Vettori 6-127) and 83-2 (**SR Tendulkar 44***, DJ Gandhi 31)
India won by 8 wickets

3rd Test. Ahmedabad. 29 October-2 November 1999
India 583-7 dec (**SR Tendulkar 217**, SC Ganguly 125, S Ramesh 110;
    DL Vettori 4-200) and 148-5 dec (SC Ganguly 53, **SR Tendulkar 15**)
New Zealand 308 (NJ Astle 74, CL Cairns 72, SP Fleming 48; A Kumble
    5-82) and 252-2 (GR Stead 78, SP Fleming 64*, CM Spearman 54*)
Match drawn

India won the series 1-0

India in Australia 1999-2000 - The Border-Gavaskar Trophy

1st Test. Adelaide. 10-14 December 1999
Australia 441 (SR Waugh 150, RT Ponting 125, SK Warne 86; BKV Prasad
    3-83) and 239-8 dec (GS Blewett 88, AC Gilchrist 43; AB Agarkar 3-43,
    J Srinath 3-64)

India 285 (**SR Tendulkar 61**, SC Ganguly 60, VVS Laxman 41; SK Warne
    4–92, DW Fleming 3–70) and 110 (SC Ganguly 43, **SR Tendulkar 0**;
    DW Fleming 5–30, GD McGrath 3–35)
Australia won by 285 runs

2nd Test. Melbourne. 26–30 December 1999
Australia 405 (MJ Slater 91, AC Gilchrist 78, RT Ponting 67; J Srinath 4–130,
    AB Agarkar 3–76) and 208–5 dec (AC Gilchrist 55, ME Waugh 51*;
    AB Agarkar 3–51, A Kumble 2–72)
India 238 (**SR Tendulkar 116**, SC Ganguly 31; B Lee 5–47, GD McGrath 3–39)
    and 195 (**SR Tendulkar 52**, HH Kanitkar 45; ME Waugh 2–12, B Lee 2–31,
    DW Fleming 2–46)
Australia won by 180 runs

3rd Test. Sydney. 2–4 January 2000
India 150 (**SR Tendulkar 45**, R Dravid 29; GD McGrath 5–48, B Lee 4–39)
    and 261 (VVS Laxman 167, **SR Tendulkar 4**; GD McGrath 5–55, B Lee
    2–67)
Australia 552–5 dec (J Langer 223, RT Ponting 141*, SR Waugh 57; J Srinath
    2–105, **SR Tendulkar 1–34**)
Australia won by an innings and 141 runs

Australia won the series 3–0

South Africa in India 2000

1st Test. Mumbai. 24–26 February 2000
India 225 (**SR Tendulkar 97**, AB Agarkar 41*; JH Kallis 3–30, AA Donald
    2–23, SM Pollock 2–43) and 113 (R Dravid 37, **SR Tendulkar 8**; SM Pollock
    4–24, WJ Cronje 3–23)
South Africa 176 (G Kirsten 50, HH Gibbs 47; **SR Tendulkar 3–10**, J Srinath
    3–45) and 164–6 (HH Gibbs 46, JH Kallis 36*; A Kumble 4–56)
South Africa won by 4 wickets

2nd Test. Bangalore. 2–6 March 2000
India 158 (A Kumble 36*, **SR Tendulkar 21**; N Boje 2–10, SM Pollock 2–26,
    M Hayward 2–40) and 250 (M Azharuddin 102, A Kumble 28, **SR Tendulkar
    20**; N Boje 5–83, AA Donald 2–56)
South Africa 479 (L Klusener 97, JH Kallis 95, N Boje 85, G Kirsten 79,
    DJ Cullinan 53; A Kumble 6–143, M Kartik 3–123)
South Africa won by an innings and 71 runs

South Africa won the series 2–0

11

THE BEST SERIES EVER

India started well under Sourav, winning the ODI series 3–2 against South Africa in March 2000. But soon afterwards cricket plummeted to a low in the wake of the match-fixing scandal. The credibility of the game had been compromised and I found the revelations about matches being thrown for money distasteful and disgusting. The whole thing was repulsive and what was seriously worrying was that fans had started to lose faith and the integrity of our sport was in doubt. We desperately needed to bring credibility back to the game and we hoped that we could do so in the course of playing the Australians at home in a much-anticipated Test series in February–March 2001. It would allow fans to move away from the sordid tales of corruption and focus on the real thing: quality Test cricket.

At the time, Steve Waugh's Australian team were hammering opposition teams both at home and away. They had won fifteen Test matches in a row when they landed in India. In Glenn McGrath, Jason Gillespie, Damien Fleming, Michael Kasprowicz and Shane Warne they had a bowling line-up capable of taking wickets in all conditions. The batting was also exceptional, with Matthew Hayden, Michael Slater, Justin Langer, the Waugh twins, Ricky Ponting and Adam Gilchrist all in good form.

A few months before the Australia series my family had relocated from Sahitya Sahawas to our new haven, an apartment at La Mer Residency in Mumbai's Bandra West, a move to which I contributed very little, I have to confess. It was Anjali who organized everything and all I did was walk into a sprawling apartment with all my things beautifully set up for me.

On the morning of 26 January 2001, just ten months after we

had moved into the new apartment, I heard Anjali screaming in fear, yelling 'Earthquake!' The building was swaying from side to side and my first thought was that the builder must have messed up with the construction. However, within moments I realized that it was far more serious than that and people from nearby buildings were all screaming '*Bhago, bhago!*' (Run, run!) Because we were on the tenth and eleventh floors, it would have taken us a few minutes to walk down with two kids, so all we did was stand in the middle of the drawing room, huddled together as a family, praying for the catastrophe to stop.

The earthquake that rocked Western India lasted less than a minute, but it left devastation in its wake. The town of Bhuj in Gujarat was almost destroyed and we in Mumbai did not escape unscathed. From my bedroom at La Mer I could see Mount Mary Church on the one side and Siddhivinayak Temple on the other and for days after the earthquake I would pray at night, urging God never to unleash such wrath on us again.

In fact, even when I played a Duleep Trophy match in Pune for West Zone against East Zone in early February, I still could not sleep properly at night. The nightmare of the quake was too fresh to forget. In Pune we were staying in an ordinary hotel but the staff did everything possible to make things comfortable for me. In fact, they overdid things on occasions and were themselves embarrassed as a result. To ensure we all had hot water, the maintenance person had switched on the boiler very early in the morning. As a result, the boiler over-heated and all we ended up with was black muddy water in the room. Being used to staying in five-star hotels, initially I was irritated with the hotel staff, but later I found it funny that they were trying so hard to make me comfortable. The effort was overwhelming and left a lasting impression.

Soon after the end of the Duleep Trophy game, in which I scored 199 in our only innings, a number of journalists asked me if we stood a chance against Australia. I said we did and felt confident we could beat them, provided we were able to put them under pressure. It seemed to me they weren't accustomed to handling pressure and it would be interesting to see how they reacted if we gained the upper hand.

First Test, Mumbai, 27 February–1 March 2001

Though we lost the first Test in Mumbai in three days, we did have our moments in the match. I scored 76 in the first innings, getting out when I went for an expansive shot to a McGrath delivery that was wide of off stump. In the Australian first innings we reduced them to 99–5, with Harbhajan Singh taking three quick wickets, before an aggressive counter-attacking partnership between Hayden and Gilchrist took the match away from us again. We dropped a few catches and they both managed to score hundreds, giving Australia a sizeable first-innings lead.

We started the second innings with thirty overs remaining in the second day and had lost two wickets by the time we came to the last over. Then the nightwatchman Nayan Mongia was hit on the finger by a ball from Gillespie and retired hurt. I had to go in and play out the last five balls, a task that is never easy, particularly with Gillespie bowling at his best. The next morning I resumed with Rahul Dravid, knowing it was going to be a stern test of our character. McGrath and Gillespie were bowling in tandem and while Rahul mostly played Gillespie, I played out a very good spell from McGrath. We hardly rotated strike, knowing that once we had played out the initial burst from these two bowlers, things would become a lot easier.

I scored a half-century but I think even my harshest critic would concede that I got out in a most unfortunate manner. I played a full-blooded pull shot to a short Mark Waugh delivery, which would have been a definite boundary had the ball not hit Justin Langer's back at forward short leg and spooned up to midwicket. Ricky Ponting ran fifteen yards and dived forward for a very good catch. The momentum had shifted and Australia soon capitalized on the advantage and closed out the game. The Australians had now won sixteen straight Tests and needed to win just one more to set a new world record.

Second Test, Kolkata, 11–15 March 2001

The Kolkata Test match was undoubtedly one of the best I played in, but it didn't start well for us. Australia scored 445 in the first innings, thanks to 110 from Steve Waugh and 97 from Matthew Hayden, and when we were at a dismal 128–8 at the end of day two, with the Australian quartet of McGrath, Gillespie, Kasprowicz and Warne all taking wickets, not even the most ardent Indian fan thought we'd be able to save the match. I had scored ten in our first innings and everybody was dejected after our frankly pathetic batting display. John Wright, our coach, was livid and took it out on a few plastic bottles in the dressing room.

The poor performance hurt even more because it followed the high of the first ever Indian hat-trick in Test cricket. Harbhajan had picked up Ponting, Gilchrist and Warne in succession on the first day, swinging the match in our favour again after Australia had reached a position of strength at 252–4. Bhajji was brilliant throughout the series and this was the very best I had ever seen him bowl. First he had Ponting lbw, then he followed up with the wicket of Adam Gilchrist. Understandably there was a lot of talk among the players before the hat-trick ball and I had an urge to tell Bhajji what I thought he should bowl to Warne, the new batsman. However, I decided not to and all I said was that he should bowl what he thought best. He ended up bowling a low full toss, which Warne played into the hands of forward short leg.

At the end of our first innings on the third morning at Eden Gardens, even though we failed to avoid the follow-on, there were signs of better things for us when Laxman, batting at six, managed to add a few runs with the tail. He scored 59 and was the last man out. There was a brief discussion in the dressing room and we all agreed that Laxman, who was obviously in good touch, should go in at three for the second innings, with Rahul moving to six. None of us had any idea that this swap would result in history being written.

Laxman and Rahul batted like champions in the second innings and I thoroughly enjoyed seeing an extraordinary batting effort unfold before my eyes. India scored 335 runs in the second innings on day four without losing a single wicket. Not to lose a wicket in a day is unbelievable and to do it against the world's best team makes the achievement all the more miraculous. Laxman played some unbelievable shots off Warne and both he and Rahul had to battle serious physical exhaustion in the intense heat and humidity, but they held on, eventually scoring 281 and 180 respectively, and by the end of the day we knew we couldn't lose the Test match. In fact, we had started to believe that we had a slim chance of winning if we bowled well on the last day. This in itself was a dramatic turnaround, because for the first time in the series we had managed to put Australia under pressure, just as I'd hoped.

We declared early on day five with a lead of 383 and knew we had a chance if we could force the Australians back with a few quick wickets. Harbhajan was bowling with exceptional skill, but we needed someone to back him up from the other end. We did not get the wickets we were after in the post-lunch session, however, and Australia went to tea with just three down. The game was drifting towards a draw unless something dramatic happened.

Wanting to try something different, Sourav decided to give my bowling a go. He hoped that a couple of breakthroughs might open up the game and he knew that the large Kolkata crowd would get behind us if they sensed an opportunity. I would always bowl for two or three overs when there were partnerships, and being an irregular bowler, I had licence to experiment. On the fifth-day pitch I decided to bowl leg-spin, pitching the ball in the rough with two left-handers at the crease. It was one of those rare days when the ball came out perfectly and I managed to take three quick wickets for the team in a five-over spell, including the wickets of in-form Matthew Hayden and the dangerous Adam Gilchrist.

However, the wicket that gave me the most satisfaction was that of Shane Warne. I tried to bowl him a googly and the ball ended up being a half-tracker, landing in the middle of the pitch before turning in to hit Warne plumb in front. Warne had perhaps misread the delivery and had first tried to cut before playing a half-pull. I had bamboozled one of the great spinners of all time!

We now had the opening we were after and Bhajji did the rest. When we finally took the last wicket of Glenn McGrath, with just three overs or so remaining in the match, the stadium went mad. Close to 100,000 spectators at Eden Gardens could not believe we had managed to win – and it was only the third time in history that a team had won after following on.

We celebrated for a long time after the match. The atmosphere in the changing room had changed completely after such an incredible win. There was a tremendous sense of positivity and we started to believe that we could go on to win the series. The Australians had collapsed in the face of sustained pressure. The myth of invincibility had been shattered. The series was now locked at 1–1, with all to play for in the third and final Test at Chennai.

The impact of the victory, celebrated all across the country, is perhaps illustrated by an incident involving SK Bansal, one of the umpires officiating in the Test. Mr Bansal later recounted to me that he had gone out for a meal after the match and his driver had mistakenly taken a wrong turn. He was heading the wrong way up a one-way street and was soon stopped by a traffic constable. Mr Bansal, dreading the consequences the driver would be subjected to, stepped out of the car to ask the constable to forgive the poor fellow. The constable, who turned out to be an ardent cricket fan, recognized Mr Bansal and promptly decided to let the driver off.

Third Test, Chennai, 18–22 March 2001

The Australians started well, with Matthew Hayden once again leading the way. He had batted wonderfully throughout the series and was the only Australian batsman who looked comfortable against Harbhajan. He scored an impressive double hundred and the Australians notched up a first-innings score of 391. I bowled a good spell on the first day, carrying on from Kolkata, and got the ball to turn sharply but did not take any wickets, but by the end of the spell, the skin of my fingers had started to peel off and I was finding it hard to grip the ball.

Australia, who were at 326–3 at the end of day one, suffered a collapse on day two, ending up with just 391. It all started with an unusual dismissal. Against skipper Steve Waugh we were trying to keep things tight and when he tried taking a single to short cover I prevented the run and said a few things to him on the lines that he was trying to get away from the strike. Rahul, fielding at leg slip, offered a few words and before long we were able to get under Waugh's skin. Finally, when Harbhajan beat him with a good off-spinner and appealed for lbw, Waugh, in a momentary lapse of concentration, moved the ball away with his hand. We appealed for handling the ball, and the Australian captain was on his way back to the dressing room. Mission accomplished, we didn't say another word to him.

I was determined to make amends for my batting failures in Kolkata and had practised hard against reverse swing in the gap between the two Test matches. I decided to follow the ball throughout my innings and not to lose sight of it at any time. To play well against reverse swing you have to keep your eye on the ball for as long as possible and that was what I did all day, as it was passed from the wicketkeeper to the slips and through the hands of various fielders back to the bowler. I focused on the ball and nothing else. The only time I was not following the ball was when I was talking to the non-striker about something. As the bowler came in to bowl I concentrated on the ball and monitored the release as closely as possible. From the arm position and the release point I could assess what was coming at me and I tried to play as late as possible.

This exercise was draining and by the end of the day I was mentally exhausted. However, I had done what the team needed me to do: I had scored a hundred. I had forged an important partnership with Rahul, which was all the more satisfying because we had to negotiate a very hostile Jason Gillespie spell with the second new ball. Gillespie, who was tired after bowling all day, wasn't bowling quite so fast with the second new ball, but suddenly he gained inspiration from an unlikely source. One solitary Australian fan, sitting at the top of the sightscreen and carrying a huge toy kangaroo, started screaming after every delivery, urging Gillespie on. He was shouting 'Come on Aussie' each time he walked back to the end of his run-up. The fan had a huge impact on him. Within minutes Gillespie started to bowl really quickly again and was all fired up. Rahul and I even discussed what had happened to him all of a sudden. It just goes to show that you don't always need thousands of fans to motivate you.

Our partnership of 169 helped the team to an important 110-run lead, giving our bowlers some runs to play with in the second innings. The match was nicely poised in our favour and we knew we had a chance to close out the series. Hayden was once again going to be the crucial wicket. He fell for 35 to the bowling of Nilesh Kulkarni. Gilchrist was the other danger man lower down the order, because we knew he could score quickly and put the pressure back on us. But Bhajji, who had a grip on Gilchrist and Ponting right through the series, once again took the bulk of the Australian wickets, finishing off with a career-best haul of 8–84 in the innings. We needed 155 runs to win the series.

The chase started well and we were cruising before Mark Waugh pulled off an unbelievable catch at short midwicket. It was a full-blooded pull shot from VVS Laxman and Waugh just flung himself at full stretch to come up with a stunning catch. Laxman had been batting brilliantly for his 66 and his dismissal left us at 135–6, changing the course of the match yet again. Suddenly we had a contest on our hands.

By this stage, the whole team was sitting nervously outside the changing room. Everyone was told not to change seating positions and we were all feeling the tension. There were not too many runs left to get, but at stake was a series win against the world's best cricket team. The crowd was cheering every Indian run. It could not get any bigger.

At a crucial time, Harbhajan Singh and Sameer Dighe, our wicketkeeper and my very close friend, put together a partnership that, though not a big one, was perhaps the most significant of the series. Fighting unbelievable pressure, they somehow held things together to take us over the line and the rest of the team were in raptures. The way the two of them ran the winning runs was almost comical, but it was an incredible feeling to know we had won the match and the series. We were all shouting with delight and handing out high-fives and hugs. We had beaten the best team in the world and it felt truly amazing to have accomplished what I had predicted before the start of the contest. We had put the Australians under pressure and had reaped the rewards for doing so. The whole team had stuck together despite losing the first Test, and this series is without doubt one of the best I have played in my career.

Coming at a critical time, the series also helped restore Indian fans' faith in the game. Cricket had once again triumphed over all odds. Both teams had played hard cricket and the passion and intensity was at a high level throughout. Played before huge crowds, it was the best possible advertisement for Test cricket. To Australia's credit, they were always competitive and had actually come close to winning in Chennai themselves, picking up eight Indian wickets in the second innings.

As we celebrated the series win I remember being very pleased to see Anil, who had not played a part in the series because of injury. He had been present in the pre-series training camp and had come along to cheer on the team during the third and deciding Test.

During the ODI series that followed, which we lost 2–3, I reached 10,000 runs in ODIs, in the third game in Indore, and in the last match in Goa I did something that I have never done again in my life. I injured my index finger and ended up bowling off-spin with my middle finger for ten overs, picking up 3–35 in the spell, including the wicket of Steve Waugh. The moment Waugh came in to bat I started gesturing towards the midwicket fielder, suggesting to Waugh that I would get him out there. It was friendly banter and Waugh retorted by saying I wasn't playing in my garden. As luck would have it, Steve tried playing a slog sweep to midwicket and was caught there by Ajit Agarkar.

Australia in India 2001 – The Border-Gavaskar Trophy

1st Test. Mumbai. 27 February–March 1 2001
India 176 (**SR Tendulkar 76**; SK Warne 4–47, GD McGrath 3–19) and 219
   (**SR Tendulkar 65**, S Ramesh 44; ME Waugh 3–40, JN Gillespie 3–45)
Australia 349 (AC Gilchrist 122, ML Hayden 119, SK Warne 39; H Singh
   4–121) and 47–0
Australia won by 10 wickets

2nd Test. Kolkata. 11–15 March 2001
Australia 445 (SR Waugh 110, ML Hayden 97, JL Langer 58; H Singh 7–123)
   and 212 (ML Hayden 67, MJ Slater 43; H Singh 6–73, **SR Tendulkar 3–31**)
India 171 (VVS Laxman 59, **SR Tendulkar 10**; GD McGrath 4–18) and
   657–7 dec (f/o) (VVS Laxman 281, R Dravid 180, SC Ganguly 48,
   SR Tendulkar 10; GD McGrath 3–103)
India won by 171 runs

3rd Test. Chennai. 18–22 March 2001

Australia 391 (ML Hayden 203, ME Waugh 70, SR Waugh 47; H Singh 7–133)
    and 264 (ME Waugh 57, MJ Slater 48, SR Waugh 47; H Singh 8–84)

India 501 (**SR Tendulkar 126**, SS Das 84, R Dravid 81, VVS Laxman 65,
    S Ramesh 61; GD McGrath 3–75) and 155–8 (VVS Laxman 66,
    SR Tendulkar 17; CR Miller 3–41, GD McGrath 2–21)

India won by 2 wickets

India won the series 2–1

12

STANDING UP FOR MYSELF

In July 2001, two months after the Australia series, we played a tri-series against the West Indies and Zimbabwe at Harare. I had trained hard in the off season and felt in good shape ahead of the series. For close to two years, between August 1999 and July 2001, I had been injury-free and the off-season training had definitely helped improve my fitness. I used to run in the mornings and do gym sessions in the afternoon to strengthen my upper body and I also kept a check on my diet. The discipline had helped and the 1999 back injury was now just a bad memory.

I started the tournament in red-hot form and scored two fifties and a century in the four pool games, being dismissed only once. But just as I had started to look forward to the final, I suffered the second major injury of my career in rather unexpected circumstances.

It happened during the last of our group matches against the West Indies on 4 July 2001. Rahul and I were batting together and we were cruising to victory. With some 20 runs left to win, I turned a ball to midwicket and set off for two runs. That's when I heard something click in my big toe. Immediately I felt a sense of discomfort and found it difficult to complete the second run. Before the next ball I walked up to Rahul and said that I had hurt my toe and that the temperature in my foot had suddenly gone up a few degrees. However, with so few runs needed, I decided to stay in and finish off the game as quickly as possible, making 122 in the process.

After the match I showed the toe to Andrew Leipus, who had taken over as our physiotherapist, and the next morning we went for an X-ray. The pain had actually increased in the interim and I was now struggling to walk properly. On our way to the hospital I asked Andrew not to tell me about the results of the X-ray, for no matter what, I wanted to play in the final. Soon after the X-ray, Andrew, looking somewhat helpless, just said to me, 'You are a crazy man.'

Before the game it was decided that Andrew would strap the toe bent down to prevent any movement and I took the field against the West Indies in considerable physical discomfort. I had been in terrific touch throughout the tournament and the thinking was that my batting was more important for the team than my fielding and bowling. Personally, I felt I would be able to make it through the game, as it happened to be the final match. After all that effort, however, I proceeded to get out for a duck and we lost the match. It turned out I had damaged my sesamoid bone, which is the bone at the connection of the big toe and the first metatarsal.

After returning to India I was prescribed total rest, but after two months I still wasn't happy with the way the recovery was going. I could barely walk without discomfort. In desperation I saw a specialist, who advised me to have surgery. We even fixed a tentative date, but that's when Anjali advised me to seek a second opinion. She felt that surgery should always be the last resort and we had to be sure there was no other way to get the injury treated.

We went to Bombay Hospital and saw one of the most senior doctors around, Dr Dholakia. He showed me a big fat book on sesamoid bones and informed me that the author of the book, who was the world expert on sesamoid injuries, wasn't a hundred per cent certain that surgery was the best way to treat them. He went on to say that I shouldn't allow anyone to touch my toe, as it might be counterproductive. There was the possibility of permanent damage, which might bring my career to an end, and that was a scary thought. On the very same day Dr Dholakia started looking into where I could go to get my toe examined by a specialist.

Eventually I found myself at the Rosebank Clinic in Johannesburg, where Dr Mark Ferguson, who had worked with a lot of sportsmen, advised me to try out a few insoles. Over a week in South Africa I went from walking for fifteen minutes to close to an hour. Back in Mumbai I continued with the routine, building up from jogging to running. Running in cricket shoes was a bit of a problem because of the spikes, so for the next few months I wore shoes with no spikes immediately under my toes. The injury, it appeared, was finally on the mend.

My first tour after the lay-off, coincidentally perhaps, was to South Africa in October–November 2001. We were playing a tri-series against South Africa and Kenya before going on to play a three-Test series against the South Africans. However, in our very first tour game against the Nicky Oppenheimer XI on 1 October, the pain in my toe resurfaced. It was a strange sensation and I left the field to get some treatment.

Luckily for me we were in Randjesfontein, which is not far from Johannesburg, so I set out for the Rosebank Clinic again. Much to my relief, I was assured there that it wasn't anything major and that a slight recurrence of pain was normal with sesamoid bone injuries. They told me that there was no need to panic. I left the clinic with a sigh of relief and was eager to get back to playing cricket again.

The first match of the tri-series was in Johannesburg on 5 October and I managed to score a hundred against South Africa. The intensity of the match pushed the thought of the injury out of my mind, but afterwards I was relieved that I'd been able to bat for so long with very little pain. It was as if I had started all over again.

India in South Africa, November 2001

Taking on South Africa in their home conditions is always challenging and it was even more so having just recovered from the toe injury. I had, however, started to feel more confident after a net session at Bloemfontein, the venue for the first of the three Tests. I distinctly remember that session because every ball hit the middle of my bat and it seemed to me that I could do no wrong.

The first Test started on 3 November and happily my touch with the bat was still there in the first innings. I made 155 out of a team total of 379, and it was the first time I played the upper cut over the slips, a shot I went on to use regularly in the second half of my career. I had come up with the idea of the shot to counter the South African fast bowler Makhaya Ntini, whose strength was to bring the ball in to the batsman from short of a length. I knew that if I played the upper cut against Ntini, it would affect his rhythm, as he was not prepared for this form of counter-attack. The pitch in Bloemfontein had a lot of bounce and in the absence of a third-man fielder the upper cut was a scoring stroke played with minimal risk. I followed the ball till late and just helped it on the way over the slip fielders, using the pace generated by Ntini.

Virender Sehwag, on his debut, also played aggressively and, had we batted a little better in the second innings, we could have saved the game. Instead, we lost by nine wickets, with Shaun Pollock taking 6–56. My partnership with Sehwag was our high point and I remember asking him if he was nervous when he walked out to bat for the first time in a Test. He admitted that he was a little and I immediately told him that was normal. In fact, it was good to be a little nervous and everyone who played Test cricket experienced similar nerves. He just needed to play his natural game and the nervousness would disappear once he'd spent a little time out in the middle. He did so and scored a fantastic hundred on debut.

Missing the comforts of home

We went to Port Elizabeth for the second Test. Sara and Arjun were both with me and on one evening before the match I asked the hotel staff to recommend a restaurant where we could go out for a good family meal. Eating together was the only way I could spend quality time with my children and I looked forward to these meals at the end of long, hard work days. The hotel staff told me about a diner that also had a fairly big play area where the children could enjoy themselves and we ended up going to the same restaurant three days in a row. It was from this restaurant that I picked up the idea of the play area that I put in my own restaurant when I created Tendulkar's in Mumbai in 2004.

Food on tour was always an important consideration for the team and to get the kind of food we liked in places such as Bulawayo in Zimbabwe and some South African cities could sometimes be a real problem.

I remember one occasion in Bulawayo when all the players were yearning for home food. We were tired of eating the same breakfast and lunch in the hotel, and the restaurants were not the best. Spotting an Indian family that had come to see us play, Sameer Dighe boldly walked up to them and said that the team was desperate to eat some good Indian food – could they help?

Jhanak bhai, the man in question, was a Gujarati settled in Zimbabwe and he ended up inviting the team to his home, where we feasted on a home-cooked meal of Gujarati-style dal, rice and ghee. We all had three spoons of ghee and pigged out on the food in front of us. It soon became a regular thing and Jhanak bhai and his family fed us many times. Others who have been kind enough to provide us with good home-cooked food in Zimbabwe and South Africa are Raj and Chester Naik and Jayesh Desai. They have selflessly helped us whenever we have toured their parts of the world and have made a major contribution to our well-being. Raj and Chester Naik also took us to play golf and we had some wonderful dinners together. Invariably Ravi Shastri would join us for these dinners because they were his friends first. I became good friends with many of them and must say I will always remember the warmth and affection I received from them and their families.

Unacceptable allegations

We managed a better batting performance in the Port Elizabeth Test, which started on 16 November 2001. Rahul Dravid and Deep Dasgupta, our wicketkeeper, played resolutely on the last day, and we saved the match comfortably in the end. However, what hit the headlines from that match were the allegations made against me by the match referee Mike Denness, who also charged five other Indian players.

The incident occurred on the third day, when I bowled a four-over spell, taking the wicket of Herschelle Gibbs. I was bowling seam-up and was getting the ball to swing both ways. During this spell I used my thumb to clean off the grass that was stuck on the seam.

Soon after the end of the day's play we were informed that the match referee had called six Indian players for a hearing and that I had been accused of ball tampering. I was shocked, because I had always played cricket with integrity and honesty and would never do such a thing.

When I met the match referee I informed him that I was merely trying to clean the seam of the ball. My mistake, which I have no hesitation in owning up to, was that I should have informed the on-field umpires under Law 42.3 when I was cleaning the seam, but I'm afraid it did not enter my mind in the intensity of the moment. I asked Mike Denness to consult the on-field umpires, because they had checked the ball every two or three overs and were in the best position to tell if the ball had been tampered with. Denness said that there was no need to consult the umpires, presumably because I had admitted altering the ball by cleaning the seam.

I found this strange, because there was no way Denness could gauge what was going on in the middle when he was sitting eighty yards away from the pitch. None of the umpires had lodged a formal complaint against me and it was humiliating to be labelled a cheat. I wasn't prepared to let it pass. I informed Mike Denness that I would complain about the allegation to the BCCI and would not keep quiet about it.

Apart from charging me with ball tampering, Mike Denness handed captain Sourav Ganguly a one-match suspended ban for failing to control the players and banned Virender Sehwag for one match on a charge of over-appealing. Deep Dasgupta, Harbhajan Singh and Shiv Sunder Das, the opening batsman, were all handed a one-Test suspended ban and fined 75 per cent of their match fee for the same offence. The team considered these punishments harsh, especially when none of the South Africans had been pulled up despite, we felt, appealing just as aggressively. It is a hard game and sometimes things get heated in the middle. But we didn't think we deserved the punishments we had been handed.

We informed the BCCI that the allegations were unsubstantiated and unfair. We were delighted when the BCCI, led by Jagmohan Dalmiya, stood steadfastly behind us and informed the ICC that the team had lost faith in the match referee. We also received support in the media; the Indian journalistic fraternity, at home and on tour, was united behind the team. We were prepared to abandon the tour if need be, but we weren't ready to be labelled cheats. It was about honour and there was no way we would allow a match referee to cast aspersions on our credibility.

Things had come to such a pass at one point that we weren't sure if the tour would actually carry on. There were conflicting reports everywhere and the atmosphere was one of mistrust and confusion. The situation came to a head twenty-four hours before the start of the third Test match, when it was finally decided by the Indian and South African boards, rather than by the ICC, that Mike Denness should not officiate in the match. Denis Lindsay, the former South African wicketkeeper, was the replacement, and the match went ahead, but it was labelled an unofficial Test match by the ICC.

Not everything was right about it after all the acrimony, which I must say was largely unnecessary. Mike Denness's decisions had led to a crisis that had ended up dividing the cricket world down the middle. It was an avoidable incident and one that left everyone bitter in the end.

India in South Africa 2001

1st Test. Bloemfontein. 3–6 November 2001

India 379 (**SR Tendulkar 155**, V Sehwag 105; S Pollock 4–91, M Hayward 3–70) and 237 (SS Das 62, V Sehwag 31, **SR Tendulkar 15**; SM Pollock 6–56)

South Africa 563 (L Klusener 108, HH Gibbs 107, G Kirsten 73, J Kallis 68, ND McKenzie 68; J Srinath 5–140, A Kumble 3–132) and 54–1

South Africa won by 9 wickets

2nd Test. Port Elizabeth. 16–20 November 2001

South Africa 362 (HH Gibbs 196, MV Boucher 68*; J Srinath 6–76, **SR Tendulkar 1–22**) and 233–5 dec (JH Kallis 89*, SM Pollock 55*; J Srinath 2–28, H Singh 2–79)

India 201 (VVS Laxman 89, SC Ganguly 42, **SR Tendulkar 1**; SM Pollock 5–40) and 206–3 (R Dravid 87, D Dasgupta 63, **SR Tendulkar 22***; M Hayward 2–58)

Match drawn

South Africa won the series 1–0

13

A GLORIOUS ENGLISH SUMMER

Within a week of returning from South Africa we faced Nasser Hussain's Englishmen at home in December 2001. Nasser, nowadays a respected commentator, played hard and came up with some ultra-defensive tactics against me. It was in this series that Nasser instructed his left-arm spinner Ashley Giles to bowl from over the wicket and consistently pitch the ball way outside my leg stump. Nasser and Giles were counting on the fact that I would have limited scoring options off balls bowled there and were hoping to frustrate me and induce me to play a false shot. They had essentially given up any attempt to get me out in favour of trying to get under my skin.

While Giles did manage to have me stumped, for the first time in my Test career, in the third Test in Bangalore, overall these tactics had little impact on the result of the series. I scored a lot of runs in all three Test matches and was declared Player of the Series.

I was reminded of this series when Nasser, who is a good friend, met me a couple of years later in South Africa during the 2003 World Cup. We were in the washroom during the inaugural function and Nasser jokingly started the conversation, saying, 'So I am in the washroom with the great Mr Tendulkar.' It was a minute-long conversation and we were both enjoying ourselves. It was friendly banter between two people who have great regard for each other. From memory, the conversation went something like this:

NASSER: You have to agree that I was successful in stopping you and getting you frustrated during the 2001 England tour of India when I got Ashley Giles to bowl to you from over the wicket.

SACHIN: You did indeed, but despite his efforts, my batting average for the series was 76, with scores of 88, 103 and 90 in the three Test matches, and I was in fact nominated Player of the Series. I would love to have that average right through my career.

We won the series 1–0, a result that gave us considerable confidence as we looked forward to the return tour of England the following summer. It looked likely to be an enthralling series.

Some thoughts on batting

It was in the early stages of the 2002 tour of England that I first gave a masterclass. It was at the Rose Bowl, where we were playing a warm-up game against Hampshire, and it was organized by Mark Nicholas for Channel 4 television. I enjoyed talking to a group of youngsters about the basics of batting, including how to grip the bat.

People have often commented on my own grip, which is very low down on the handle. It all goes back to when I started playing cricket when I was eleven with my brother Ajit, who is ten years older. As I didn't have a bat of my own, I had to use Ajit's full-size bat and the only way I could cope with the weight at that age was to hold the bat right at the bottom of the handle. Some coaches suggested changing my grip, and I did experiment, but it never felt right. I had got used to feeling the end of the handle pressing against the inside of my forearm and if I gripped the bat further up I didn't have that, and batting just didn't feel natural.

That's not to say that my technique didn't change at all, though. Throughout my career, I was always looking to improve and constantly tried new things to cope with different situations. My backlift changed significantly over the years, for example. I used a pretty heavy bat and I was sometimes encouraged to move to a lighter one. Again, I did try but I never felt comfortable, as my whole bat swing depended on that weight. When I was hitting a drive, I needed the weight to generate the power. It was all to do with the timing. To me the bat should be an extension of your arm, and if you've reached the stage where it's become an extension of your arm, why do you need to change?

What mattered to me most when I was batting was feeling comfortable. As long as I felt comfortable, it didn't matter where I was playing or who I was playing against. If you make technical adjustments, such as moving to a lighter bat, to cope with different conditions, there's a risk of making yourself feel uncomfortable and of thinking too much about your technique. I've always felt that I've batted best when my mind has been at the bowler's end of the pitch, not at my end. In fact, for both batsmen and bowlers, I've always believed that cricket is played best when your mind is at the opposite end and that problems occur when your mind is stuck at your own end.

For example, if a bowler is thinking too much about bowling no-balls, he's not going to be able to bowl what he wants to bowl. Instead, his mind should be at the batsman's end, focusing on where he's going to pitch the ball, which way he's going to swing it and so on. As a batsman, if I'm not consciously worrying about my footwork or my backlift or my wrist-work, then I know that I'm in the right space, because my mind needs to be at the opposite end, figuring out what the bowler is trying to do. There's no time to think about both ends at the same time. So in general it always seemed to me that if I was comfortable with my gear, it would allow my mind to be at the opposite end and I had a better chance of playing well.

India in England, the Test series, July–September 2002

I have always enjoyed playing in England, but on the 2002 tour it took the team a little time to adjust to the conditions. The first of the four Tests, at Lord's, started on 25 July 2002 and England won pretty convincingly, with Hussain making his highest score for five years and Michael Vaughan also contributing a century. For India, the high point was my friend Ajit Agarkar's second-innings hundred, and I was delighted to see his name go up on the famous honours board in the dressing room.

We knew we needed to be more competitive in the next Test at Trent Bridge ten days later if we were to stay alive in the four-match series. Once again England posted a huge score, with Vaughan again in good form, and we were faced with batting out the last day to survive. The pitch was assisting the bowlers and quite a few balls were taking off from a good length, while some were keeping low. In difficult circumstances, Rahul and I put together an important partnership. There were occasions when we were beaten by balls which had either taken off or kept low and all we did was smile. We chatted at the end of every over but never once talked about the deliveries we had missed. It was natural that the ball would occasionally beat us on a fifth-day wicket offering uneven bounce; we enjoyed the challenge.

Rahul got a hundred and both Sourav and I fell in the nineties. Sourav was out for 99 while I was bowled for 92 by part-time off-spinner Michael Vaughan to what was probably the best ball he ever bowled. The ball pitched in the rough outside my off stump and turned a long way to go through the gap between bat and pad to hit the stumps. That we managed to hold on for a draw, thanks to some dour resistance from wicketkeeper Parthiv Patel, a teenager at the time, was an important statement and it laid the foundation for the fightback at Headingley in the third Test.

There was a long gap between the second and third Tests,

which allowed us to unwind and refocus. By now we had come to terms with the conditions and were feeling more relaxed. We were enjoying ourselves socially, going out to interesting restaurants to try out different types of food and spending a lot of time together, which is always essential in the middle of a difficult tour.

It was around then that a friend of mine suggested visiting the famous Harry Ramsden's, in Guiseley in West Yorkshire. This restaurant, I was told, served great fish and chips and Ajit Agarkar and I decided to try out the fare. There was one item on the menu titled Harry's Challenge, which invited the customer to eat a giant portion of fish, either cod or haddock, served with chips, bread and butter and two other side dishes. If successful, the head chef would personally sign a certificate for the customer. I've always been a big eater, so I decided to take on the challenge. I must say I managed the giant portion of fish fairly comfortably and also polished off the salad and other side dishes served to me. The only thing I did not eat was the chips, which I thought might be just a little too fattening. Impressed with my performance, the chef signed my Harry's Challenge certificate all the same.

Third Test, Headingley, 22–26 August 2002

The wicket was very damp at the start of the Headingley Test on 22 August 2002. Despite this, we decided to bat first after winning the toss. We were all in agreement that we should put runs on the board and try to put the English under pressure. Sehwag got out early but then Rahul Dravid and Sanjay Bangar, our makeshift opener for the game, put together an excellent partnership of 170 that turned things our way. Batting wasn't easy on a fresh wicket and they both played exceptionally well, leaving a lot of balls outside the off stump.

I went in to bat in the last session of day one and decided to wear an inner-thigh guard. I had never used one before, even in practice, but Andrew Flintoff was getting the ball to jag back in to the batsmen and I thought the inner-thigh guard might be a sensible protection against injury. However, I soon realized that my stance had completely changed. Normally the forearm of my bottom hand rests on my thigh while I take stance, but at Headingley it felt completely different because of the new guard. I immediately decided to get rid of it and the experiment was never tried again.

In this innings I was circumspect to start with and decided to play out the day, waiting for my opportunity the next morning. Flintoff bowled a hostile spell and I really had to knuckle down. He was getting the ball to swing and bounce and there was not much I could do but defend. The following morning Matthew Hoggard, who had the ability to swing the ball both ways, also bowled impressively, getting the ball to move away from the bat at good pace. Quality outswing is difficult to negotiate and I had to be watchful while playing big drives on the rise. Shot selection in this innings was the key.

Andrew Flintoff produced another really probing spell. He was bowling into Sourav's body and it was decided that I would face up to him while Sourav, a left-hander, took as much strike as possible against Ashley Giles, who was once again bowling a defensive line to me outside my leg stump. When we went back for tea to the dressing room, Sourav said, 'Woh beech wale Flintoff ka spell humne kya jhela yaar.' (We did really well to see off Flintoff's spell.) I couldn't resist pulling his leg and jokingly said to him, 'Humne jhela? Saala maine jhela hain!' (Did we? I was the one who negotiated Flintoff!) The whole dressing room burst out laughing.

In the third session of the day we shifted gears and launched into the English bowlers, who were gradually starting to tire. It was one of those rare matches in which we refused to take the light even when the umpires offered it to us. We were dominating proceedings and there was no reason to go off.

In the end the umpires came up to us and said that as they

could not see the ball they were calling it a day. I was unbeaten on 185 and we had a mammoth score on the board. We could not lose the Test match from that position and we already had enough runs for our bowlers to play with. By the time England's turn came, their task would be even more difficult, because the wicket was becoming uneven and the odd ball had started to keep low. In fact, it was a low bounce that cost me my wicket on the morning of the third day, when I was lbw to Andrew Caddick for 193. We finally declared our first innings at 628–8, one of our highest ever scores on English soil.

The bowlers took over and from the start of the English innings managed to put them under pressure. Kumble and Harbhajan bowled beautifully in tandem in conditions that were not so helpful for spinners and picked up three wickets each in the innings. There were no big partnerships and we kept taking wickets at regular intervals, finally bowling England out for 273 and then enforcing the follow-on. Our huge first-innings score had allowed us to put a lot of fielders in catching positions and we attacked the whole time.

In the second innings, with close to 400 runs in the bank, we kept up the pressure and gave each English batsman a hard time. Even Nasser, who scored a hundred in the second innings, wasn't spared and there was a lot of banter in the middle. We were all extremely motivated and did not want a single English batsman to settle down and take control. Nobody held back and our bowlers made regular inroads into the English batting. Each wicket was followed by a lot of talk and the new batsman was given a rousing welcome. When Andrew Flintoff got out for a pair, caught by Dravid at slip off Zaheer Khan, our left-arm fast bowler, we knew we were within striking distance of a famous victory. Anil did the rest, picking up four wickets, and we bowled England out for 309, winning the match by an innings and 46 runs.

At Trent Bridge in the previous Test we had played well to draw the match and now we had cashed in at Headingley. Kumble bowled his heart out for his seven wickets in difficult conditions and all the other bowlers – Zaheer, Ajit Agarkar, Sanjay Bangar and Harbhajan – chipped in with important wickets.

Fourth Test, The Oval, 5–9 September 2002

We followed up with another very good performance at The Oval. Rahul played a gem of an innings and his 217 allowed the rest of the batting to revolve around him. This match had special significance for me because it was my 100th Test. I was nervous and excited on the morning of the game and the chief executive of Surrey County Cricket Club, Paul Sheldon, presented me with a commemorative plaque. A special announcement was made and when it was my turn to bat people were expecting me to carry on from where I had left off at Headingley. I hit some good shots on my way to my half-century, but then I unexpectedly got out to a ball I completely misread.

I could see the ball in Caddick's hand as he was about to start his run-up and it was clear that the shiny side was on his right side, or the on side. With normal swing, that would indicate an outswinger, so I said to myself here's an opportunity for a big drive and I was ready to play the ball between mid off and cover. To my complete surprise, the ball came *in* a long way and hit me on my heel. I have rarely been beaten so comprehensively and was out plumb lbw. The ball had reverse-swung and it was the first and only ball that did so in the innings. In normal circumstances Caddick didn't bowl big inswingers, but got the ball to cut in to the batsmen. On this one occasion he somehow got the ball to reverse-swing a mile. It was particularly difficult to deal with because it was a Yorker-length delivery.

It was unusual for me to misread a bowler's swing in that way, as I normally backed myself to work out what the bowler was up to by watching the ball in his hand. For example, every time Ben Hilfenhaus, the Australian fast bowler, held an old ball cross-seam,

I knew he would bowl a bouncer – and I would be prepared for it. This strategy came in handy during the India–Australia series in India in 2010, when I managed to score a double hundred in Bangalore. Similarly, I noticed that the Pakistan fast bowler Shoaib Akhtar would swing his bowling arm twice before he delivered his effort ball as he tried to generate more pace into the delivery. Again, I would be prepared for it.

As for spin bowlers, I have always monitored a bowler's release point to work out what the bowler was planning. In the case of the Sri Lankan legend Muttiah Muralitharan, he would have his thumb on top of the ball when bowling a doosra. For his normal off-spin deliveries, he had his thumb below the ball. We once had a conversation in the dressing room on how to pick Murali's doosra and I told everyone that all they needed to do was watch his thumb. One day, we were practising at the SSC Ground in Colombo when Murali came to the ground. Bhajji decided to go up and ask him how to bowl the doosra. Murali told Bhajji to use his thumb to support the ball from the top – that was the secret. I had no idea about this conversation until Bhajji told me later. I felt very gratified that I had worked it out for myself.

Being able to spot the doosra helped me a lot, and not just when I was batting. When I did an over of commentary during the final of the IPL in May 2013, I said on air that Bhajji had just bowled a doosra to dismiss the South African fast bowler Chris Morris. Morris had played for conventional off-spin when the ball had actually gone the other way. The commentators, including Harsha Bhogle on air, said they were impressed because they had not been able to pick the doosra and the replay had not yet been shown.

I should also say here that there were other occasions when I found it difficult to figure out what a bowler was planning to do. One bowler I found particularly challenging in this respect when I first faced him was the New Zealand fast-medium bowler Dion Nash. His action was such that I thought he would bowl inswingers at me, which he never did. I got out to Nash on the flattest of decks because I played for the inswinger when the ball was actually an outswinger. Eventually I worked him out, and even got a hundred against him in Wellington, but it did take me a while to do so.

Another bowler I had great difficulty picking at first was the West Indian left-arm fast bowler Pedro Collins. I had first seen Collins in a practice match during our May–June 2002 tour of the West Indies, when he bowled our opening batsman Wasim Jaffer with a big inswinger. I made a note that here was a bowler who started with inswing early on. Accordingly, in the next few innings I played for this inswing, only to see the ball leaving me and I ended up nicking deliveries behind the wicket. I was out to him three times and didn't last more than two or three balls in each of these innings. Midway through the series, I spoke with a number of West Indies players and I was told that actually Collins hardly ever bowled inswing – he normally got the ball to angle away from the right-hander. So by the time of the final Test in Jamaica I was more confident against him and I managed to score 86.

The best bit about dealing with Collins, however, happened in India when the West Indies visited in November 2002. By then I had fully worked him out and had started to consciously watch the shine to tell which way the ball would be moving, because he was reverse-swinging the ball. If the shine was on the outside I would even leave balls pitched on middle stump because I knew that by the time the ball passed the stumps it would be close to the sixth or seventh stump. This frustrated Collins and after a while he realized my strategy and decided to go round the wicket. That's when the mind games started. He did all he could to stop me seeing the shine of the ball. He ran in from right behind the umpire so that he wasn't in my line of vision. To counter this strategy, I deliberately pulled away once or twice and subsequently asked the umpire to crouch. I said I wasn't able to see the bowler and did not know when he was about to deliver the ball.

Then I did something completely unorthodox. I decided not to take my stance when Collins was at the top of his run. Instead,

I moved to the off side so that I could see how Collins was holding the ball. I knew once he started running in he couldn't change the grip and I had just enough time to come back and take my stance. It was actually hilarious: a batsman standing wide of off stump, craning his neck to see a bowler's grip. It's not an everyday sight in international cricket. The strategy worked surprisingly well and I more than made up for my bloopers against him in the West Indies earlier in the year.

NatWest Series, June–July 2002

The Headingley win, which helped us to draw the Test series, followed a memorable victory in the NatWest tri-series, making it a fabulous English summer for India. England, Sri Lanka and India were the three teams playing for honours and we met England in the final after playing each other three times in a round-robin format. The final on 13 July was one of the most exciting one-day internationals of my career, and it is still fondly remembered by scores of Indian cricket fans.

All the way through the NatWest series I had been in good form, with two hundreds in the six pool games. We had success-fully chased down several high scores and we weren't overawed by the England total at Lord's. Rather, we were silently confident of reaching the steep target of 325. We started the run chase well, with Sehwag and Sourav scoring freely and laying a brilliant foundation. However, as often happens in cricket when you are chasing a big total, we lost a number of quick wickets and slipped to 146–5 in no time. I was out bowled trying to cut a ball from Ashley Giles. By now the mood in the dressing room had turned sombre and nobody was speaking – until Yuvraj Singh, the talented left-handed batsman, and Mohammad Kaif, a right-handed middle-order batsman and excellent fielder, started an unlikely recovery act. They were scoring boundaries freely and at no point did the asking rate go beyond manageable limits.

Once the partnership had started to blossom I had a feeling that something dramatic might happen. I can't explain why, but I was convinced it was not all over for us yet. The rest of the team sensed the opportunity too and soon each run was cheered in the dressing room. I was sitting on a table in the middle of the room and was eating one energy bar after another. I was not particularly hungry but in the intensity of the moment kept polishing off the bars. Before long the atmosphere had changed dramatically and everyone was engrossed in the game. Cricketers are a superstitious lot and no one was allowed to shift position. If someone wanted to go to the toilet, he wasn't allowed to do so in the middle of an over; he could only go at the end of an over and had to come back before the start of the next.

By the fortieth over, Yuvraj and Kaif had got the measure of the English bowling and we realized we had a real chance of winning the title. The next few batsmen were all charged up and even when Yuvraj got out for 69 there was no dip in intensity. Kaif was still out there and we knew that the target was within reach. Finally, when Zaheer and Kaif ran the winning runs in the last over of the match, the dressing room leaped in delight. We could not stop smiling and hugging each other – and Sourav did the unthinkable of taking off his shirt and waving it above his head as he stood bare-chested on the Lord's balcony. It is an iconic image now but for some reason Sourav is always much too embarrassed to talk about it whenever I ask him!

We stayed in the dressing room for hours, picking over the finer points of the victory. We'd heard that the England team had ordered champagne by the middle of our innings and had put a number of bottles on ice. With India at 146–5, an English win was deemed a mere formality. I don't know if this story is true, but a number of our players suggested to the England team at the end of the game that it was time to pass the champagne over to us. We would be happy to take care of it. A number of bottles did make their way to our dressing room and we finished them off before we left Lord's.

There were Indian supporters everywhere and the stretch from the WG Grace Gate to St John's Wood Tube station was packed with fans waving the tricolour and celebrating. The traffic had come to a standstill, with people playing music on the road and enjoying the moment. The police were extremely patient and realized it was a special occasion. A large crowd had waited for us to leave and were all waving at the team bus and taking pictures as we finally left Lord's with the trophy. It was a day few of us would forget.

The victory, which had seen youngsters like Yuvraj and Kaif come to the fore, suggested that the core of India's team for the 2003 World Cup was gradually coming together. It also proved that we had a side capable of doing well in overseas conditions. In Zaheer Khan, Ashish Nehra, Javagal Srinath, Anil Kumble and Harbhajan Singh we had a more than competent bowling line-up, and with Sehwag, Sourav, Rahul, Yuvraj, Kaif and myself, we were capable of out-batting any opposition. Now it was important to sustain the momentum and peak at the right time to have a crack at the world title that had eluded us for so long.

England in India 2001

1st Test. Mohali. 3–6 December 2001
England 238 (N Hussain 85, ME Trescothick 66; H Singh 5–51) and 235
    (GP Thorpe 62, ME Trescothick 46; A Kumble 6–81)
India 469 (D Dasgupta 100, **SR Tendulkar 88**, R Dravid 86, SC Ganguly 47;
    RKJ Dawson 4–134, M Hoggard 3–98) and 5–0
India won by 10 wickets

2nd Test. Ahmedabad. 11–15 December 2001
England 407 (C White 121, ME Trescothick 99, MA Butcher 51; A Kumble
    7–115, **SR Tendulkar 1–27**) and 257 (MA Butcher 92, N Hussain 50;
    H Singh 5–71, A Kumble 3–118)
India 291 (**SR Tendulkar 103**, VVS Laxman 75; AF Giles 5–67) and 198–3
    (D Dasgupta 60, SS Das 58, **SR Tendulkar 26**; RKJ Dawson 2–72)
Match drawn

3rd Test. Bangalore. 19–23 December 2001

England 336 (MP Vaughan 64, MR Ramprakash 58, JS Foster 48; J Srinath
    4–73, S Singh 3–54) and 33–0

India 238 (**SR Tendulkar 90**, V Sehwag 66; A Flintoff 4–50, MJ Hoggard 4–80)
Match drawn

India won the series 1–0

India in England 2002

1st Test. Lord's. 25–29 July 2002

England 487 (N Hussain 155, JP Crawley 64, A Flintoff 59; Z Khan 3–90,
    A Kumble 3–128) and 301–6 dec (JP Crawley 100*, MP Vaughan 100;
    A Kumble 3–84)

India 221 (V Sehwag 84, R Dravid 46, **SR Tendulkar 16**; MJ Hoggard 3–33,
    A Flintoff 2–22) and 397 (AB Agarkar 109*, VVS Laxman 74, R Dravid 63,
    W Jaffer 53, **SR Tendulkar 12**; MJ Hoggard 4–87)

England won by 170 runs

2nd Test. Nottingham. 8–12 August 2002

India 357 (V Sehwag 106, SC Ganguly 68, H Singh 54, **SR Tendulkar 34**;
    MJ Hoggard 4–105, SJ Harmison 3–57) and 424–8 dec (R Dravid 115,
    SC Ganguly 99, **SR Tendulkar 92**; DC Cork 2–54, SJ Harmison 2–63,
    MP Vaughan 2–71)

England 617 (MP Vaughan 197, C White 94*, AJ Stewart 87, MA Butcher 53;
    Z Khan 3–110, H Singh 3–175)

Match drawn

3rd Test. Leeds. 22–26 August 2002

India 628–8 dec (**SR Tendulkar 193**, R Dravid 148, SC Ganguly 128, SB Bangar
    68; AR Caddick 3–150)

England 273 (AJ Stewart 78*, MP Vaughan 61; H Singh 3–40, A Kumble 3–93)
    and 309 (f/o) (N Hussain 110, AJ Stewart 47; A Kumble 4–66, SB Bangar
    2–54)

India won by an innings and 46 runs

4th Test. The Oval. 5–9 Sep 2002

England 515 (MP Vaughan 195, ME Trescothick 57, MA Butcher 54; H Singh
    5–115, SB Bangar 2–48, Z Khan 2–83) and 114–0 (ME Trescothick 58*,
    MP Vaughan 47*)

India 508 (R Dravid 217, **SR Tendulkar 54**, SC Ganguly 51; AR Caddick 4–114)
Match drawn

Series drawn 1–1

14

WORLD CUP 2003

India's preparation for the 2003 World Cup in South Africa and Zimbabwe really started during the tour to New Zealand in December 2002. We lost to the Kiwis in both formats of the game and while those defeats were demoralizing, as defeats always are, they helped the team to focus with just a month to go before the World Cup.

We played two Test matches in New Zealand and lost both. In the first Test at Wellington, which started on 12 December, we were beaten by ten wickets, with the match finishing in just three days. The pitch offered a lot of assistance to the fast bowlers and even Parthiv Patel, our wicketkeeper, was getting the ball to swing prodigiously in the nets.

I played the first Test with an injured finger, which I had hurt during practice. On the first morning, when the rest of the team were on the ground preparing to play, I was in hospital with Andrew Leipus getting my finger checked. The pain was getting severe and I was finding it impossible to catch the ball. Even when a fielder gently tossed the ball to me to pass on to the bowler I was having difficulty catching it. Batting was not so much of a problem, as I could grip the bat as normal, but fielding was a real issue. I asked the doctor to numb my finger, but he refused, saying I would have no idea where my finger was and might break it if I didn't catch the ball properly. All I could do was put up with the pain.

When I got back to the ground, I went up to captain Sourav Ganguly and suggested I should field at short leg. In that position, the ball would either lob to me or, if it was a firm hit, I would receive the blow on my body instead of attempting to catch it. Both of these possibilities were fine by me. At short leg no one expects you to stop a full-blooded shot with your hands. It was one of the few times I stood in that position in the second half of my career.

Although the second Test match at Hamilton the following week was a low-scoring game, in the end it turned out to be a competitive one. On reaching Hamilton, we were shocked to see the track had been watered so much that the pitch was incredibly damp two days before the Test match. Then a lot of rain fell and the covers couldn't be removed to allow it to dry properly. John Wright, our coach, tried inserting a key into the pitch the day before the match and the whole key went in without any effort. It was anything but a good Test wicket.

The dampness delayed the start by four hours on the first day, despite it being bright and sunny in Hamilton. The umpires did the right thing by waiting, as there was no way Test cricket could be played in such conditions. The crowd was getting restless but there was nothing the umpires or players could do. When the match finally started we lost the toss and were sent in to bat first in nigh-on impossible batting conditions. We were bowled out for 99, with no one managing to get in.

I was sitting next to John Wright when Harbhajan was going out to bat, with India six wickets down. John, a New Zealander, had tried telling us that we needed to stay at the wicket and that batting was expected to become easier with time. I told John not to say anything to Harbhajan about digging in. Far better that he should just go out and swing his bat. Time wasn't a factor, as the match was not likely to last the full five days anyway, and whatever runs he managed to score would be valuable. Harbhajan went on to make a quick 20, all in boundaries, and got out trying to defend the ninth ball he faced. His innings gave John a good laugh amidst all the disappointment of the low score. While Bhajji had scored 20 in no time, all the batsmen who had tried to stick around struggled to reach double figures.

New Zealand didn't do any better; in fact, we managed to get a first-innings lead of five runs, which just goes to show the nature of the wicket. In the second innings Rahul and I had a pretty good partnership but neither of us managed to kick on for a big score. After the partnership was broken, wickets fell in a heap and we finally set New Zealand a target of 160.

I must mention the unique feat of Ashish Nehra in this game. He was the first man to bat twice and bowl in two innings on the same day in Test cricket. We had scored 92–8 by the end of the first day's play and Ashish was one of the not-out batsmen. He resumed his innings on the second day but we were soon all out for 99. He was then part of our attack as we bowled New Zealand out for 94 in their first innings, before we ourselves were bowled out in our second innings for 154. Finally, when New Zealand came out to bat in the fourth innings of the match, Ashish had another bowl at them in the final moments of the day.

We discussed his feat in the dressing room and wondered if anything of the sort had happened before. A total of twenty-two wickets had fallen in a day and there wasn't much that the batsmen on either side could do in such conditions. It was disappointing for the crowd, who had come to watch a five-day game. Their only consolation was that the match was very close in the end and the home team won by four wickets.

Fighting for fitness

With both Test matches over early, I decided to spend a lot of time in the gym working on my fitness ahead of the World Cup. Sehwag was my training partner and we used to award marks. We worked on specific body parts each day and rated each other for the effort put in. We even joked that we were perhaps scoring more marks in the gym than the total runs we had scored in the series. But both Sehwag and I were confident that the effort put in would pay off sooner or later.

After the Test series was wrapped up we played a seven-match one-day series, losing 2–5. Again, most of the wickets weren't really suitable for international cricket. I did not feature in the first four matches because of an ankle injury, which I sustained in practice on the eve of the first one-dayer at Auckland. It was one of the few freakish injuries I have had in my career. I had just finished bowling a long spell to each of our batsmen when Srinath called out, 'Last ball, with four runs to win.' I picked up the ball again to bowl one final delivery at him. I had not noticed a big hole in the corner of the practice pitch and, unluckily for me, as I ran to stop Srinath's shot, my foot landed in the hole and I slumped to the ground in agony. After a frustrating couple of weeks, I eventually made a comeback in the fifth match of the series, at Wellington, and was promptly out for a duck. In fact I scored just one run in each of the next two matches and Anjali and I joked about my scores – which read 0, 1, 1 – which reads more like a dialling code than anything else!

The New Zealand experience was best summed up by the home captain Stephen Fleming. At the end of the tour Fleming stated that the tour had done enough to breed a false sense of complacency among the bowlers, while the batsmen were now worrying about flaws in technique that weren't really there. The conditions were simply not good enough for international cricket and the series was not the best advertisement for the game.

Warming up

There was no doubt I was not in the best physical shape when the team left for the World Cup in South Africa and Zimbabwe in February 2003. I was recovering from three injuries: the finger, the ankle and a strained hamstring. As a result, at our training camp in Paarl, in the Western Cape, I was not able to run with the team and spent my time cycling to keep up my cardio exercises. It was frustrating, but I knew I had to push myself to get back to fitness before the first match of the tournament against the Netherlands on 12 February.

The injury that bothered me most was the ankle. It had not fully healed and I had to strap it before every practice session and match. Strapping the ankle all the time became an ordeal and it started to frustrate me. So much so that one day I was careless when removing the strapping after training and suddenly felt a strange sensation in my hand. I was holding the strapping, which had a thick layer of my skin on it, which had come off my heel. The skin was stuck to the tape and I ended up putting it back because otherwise there would have to be a hole in a sensitive area of the foot. I know it sounds gruesome, but there was little else I could do in the circumstances. After that it was particularly painful when I had to go into the sea with the rest of the team as part of our recovery routine and the salty water would really sting. The incident at least taught me to be more careful about handling my injuries, however frustrating they might be.

We played two practice games, both against the KwaZulu-Natal side. While we batted reasonably in the first game on 4 February in Pietermaritzburg, with Yuvi and Dravid both doing well, the game on 6 February at Chatsworth didn't go according to plan. We managed to get the opposition out fairly cheaply, and I remember Sourav saying that, because we needed as much batting practice as possible, the opposition should bowl the full quota of fifty overs to us, even if we'd achieved the target. In fact, towards the end of the Natal innings we were all trying to give them some extra runs and Sourav kept close-in fielders in the ring to allow them to score freely, so that we would have a decent total to chase down. But in our reply we collapsed well before the fifty overs and the question of the opposition bowling the full quota never arose! We were all out for 158 and lost the match by 32 runs.

In both matches I had batted at number three, which was the

result of a decision that had been taken soon after we had reached South Africa. There had been a meeting of the senior players and the coach, and most of my team-mates, including Sourav, Rahul and Srinath, felt I should bat at number three in the competition. Only Anil suggested that I should open. The majority argument was that at the top of the order I might get a good ball early on and get out, which would end up putting the team under pressure. After the second practice game John Wright came to my room and asked me if I was really happy batting in the number three position. I assured him that I would bat anywhere the team wanted me to. John, however, insisted that I should voice my personal opinion as a player, so I said that, if it were up to me, I would prefer to open. I went on to say that I felt I could control the game from that position, and I also told him that there was no guarantee anyway that I wouldn't get out early if I was batting at number three or four, as it only takes one good ball. So I thought my best opportunity to set up the match for India was as an opener. John agreed with me and finally convinced Sourav and the rest of the team that having me at the top of the order was our best option.

The pool games

The less-than-impressive performances in our warm-up matches had made the first pool match on 12 February 2003, against the Netherlands, extremely important. We had to start well to give ourselves a fighting chance in the tournament. Even if the Netherlands were not the best opposition in the world, they had some good players in their team who had experience of playing on the county circuit in England. As I went out to bat, I was unusually nervous. The expectations in India were huge and the dressing room was also expecting a lot from me, now that they'd agreed to my wish to open the batting. I'd caused our plans to be changed completely and now it was up to me to deliver.

I was deliberately conservative in my approach at the start and set out to build a solid foundation before we went on the attack. We had been getting out for scores of 150 and less and it was important that we batted the full fifty overs and posted a reasonable total. I managed to score a half-century and, with Mongia contributing 42 runs down the order, we just passed the 200-run mark, making 204 all out. It wasn't a score to rave about and we knew that with one good innings from a Netherlands batsman we might have a contest on our hands. At the team meeting before the start of their innings we agreed that we should play as if we had to bowl the opposition out for 150, to force us to apply ourselves properly. Eventually, it was Srinath and Kumble, with four wickets each, who helped us achieve that aim as we bowled them out for 136. We had not played our best but had still managed to win.

Our next match was against defending champions Australia at Centurion on 15 February. They were playing excellent cricket and were firm favourites to win the tournament again. We played a very bad game from the start and lost a heap of early wickets. I scored 36 and we were bowled out for a very poor 125 and lost the game by nine wickets.

Our underwhelming performances in South Africa so far were not going down well with supporters at home and we heard that some irate fans had vented their fury that evening by throwing tar at Mohammad Kaif's home in Uttar Pradesh. It was alarming to read about the hostile reaction in India and I eventually had to issue a formal appeal, in the form of a media release, to try to pacify the fans. I stated that we were all trying our best and there was no dearth of commitment at our end. This had some effect and we were able to concentrate once again on the task at hand.

Stopping the rot

In 2003 Zimbabwe were a very good side in home conditions, and included some very talented players in their ranks. It was only after 2004–5, when the country was laid low by political turmoil, that many of these players stopped playing for Zimbabwe. In our pool game against them in Harare we played well from the start and won by 83 runs in the end. We could sense that we were getting back into form and it was surprising how one good win could boost a team's confidence. I scored 81 off ninety-one balls and Bhajji picked up the crucial wicket of Andy Flower, Zimbabwe's best batsman. Now we needed to carry this form forward, as we would soon be playing England in what was likely to be a crucial match for us, one that could guarantee a place in the Super Six.

Before the England match, however, we had to play Namibia on 23 February and it was important not to take it easy against a relatively weak team. We kept the pressure up and scored 311–2, with Sourav and me both scoring hundreds. Our bowlers then dismissed the opposition for 130, with Yuvraj Singh taking four wickets for six runs, and though not much could be read into our performance against a team like Namibia, it was apparent that things were moving in the right direction.

The build-up to the England game at Durban on 26 February was something else. England versus India is always a big game, but this time it was the World Cup and it was a must-win game for both teams. Apparently, Andrew Caddick said a number of things before the game and our players who read those statements were fired up on the eve of the match. I had not read them and to this day don't know exactly what was said. I had scored runs in all three matches so far and was simply looking forward to another opportunity.

We won a very important toss and decided to bat first. Batting under lights at Durban is always a challenge and winning the toss had given us the early advantage. Our plan was not to give away early wickets, even if we didn't score quickly. Once the first five or six overs had gone by we started shifting gear and looking for runs, passing 50 in no time. Durban always offers something for the fast bowlers and I knew that Caddick and the other tall England bowlers would look to exploit the extra bounce by bowling short of a length. I was ready for the short ball and it finally came in the ninth over of the innings when Caddick bowled one a foot and a half outside the off stump. It was exactly what I was waiting for and I swivelled back and hit him over midwicket for six. The moment the ball hit my bat I knew it was going the distance.

In his next over I played one of my favourite shots of the World Cup. I was hoping Caddick would over-compensate and bowl a fuller delivery, which he did. It wasn't a bad ball but I managed to play an off drive on the up, bisecting mid off and the bowler for four. The timing and impact felt wonderful. I hit two more boundaries in the same over and we raced to 75 off just eleven overs.

It was a dream start in a very big game and it took a great spell from Andrew Flintoff to bring England back into the match. He conceded just 15 off his ten overs and picked up two wickets. He caught and bowled Sehwag for 23 and then had me caught by Collingwood at point for 50. It was an extraordinary spell that undid our good start. At this point Yuvraj was getting increasingly restless in the dressing room and I remember saying to him that it had to be his day. It was now his responsibility to finish the innings off with a flourish and make sure that we did not squander the early advantage. Yuvraj and Rahul went on to bat beautifully to take us to 250 at the end of our innings, but we still felt we were 20 runs short.

The England innings started well for us with an incredible piece of fielding by Mohammad Kaif. Nick Knight, the left-handed opening batsman, had played the ball off the back foot and was running a quick single when Kaif swooped in from cover to pick up the ball and dived full-length to break the wicket. England were 6-1 and we had an early breakthrough. It was an excellent piece of athleticism from one of our best fielders.

We picked up Marcus Trescothick, the other opener, when he mistimed a pull off Zaheer and ended up giving me an easy catch at backward square. It was then that Ashish Nehra took over. It was easily the best I have seen Ashish bowl and he looked a man possessed that night in Durban. He was getting the ball to move both ways and was bowling at speeds between 140 and 145 kph, making it extremely difficult for the England batsmen to negotiate his pace and swing. It must be one of the best spells of fast bowling by an Indian bowler in a limited-over international. By the thirtieth over England were eight wickets down with more than 140 runs still required. Rahul, who was keeping wicket in that tournament, and Sehwag took some good catches off Ashish's bowling and the whole team was fired up. We could sense we were knocking on the door of the Super Six stage.

India eventually won the match by 82 runs. It was now a question of sustaining the momentum for the rest of the tournament. This time there were great celebrations back home and India were suddenly the team to beat in the competition. While Durban had set us on course, our next match against Pakistan was just massive. It was one of the most high-pressure cricket matches I have played in and had enormous significance for our fans back home. Without doubt it was the match of the World Cup.

Battlefield Centurion

The first time I heard people talking about the India–Pakistan fixture at Centurion Park on 1 March 2003 was exactly a year earlier, when some of my friends had been discussing it with great excitement. It was always going to be a huge game for both teams. The intensity was such that I could not sleep properly for three nights before the game. If there was ever a match we wanted to win, it was this one. The nation would brook no failure and for many of our fans this was the true final. It really did not matter to them what happened in the rest of the tournament, as long as we managed to beat Pakistan at Centurion.

The ground was buzzing hours before the match. It was sport at its best. This is why I played cricket, to be out in the middle for my team, on the world's biggest cricketing stage, against India's arch rival. Listening to the national anthem and singing the words gave me goose bumps.

Pakistan batted first after winning the toss and put together a very good score. Saeed Anwar held the innings together and made a very important hundred for his team. Their total of 273 was at least 20 runs more than we wanted to chase. As we were walking off the pitch, Sourav asked me if we should hold a brief team meeting. I said there was no need. Everybody knew what to do and it was now time to go out there and do the job.

During the break I hardly spoke to anyone at all. Nor did I eat much. In fact, for most of the time I had my headphones on and listened to music, trying to work myself into the right frame of mind. I just had a big bowl of ice cream and a banana to give myself some energy and asked one of the players to let me know as soon as the umpires had walked out to the middle. When they were in position, I picked up my bat and went out to start the run chase.

Generally it was Sehwag who took first strike, but this was a day with a difference. On the way out I told him that I would take strike and said that we needed to play out the initial burst from the Pakistani fast bowlers before we started attacking. Needless to say, Wasim Akram, Waqar Younis and Shoaib Akhtar were capable of doing a lot of early damage.

That's not how it turned out, however. In the very first over of our innings, I drove Wasim to the cover boundary. Then I took a single off the next ball and Sehwag scored a boundary off the final delivery. Shoaib Akhtar bowled the second over and in many ways it turned out to be the defining over of the match. His first ball to me was a wide. The next ball I played watchfully. I scored a single off the third ball and then he bowled another wide to Sehwag, which also allowed us to go through for a single. It was his sixth ball that allowed me to go after him. It was short and wide. I sighted the ball early and within a fraction of a second had made up my mind to go over third man. It wasn't exactly the upper cut but more of a hard slash over the third-man fielder that sailed over the boundary. Trying to compensate for the short ball, Shoaib bowled the next one on a length on the off stump and I shuffled across and flicked him behind square for four.

It was a dream start. We had shed our initial inhibition and had started to attack. Having already scored 10 off his last two balls, I was intent on playing the final ball of the over cautiously, so I just punched it back towards mid on. It was a defensive stroke, but the timing was such that it sped across the turf to the long-on boundary. We had scored 18 off the over.

Pakistan were obviously feeling the pressure when Waqar came on to bowl in the fourth over, giving Shoaib a break after one disastrous over. Sehwag launched Waqar's first ball for six over third man and we attacked him straight away. We were now egging each other on and were speaking to each other loudly in Hindi, which the Pakistanis could understand, of course. Our body language had turned aggressive and when I finished off the Waqar over with another four we were firmly in control. We had not allowed the bowlers to settle down and had seized the advantage. It was the best early assault against Pakistan that I had been involved in and it could not have come at a more important time. We reached 50 in just five overs and the target of 273 was no longer the huge mountain it had seemed at the start of our innings.

As with most India–Pakistan matches, however, there had to be a shift in momentum and against the run of play Pakistan picked up two wickets in Waqar's next over – first Sehwag and then Sourav with the very next ball. Pakistan were back in the match. Mohammad Kaif came in next and it was important for us to put together a partnership and also not to get bogged down. Kaif played well and ran hard between the wickets to make sure I had as much of the strike as possible. The run rate had not dipped and I reached my fifty with a scoring rate of over 150 for the innings.

This innings must rank as one of the best I have played because of the immense pressure it was played under. Each boundary brought me an ovation from the raucous crowd. Wearing the tricolour on my helmet on sport's biggest stage against the nation's premier opposition while being watched by close to a billion fans – what more could I have asked for? I just had to bat Pakistan out of the game.

It was in my seventies that I started cramping up. I received some treatment but refused to have a runner as I have always been uncomfortable with someone else running for me. My concentration was affected and much as I would have liked to power on, it wasn't possible. I eventually got out to a short ball from Shoaib Akhtar for 98. In that physical state I found it difficult to get up on my toes to keep the rising ball down. I walked back to a standing ovation.

Importantly, we still had a deficit of 96 runs and my innings would have little value if we lost a couple of quick wickets. There was no need to fear, as Rahul and Yuvraj took control and finished the match with almost five overs to spare. They both made half-centuries and India had won a famous contest, continuing our run of success against Pakistan in World Cups.

I felt very proud when I went out to receive the Man of the Match award, a watch. It was one for all our passionate fans back home. I called a number of my friends in India and was told that the country had erupted in celebrations. We were glad we could give our people such a moment to cherish.

Nobody wanted to call a halt to the celebrations in the dressing room, until finally the team decided to go out for something to eat, as we were all starving. It was close to midnight and we ended up going to a roadside stall for Chinese food. My friends Sunil Harshe and Sanjay Narang, there to cheer on the Indian team, also came along, and it was over our dinner of noodles that I decided to give Sanjay my Man of the Match watch to take back to Mumbai.

Some time later, after we had finished dinner and were on our way back to the hotel, Sanjay panicked. He told me that he had left the watch at the Chinese food stall. At first I thought he was joking, but he wasn't and he said he would never joke about something as precious as a World Cup Man of the Match award. He immediately called the stall and told them he had left his Adidas bag behind, saying that it contained his shoes rather than a gold watch. Then we rushed back and, to our enormous relief, the elderly lady who ran the stall handed over the bag with a smile.

The road to the final

Our next three matches were against Kenya, Sri Lanka and New Zealand and we won them all convincingly. India were playing fantastic cricket and we had started to believe that we could give Australia a run for their money, if we made the final. Here I am a bit embarrassed to reveal a very personal secret relating to the Sri Lanka match. On the eve of the match I had a bad stomach and was feeling dehydrated. This happened because I had not yet fully recovered from the cramps I had suffered while playing Pakistan and as a result had had a lot of isotonic drinks. I also added a teaspoon of salt to the energy drinks, thinking it would help the recovery, and that caused a tummy upset. In fact, the situation was so bad that I had to bat with tissues inside my underwear. I even had to go back to the dressing room during one of the drinks breaks and was feeling extremely uncomfortable in the middle. I somehow scored 97, but batting with stomach cramps wasn't a pleasant experience. I was pushing myself to the limits of endurance and in the end I was glad that the effort paid off.

India were now in the semi-final and we were drawn to play Kenya, who had caused a stir by beating a few of the top-ranked teams. In fact, during the match between Kenya and Sri Lanka, which we watched in the games room in our hotel, a rather odd thing happened. Every time we said something good about a Sri Lankan player, the player got out. It was strange and in no time Kenya had caused a huge upset.

We played our semi-final against Kenya at Durban and managed to win the match comfortably. Sourav and I had a very good partnership and the team managed 270 in our fifty overs before bowling the Kenyans out for 179. We were in the World Cup final, with eight straight wins behind us. The defeat to Australia in the qualifying rounds seemed a lifetime away. Now we were playing them in the final and we were convinced we had the team to stop them from winning back-to-back world titles.

So near and yet so far

Up till then, all of the players in the team had only watched others take part in a World Cup final. Now it was our turn. The excitement back home was extraordinary and a huge number of people had come to South Africa to cheer on the team. We had peaked at the right time and were playing some really good cricket. Naturally we were all determined to give our best in the final but perhaps we got ourselves too wound up. The evening before the final the team decided to spend some time in the pool. To our surprise, the water was freezing but that did not stop us from jumping in together. I didn't sleep well that night.

When we got to the ground the next morning, we immediately went over to take a look at the surface. It was apparent to us all that there was moisture in the pitch and, given it was a day game, the fast bowlers were sure to get some early assistance. It would not be a bad idea to field first if we won the toss. That's what we did, but the decision turned out to be a disaster, with Ricky Ponting playing one of the best one-day innings of all time, making 140. Australia scored a mammoth 359 in their fifty overs and had almost batted us out of the game.

In hindsight, I would still have opted to field. It was because we could not keep a lid on our excitement that we lost the plot early on. Zaheer conceded 15 runs in the first over and though we still felt we could make a comeback after that one bad over, it just didn't happen. Towards the concluding stages of their innings, every big shot that Ponting played made our task that much more difficult. In a final, every run scored after the total passes 300 is worth double and 358 was an intimidating target against a fantastic Australian bowling attack. In the team discussion at the interval we reckoned that we needed to hit one boundary every over and then score the remaining 160 runs in 250 balls. It was an attempt to be positive, as there was no other option left to us at that point.

I took first strike again and managed to score a four with a mistimed pull off McGrath. When I attempted a second pull shot I got a top edge and felt utterly dejected to see McGrath settle down under the ball to take the catch. In situations like those you can only pray that the ball falls in no man's land or that the fielder makes a mistake. It was not to be and I was on my way to the pavilion. While walking back, I kept asking myself why on earth I had played that shot. Maybe I should have given myself two or three overs to settle down, but the pressure of the chase was such that attack seemed the only option.

In the middle of the innings there was some light drizzle and it turned really dark. My thoughts went back to the South Africa series in January 1997 when rain had denied us victory. This time I was praying for rain and hoping that the match would be washed out, forcing a re-match the next day. We were not so lucky and were eventually all out for 234.

At the presentation it was difficult to watch the Australians celebrate while our own camp was feeling the pain of defeat. When my name was called to collect the Man of the Tournament award for the 673 runs I had scored, it didn't give me much excitement. I am not suggesting that I did not feel honoured or proud, but the feeling was overshadowed by the loss. Now we would have to wait four years before we could have another crack at the World Cup.

In my disappointment, I had not even noticed that the bat I was presented with as the Man of the Tournament was made of gold and I just stuffed it in my kitbag and checked it in as luggage on the way back. Only when people asked to see the bat after we landed in Mumbai did I realize it was gold and had been specially crafted. All I did on the flight back was sleep. Most of the players were still upset and were in no mood to talk. It would take a long time to get over the disappointment.

Looking back, the 2003 World Cup remains a bitter-sweet memory. We played some excellent cricket as a team and I contributed well in almost all of the matches – but not in the final. Beating England and Pakistan were unforgettable high points, but the World Cup trophy was still eluding me.

India in the 2003 World Cup

7th match. India v Netherlands at Paarl. 12 February 2003
India 204 (48.5/50 ov); Netherlands 136 (48.1/50 ov)
India won by 68 runs

11th match. Australia v India at Centurion. 15 February 2003
India 125 (41.4/50 ov); Australia 128–1 (22.2/50 ov)
Australia won by 9 wickets (with 166 balls remaining)

17th match. Zimbabwe v India at Harare. 19 February 2003
India 255–7 (50/50 ov); Zimbabwe 172 (44.4/50 ov)
India won by 83 runs

25th match. India v Namibia at Pietermaritzburg. 23 February 2003
India 311–2 (50/50 ov); Namibia 130 (42.3/50 ov)
India won by 181 runs

30th match. England v India at Durban. 26 February 2003
India 250–9 (50/50 ov); England 168 (45.3/50 ov)
India won by 82 runs

36th match. India v Pakistan at Centurion. 1 March 2003
Pakistan 273–7 (50/50 ov); India 276–4 (45.4/50 ov)
India won by 6 wickets (with 26 balls remaining)

2nd super. India v Kenya at Cape Town. 7 March 2003
Kenya 225–6 (50/50 ov); India 226–4 (47.5/50 ov)
India won by 6 wickets (with 13 balls remaining)

4th super. India v Sri Lanka at Johannesburg. 10 March 2003
India 292–6 (50/50 ov); Sri Lanka 109 (23/50 ov)
India won by 183 runs

7th super. India v New Zealand at Centurion. 14 March 2003
New Zealand 146 (45.1/50 ov); India 150–3 (40.4/50 ov)
India won by 7 wickets (with 56 balls remaining)

2nd semi-final. India v Kenya at Durban. 20 March 2003
India 270–4 (50/50 ov); Kenya 179 (46.2/50 ov)
India won by 91 runs

Final. Australia v India at Johannesburg. 23 March 2003
Australia 359–2 (50/50 ov); India 234 (39.2/50 ov)
Australia won by 125 runs

15

AWAY WINS

As soon as the World Cup was over I consulted a series of specialists and was advised to have an operation on the ring finger of my left hand because of calcification. There was no other option and in April 2003 I travelled to Baltimore, USA, with my family to get the surgery done. Dr Anant Joshi, as on many occasions in the past, was with me, and his reassuring presence, together with that of my friends Vini Desai and Paresh Bhakta, was always a great source of strength in moments like these.

The surgical process turned out to be slightly out of the ordinary because I was not the best patient. I was extremely worried that the doctors would cut open my palm. Cutting the palm would mean substantially altering my grip, which I really didn't want to do. I explained to both my surgeons the nuances of cricket and urged them to cut open the back of the hand. I was so obsessed with this issue that I woke up during the surgery and asked them to show me where they had made the incision. Dr Joshi later told me that they were all surprised to see me awake despite the anaesthesia. The doctors showed me that my palm had been left untouched and told me to calm down and allow them to carry on. Satisfied, I instantly drifted back to sleep.

The surgery kept me off the field for close to four months. There was not much cricket scheduled then and I missed only one tour, of Bangladesh, in the period I was out. The recovery was painful and, as often happens, I jarred the hand on a number of occasions during the period of convalescence. The one time I hurt it really badly was when I was holidaying in London in June 2003. Anjali and I went out for dinner and then took a taxi back to the hotel. While paying the taxi driver my finger got stuck in the glass of the window and I fell to the ground in severe pain. The taxi driver was alarmed but Anjali assured him that it was not his fault and told him to carry on. After a few painful minutes I finally managed to walk back to the hotel.

India in Australia, November 2003–February 2004

So far, 2003 had turned out to be a good year for Indian cricket. Making the World Cup final was something to be proud of, but there were still plenty of challenges ahead. We were due to play a Test series against the world champions in Australia at the end of the year and that tour was to be followed by one to Pakistan in early 2004.

Before leaving for Australia we played a one-day tri-series at home against Australia and New Zealand in October and November 2003. I was in good form and scored a couple of hundreds on the way to the final. Though we lost to Australia at Eden Gardens, I came away from it feeling confident of doing well in front of big Australian crowds.

Unfortunately my series Down Under started in the worst possible fashion at the Gabba on 4 December 2003. I lasted just three balls and was given out lbw to Jason Gillespie when the ball struck the top flap of my pad. I thought it would have gone over the stumps by six inches or more and I was disappointed to see the umpire raise his finger. Sourav and VVS Laxman managed to steady the ship, and Sourav, captaining India for the first time in Australia, duly played one of his finest Test innings. His 144 at Brisbane helped to set the tone for the series. At the end of the day's play he was ecstatic and had every reason to be so.

The first Test was drawn and we moved to Adelaide for the second Test on 12 December. The Adelaide wicket was good for batting and the Australians made the most of their opportunity. When they scored 400 runs on the first day, I clearly remember the Australian team standing up on the dressing-room balcony and cheering the batsmen off the field. Day two started better for us and, with Anil bowling beautifully, we managed to restrict Australia to 556 in their first innings. With the good batting conditions and a lot of time still left in the match, there was every chance we could make a contest of it if we batted well enough.

Rahul was outstanding and his double hundred helped us get close to the Australian first-innings total. Laxman too was majestic and it reminded us of the incredible partnership Rahul and Laxman had put together at Eden Gardens in March 2001, only this time the roles were reversed, with Rahul getting a double hundred and Laxman a hundred. I lasted just six balls before I was caught by Gilchrist off the fast bowler Andy Bichel. It was an annoyingly soft dismissal.

The Australian second innings belonged to Ajit Agarkar, my team-mate from Mumbai. He produced his best ever spell to set up the match for us. He took six Australian wickets for just 41 runs as we bowled the Australians out for 196, leaving us with 230 to chase. We fielded brilliantly in this innings and took some amazing catches, Aakash Chopra's catch of Ponting at point off Ajit being the stand-out. I chipped in with two crucial wickets, bowling leg-spin. Steve Waugh and Damien Martyn had put together a good partnership and it was immensely satisfying to be able to get both of them out caught in the slips. It was time for the batsmen to close out the game.

Rahul was yet again the star performer and I managed to contribute 37 before falling lbw to leg-spinner Stuart MacGill. We had put together a 70-run partnership at a critical time in the match, which was particularly satisfying. Rahul hit the winning runs for us, remaining unbeaten on 72, and the team was thrilled to have taken a 1–0 lead in the series. We stayed in the dressing room till late and thoroughly savoured the moment. Never in our history had we managed a 1–0 lead against Australia, in Australia. We had matched the Australians in every aspect of the game and had a very good chance of winning the series if we continued to play at our best. Rahul and Laxman were in imperious form; Sehwag and Sourav had made important contributions in both Tests; Aakash Chopra, our second opener, had done a good job of blunting the new ball.

On the eve of the next game – the Boxing Day Test in Melbourne – I decided to take Anjali, Sara and Arjun out onto the ground, just to give them a feel of what it is like to be inside a stadium. Standing in the middle of the MCG, they could imagine for themselves what we go through with more than 80,000 people in the stands. It was Arjun's first visit to a stadium.

We batted first after winning the toss on 26 December and Virender Sehwag played what must be one of the best Test innings ever seen at the MCG. He was in his attacking mode and played some strokes that only he can play. I have no doubt that Sehwag at the top of the order was one of the best things to happen to Indian cricket and he played a key role in leading us to the top of the world Test rankings in 2009. He really should have got a double hundred at the MCG, but was out for 195 hitting a Stuart MacGill full toss to long on.

The rest of the batsmen unfortunately failed to capitalize on the start Sehwag and Aakash Chopra had given us and we were all out for 366, allowing Australia back into the game. I faced only one ball, getting a faint tickle down the leg side to Gilchrist, who was standing way back to Brett Lee. I turned around to see the ball travelling to Gilchrist and knew that it was the end of me. That is one of the worst ways of getting out and I felt embarrassed. I felt even worse when I was told that Anjali had come to the MCG to watch after being persuaded by some of the other players' wives. I heard that she left the ground the moment I was out and walked all the way back to the hotel. I couldn't help reflecting on the occasionally cruel and unpredictable nature of our much-loved game.

Australia responded impressively, playing brilliantly in their first innings and, with Ponting scoring 257 and Hayden 136, effectively batted us out of the game with their 558 total. Close to 200 runs behind, we would have to bat exceptionally well to save the match. We did not, and the series was 1–1 with one Test to play.

Once again, I did not make the contribution I had hoped for in the second innings at the MCG. To change things a bit, I asked Sourav what he thought about batting ahead of me. It was towards the end of the third day's play and Sourav, who was in good form, agreed to step up, allowing me the cushion of going in to bat the following morning at number five. The ploy seemed to work and all was going well until I got out for 44, caught by Gilchrist off the fast bowler Brad Williams. I had been in control until I played one false shot, the feature of my batting in the series. It seemed that every time I tried to move up a gear, I lost my wicket.

It all comes down to Sydney

On the eve of the fourth and final Test match in Sydney at the beginning of January 2004, John Wright came to my room to try to get me to think positively and boost my confidence, which was a great help. I had also had a long conversation with Ajit, and one challenge he put in front of me was to try to remain not out in both innings. He said that I was allowing myself to get out to bowlers, rather than making them have to take my wicket, and that if I decided to rein myself in, no bowler would be able to get me out. I took up the challenge and decided to play a waiting game. Even if I looked ugly in the middle I was intent on sticking to my plan. Having got out twice in the series playing aggressive shots, I was simply not going to try anything extravagant at the SCG. True to my promise, I played what was in some ways one of my most difficult Test innings. I consciously checked my shots and was determined not to get out. In more than ten hours at the crease I did not play a single cover drive. When the Australian bowlers cracked a few jokes at my expense,

I remained focused. It was a real test. Even when balls were there for the drive, I let them go. It was all totally against my natural instincts and it left me drained but immensely satisfied. At the end of our first innings, I was not out on 241 and had taken the team score past 700.

When I think about this Test, I can't help remembering that for some reason I turned unusually superstitious. Anjali, her parents, Sara and Arjun were with me on the eve of the match and we decided to go to a Malaysian restaurant for dinner. The food was excellent and we ended up ordering noodles, chicken and a host of other dishes. My family then left for India the next morning, but I had a very good first day and was unbeaten on 73. In the evening I decided to stick to the routine of the previous night and went to the same Malaysian restaurant, this time with Ajit Agarkar and a couple of other players. Not only did we sit at the same table, but I had exactly the same food. The next day went even better and I was not out on 220. That night, I again went to the same restaurant and occupied the same table and ate the same food. On the third day of the match, with the Test match going really well for us, we went to the same restaurant one final time. The restaurant manager must have thought we were mad. At the same time he must have been elated at the thought that we had returned because of the food. Little did he know the real reason for our fourth consecutive visit!

After my double century, I was sent to address the media. A local journalist said that I had been getting a lot of flak in the press recently but, now that I had scored an unbeaten double hundred, would I be reading the papers the following morning? All I said to him was that I had not read anything during the series – which was my way of keeping myself insulated from all the hype – and I was not aware of what they had written about me. I didn't have a problem with getting flak if I had not performed. The media needed to do its job, after all. But I was not looking forward to reading the papers just because I had scored some runs

– I did not need validation from the media. Criticism and praise are two sides of the same coin and, having played international cricket for fifteen years, I had learnt to take these things in my stride.

We backed up the first-innings batting performance with a very good bowling effort and dismissed Australia for 474, with Anil taking a remarkable 8–141. We were ahead by 231 and now we needed quick runs to give our bowlers time to close out the match. Yet again we batted well and Rahul and I were in the middle of a good partnership when Sourav sent two or three messages out to check when we should declare. Rahul was the vice captain of the team and I said to him that it was his decision as much as Sourav's. I was ready to go off whenever they wanted. Rahul was keen to bat on for a little longer and we finally declared just after he was hit on the head by a Brett Lee bouncer when he was on 91 and I was on 60 not out. In hindsight I must say we delayed the declaration too long. The ball was turning and bouncing, and we should have given Anil and the bowlers a few more overs on the fourth evening than the four they eventually bowled.

Set 443 to win, Australia were under pressure throughout their second innings. Anil bowled a marathon spell of forty-two overs, picking up four more wickets on the fifth day. In his final innings in Test cricket Steve Waugh played well to save his team some blushes. He was eventually out for 80, caught by me at deep square leg off Anil. The crowd was desperate for a final Steve Waugh hundred but it didn't work out that way. Straight after taking the catch, I ran over to Steve and congratulated him on a fantastic career and wished him all the best for his future endeavours as he received a standing ovation from the Sydney crowd.

Australia held on for a draw and the series finally ended 1–1. Personally, it had been a great Test match for me and I was satisfied at having kept my promise to Ajit not to get out in both innings. It had been extremely difficult to go against my natural instincts. But it was a series we really should have won. We were the better team for most of it and had played exceptional cricket in patches. Had the declaration on the fourth evening come a little earlier, and had we grabbed more of the chances that came our way, we might have made history. Despite missing out on a series win, we still had reason to be happy and were looking forward to the tour of Pakistan that was just round the corner.

India in Pakistan, March–April 2004

There was a lot of excitement about our tour to Pakistan. Playing Pakistan is always a big occasion for an Indian cricketer, and this was the first time we had played them in Pakistan since my debut series in 1989. The tour also seemed to have come at the best possible time for India; we had done well in the series Down Under and most of the players were in good form.

As soon as we landed in Pakistan we realized just how different this tour would be. Unlike the first time, when I was just sixteen, in 2004 I understood the full significance of an India–Pakistan series. The security was simply unbelievable. We were whisked through immigration and on our way to the hotel we had a security vehicle ahead of the team bus. There were also bikes escorting the bus and we even had a chopper flying above us. In the hotel we were received warmly and given instructions about the security protocols we were expected to follow. We were informed that the first room on our floor was to be occupied by security personnel, who would check every visitor who came to the floor. The floors above and below us had been sealed off. I had not experienced security like that before and it was a very strange feeling, because we were just sportsmen who had come to Pakistan to play cricket.

Leaving the hotel wasn't an option and this meant the players spent a lot of time in each other's rooms having dinner, playing cards and watching movies. It was always fun to be able to spend time together and the spirit of the team was excellent as we prepared for the first one-day international in Karachi on 13 March 2004.

It was the best possible start to the series, with the match decided on the very last ball. After we had scored 349 batting first, Pakistan responded well but came up short, with 344 in their fifty overs. Unfortunately, we lost the next two matches, but we did well to come back with victories in the final two games, winning the series 3–2. The final match was a thriller and we beat Pakistan by 40 runs in the end. I have fond memories of this match, having taken a very good catch to dismiss the Pakistan captain Inzamam-ul-Haq. In this series Inzamam would invariably try and hit the slow bowlers straight back over the bowler's head, so before the fifth ODI Murali Kartik and I made a plan for him. We agreed that I would stand far straighter than normal at long on and would be ready to move towards the sightscreen the moment Inzamam was on strike. Sure enough, he hit Kartik straight back over his head and I was ready for the opportunity. I caught the ball above my head just inches from the boundary rope and then sprinted towards my team-mates in the middle, knowing we had managed to prise out the most important Pakistan wicket. In the end it was a terrific result and it gave us tremendous confidence ahead of the first Test at Multan.

Australia v India

(4th Test)

Played at Sydney Cricket Ground, Sydney, on 2–6 January 2004

Umpires: BF Bowden & SA Bucknor (TV: PD Parker)
Referee: MJ Procter
Toss: India

INDIA

AS Chopra	b Lee	45	c Martyn b Gillespie		2
V Sehwag	c Gilchrist b Gillespie	72	c Gillespie b MacGill		47
RS Dravid	lbw b Gillespie	38	not out		91
SR Tendulkar	not out	241	not out		60
VVS Laxman	b Gillespie	178			
SC Ganguly*	b Lee	16			
PA Patel†	c Gilchrist b Lee	62			
AB Agarkar	b Lee	2			
IK Pathan	not out	13			
A Kumble					
M Kartik					
Extras	(b 4, lb 5, w 4, nb 25)	38	(lb 3, w 1, nb 7)		11
Total	(for 7 wkts dec)	**705**	(for 2 wkts dec) (43.2 overs)		**211**

AUSTRALIA

JL Langer	c Patel b Kumble	117	c Sehwag b Kartik		47
ML Hayden	c Ganguly b Kumble	67	c Dravid b Kumble		30
RT Ponting	lbw b Kumble	25	c and b Pathan		47
DR Martyn	c and b Kumble	7	c sub (Yuvraj Singh) b Kumble		40
SR Waugh*	c Patel b Pathan	40	c Tendulkar b Kumble		80
SM Katich	c Sehwag b Kumble	125	not out		77
AC Gilchrist†	b Pathan	6	st Patel b Kumble		4
B Lee	c Chopra b Kumble	0			
JN Gillespie	st Patel b Kumble	47	(8) not out		4
NW Bracken	c Agarkar b Kumble	2			
SCG MacGill	not out	0			
Extras	(b 6, lb 9, w 3, nb 20)	38	(b 6, lb 7, w 2, nb 13)		28
Total	(117.5 overs)	**474**	(for 6 wkts) (94 overs)		**357**

AUSTRALIA	O	M	R	W		O	M	R	W	Fall of wickets:				
Lee	39.3	5	201	4		12.2	2	75	0		Ind	Aus	Ind	Aus
Gillespie	45	11	135	3		7	2	32	1	1st	123	147	11	75
Bracken	37	13	97	0	(4)	8	0	36	0	2nd	128	214	73	92
MacGill	38	5	146	0	(3)	16	1	65	1	3rd	194	229	–	170
Waugh	2	0	6	0						4th	547	261	–	196
Katich	17	1	84	0						5th	570	311	–	338
Martyn	9	1	27	0						6th	671	341	–	342
										7th	678	350	–	–
INDIA	O	M	R	W		O	M	R	W	8th	–	467	–	–
Agarkar	25	3	116	0		10	2	45	0	9th	–	473	–	–
Pathan	26	3	80	2	(3)	8	1	26	1	10th	–	474	–	–
Kumble	46.5	7	141	8	(2)	42	8	138	4					
Kartik	19	1	122	0		26	5	89	1					
Ganguly	1	1	0	0										
Tendulkar					(5)	6	0	36	0					
Sehwag					(6)	2	0	10	0					

Close of play: Day 1:   Ind (1) 284–3 (Tendulkar 73*, Laxman 29*, 90 overs)
                     Day 2:   Ind (1) 650–5 (Tendulkar 220*, Patel 45*, 180 overs)
                     Day 3:   Aus (1) 342–6 (Katich 51*, Lee 0*, 80 overs)
                     Day 4:   Aus (2) 10–0 (Langer 4*, Hayden 1*, 4 overs)

Man of the Match: SR Tendulkar
Result: **Match drawn**

First Test, Multan, 28 March–1 April 2004

At Multan, Virender Sehwag played a blinder. We won the toss and from the word go he was in control. He played some outstanding shots and his innings had the effect of demoralizing the opposition on the very first day of the series. He flayed the Pakistani bowlers to all parts of the ground and by the time I joined him in the middle he was already well past his century.

I remember that just after tea Sehwag seemed to lose concentration. He began trying to hit every ball and looked a bit agitated. I walked up to him to calm him down and told him that he just needed to hang in there and let this spell pass. I also said to him that he should check himself a bit, as something big was about to happen. It was important to grab this opportunity and not let it slip away. I was glad to see him grind it out on his way to a double hundred. As soon as he reached the milestone, he was back in his groove and the shots started to flow again. I was even more delighted when he managed to get to a triple hundred on the second morning. It was an incredible effort and coming against Pakistan made it all the more special.

By the time Sehwag reached that landmark, I had made a century. I had paced my innings nicely and we were now firmly in the driver's seat. At teatime I asked stand-in skipper Rahul Dravid, who was in charge because Sourav was out with a back injury, and coach John Wright what the plan was. I was informed that we were looking to give Pakistan an hour to bat and so would put them in with fifteen overs left on the second day.

It was perfectly sensible and I went about my business after tea with this plan in mind. In fact, I was pacing my innings so that I could reach my double hundred and we could still give Pakistan fifteen overs to bat, as was the plan. But then, a little more than half an hour into the post-tea session, Ramesh Powar, who was substituting in the game, came onto the field and asked me to accelerate. I even joked with him, saying I was aware that we needed quick runs but with the field totally spread out, there was only so much we could do.

A little later, when I was on 194, he came out again and said that I should try and get to my double hundred in that over itself because Rahul had decided to declare. I was startled, to say the least, because in my mind I still had twelve balls in which to score the remaining six runs before fifteen overs were left for the day. However, as it happened, I did not get to play a single ball in that over, with Yuvraj on strike against Imran Farhat, Pakistan's opening batsman and part-time leg-spinner. He blocked the first two balls before picking up two runs off the third ball. He once again blocked the fourth ball and was out to the fifth ball. Then, just as Parthiv Patel, the next batsman, started to come out, I saw Rahul gesturing us to go back to the pavilion. He had declared the innings with me stranded on 194 and with sixteen overs still left for the day, one more than we had agreed at tea. I was shocked, as it did not make any sense. It was day two of the Test match and not day four, as it had been in Sydney a month earlier.

Disappointed and upset, I made my way back to the dressing room and could sense that the whole team was surprised at the decision. Some of my team-mates perhaps expected me to throw my gear about in the dressing room in disgust and create a scene. However, such things are not in me and I decided not to say a word to anyone about the incident. I calmly put my batting gear away and asked John Wright for a little time before I went out to field because I was feeling a little tight after batting for so long. Inside I was fuming.

Just as I was washing my face in the bathroom, John walked up to me and apologized. He was sorry about what had happened and said he had not been party to the decision. I was surprised and said to him that as coach he was one of the decision-makers and there was no reason for him to be sorry if he believed in what had been done. I also said that what was done could not be reversed and it was best to leave it alone. Finally, I couldn't help reminding him that the declaration was contrary to what had been discussed at tea and it was strange that I was not given even one ball to get to my double hundred after a message had been sent out asking me to get there as quickly as possible.

Soon after my exchange with John, Sourav came up to me and said he was very sorry at what had happened and that it wasn't his decision to declare. This was a little surprising because Sourav, as the skipper, was part of the teatime discussion and was also present in the dressing room at the time of the declaration. I said to him there was no point going over it any more.

At the end of the day's play I was asked by the press if I was disappointed by the declaration and I had no reason to shy away from the truth. Soon after the press conference I put my headphones on and listened to music all the way back to the hotel. Then I hit the gym to work out my frustration. Some of the Pakistan players were also in the gym but none of them spoke to me, sensing the state of mind I was in. I worked myself hard, trying to get the declaration out of my mind, then headed up to my room for some time alone.

In the evening Professor Ratnakar Shetty, our manager, came to my room for a chat. I had known Professor Shetty since I was a youngster in Mumbai. He apologized for what had happened and said he did not agree with the declaration. However, it was a cricketing decision and he did not ever interfere with cricketing decisions as manager. I assured him that it was over and done with and would not affect my contribution to the team.

It was when I was talking to Professor Shetty that Sanjay Manjrekar, who was in Pakistan as a commentator, turned up in my room. Sanjay said that it had been a brave decision to declare and that it was a good sign for Indian cricket. He carried on in that vein until I asked him if he really knew what he was talking about. I explained to him that he was not aware of what had transpired in the dressing room and had arrived at his judgement without knowing the real facts of the matter. I made it clear that

I did not appreciate his opinion, which I thought was a deliberate attempt to be different.

The following morning, Rahul finally came to me and said he had heard that I was upset and wanted to have a chat. I informed him that I was indeed upset and there was no way I would pretend otherwise. I asked him what the thinking was behind declaring at the time that he did. It wasn't as if we were pressing for a win, and one over wouldn't have made much difference. We had agreed to a plan at tea and I was doing exactly as I had been told.

Rahul said that the call was taken with the interests of the team in mind. It was important to demonstrate to the Pakistanis that we meant business and were keen to win. I wasn't convinced. First, I said to him that I was batting for the team as well. Yes, I had scored 194, but the 194 was meant to help the team and it was my individual contribution to the team's cause. So to say that the decision was taken in the best interests of the team wasn't altogether correct.

I reminded him of what had happened in Sydney less than a month earlier, when we had both been batting on the fourth evening and Sourav had sent out two or three messages asking when we should declare and Rahul had carried on batting. The two situations were comparable and, if anything, the Sydney declaration was far more significant and may have cost us a Test match and series victory. If Rahul was so keen to show intent here in Multan, he should have done the same in Sydney.

Rahul didn't say anything to this and stated that I would surely get another opportunity to score a double hundred. I disagreed, saying it would not be the same. I would have to bat from zero to score a double century and would not be starting my innings at 194. Before I brought the conversation to a close, I assured Rahul that the incident would have no bearing on my involvement on the field, but off the field I would prefer to be left alone for a while to come to terms with what had happened.

Despite this incident, I am glad to say Rahul and I remain

good friends, and even on the field our camaraderie remained intact until the end of our careers. We continued to have some good partnerships and neither our cricket nor our friendship was affected.

Learning from history

A very similar situation arose a few years later, in December 2008, when we were playing England at Mohali. It was the last day of the Test match and Gautam Gambhir and Yuvraj were both in the seventies. Yet again there was talk of a possible declaration in the dressing room. It was being argued that we needed to declare immediately and put the English in for some thirty overs so that we could try and force a win.

I intervened and stopped the declaration. Dhoni was our captain then and Gary Kirsten our coach. I said that I had been in this situation before and did not want a repeat of what had happened to me. There was no way we could win the game by putting the English in after lunch. There was not enough time – particularly because on each day so far, play had finished early because the light in Mohali did not last long and the last day was expected to be no different. In such a situation, what was the point of declaring and depriving the two batsmen of the chance to get their hundreds? Gautam had already scored one in the first innings, so he had a rare opportunity to make a hundred in each innings. Yuvraj, on the other hand, had played a key role in winning us the first Test at Chennai and it was only fair to give him the chance of a Test hundred.

Finally, I said it was our responsibility to look after the interests of all individuals who were part of the team, because a bunch of happy individuals make a happy team. I wasn't suggesting that we should place individual interest ahead of team interest. However, in a situation where there was no chance of winning the match, it was essential to give both batsmen a chance to get their hundreds. I convinced Gary that it was the right thing to do for the team and was glad that he agreed with me.

Unfortunately, however, both Yuvraj and Gautam missed their hundreds. Yuvi was run out for 86 and then Gautam was out for 97, which was when we finally declared the innings at 251–7. Soon afterwards, I joked with Yuvraj and Gautam, complaining that I had delayed the declaration for them both and yet they had not scored their hundreds. In fun, I said to Yuvraj, *'Tumhe main ek laath doonga. Maine tumhare liye declaration roka, aur tum 86 par run out ho kar aa gaye!'* (I will kick you. I stopped the declaration for you and you got run out for 86!)

A series win to remember

In the end it took us just thirty minutes on the final day to wrap up that first Test at Multan in 2004. Before that I had had a part to play with the ball against Pakistan wicketkeeper Moin Khan. I had dismissed Moin before in exhibition games and started playing mind games with him, telling one of my teammates, *'Main ise pehle bhi out kar chuka hoon. Aaj bhi main isko out karunga.'* (I have dismissed him before and today also I will get him out.) Moin heard the conversation and smiled at me, saying, *'Aaj toh main tujhe chhakka marunga.'* (Today I will hit you for six.) I told him that I promised to flight the ball, so *'Chalo mar ke dikhao.'* (Come on, try and hit me.) Then I shouted to my teammates to give Abdul Razzaq a single and get Moin back on strike. For the last ball of the day, I decided to bowl him a googly, because he was trying to pad up to every delivery. The ball pitched on off stump, turned exactly as I had hoped and went through his legs to hit leg stump. It was a key wicket and helped to swing the momentum in our direction. In the second Test at Lahore, however, we were outplayed. Though Yuvi scored a very good hundred for us, we were always playing catch-up and were never in the contest.

The third and deciding Test at Rawalpindi started on 13 April. Sourav was back in the side and to maintain balance we decided to open with Parthiv. Lakshmipathy Balaji and Irfan Pathan, our two swing bowlers, bowled very well throughout the series and this match was no different. Balaji picked up four wickets and we restricted Pakistan to 224 in the first innings. Then, with Rahul leading the way with a spectacular double hundred, we put 600 on the board in reply.

This time Pakistan had been outplayed and we finished the formalities on day four by bowling them out for 245. Anil took four wickets and I took the tenth and final wicket of the innings bowling leg-spin. Though the match was over on the fourth day, it was not without drama or embarrassment. That morning we spilled four catches, one after the other. They weren't difficult and we all seemed to be dropping the ball like a hot potato.

It was a terrific series win and our first in Pakistan in fifty years. Coming on the back of the 3–2 ODI series win, it marked the end of a brilliant tour.

India in Australia 2003–04 – The Border-Gavaskar Trophy

1st Test. Brisbane. 4–8 December 2003
Australia 323 (JL Langer 121, RT Ponting 54; Z Khan 5–95, AB Agarkar 3–90) and 284–3 dec (ML Hayden 99, DR Martyn 66*, SR Waugh 56*, RT Ponting 50)
India 409 (SC Ganguly 144, VVS Laxman 75, **SR Tendulkar 0**; JN Gillespie 4–65, SCG MacGill 4–86) and 73–2 (R Dravid 43*; NW Bracken 2–12)
Match drawn

2nd Test. Adelaide. 12–16 December 2003
Australia 556 (RT Ponting 242, SM Katich 75, JL Langer 58; A Kumble 5–154) and 196 (AC Gilchrist 43, SR Waugh 42; AB Agarkar 6–41, **SR Tendulkar 2–36**)
India 523 (R Dravid 233, VVS Laxman 148, V Sehwag 47, **SR Tendulkar 1**; AJ Bichel 4–118) and 233–6 (R Dravid 72*, V Sehwag 47, **SR Tendulkar 37**; SCG MacGill 2–101)
India won by 4 wickets

3rd Test. Melbourne. 26–30 December 2003

India 366 (V Sehwag 195, R Dravid 49, A Chopra 48, **SR Tendulkar 0**;
SCG MacGill 3–70) and 286 (R Dravid 92, SC Ganguly 73, **SR Tendulkar
44**; BA Williams 4–53)

Australia 558 (RT Ponting 257, ML Hayden 136; A Kumble 6–176,
SR Tendulkar 1–57) and 97–1 (ML Hayden 53*, RT Ponting 31*)

Australia won by 9 wickets

4th Test. Sydney. 2–6 January 2004

India 705–7 dec (**SR Tendulkar 241***, VVS Laxman 178, V Sehwag 72,
PA Patel 62; B Lee 4–201, JN Gillespie 3–135) and 211–2 dec (R Dravid 91*,
SR Tendulkar 60*, V Sehwag 47)

Australia 474 (SM Katich 125, JL Langer 117, ML Hayden 67; A Kumble
8–141) and 357–6 (SR Waugh 80, SM Katich 77*; A Kumble 4–138)

Match drawn

Series drawn 1–1

India in Pakistan 2004

1st Test. Multan. 28 March–1 April 2004

India 675–5 dec (V Sehwag 309, **SR Tendulkar 194**, Y Singh 59; M Sami
2–110)

Pakistan 407 (Y Hameed 91, Inzamam-ul-Haq 77, A Razzaq 47; IK Pathan
4–100, **SR Tendulkar 2–36**) and 216 (f/o) (Y Youhana 112; A Kumble 6–72,
IK Pathan 2–26)

India won by an innings and 52 runs

2nd Test. Lahore. 5–8 April 2004

India 287 (Y Singh 112, IK Pathan 49, **SR Tendulkar 2**; Umar Gul 5–31) and
241 (V Sehwag 90, PA Patel 62*, **SR Tendulkar 8**; D Kaneria 3–14, S Akhtar
3–62)

Pakistan 489 (Inzamam-ul-Haq 118, I Farhat 101, A Kamal 73, Y Youhana 72;
L Balaji 3–81, IK Pathan 3–107, **SR Tendulkar 1–38**) and 40–1

Pakistan won by 9 wickets

3rd Test. Rawalpindi. 13–16 April 2004

Pakistan 224 (M Sami 49; L Balaji 4–63, IK Pathan 2–49, A Nehra 2–60)
and 245 (A Kamal 60*, Y Youhana 48; A Kumble 4–47, L Balaji 3–108,
SR Tendulkar 1–1)

India 600 (R Dravid 270, SC Ganguly 77, VVS Laxman 71, PA Patel 69,
SR Tendulkar 1; S Akhtar 3–47)

India won by an innings and 131 runs

India won the series 2–1

16

UNDER THE KNIFE

It started in Amsterdam, of all places. It was just another net session before the Videocon Cup tri-series involving Australia and Pakistan towards the end of August 2004. Ajit Agarkar was bowling to me and bowled a short one, which I fended off with one hand. I instantly realized I had done something to my elbow. Andrew Leipus, our physio, didn't like the look of it at all. It turns out he was right to be concerned.

It was an unfortunate situation because my in-laws had travelled to Amsterdam with their friends from London to see me play and here I was nursing what was later diagnosed as tennis elbow. To complicate matters, I also had a virus and for a good three days couldn't set foot outside my hotel room. I was desperate to get back in shape as quickly as possible because the ICC Champions Trophy in England started in September and in October Australia were due to arrive in India for a four-Test series.

I did all I could to get the elbow injury treated. An expert in Amsterdam tried to help it by manipulating my wrist. He suspected the elbow was being overloaded because of stiffness in my wrist, but unfortunately those painful sessions didn't help much. Then I tried shockwave therapy, which involved a machine that looked like a hairdryer being placed on my elbow. The feeling reminded me of inflating a balloon and at one point I thought my elbow was going to burst under the pressure.

Anjali was about to join me in England and I called her to say she should bring a video camera along. I remember telling her that she would never see me in more physical pain, and we videoed one of the sessions to keep a record of what I had to go through. I was due to undergo three sessions but I urged the doctor to administer a fourth one if he thought it would help me get fit quicker. Anjali's presence had given me the courage to press on with the recovery and I was desperate to get fit, particularly for the Test series against Australia. Seeing my desperation, one of the doctors asked me how important that series was for me and why I was so determined to play. I said that it would be like missing my own wedding reception and there was no way I would want to do that!

Despite all my efforts, I was in no condition to take part in the Champions Trophy and I also had to miss the first two Tests against Australia. It was extremely frustrating to be forced to sit out and watch Clarke and Gilchrist score centuries to set up a 217-run victory for Australia in the first Test at Bangalore, despite eleven wickets in the game for Harbhajan Singh. I even had a steroid injection on the eve of the second Test match in Chennai, but it didn't work. The Chennai Test was a draw and then finally, after two weeks of complete rest, the pain had subsided enough for me to return for the third Test at Nagpur on 26 October 2004. It wasn't the greatest comeback match. On a seaming pitch, Gillespie took nine wickets and Damien Martyn just missed out on a century in both innings, as Australia won by 342 runs. My contribution was a disappointing total of ten runs.

In the final Test at the Wankhede Stadium the following week, Rahul and I were at the crease in the second innings when all of a sudden I felt a searing pain in my elbow again. It was at a critical stage in a low-scoring match and I was worried that I had rushed the comeback and was going to let my team down. I immediately asked for some painkillers and, thinking to myself that it would have an instant effect, decided to chew the two tablets rather than gulping them down. Gritting my teeth, I dug in and managed to battle my way to 55. With Laxman scoring a brilliant 69, we set Australia a target of 107 in the fourth innings. Helped by another five-wicket haul from Harbhajan and three from the left-arm spinner Murali Kartik, who was the Player of the Match, we proceeded to bowl Australia out for just 93 and won the match by 13 runs. The pain was definitely worth it. Unfortunately for Kartik, he did not get another chance to play Test cricket for India after that.

We followed the Australia series with two home Tests against South Africa in November 2004. The first at Kanpur was a draw, but the second at Kolkata, starting on 28 November, brought a very satisfying victory, with Bhajji proving a match-winner again, this time taking seven wickets in the South African second innings.

Even though I was still not fully fit, my contribution was gradually improving and by the time of the first match in a two-Test series in Bangladesh in December, I was in good enough form to make my highest Test score – 248 not out – at Dhaka. It was also my thirty-fourth Test hundred, equalling Sunil Gavaskar's world-record tally. He was actually commentating in Bangladesh at the time and he graciously sent me a fabulous gift of thirty-four bottles of champagne to make it a truly memorable day in my career.

The elbow surgery

In March 2005 Pakistan were scheduled to visit us at home for three Tests and seven ODIs. It was a tour I really did not want to miss and I pushed myself as hard as I could, trying to ignore the soreness, but I eventually realized that I was struggling for form and I wasn't doing my elbow any good. It was time to face the prospect of surgery, something I'd hoped to avoid.

The procedure was carried out on 25 May 2005 and I was told it would be four and a half months before I could hold a cricket bat. Those months were extremely difficult. I couldn't help worrying that my career might be over and would often pray to God that my career should not come to an end like this. It was very frustrating not doing anything and at one point I hung a ball in a sock below our apartment and tried doing some shadow practice with a plastic bat, but even that was really painful. The last two months were the hardest. I could barely sleep and would have to go out for long drives in the middle of the night with my friend Faisal Momen just to try and calm down a little.

The first games I played after the surgery were in a domestic competition, the limited-overs Challenger Trophy in Mohali in October 2005. The elbow was not completely back to normal but I felt it was time to try it out. On my very first day of practice I experienced some pain in my shoulder after a throw. Here I was recovering from surgery on my left elbow and now my right shoulder was hurting. I put it down to my prolonged absence from the game and went ahead with the games, but the pain increased with each passing day and I even started having problems with my right elbow.

I was in Baroda when I got to know that my surgeon, Dr Andrew Wallace, was in Delhi for a day. However, with no flight connections to Delhi from where I was, I was beginning to get worried about how to get to him before he left. That's when my good friend Amit Bhatia stepped in. Amit, who is an ardent cricket fan, gave me a ride in his private jet and made sure I reached Dr Wallace in good time. On examining my shoulder, Dr Wallace said that during rehabilitation athletes often put too much load on the non-injured limbs to compensate and it was likely that's what had happened to me. He asked me to have a few scans, to figure out the nature of the problem. I did not want to fuel more speculation in the media about my injury, so when I went to get the scans done, I resorted to wearing a burkha, which shows how difficult things were at the time! John Gloster, our new physio, accompanied me to the hospital and the scans revealed a small cyst next to a nerve. I was told I needed to get it removed as soon as possible, though I could play on for the moment.

My return to international cricket finally happened on 25 October 2005 in the first ODI of a series against Sri Lanka. It was a truly emotional moment when I took the field after six months out and the first thing I did was to look up to the heavens and thank God for giving me another opportunity. I scored 93 and this time it was exactly the sort of comeback I had hoped for. My first scoring shot was a cover drive for four against the medium-pacer Farveez Maharoof and I flicked the next ball to square leg for another boundary. I was determined to make the most of this lifeline. We won the match by 152 runs and went on to take the series 6–1.

In the three-Test series that followed in December 2005 I scored my thirty-fifth Test century, making the world record my own. The hundred had eluded me for a while and at Chennai, the venue for the first Test, I was beginning to wonder how long I would have to wait. Though most of the drawn Chennai Test was lost to rain, something happened there that put me in good spirits: I had a dream in which I saw myself scoring the thirty-fifth hundred in Delhi, the venue of the second Test.

I didn't really expect it to work out that way, of course, but then towards the end of 10 December, the very first day of the Delhi Test, I found myself in the nineties as the light began to fade rapidly. The umpires were discussing whether to stop play, but I was desperate to stay out there and was praying that they would continue the match for just another few minutes. They did so and Chaminda Vaas, the left-arm fast-medium bowler, was put on to bowl. Vaas was bowling wide of my off stump with a packed off-side field and I knew I had to try something different. I decided to play a chip shot behind the wicket from way outside off stump, a shot no one would expect me to play just a few runs short of my century. I got it just right and to everyone's surprise reached 97 with a well-calculated risk.

The umpires checked the light again at the end of the over and to my relief decided to carry on. I knew I had at least a few more minutes to get to the hundred. In the next over from Vaas, by which time I had picked up two more singles, I had already made up my mind not to repeat the shot. I predicted that Vaas would be expecting me to paddle-sweep and would change his line and bowl to me on the stumps. I was proved right and he bowled a ball on middle stump which I played towards square leg for a single.

I was so delighted at reaching the century that I did something very out of character. I shouted in jubilation and celebrated in a manner I had hardly ever done in my career. I was very proud of the achievement. We went off shortly afterwards and when I got back to the dressing room I couldn't control my emotions. With tears flowing down my cheeks, I made four phone calls – to Anjali, Ajit, my mother and Achrekar Sir – to thank them for all they had done.

While I managed to play in the Sri Lanka series, followed by three Tests against Pakistan in January 2006 and England in March 2006, Tests in which I didn't do a great deal, I realized that shoulder surgery was unavoidable if I harboured any ambition of going to the West Indies for the Test series in May. I decided not to play in the one-day series against England and went ahead with the operation on 27 March in London.

The shoulder operation

It wasn't quite as straightforward as planned. As normal, I was sedated before being moved to the operating theatre, but for some reason I suddenly woke up on the trolley and asked the nurse if the operation was over. She was shocked to see me awake and told me that it had not even started. There had been some complication with the previous operation and mine had been delayed. I drifted back to sleep but a little later woke up again and asked a doctor if the ordeal was finally over. To my surprise I was told that this time they had had to wake me because of an unexpected discovery. They had spotted a ruptured tendon in my right biceps and needed my consent to fix it while they did the shoulder surgery. I agreed, but asked them to make sure I recovered in time for the West Indies series! In fact, as soon as

I'd got back to my room from the operating theatre, I cried and cried because I thought I was going to miss the West Indies series, which I was very eager to play in.

Within five weeks of the surgery, I picked up a cricket bat and even played a few shots to tennis balls. My family and friends Atul Ranade and Jagdish Chavan were with me throughout the recovery and I got them to bowl at me from 18 yards to get used to the extra pace that I was likely to encounter in the West Indies. In hindsight I concede that I probably pushed myself too hard. When my physio and doctors asked me to play thirty balls a day, I played sixty.

After practising to short-pitched bowling for four days, I asked one of my friends to bowl at me from the full 22 yards, to get used to swing and seam movement. All was fine until I felt a sudden jerk. I immediately stopped and one look was enough to frighten me. My biceps was hanging like a hammock and my immediate apprehension was that I had ruptured it again. I was desperate to speak to John Gloster and report what had happened, but John was then in the West Indies with the team and, because of the time difference, I had to wait eight or nine hours before I was able to speak to him. Those hours were a real nightmare. John advised complete rest for the next few days. The incident had really shaken me up. A week later I went to Chennai and met up with our trainer, Ramji Srinivasan. I wanted to work on my physical fitness, even if I couldn't bat. I trained hard for a week but it was to no avail. I had lost confidence completely and decided not to go to the West Indies for the June 2006 Test series.

Led by Rahul Dravid, who had replaced Sourav Ganguly as captain, the team played outstandingly well. Rahul batted brilliantly in truly trying conditions and we won the four-Test series 1–0. It was our first series win in the Caribbean for thirty-five years – and I was frustrated at missing every single bit of the action. I called my team-mates after the victory and congratulated them on a fantastic series win.

By the time the team returned from the West Indies and were ready to go to Sri Lanka for three ODIs in August, I had recovered enough to join them, though throwing was still a bit of an issue. Disappointingly, the Sri Lanka series was a washout – only twenty-two balls were bowled in the first game because of rain and the second and third games were abandoned completely – although it did at least allow me more time to recover. Frustrated because of all the rain, we ended up sitting out on the hotel-room balcony playing carrom.

The next tournament was a tri-series in Malaysia in September 2006 against Australia and the West Indies, and I was delighted to score a big hundred in the first game of the competition against the West Indies. My innings of 141 not out finally put all my injury concerns to rest, though it was disappointing to lose the rain-shortened match by the Duckworth-Lewis method.

Heartened by my successful comeback, I kept promising my team-mates that I would get them a run-out in the tournament. I said that all the opposition players were aware of my injuries and were bound to take some risks against me, assuming I wouldn't be able to throw hard. It happened exactly as I had predicted and I got Australia's Damien Martyn run out when he took on my arm while fielding at third man. I celebrated by sprinting back to the wicket and my team-mates were delighted that I had kept my promise. I was back.

Australia in India 2004 – The Border-Gavaskar Trophy

1st Test. Bangalore. 6–10 October 2004
Australia 474 (MJ Clarke 151, AC Gilchrist 104, SM Katich 81, JL Langer 52;
    H Singh 5–146, A Kumble 3–157) and 228 (DR Martyn 45, SM Katich 39;
    H Singh 6–78)
India 246 (PA Patel 46, SC Ganguly 45; GD McGrath 4–55) and 239 (R Dravid
    60, IK Pathan 55; JN Gillespie 3–33)
Australia won by 217 runs

2nd Test. Chennai. 14–18 October 2004
Australia 235 (JL Langer 71, ML Hayden 58; A Kumble 7–48) and 369
    (DR Martyn 104, AC Gilchrist 49; A Kumble 6–133, H Singh 3–108)
India 376 (V Sehwag 155, M Kaif 64, PA Patel 54; SK Warne 6–125,
    JN Gillespie 2–70) and 19–0
Match drawn

3rd Test. Nagpur. 26–29 October 2004
Australia 398 (DR Martyn 114, MJ Clarke 91, DS Lehmann 70; Z Khan 4–95,
    M Kartik 3–57) and 329–5 dec (SM Katich 99, DR Martyn 97, MJ Clarke 73;
    Z Khan 2–64, M Kartik 2–74)
India 185 (M Kaif 55, **SR Tendulkar 8**; JN Gillespie 5–56, GD McGrath 3–27)
    and 200 (V Sehwag 58, AB Agarkar 44*, **SR Tendulkar 2**; JN Gillespie
    4–24)
Australia won by 342 runs

4th Test. Mumbai. 3–5 November 2004
India 104 (R Dravid 31*, **SR Tendulkar 5**; JN Gillespie 4–29, NM Hauritz 3–16,
    MS Kasprowicz 2–11) and 205 (VVS Laxman 69, **SR Tendulkar 55**;
    MJ Clarke 6–9, GD McGrath 2–29)
Australia 203 (DR Martyn 55; A Kumble 5–90, M Kartik 4–44) and 93
    (ML Hayden 24; H Singh 5–29, M Kartik 3–32)
India won by 13 runs

Australia won the series 2–1

South Africa in India 2004

1st Test. Kanpur. 20–24 November 2004
South Africa 510–9 dec (AJ Hall 163, Z de Bruyn 83, HH Dippenaar 48;
    A Kumble 6–131) and 169–4 (GC Smith 47; M Kartik 2–17, H Singh 2–39)
India 466 (V Sehwag 164, G Gambhir 96, SC Ganguly 57, R Dravid 54,
    SR Tendulkar 3; AJ Hall 3–93, M Ntini 3–135)
Match drawn

2nd Test. Kolkata. 28 November–2 December 2004
South Africa 305 (JH Kallis 121, JA Rudolph 61; Z Khan 3–64, IK Pathan
    3–72) and 222 (GC Smith 71, JH Kallis 55; H Singh 7–87, A Kumble
    3–82)

India 411 (V Sehwag 88, R Dravid 80, **SR Tendulkar 20**; M Ntini 4–112) and
   120–2 (R Dravid 47*, **SR Tendulkar 32**)
India won by 8 wickets

India won the series 1–0

India in Bangladesh 2004

1st Test. Dhaka. 10–13 December 2004
Bangladesh 184 (M Ashraful 60*, M Rafique 47; IK Pathan 5–45) and 202
   (MI Rana 69, N Iqbal 54; IK Pathan 6–51)
India 526 (**SR Tendulkar 248***, SC Ganguly 71, G Gambhir 35, VVS Laxman 32)
India won by an innings and 140 runs

2nd Test. Chittagong. 17–20 December 2004
India 540 (R Dravid 160, G Gambhir 139, SC Ganguly 88, H Singh 47,
   SR Tendulkar 36; M Rafique 4–156, M Mortaza 3–60)
Bangladesh 333 (M Ashraful 158*, A Ahmed 43; A Kumble 4–55) and 124
   (f/o) (T Jubair 31; IK Pathan 5–32, **SR Tendulkar 1–27**)
India won by an innings and 83 runs

India won the series 2–0

Pakistan in India 2005

1st Test. Mohali. 8–12 March 2005
Pakistan 312 (A Kamal 91, Inzamam-ul-Haq 57, T Umar 44; L Balaji 5–76) and
   496–9 dec (K Akmal 109, Inzamam-ul-Haq 86, A Razzaq 71, Y Youhana 68;
   L Balaji 4–95, A Kumble 4–160)
India 516 (V Sehwag 173, **SR Tendulkar 94**, VVS Laxman 58, R Dravid 50;
   D Kaneria 6–150) and 85–1
Match drawn

2nd Test. Kolkata. 16–20 March 2005
India 407 (R Dravid 110, V Sehwag 81, **SR Tendulkar 52**; A Razzaq 3–62,
   S Afridi 3–80, D Kaneria 3–136) and 407–9 dec (R Dravid 135, KD Karthik
   93, **SR Tendulkar 52**; A Razzaq 3–80, M Sami 3–82, D Kaneria 3–123)
Pakistan 393 (Y Khan 147, Y Youhana 104; A Kumble 3–98) and 226 (S Afridi
   59, A Kamal 50; A Kumble 7–63)
India won by 195 runs

3rd Test. Bangalore. 24–28 March 2005
Pakistan 570 (Y Khan 267, Inzamam-ul-Haq 184; H Singh 6–152) and 261–2
   dec (Y Khan 84*, Y Hameed 76, S Afridi 58; **SR Tendulkar 1–62**)
India 449 (V Sehwag 201, VVS Laxman 79*, **SR Tendulkar 41**; D Kaneria
   5–127) and 214 (G Gambhir 52, **SR Tendulkar 16**; S Afridi 3–13, A Khan
   2–21, D Kaneria 2–46)
Pakistan won by 168 runs

Series drawn 1–1

Sri Lanka in India 2005

1st Test. Chennai. 2-6 December 2005
India 167 (V Sehwag 36, **SR Tendulkar** 22; WPUJC Vaas 4-20, M Muralitharan
    2-60)
Sri Lanka 168-4 (DPMD Jayawardene 71; A Kumble 3-41)
Match drawn

2nd Test. Delhi. 10-14 December 2005
India 290 (**SR Tendulkar** 109, VVS Laxman 69; M Muralitharan 7-100)
    and 375-6 dec (IK Pathan 93, Y Singh 77*, R Dravid 53, MS Dhoni 51*,
    SR Tendulkar 16)
Sri Lanka 230 (MS Atapattu 88, DPMD Jayawardene 60; A Kumble 6-72,
    IK Pathan 3-34) and 247 (MS Atapattu 67, DPMD Jayawardene 67;
    A Kumble 4-85, H. Singh 3-70)
India won by 188 runs

3rd Test. Ahmedabad. 18-22 December 2005
India 398 (VVS Laxman 104, IK Pathan 82, MS Dhoni 49, **SR Tendulkar** 23;
    SL Malinga 3-113, M Muralitharan 3-128) and 316-9 dec (Y Singh 75,
    AB Agarkar 48, **SR Tendulkar** 19; HMCM Bandara 3-84, M Muralitharan
    3-90)
Sri Lanka 206 (TM Dilshan 65, KC Sangakkara 41; H Singh 7-62, A Kumble
    2-87) and 249 (TM Dilshan 65, DPMD Jayawardene 57, WU Tharanga 47;
    A Kumble 5-89, H Singh 3-79)
India won by 259 runs

India won the series 2-0

India in Pakistan 2006

1st Test. Lahore. 13-17 January 2006
Pakistan 679-7 dec (Y Khan 199, M Yousuf 173, S Afridi 103, K Akmal 102*,
    S Malik 59; AB Agarkar 2-122)
India 410-1 (V Sehwag 254, R Dravid 128*; Naved-ul-Hasan 1-94)
Match drawn

2nd Test. Faisalabad. 21-25 January 2006
Pakistan 588 (S Afridi 156, Inzamam-ul-Haq 119, Y Khan 83, M Yousuf 65;
    Z Khan 3-135, A Kumble 3-150) and 490-8 dec (Y Khan 194, M Yousuf
    126, K Akmal 78; Z Khan 4-61)
India 603 (MS Dhoni 148, R Dravid 103, VVS Laxman 90, IK Pathan 90,
    SR Tendulkar 14; D Kaneria 3-165) and 21-0
Match drawn

3rd Test. Karachi. 29 January-1 Feb 2006
Pakistan 245 (K Akmal 113, A Razzaq 45, S Akhtar 45; IK Pathan
    5-61, RP Singh 3-66) and 599-7 dec (F Iqbal 139, M Yousuf 97, A Razzaq
    90, Y Khan 77, S Afridi 60, I Farhat 57, S Butt 53; A Kumble 3-151)
India 238 (Y Singh 45, IK Pathan 40, **SR Tendulkar** 23; M Asif 4-78, A Razzaq

3–67) and 265 (Y Singh 122, **SR Tendulkar 26**; A Razzaq 4–88, M Asif 3–48)

Pakistan won by 341 runs

Pakistan won the series 1–0

England in India 2006

1st Test. Nagpur. 1–5 March 2006

England 393 (PD Collingwood 134*, AN Cook 60; S Sreesanth 4–95, IK Pathan 3–92) and 297–3 dec (AN Cook 104*, KP Pietersen 87, AJ Strauss 46; IK Pathan 2–48)

India 323 (M Kaif 91, W Jaffer 81, A Kumble 58, **SR Tendulkar 16**; MJ Hoggard 6–57) and 260–6 (W Jaffer 100, R Dravid 71, **SR Tendulkar 28***; SJ Harmison 2–48, A Flintoff 2–79)

Match drawn

2nd Test. Mohali. 9–13 March 2006

England 300 (A Flintoff 70, KP Pietersen 64, GO Jones 52; A Kumble 5–76, MM Patel 3–72) and 181 (IR Bell 57, A Flintoff 51; MM Patel 4–25, A Kumble 4–70)

India 338 (R Dravid 95, IK Pathan 52, **SR Tendulkar 4**; A Flintoff 4–96) and 144–1 (V Sehwag 76*, R Dravid 42*; MJ Hoggard 1–24)

India won by 9 wickets

3rd Test. Mumbai. 18–22 March 2006

England 400 (AJ Strauss 128, OA Shah 88, A Flintoff 50; S Sreesanth 4–70, H Singh 3–89) and 191 (A Flintoff 50, OA Shah 38; A Kumble 4–49, H Singh 2–40)

India 279 (MS Dhoni 64, R Dravid 52, **SR Tendulkar 1**; JM Anderson 4–40, MJ Hoggard 2–54) and 100 (**SR Tendulkar 34**; SD Udal 4–14, A Flintoff 3–14, JM Anderson 2–39)

England won by 212 runs

Series drawn 1–1

17

'ENDULKAR'

My primary goal now was to win the 2007 World Cup in the Caribbean. We had made the final four years earlier and had faltered at the very last hurdle. We were all desperate to go one better this time and expectations at home were very high.

We played well in our two practice matches against the Netherlands and the West Indies in Jamaica in early March. We scored 300 batting first against the Netherlands, for a decisive 182-run win, and in the next match our bowlers polished off the West Indies for 85, setting up a nine-wicket victory. We seemed to be getting into a good rhythm for our first group match against Bangladesh on 17 March, but at the same time there was no question of being complacent or taking them lightly. Bangladesh had beaten decent opposition before.

The match was tough for many reasons. When we batted, the pitch was damp and it was extremely difficult to play shots in the first ten overs. Mashrafe Mortaza, Bangladesh's medium-fast bowler, was performing well and we had lost two early wickets when I went in to bat. I was batting at number four in this competition, as requested by the team management. I was perhaps a little surprised to bat in that position, because we had experimented with my batting position before, on the eve of the 2003 World Cup, only to agree that I could contribute most as an opener. But the team management's theory was that the tracks in the West Indies would be slow and low and I would be able to manoeuvre the spinners in the middle of the innings. As it turned out, almost all the wickets had bounce and movement and the strategy backfired on us.

My plan was to see off the new ball before gradually picking up the scoring rate. Sourav and I successfully negotiated the early swing and, with the spinners on, I decided to play an inside-out shot over extra cover. Unfortunately the ball from left-arm spinner Abdur Razzak hit the inside edge of my bat, ricocheted into my pad and went on to hit the stumps. It was not the start to the World Cup I had hoped for.

Not much went right for us on the day. Although Sourav scored 66 while opening the batting, Rahul, the captain, made only 14 and then Dhoni got out for a duck trying to play a cut shot, caught at short third man. It was one of those days when things just didn't click and we ended up with a below-par score of 191. In reply Tamim Iqbal, the left-handed opening batsman, gave Bangladesh a quick start and they managed to reach the target fairly easily in the end, with five wickets to spare.

Not all was lost after one defeat, however, and there was still time to pull things round. We knew we had to win the two remaining group matches and that the run rate might come into the equation. In our second match against Bermuda, we went out and played our shots and won by 257 runs. Thanks to our total of 413, the net run rate had been beefed up and we only had to beat Sri Lanka to progress to the next stage.

We started well against Sri Lanka on 23 March and kept their score to a manageable 254. There's little doubt that we were capable of chasing down that total, but despite our best efforts things did not go to plan. I got an inside edge to a ball from fast bowler Dilhara Fernando; hearing the ball hitting the stumps in such a crucial match was devastating. When we were all out for 185 the dressing room was in shock and some of the players were in tears. Most were just completely silent. I found it very difficult to get over the disappointment. It was definitely one of the lowest points of my cricket career.

A difficult homecoming

After we returned to India, the media followed me back home and it hurt when I heard my own people doubting the commitment of the players. The media had every right to criticize us for failing, but to say we were not focused on the job was not fair. We had failed to fulfil the expectations of the fans, but that did not mean we should be labelled traitors. At times the reaction was surprisingly hostile and some of the players were worried about their safety.

Headlines like 'Endulkar' hurt deeply. After eighteen years in international cricket, it was tough to see things come to this and retirement crossed my mind. My family and friends like Sanjay Nayak did all they could to cheer me up and after a week I decided to do something about it. I started to do some running, to try to sweat the World Cup out of my head.

On top of all this our coach, Greg Chappell, was publicly questioning our commitment and instead of asking us to take fresh guard, was making matters worse. It seems to me that Greg Chappell must take a lot of responsibility for the mess. I don't think I would be far off the mark if I said that most of us felt that Indian cricket was going nowhere under Chappell.

In my opinion, Indian cricket benefited significantly when the BCCI decided to end Chappell's tenure in April 2007. Several of our senior players were relieved to see him go, which was hardly surprising because, for reasons hard to comprehend, he had not treated them particularly fairly. His attitude towards Sourav, for example, was astonishing. Chappell is on record as saying that he may have got the job because of Sourav but that did not mean he was going to do favours to Sourav for the rest of his life. Frankly, Sourav is one of the best cricketers India has produced and he did not need favours from Chappell to be part of the team.

Chappell seemed intent on dropping all the older players and in the process damaged the harmony of the side. On one occasion, he asked VVS Laxman to consider opening the batting. Laxman politely turned him down, saying he had tried opening in the first half of his career because he was confused, but now he was settled in the middle order and Greg should consider him as a middle-order batsman. Greg's response stunned us all. He told Laxman he should be careful, because making a comeback at the age of thirty-two might not be easy.

Unlike John Wright and Gary Kirsten, who coached India before and after Greg and made a priority of keeping the players happy, Greg was like a ringmaster who imposed his ideas on the players without showing any signs of being concerned about whether they felt comfortable or not. In fact, I later found out that Greg had spoken to the BCCI about the need to remove the senior players, no doubt hoping to refresh the team.

I also remember that every time India won, Greg could be seen leading the team to the hotel or into the team bus, but every time India lost he would thrust the players in front. In general John and Gary always preferred to stay in the background, but Greg liked to be prominent in the media.

Just months before the World Cup, Chappell had come to see me at home and, to my dismay, suggested that I should take over the captaincy from Rahul Dravid. Anjali, who was sitting with me, was equally shocked to hear him say that 'together, we could control Indian cricket for years,' and that he would help me in taking over the reins of the side. I was surprised to hear the coach not showing the slightest amount of respect for the captain, with cricket's biggest tournament just months away. I rejected his proposition outright. He stayed for a couple of hours, trying to convince me, before finally leaving.

A few days after Greg had come to my house, I suggested to the BCCI that the best option would be to keep Greg back in India and not send him with the team to the World Cup. I also said that we as senior players could take control of the side and keep the team together. That's not what happened, of course, and the 2007 campaign ended in disaster.

Greg has since written a lot of things about the Indian cricket team. Perhaps it is time to set matters straight. It came to light later that Greg was being filmed for a documentary, *Guru Greg*, during this period which went into a lot of detail about what was happening behind the scenes. It says a great deal about his tenure as coach that most of the players, including me, did not even know about this. Why were the players not asked if they felt comfortable with this? I wonder if he even had permission from the BCCI to record this documentary. Wasn't it a clear infringement of the players' privacy?

While we may never get answers to these questions, suffice to say that Greg's tenure as coach was the worst of my career. There is no doubt we failed as a collective in 2007, but his high-handed manner added to our disappointment and, in the immediate aftermath of defeat, had a harmful impact on Indian cricket.

Unwelcome opinions

The outrage in India after the 2007 World Cup was not helped by armchair experts who were sitting thousands of miles away but still passing judgement on Indian cricket and suggesting I should 'have a good long look in the mirror' and think about retiring. Such opinions, which were published in Indian newspapers, provoked fans across the country. I have never quite understood why Ian Chappell, who was merely reporting on the game, should have got a headline in the Indian press. Would any of our former players commenting on Ricky Ponting or Michael Clarke have had a headline in the *Melbourne Age* or the *Sydney Morning Herald*? Chappell would have done better to stick to Australian cricket.

I remember meeting Ian Chappell in Durban in 2010 during the Champions League Twenty20 and having a most interesting discussion with him. I bumped into him as I was coming out of a health club after a session in the gym with my physio, Nitin Patel, who was party to the entire exchange. Ian started the conversation by saying that now he knew the secret behind my scoring big runs. I reminded him that he was conveniently changing his stand, considering what he'd written about mirrors and retirement in 2007. I said to him that I had not done what he suggested back then because I was well aware of what I needed to do and how much cricket I had left in me.

I also said that critics like him change with the wind. When the going is good, they write positive things and when the going gets tough, they start making a lot of negative comments without ever trying to find out what actually is going through a player's body or mind. He then asked me if I had changed the weight of my bat. I told him that I hadn't changed a thing and was doing exactly what I had been doing for twenty long years. He was the one who had conveniently changed his opinion because I had been scoring heavily between 2008 and 2010.

Finally the conversation moved to Greg. I told Ian bluntly that Greg had not been popular and I would not want to share a dressing room with him again. Ian attempted to argue that Greg had always had a problem trying to understand failure and had had issues as captain of Australia. I said that that was not my concern and all that mattered to me was that he had failed to take Indian cricket forward. Ian was most surprised to hear all this. In fact, Nitin Patel told me soon after that I was the last person he had expected to lash out like this.

A welcome phone call

All in all, I was in a bad state after the 2007 World Cup. I was not enjoying my cricket at all and was thinking about retiring – until I received some encouraging words from Viv Richards. Out of the blue, he called me in India from the West Indies and we spoke for about forty-five minutes. He assured me that there was a lot of cricket left in me and insisted that I shouldn't even think about stopping playing.

Viv was my hero when I was growing up and he will always be a hero, no matter what success I've achieved myself. We have got to know each other well over the years and whenever we meet, he treats me like his younger brother and I treat him like my older brother. I've always respected him and his views, so when he chose to call me and spend all that time convincing me to carry on, it meant a great deal to me. When I finally got back into some good form and put together a very satisfying century in Sydney at the beginning of 2008, I made a point of calling Viv to thank him for his crucial support.

India in the 2007 World Cup

8th match, Group B. Bangladesh v India at Port-of-Spain. 17 March 2007
India 191 (49.3/50 ov); Bangladesh 192-5 (48.3/50 ov)
Bangladesh won by 5 wickets (with 9 balls remaining)

12th match, Group B. Bermuda v India at Port-of-Spain. 19 March 2007
India 413-5 (50/50 ov); Bermuda 156 (43.1/50 ov)
India won by 257 runs

20th match, Group B. India v Sri Lanka at Port-of-Spain. 23 March 2007
Sri Lanka 254-6 (50/50 ov); India 185 (43.3/50 ov)
Sri Lanka won by 69 runs

Final. Australia v Sri Lanka at Bridgetown. 28 April 2007
Australia 281-4 (38/38 ov); Sri Lanka 215-8 (36/36 ov, target: 269)
Australia won by 53 runs (D/L method)

18

BAD LANGUAGE

The process of getting Indian cricket back on track after the World Cup started with a two-Test series in Bangladesh in May 2007, which we won 1–0. Ravi Shastri, who was interim coach, played a key role in helping us put the disappointment of the Caribbean behind us. Personally, it was a welcome change, because Ravi and I have always been very good friends. Not only did we play together in the early years of my career, but even after Ravi's retirement we spent a reasonable amount of time together on tours when he was commentating. He has an astute cricket brain, and, with his straightforward and transparent attitude, we felt that we finally had a coach we could confide in.

In June we went to Ireland for a limited-overs series against South Africa. I was particularly excited about visiting Ireland because my favourite rock band, U2, come from there. The series posed an unusual challenge for us because it was freezing cold and it took us a while to get used to the conditions. Despite the weather, I had a good outing and twice got out in the nineties in the three-match contest, which we won 2–1.

I also remember the series for an incident with Yuvraj during dinner in Belfast. I suggested to some of my team-mates, including Yuvraj and Zaheer, that we should have some Japanese food one evening and we found a restaurant that served Thai, Chinese and Japanese cuisines. We ordered a number of entrées, including some sushi and sashimi. They served wasabi with the sushi and also gave us some bread rolls to go with the other starters.

I asked Yuvi if he liked wasabi and he swore that he did. To our amazement, he then proceeded to spread the hot wasabi on a roll as if it was butter and was just about to pop it in his mouth when I stopped him. Zaheer was kicking me under the table, telling me to let him eat it, just to see what happened. The wasabi was very strong, though, and there is no doubt that if he had eaten that roll he would have been in serious trouble!

We forced Yuvi to admit that he had never tried wasabi before and we ribbed him mercilessly, though he tried to put on a brave face.

India in England, July–August 2007

After the Ireland tour we went to England for a series of Tests and ODIs. The first Test started on 19 July 2007 and I have to say we were fortunate to avoid defeat after Michael Vaughan's England had put themselves in a good position. Anderson and Sidebottom had taken nine wickets between them as we were dismissed for 201 in our first innings, and Kevin Pietersen's spectacular 134 had helped to set us a target of 380 in our second innings. On the last day of the match we were nine wickets down and struggling when Steve Bucknor ruled Sreesanth not out, even though it appeared that he had been hit right in front of middle stump. The match was stopped shortly afterwards because of rain and it was a lucky escape.

We played much better in the second Test at Nottingham a week later, and on the first day, which was also curtailed because of rain, we took control. We dismissed England for under 200, thanks to excellent bowling from Zaheer Khan and Anil Kumble, with good support from RP Singh and Sreesanth, and followed up with a total of 481. Five out of our top six batsmen passed 50 without going on to make a century. I contributed 91 before being given out lbw by Simon Taufel. He later came to see me to admit that it had been a mistake on his part and that he had seen from replays that the ball was clearly missing the stumps. It added to my respect for Simon and we are still good friends today.

Our innings was tinged with controversy when Zaheer Khan had an unusual welcome to the middle. When he reached the wicket, Zaheer saw several jelly beans sprinkled on the crease. Clearly it was a prank by one of the England players. Zaheer removed the jelly beans but they reappeared as soon as he was back on strike. Zaheer directed a few words at Kevin Pietersen at gully – though it was never clear who was actually involved – and when he came back to the pavilion he was furious. He shouted to the team that we needed to play aggressive cricket and finish England off in the second innings. Zaheer is normally a cool guy and he very rarely gets angry. It was a blessing in disguise for us, as Zaheer backed up his words with one of his best ever spells in Test cricket, taking five wickets and leading us to a famous victory. We went on to win the Test series 1–0 and the recovery that had started in Bangladesh was complete.

We celebrated heartily, in which we were greatly helped by Rajiv Shukla, our manager for this tour. Rajiv was a positive presence throughout the tour, and had been part of the team in some of our most crucial away victories, including the NatWest tri-series win in 2002. On that occasion he took the entire team out to dinner at the Four Seasons to celebrate the victory and also organized a special performance of the musical *Bombay Dreams*, something we very much enjoyed.

We were playing some very good cricket by now and were looking forward to taking on Australia in October 2007 in a series of ODIs in India before heading Down Under for a full tour a couple of months later. Before that ODI series, however, Indian cricket received a huge fillip when we won the inaugural World Twenty20 in South Africa in September under MS Dhoni. I was not part of the Twenty20 team, of course, but I watched the team's progress with great interest. The Twenty20 win helped restore the nation's passion for cricket and the players received a hero's welcome on their return to India.

India in Australia, December 2007–January 2008

India's tour to Australia in 2007–08 was perhaps the most eventful series of my career. While we had come close to beating Australia in 2003–04, drawing the series one apiece and dominating the last Test in Sydney, we played even better in 2007–08. Even though the Test series is still talked about because of an incident involving Andrew Symonds and Harbhajan Singh in Sydney, a lot of other issues combined to make it an extremely intense couple of months.

We were full of confidence by the time we set off for Australia. After the series of ODIs in India in October, which Australia won 4–2, we had played Pakistan at home in November and early December 2007 and won the three-Test series 1–0. Most of the batsmen were in good form and we were hopeful of achieving our first ever series win Down Under. Unfortunately, before the first Test at the MCG there was only one warm-up game, as is often the case with scheduling these days, and even that was a near washout because of a storm, which meant we had very little chance to adjust to Australian conditions.

First Test, Melbourne, 26–29 December 2007

We had a reasonable first day at the MCG, picking up nine Australian wickets, and we quickly finished off their innings the next morning for 343. Anil and Zaheer had bowled well and now it was down to the batsmen. I came in with the score at 31–2.

I had thought carefully about the way I would approach my innings and had a plan for each Australian bowler. In fact, a glance at my scoring chart for the series will show where I played the big shots: I really went after the bowling in the area between long on and midwicket. This was based on my experience of playing the Australian attack in the one-dayers in India a couple of months before, when the left-arm chinaman bowler Brad Hogg had caused us problems. I was determined to attack him because I knew it would force the Australians to rethink their plans. If they couldn't rely on Hogg, the fast bowlers would have to bowl longer spells than expected and we could attack them when they got tired in the hot and testing conditions. I went into the Melbourne Test with a set plan against Hogg. However, once in the middle, I realized that I needed to play differently and changed my plan on the ground itself. Looking at his field placements, I started taking the aerial route and hit him in the area between deep midwicket and long on, forcing him to change his game plan and remove the close-catching fielders. This strategy paid off and I could subsequently milk singles, with no men close on the leg side. For other bowlers, however, I stuck to the same game plan that I had originally decided.

Brett Lee bowled at his best in this series. Back in 1999 Lee had been fast but raw; in 2008 he was the complete package. He had real pace, a vicious bouncer, a yorker, a fast swinging delivery and also a slower ball. He was consistently clocking 145 kph and I relished my contests with him. Among the other bowlers, Mitchell Johnson bowled some incisive spells, while the accurate Stuart Clark had the job of trying to keep things tight. To his credit, he also picked up some key wickets.

I went after the bowling from the start of my innings. I was feeling good and was set to kick on for a big score. However, you don't always get a hundred just because you're feeling good and I got out after scoring 62. We were all out for 196, which was nowhere near enough. Australia soon managed to establish a stranglehold over us, eventually winning the Test in four days. It was not the start we had hoped for.

Red faces all round

Something unexpected that I had to deal with at the time of the Melbourne Test was a severe allergic reaction. On our way to Australia, Harbhajan Singh and I had bought a newly launched moisturizing cream at Singapore airport and for the first few days I had no problems using the cream. It was during the first Test that I started feeling a severe burning sensation on my face. Harbhajan did not have any such problem, so at first I attributed my reaction to a massage. I had had to lie down with my face on a towel and I thought it must have been something to do with the detergent used on the towel.

The problem started to bother me on the third day and I remember putting more cream on my face before going to bed, thinking it would help. The next morning I awoke in agony. My face was on fire and it was as if someone had pushed it into a barbecue. It was even worse by the evening with my face all red and swollen. So much so that I was too embarrassed to go out in public and had to hide behind large sunglasses.

Anjali was arriving in Sydney the next day. With the Melbourne Test over on the fourth day, I got permission to fly to Sydney a little earlier than planned and met up with her and the children at the airport. They were horrified by my face and asked what on earth I had done to it. I was not in the best of moods and wanted to get to the hotel as quickly as possible. When we finally arrived, after a forty-five-minute drive because of the traffic, I was really irritable. The hotel staff then took a long time to give us our rooms and I ended up shouting at the hotel manager. By the time we got to the room I had started to feel worse and told Anjali to ask the kids to sit in the adjoining room and leave me alone. The poor kids were wondering what was causing me to behave in this way. By then, my face was troubling me even more. We called Reception and asked for a doctor to come to my room but were told that there wasn't one available at that hour. I asked where the nearest hospital was and went there immediately. After a brief examination, I was given a lotion for the night and was asked to come back the following morning.

We got a taxi from the hospital and after a few minutes the driver said to me in Hindi, '*Aap wohi ho jo main samaj raha hoon?*' (Are you the person I think you are?) I admitted that I was and he offered to show us around Sydney, which I was in no mood to do. I asked him if he wouldn't mind taking us to a fast-food place instead and Anjali got out to get some burgers for dinner while I waited in the cab. The driver accompanied her and when they returned she told me that he had insisted on paying for the food. He also refused to take any money from us after dropping us off at the hotel and left his number in case we needed to go anywhere else in Sydney during our stay. I was very touched by the gesture and told him that I would leave match tickets for him at Reception. Later, I got one of my Test shirts signed by the team and left it with the tickets.

I returned to the hospital the following morning and asked the doctor to do whatever he thought necessary to give me some quick relief, as I had a Test match to play the following morning. The doctor was a little taken aback, considering my condition, but I was absolutely determined to play. That afternoon we were supposed to be practising but I was in no state to stay out in the sun. I ended up batting against my dear friend Subroto Banerjee, the former India medium-fast bowler, who was then a resident of Sydney, in the indoor nets for a good forty-five minutes. I managed to take the field the next day, however, and that was the first time I wore a floppy white hat, which from then on became my trademark on the field. I applied a lot of ice to my face and then plastered it with zinc cream. It looked ridiculous but that didn't bother me.

After a couple of days, it finally started to settle down and I looked almost human again.

Second Test, Sydney, 2–6 January 2008

We suffered a blow on the eve of the Sydney Test when Zaheer was forced to return to India with a heel injury. Someone's loss is always another person's gain, however, and Zaheer's return meant young Ishant Sharma would get an opportunity to play in Australia for the first time.

On the first day, we started well and soon had the Australians on the ropes, with six wickets gone for only 134, four of which were taken by RP Singh. Just when we seemed to be in control and were trying to press home the advantage, what seemed to us to be an error by umpire Steve Bucknor caused a shift in momentum. Andrew Symonds was ruled not out after he had very clearly edged the ball to Dhoni off Ishant – the sound was heard not just by the players but also by the spectators. My son heard the sound of the edge sitting in the stands and reminds me whenever we discuss the Sydney Test match. Symonds stood his ground and, riding his luck, got a very important century for Australia. His 162 changed the course of the game and Australia managed to put together a total of 463 after being in a lot of trouble. That wasn't their only piece of luck, though. Even before Symonds had been given this reprieve, Ricky Ponting had been adjudged not out by umpire Mark Benson after he seemed to edge a ball down the leg side.

The best response was to go out and make some runs. I was glad to make amends for missing out in Melbourne by making 154, and it was a delight to watch Laxman score a hundred at the other end, with Rahul and Sourav also chipping in with half-centuries. But just when the momentum seemed to be swinging our way, Andrew Symonds started swearing at Harbhajan, who was batting with me and playing really well.

Bhajji had gone past 50 when it all started. For a number of overs he had been telling me that Andrew Symonds was trying to get him riled. I asked Bhajji not to rise to it but to continue batting the way he was. I knew only too well that by retaliating he would just play into the Australians' hands. The best thing to do is to ignore such provocation. That's easy enough to say, but of course it's not always so easy to keep your cool at moments of intense pressure.

Bhajji was doing his best and was actually trying to be civil with some of the Australian players, including Brett Lee, when all hell broke loose. Bhajji had playfully tapped Lee on the back after completing a run and Symonds at mid off took exception to this. He apparently did not want an opposition player meddling with Lee and once again hurled abuse at Bhajji. Bhajji is an impulsive and passionate individual and it was only a matter of time before he would retaliate, which he soon did. That was the start of the controversy that almost caused the tour to be called off.

I want to state very clearly that the incident arose because Andrew Symonds had been continually trying to provoke Bhajji and it was inevitable that the two would have an altercation at some point. While walking up to Bhajji to try to calm things down, I heard him say '*Teri maa ki*' (Your mother . . .) to Symonds. It is an expression commonly used in northern India to vent one's anger and to me it was all part of the game. In fact, I was surprised to see umpire Mark Benson go up to Bhajji and speak to him. While the umpire was talking to Bhajji, some of the Australian players started to warn him of the dire consequences of his words, presumably to rattle him and disturb his concentration. The ploy paid off when a few overs later Bhajji was out for 63.

I thought the matter had ended with Bhajji's dismissal and later I was surprised when told that the Australians had lodged a formal complaint at the end of that day's play, apparently alleging that Bhajji had called Symonds a 'monkey', which was being treated as a racial insult. What surprised me most was the haste with which the Australians had lodged their complaint. I was later informed that it had apparently been agreed between the Australian and Indian boards during their tour of India in October 2007, following an incident in Mumbai, that the respective captains were to report to the match referee any incident with a racial element. Even so, I still believe that the matter would not have been blown out of proportion if Ponting had discussed it with the captain Anil Kumble, Harbhajan and the Indian team management before reporting the incident to Mike Procter, the match referee. In turn, Mike Procter could also have handled the matter with a little more sensitivity.

Soon after the end of play on the third day we were informed by Mike Procter that there would be a formal hearing on the incident at the end of the fourth day, which was later changed to the end of the match. It did not leave us in the best frame of mind in the middle of an intense contest. While it was distressing to hear that Symonds felt he had been racially abused, it was equally distressing to observe what Bhajji was going through. As far as we were concerned, he had retaliated in the face of provocation, which was par for the course in an Australia–India cricket match. But he did not racially abuse another cricketer.

With the controversy overshadowing everything, the Test match assumed a completely different character. By the fifth day we were batting to save the game. Mind you, there is little doubt in my mind that we would have drawn had it not been for what seemed to us to be mistakes by the umpires and some rather unsportsmanlike conduct by a few of the Australian players.

Rahul Dravid was given out caught behind off Symonds for 38 by umpire Bucknor when his bat seemed to be a fair distance away from the ball. The wicketkeeper Adam Gilchrist was standing up to the stumps at the time and was in the best position to see if the ball had touched Rahul's bat. Yet he who prided himself on walking off if he nicked the ball appealed for the caught-behind and to our disbelief we saw the umpire raise the finger. It was a shocking decision. Some of us actually wondered if Rahul had been given out lbw.

A few overs later, Sourav was given out by umpire Benson after Michael Clarke and Ricky Ponting decided to appeal for what we thought was a grassed catch at slip. Finally, umpire Bucknor gave Dhoni out leg-before when to us the ball would clearly have missed the stumps. It seemed that every decision that could go against us had done so.

After the Test had ended with an Australian victory in the dying minutes of the fifth day, the Indian team were instructed to stay behind at the ground for the Bhajji hearing. Despite this, however, I was the first person to go out and congratulate the Australians, regardless of all the controversy and disappointment. In those circumstances, to have to hang around in order to testify on an important incident like that wasn't ideal, to say the least.

The hearing was conducted rather strangely, it seemed to me, with the Australians and Indians asked to testify separately, without the other side being present in the room. This certainly didn't improve the trust between the Indian and Australian players. I was the principal witness because I was batting at the other end from Bhajji and I recounted the incident to the match referee in detail. Apart from Bhajji himself, Chetan Chauhan, our manager on this tour, MV Sridhar, the media manager, and Anil Kumble, the captain, were also called.

Mike Procter did not look very convinced by our version of events and we found it surprising that he asked us to wait in our dressing room till well past midnight. In fact, it was not until 2 a.m. that we were allowed to return to our hotel. The controversy had started to cast a pall over the series. After the hearing there was serious ill-feeling between the two teams and we felt betrayed by the turn of events.

Standing up for justice

We were preparing to travel to Canberra the day after the Sydney Test to play a first-class fixture when we heard that Bhajji had been banned for three matches. We had had enough. It was just not acceptable and we decided it was time to take a stand against the judgement. We did not agree with what the referee had done and felt that the hearing at Sydney had been something of a farce. We informed the BCCI of the players' feelings and held a team meeting to decide what to do about it.

Anil Kumble and I took the lead and it was unanimously decided that we would boycott the tour if Bhajji's ban was upheld. Anil is one of the politest cricketers I have known but he is also very strong-minded. I have great admiration for the role he played as captain during this controversy. We decided to lodge an appeal against the ban and, in a gesture of protest, we also decided not to travel to Canberra – even though we had already loaded all our cricket gear into the bus. It was time for stern words and strong action.

The BCCI was behind us all the way and duly lodged a formal appeal contesting the ban. Mr VR Manohar, one of India's legal luminaries, was handling our case. We had regular conversations with him and provided him with all the relevant details. I must reiterate that we were very serious about the boycott. If Bhajji's ban was upheld, it would mean an acceptance of guilt and imply that Bhajji had racially abused Symonds, which he most certainly had not. We were fully prepared to accept the consequences of walking out of a tour, knowing that such an action might have resulted in the ICC banning the Indian team. The issue was now bigger than just Bhajji. Indians all over the world felt slighted and we felt it was our responsibility to stand up for our cause.

Having made our decision, we needed to find some way of reducing the tension. In the end we went to Bondi Beach and played a game of volleyball. It had a magical effect. It served as a fantastic team-bonding session and helped give us the determination to carry on. Unsurprisingly, perhaps, the media followed us wherever we went, particularly Bhajji. On a lighter note, I remember saying to him that he must be the second most popular man in the world after Michael Jackson, with so many cameras following him. In fact, I called him MJ for some time during and after the controversy.

Third Test, Perth, 16–19 January 2008

Once we had lodged our appeal, we agreed to go to Perth for the third Test. On the eve of the match the ICC had flown in Ranjan Madugalle, its senior match referee, in an attempt to defuse the simmering tension between the two teams. A meeting was staged between the two captains at the Hyatt Hotel in Ranjan's presence and Anil and Ricky shook hands for the cameras. In reality nothing had changed. The unpleasantness of Sydney would not go away and a number of issues remained to be straightened out at the WACA, where India had never won a Test.

The Perth Test turned out to be one of the best Test matches I was involved in. There is little doubt in my mind that the controversy had brought us together as a team. Sehwag was back and he gave us a quick start against Brett Lee, Mitchell Johnson, Shaun Tait and Stuart Clark on the first morning, helping us to win the first skirmish. He only scored 29 but it was enough to set the foundation for the middle order. Rahul and I then put together a very important partnership of 139.

It was in this innings that I had one of my toughest contests with Brett Lee. He bowled at real pace and I had to be at my best. I hadn't been in long when Lee bowled a fast bouncer. The shot I played still gives me a lot of satisfaction. I readied myself to play the upper cut over the slips, but then I realized that the ball was jagging back at me at furious pace. Within a fraction of a second the ball was just inches away from my head. I kept my eyes on the ball and was leaning back at almost 45 degrees when I finally met the ball with the bat right in front of my eyes. The ball flew over the wicketkeeper's head to the boundary. After that, I had a feeling it was going to be a good day. I went on to make 71 in our score of 330, with Dravid contributing 93.

Anil picked up his 600th Test wicket in Australia's first innings when he had Symonds caught by Rahul at slips. Anil's uncharacteristically exuberant celebration was an eye-opener for all of us and showed how much the wicket meant to the team after the Sydney Test. Breaking the partnership between Symonds and Gilchrist proved crucial. We went on to bowl Australia out for 212, with RP Singh taking four wickets, giving us a 118-run lead. We had set Australia a target of 413 and were beginning to scent victory. But there was still a job to be done and there was no room for complacency.

The final day was a classic piece of Test cricket. In fact, Ishant Sharma's spell of fast bowling that morning was one of the best spells by an Indian bowler in all my years of international cricket. Ponting and Michael Hussey came in intent on staging a fightback after Irfan Pathan had picked up the two openers the previous evening. Anil had set a good field to Ponting and Ishant was given the ball. It was inspiring to see an Indian fast bowler bowl at real pace to one of the world's premier batsmen and mesmerize him with balls that came in from a good length.

The length Ishant was hitting was the key. I was standing at mid on and kept reminding him to bowl the same line and length over and over again. There was no need for anything fancy, as he already had Ponting in some difficulty. I could also sense Ponting trying to upset Ishant by threatening to come forward, to force him to alter his length. It was a true test between bat and ball and I was impressed to see Ishant stick to doing exactly what had been asked of him.

By the end of eight overs Ishant showed no reduction in pace. He had beaten Ponting on numerous occasions but somehow the batsman had survived. It was an important moment. If he managed to play Ishant off, Ponting would be able to relax and we would have missed an opportunity. Anil, however, was tempted to give Ishant a rest – until some of the senior players persuaded him to allow Ishant one more go at Ponting.

The gamble paid off and Ishant finally got Ponting to edge one to Rahul at slip. It was a just reward for a great piece of fast bowling. We had our man and could now have a crack at the Australian middle order. We kept taking wickets at regular intervals and in the end it was the left-arm seamer RP Singh who clean-bowled Stuart Clark to give us an amazing victory.

Reasons to be cheerful

After the game a number of bottles of champagne were opened in the dressing room and one was also sent across to the touring Indian media contingent, who had played a very important role in standing behind us during the Sydney controversy. I'm pleased to say that Brett Lee and Adam Gilchrist also came to our dressing room to congratulate us and it was a gesture that was much appreciated.

As I look back at the Perth Test a few things stand out. We arrived in Perth with a sense of purpose. We all felt hurt by what had transpired in Sydney and the best way to vent our anger was on the cricket field. And that is what we did.

The second thing I remember about Perth is the arrival of Gary Kirsten, who had been nominated as coach of India but who was yet to take charge. Gary did not say much at first and just wanted to observe how the Indian players went about their routines. It was Gary who suggested that the team should go cycling in Perth, to get our minds off cricket for a while. It certainly did us a lot of good. At such times net practice is not always the only answer. No one will ever become a Sunil Gavaskar or a Kapil Dev in two days of practice. It is just as important to recharge mentally and it often helps to spend some time together away from the cricket field.

Finally, the support of the fans was particularly memorable.

We were 2–0 down in the series and a lot had been written about the fragility of the team on the fast and bouncy WACA track. None of this gloomy talk stopped the Indian fans from coming and lending their support. It was terrific to see the tricolour being waved in the stands and it was a reminder of what the game meant to Indians all round the world. It felt good to have made them proud.

We had proved that the Indian team could play within the spirit of the game both on and off the field.

Fourth Test, Adelaide, 24–28 January 2008

As we prepared for the final Test at Adelaide, Gary asked me if I wanted to bat in the nets and I said I'd prefer to practise to some short-pitched throw-downs. This was the start of a ritual that continued for four years, with Gary throwing hundreds of balls to me before every game. He never seemed to get tired and his commitment to the job was amazing.

When he asked me at Adelaide if I wanted to practise against short throw-downs, I asked him to throw full and fast at me, because I had a feeling Brett Lee would bowl a full-length delivery the moment I went in, as he had got me out with a full delivery at Perth. Sure enough, as soon as I walked out to bat at the Adelaide Oval, Lee bowled a delivery at my pads. I was prepared and instead of playing square, which perhaps he was expecting me to do, I played a straight drive past the umpire for four. After the stroke I looked towards Gary in our dressing room.

I went on to score 153 and we put more than 500 runs on the board, with Sehwag and Bhajji both scoring 63 and Kumble playing a captain's innings down the order of 87. Australia batted just as well in response, with Hayden, Ponting and Clarke all making hundreds, and the match ended in a draw – but only after Sehwag had added an impressive 151 in our second innings.

We had not managed to level the series but we had won back credibility and respect.

The final verdict

Before bringing down the curtain on the controversial 'Monkeygate' saga, as it had been dubbed in the press, Justice John Hansen heard everybody's evidence in the appeal on 28 January 2008. I stated exactly what I had heard and seen and also said that I had taken exception to us being labelled 'liars' by the match referee, Mike Procter, who had mentioned in his statement that 'I believe one group is telling the truth'. That he banned Bhajji for three Test matches seemed to us to show which group, in his opinion, was lying. It is never a pleasant thing to be called a liar and I was extremely angry.

In the end, justice prevailed. The verdict of the appeal was that there was no evidence to suggest the use of a racist remark by Bhajji and the ban was lifted. Instead Bhajji was fined half of his match fee for using abusive language against Symonds. Bhajji could finally breathe a sigh of relief and we as a team felt vindicated.

India in Bangladesh 2007

1st Test. Chittagong. 18–22 May 2007

India 387–8 dec (**SR Tendulkar 101**, SC Ganguly 100, R Dravid 61, KD Karthik 56; M Mortaza 4–97, S Hossain 3–76) and 100–6 dec (**SR Tendulkar 31**; M Rafique 3–27, S Hossain 2–30)

Bangladesh 238 (M Mortaza 79, R Saleh 41; RP Singh 3–45, VRV Singh 3–48, **SR Tendulkar 1–15**) and 104–2 (J Omar 52*, H Bashar 37)

Match drawn

2nd Test. Dhaka. 25–27 May 2007
India 610–3 dec (W Jaffer 138, KD Karthik 129, R Dravid 129, **SR Tendulkar
122***, MS Dhoni 51*; M Rafique 2–181)
Bangladesh 118 (Shakib-Al-Hasan 30; Z Khan 5–34, A Kumble 3–32) and 253
(f/o) (M Mortaza 70, M Ashraful 67; RR Powar 3–33, **SR Tendulkar 2–35**)
India won by an innings and 239 runs

India won the series 1–0

India in England 2007 – The Pataudi Trophy

1st Test. Lord's. 19–23 July 2007
England 298 (AJ Strauss 96, MP Vaughan 79; S Sreesanth 3–67) and 282
(KP Pietersen 134, MJ Prior 42; RP Singh 5–59, Z Khan 4–79)
India 201 (W Jaffer 58, **SR Tendulkar 37**; JM Anderson 5–42, RJ Sidebottom
4–65) and 282–9 (MS Dhoni 76*, KD Karthik 60, **SR Tendulkar 16**; CT
Tremlett 3–52, RJ Sidebottom 2–42, MS Panesar 2–63, JM Anderson 2–83)
Match drawn

2nd Test. Nottingham. 27–31 July 2007
England 198 (AN Cook 43; Z Khan 4–59, A Kumble 3–32) and 355
(MP Vaughan 124, PD Collingwood 63, AJ Strauss 55; Z Khan 5–75,
A Kumble 3–104)
India 481 (**SR Tendulkar 91**, SC Ganguly 79, KD Karthik 77, W Jaffer 62,
VVS Laxman 54; MS Panesar 4–101, CT Tremlett 3–80) and 73–3
(KD Karthik 22, W Jaffer 22, **SR Tendulkar 1**; CT Tremlett 3–12)
India won by 7 wickets

3rd Test. The Oval. 9–13 August 2007
India 664 (A Kumble 110*, MS Dhoni 92, KD Karthik 91, **SR Tendulkar 82**,
R Dravid 55, VVS Laxman 51; JM Anderson 4–182) and 180–6 dec
(SC Ganguly 57, **SR Tendulkar 1**; PD Collingwood 2–24, JM Anderson
2–34, CT Tremlett 2–58)
England 345 (IR Bell 63, PD Collingwood 62, AN Cook 61; Z Khan 3–32,
A Kumble 3–94, **SR Tendulkar 1–26**) and 369–6 (KP Pietersen 101, IR Bell
67; S Sreesnath 3–53)
Match drawn

India won the series 1–0

India in Australia 2007–08 – The Border-Gavaskar Trophy

1st Test. Melbourne. 26–29 December 2007
Australia 343 (ML Hayden 124, PA Jaques 66; A Kumble 5–84, Z Khan 4–94)
and 351–7 dec (MJ Clarke 73, PA Jaques 51; H Singh 3–101).
India 196 (**SR Tendulkar 62**, SC Ganguly 43; SR Clark 4–28, B Lee 4–46) and
161 (VVS Laxman 42, SC Ganguly 40, **SR Tendulkar 15**; MG Johnson 3–21,
B Lee 2–43, GB Hogg 2–51)
Australia won by 337 runs

2nd Test. Sydney. 2–6 January 2008

Australia 463 (A Symonds 162*, GB Hogg 79, B Lee 59, RT Ponting 55;
    A Kumble 4–106, RP Singh 4–124) and 401–7 dec (MEK Hussey 145*,
    ML Hayden 123, A Symonds 61; A Kumble 4–148)

India 532 (**SR Tendulkar 154***, VVS Laxman 109, SC Ganguly 67, H Singh 63,
    R Dravid 53; B Lee 5–119) and 210 (SC Ganguly 51, A Kumble 45*,
    SR Tendulkar 12; MJ Clarke 3–5, A Symonds 3–51)

Australia won by 122 runs

3rd Test. Perth. 16–19 January 2008

India 330 (R Dravid 93, **SR Tendulkar 71**; MG Johnson 4–86, B Lee 3–71) and
    294 (VVS Laxman 79, IK Pathan 46, **SR Tendulkar 13**; SR Clark 4–61, B Lee
    3–54)

Australia 212 (A Symonds 66, AC Gilchrist 55; RP Singh 4–68, I Sharma 2–34,
    A Kumble 2–42) and 340 (MJ Clarke 81, MG Johnson 50*, MEK Hussey 46;
    IK Pathan 3–54, V Sehwag 2–24)

India won by 72 runs

4th Test. Adelaide. 24–28 January 2008

India 526 (**SR Tendulkar 153**, A Kumble 87, V Sehwag 63, H Singh 63,
    VVS Laxman 51; MG Johnson 4–126, B Lee 3–101) and 269–7 dec
    (V Sehwag 151, **SR Tendulkar 13**; MG Johnson 2–33, B Lee 2–74)

Australia 563 (RT Ponting 140, MJ Clarke 118, ML Hayden 103, PA Jaques 60;
    IK Pathan 3–112, I Sharma 3–115, V Sehwag 2–51)

Match drawn

Australia won the series 2–1

19

BOUNCING BACK

The 2008 one-day tri-series in Australia with Sri Lanka as the third team was a hard-fought competition. A lot of the tension from the controversial Test series that preceded it was carried into the limited-overs arena and the Indian team under new captain MS Dhoni were determined to return to India with the Commonwealth Bank trophy.

The pitch at the MCG on 10 February was one of the fastest I've played on. We fielded first and Dhoni was standing way back and still had to catch most balls at chest height. I was standing at slip, which was at the edge of the thirty-yard circle, an indication of the pace and bounce of the pitch. I remember mentioning to Dhoni, after an outside edge off Matthew Hayden's bat flew past me, that the pitch was going to favour the fast bowlers throughout the match and no chase was going to be easy.

Our bowlers used the conditions well and dismissed Australia for only 159. Ishant bowled beautifully again to pick up 4–38 and Sreesanth also did well, taking 3–31. At the break our dressing room was buoyant, though we knew that their fast bowlers would enjoy the conditions just as much. Sure enough, in the third over of the innings Lee bowled a fast short ball that flew off the shoulder of my bat over slip towards third man. Just as I was completing the single, Lee walked up to me and casually said with a smile that he was feeling very good and was going to bowl really fast at me. Lee has always been a good friend and while it wasn't exactly sledging, it was enough to fire me up. As he walked past I just muttered to myself that, come what may, I was going to take him on. It turned out to be one of our most memorable contests.

My chance came in the fifth over. Sehwag had just been dismissed at the other end, lbw to left-arm seamer Nathan Bracken for 11, and Lee was steaming in. His second ball was slightly wide but I still decided to go for a drive through cover. I connected moderately well and the ball raced to the fence. Lee just gave me another smile and walked back to his mark. I thought I knew what he would try next. He ran in fast and, as anticipated, bowled a fuller-length ball. I came down hard at it and hit it straight back at him. It must have been one of the most powerful shots I have hit in my life. Lee didn't have a hope of bending down to stop the ball. In fact, the ball had reached the boundary by the time he finished his follow-through.

By now Lee was even more pumped up and the next ball was a 151 kph delivery, which I defended off the back foot. I was determined to keep attacking and I got another opportunity off the fifth ball of the over. It was full and fast and again I hit it back past Lee for four. While the first straight drive had gone to the left of the bowler, this one went to his right. Those two drives gave me a lot of confidence and I went on to make 44. When I got out in the twenty-sixth over we needed 64 runs and Rohit Sharma and Dhoni played well to finish off the job.

Immediately after the match, I started to feel some soreness in my adductors, the muscles in the groin, and informed John Gloster about the problem. We took remedial steps but the pain refused to go away and I was still feeling it when we played our last pool match against Sri Lanka on 26 February in Hobart. It was a game we had to win to qualify for the three-match final against Australia. Sri Lanka scored 179, with Ishant Sharma and Praveen Kumar both taking four wickets, and when our innings started I managed to connect well from the off and went on to make 63 as we knocked off the runs in thirty-three overs. It felt good to spend time out in the middle again after several low scores and I headed to Sydney for the first final, relieved at having scored some runs.

Don't be fooled by the smile! This was one of the scariest experiences of my life – the Sky Walk on the ramp at the Sky Tower in Auckland.

Facing Australia in 2003–4. Making runs against the world's best team was always enjoyable.

Shaking hands with an old adversary. The 2004 Sydney Test marked the end of Steve Waugh's fantastic career.

This is where Daddy works. With Anjali, Sara and Arjun, as well as Anand and Annabel Mehta at the MCG in December 2003. It was the first time I had taken Arjun and Sara inside a stadium.

Above: With Anil Kumble: one of the best triers on the field.

Right: Congratulating Virender Sehwag on reaching 300 in Multan in 2004 – a terrific Test innings.

Below: With Indian and Pakistani soldiers at the Wagah border in 2004.

It meant a lot when my batting hero, Sunil Gavaskar, congratulated me on reaching his record of 34 Test hundreds.

John Wright and I are great friends. John, why did you have to take that catch in New Zealand in 1990?

With one of the best batsmen of all time and a very good friend, Brian Lara.

With Mark Knopfler of Dire Straits, one of my all-time favourite bands, in Mumbai. I treasure the guitar he gave me.

With Amitabh Bachchan: one of India's biggest cultural icons.

Playing chess with the legendary Viv Richards in Sri Lanka. If only I could bat like my hero!

Left: Andrew Symonds and Harbhajan Singh during the controversial Sydney Test in January 2008.

Above: Do you recognize this face? I had to play a Test match the next day!

Below left: Playing an upper cut to Brett Lee on the way to a very satisfying 154* at Sydney.

Below right: Congratulations from Ricky Ponting after I passed Brian Lara's record of Test runs at Mohali in October 2008.

With Rahul Dravid, Sourav Ganguly and VVS Laxman. We spent many memorable years together.

Another peak scaled. We are the number one Test side after beating Sri Lanka in Mumbai in 2009.

At a party organized by Mukesh and Nita Ambani to celebrate my twenty years in international cricket in 2009.

Celebrating the IPL win with the Mumbai Indians in 2013. Which cricketer hit a six off the last ball he played in the IPL? Answer: yours truly!

While I was looking forward to the finals, I was conscious that the pain in my adductors was getting worse after every practice session. I was having problems with running, twisting and even bending down to pick up a ball. It reached a stage where in fielding practice I had to just stand at the stumps while my team-mates threw the ball in. With the final just a day away, painkillers were the only remedy.

CB Series, first final, Sydney, 2 March 2008

Before the finals, the atmosphere got a little heated again when Ricky Ponting declared that Australia would have to play only the first two of the three finals, as that was all it would take to send India packing. His comments only added to our determination.

Australia batted first at the SCG after winning the toss. It's usually a sensible ploy to bat first in a big final, because even a mediocre score can be made to look good in a must-win situation. Australia made 239 on the day, with Matthew Hayden contributing 82, and we didn't think it was a bad total in good bowling conditions.

Robin Uthappa was opening the batting with me and our first task was to see off the new ball. We knew that if the team batted our full fifty overs, we should win the match, and I advised Robin to be patient and not to be aggressive early in the innings. Being a naturally attacking batsman, Robin was itching to play his shots and at one point I had to get a little angry with him, telling him not to do anything rash. We managed not to lose a wicket until the eleventh over, when Robin played his first big pull shot to deep square leg, where Mike Hussey caught the ball low down. Robin might have scored only 17, but he had helped see off the new ball and we had put together a 50-run first-wicket partnership.

I sensed that the match would be ours if we kept our nerve. Unfortunately for us, we lost Gautam Gambhir and Yuvraj within a few overs and needed another partnership to rebuild the innings. Rohit Sharma had come out to bat and I asked him to play straight and not try any fancy shots early on. He batted brilliantly and soon we were in a position to grind down the opposition. Rohit finally got out to the all-rounder James Hopes for 66, just after I had reached my century.

Dhoni came out next and we knocked off the 30 runs needed to finish the match quite easily in the end. The only scare was a beamer from Brett Lee that hit me on the side of my helmet grille and the top of my left shoulder. The ball had slipped out of his hand and could very easily have injured me. I felt a little dizzy and jokingly suggested to Lee that he would have to answer to my son Arjun when he next went to Mumbai. Lee knew Arjun well and had spent some time with my family when we had filmed a *Boost* commercial together. He apologized immediately and the matter was put to rest there and then. It was an accident, of course, but the shoulder felt sore and the area between shoulder and elbow turned black.

It was a very satisfying feeling to bat through the innings. It was a big match but we decided not to celebrate too much because the second final in Brisbane was only a day away and we knew it was going to be tough because of the high humidity.

I could not sleep a wink that night and ached all over. The pain in my groin had increased and I was starting to get scared. The next morning I could barely walk and it was an ordeal boarding the early-morning flight. In Brisbane I was given a long massage as soon as we reached the hotel. Seeing my condition, Dhoni suggested that maybe I should miss the second final and play in the third if needed. I said to him that '*Sher jab gira hua hota hai use tabhi maar dena chahiye*' (You can't give a wounded tiger a second chance.) He agreed with me that it would be better to close out the competition in Brisbane if we could.

CB Series, second final, Brisbane, 4 March 2008

When we arrived at the Gabba we found that there was a lot of moisture in the pitch. It was bound to be difficult for batting early on and the obvious plan was to field first if we won the toss – but I urged Dhoni not to do so. I reckoned that the Australians might well want to bat first, preferring to bat without the pressure of chasing a target. I thought it would be better if we set a target, even if it meant struggling through the initial period of dampness on the wicket.

Dhoni agreed and we batted first. Again, I told Robin Uthappa in no uncertain terms not to risk a single expansive shot till we had played out the first ten overs. In those conditions not losing wickets was far more important than trying to score runs. Robin successfully held back and we survived the first twenty overs intact, giving us a solid foundation to launch an assault. We then scored at almost six runs an over and ended up with 258, a reasonable score to defend in the circumstances.

I was pleased to score 91, but by the end of the innings I also knew that my body was in bad shape and if we weren't able to win in Brisbane I would be in no condition to play the third final. In fact, I was forced to leave the field in the fourth over of the Australia innings, when Dhoni dived to catch Hayden off Sreesanth and the ball ricocheted and hit me exactly where I had been hit by the Lee beamer.

Meanwhile our opening bowler Praveen Kumar produced a great spell and picked up three crucial Australian wickets. Hayden and Symonds then put together a big partnership and the stage was set for Bhajji to have the final word on Australian soil. First he ran Hayden out, following a misunderstanding with Symonds, and then just two balls later Symonds missed a ball that turned a long way and was trapped lbw. Unsurprisingly, Bhajji enjoyed his wicket more than any other.

The match wasn't over yet, however, with James Hopes playing some aggressive strokes. In the end, Hopes was out last, for 63, but by picking up wickets regularly at the other end we had ensured that he was constantly under pressure. Nevertheless, the match was closer than expected and when the final wicket fell, Australia were only ten runs away from winning the game.

It was a great feeling to win, and seeing the tricolour being waved all over the Gabba was a terrific sight. We had beaten Australia in Australia and were also delighted to have proved Ricky Ponting right. He did not have to play a third final, just as he had predicted.

Grasping the nettle

My physical condition was deteriorating by the day. It didn't help that the problem still hadn't been diagnosed properly and I didn't know exactly what I was suffering from. In any case, there wasn't much time to do anything about it as the first of three home Tests against South Africa was due to start at Chennai a couple of weeks later, on 26 March 2008.

After getting as much rest as I could, I went to Chennai, and in the evening before the game had three injections in my groin. The doctors sounded confident that these would enable me to play the next day. When I got up the following morning the pain was substantially reduced, but John Gloster and I decided I should undertake a fitness test. I found I was able to run around during practice and also played our customary game of football without feeling too much discomfort. John declared me fit to play.

It was unlucky for me that South Africa won the toss and then batted for two long days as they compiled 540, with Amla making 159. Fielding in the heat quickly brought back the pain and when I finally batted on the fourth day I was so stiff and sore that I got out without scoring to Makhaya Ntini, caught by Kallis at second slip. At the end of the match, which was a high-scoring draw, I told Anil Kumble and John Gloster that there was no point in pushing my body any further.

I flew back to Mumbai and embarked on a process of rehabilitation under Nitin Patel, the physio of the Mumbai Indians, the IPL team of which I had been made captain. The first season of the IPL was just round the corner and my initial aim was to get fit for the first match. Despite all my efforts, however, I was only able to play the last seven matches, and even then I was not one hundred per cent fit.

The lack of a diagnosis led to some unhelpful speculation. Apparently, one doctor in Mumbai suggested to a member of the Mumbai Indians management that the problem was actually in my head. I found out about it when one night Anjali asked me if the problem was really bad enough for me not to play. How could Anjali ask me such a question? I said to her that I had played with broken fingers and toes, and even played a few days after my father's demise, so how could she, of all people, doubt my physical condition? It was not until the competition had finished that Anjali told me what she had heard from a Mumbai Indians official about what the doctor had said. Frankly, I was shocked, but I was also glad she didn't tell me until the end of the tournament, because I was trying everything possible to get fit and play, and it would have been very upsetting to hear that.

Unfortunately for me, no one in Mumbai could diagnose the problem, despite the fact that I'd undertaken various forms of treatment. Finally, it was in London, when I was there for a family holiday, that I met up with my surgeon Andrew Wallace and explained my condition. He recommended Prof. Cathy Speed, who, on seeing the case history, immediately identified my problem as Gilmore's Groin, or Sportsman's Hernia, and referred me to Dr Ulrike Muschaweck in Germany. Prof. Speed also prescribed a few medicines and gave me some exercises to do and I felt in good enough shape to go to Sri Lanka with the team for the Test series in July and August 2008. I managed to get through the series, which we lost 2–1, without too much trouble, but before the start of the one-day series it was apparent to me that I had to do something about the condition.

On 13 August 2008, I left for Munich alone to get myself treated by Dr Muschaweck at the Munich Hernia Centre. It was a great revelation for me to discover this specialized centre for hernia treatment. Dr Muschaweck was highly recommended by Prof. Speed. She has been specializing in hernia surgery for close to two decades and has developed some new repair techniques in recent years that have considerably improved the recovery process. She immediately makes her patients feel at ease and she was quick to assure me that there was no chance of recurrence once she had operated on me. To my delight she was proved right.

I had the first operation on 14 August and must say the pain was perfectly bearable. I had asked Dr Muschaweck if both sides of the groin could be done on the same day but was told that it wasn't feasible because there would be far too much pain. Anjali hadn't been able to accompany me initially because of Sara's examinations, but she joined me on the evening of the 14th and I underwent my second operation on the morning of the 15th. I had insisted on having the two operations on consecutive days to cut down the recovery time, in the hope of getting fit for the Australian Test series. This time the pain was excruciating. Cleaning myself was quite an ordeal because of the serious pain in my abdomen and I wasn't able to eat a thing. I was given a laxative and this, a sugary syrup with a welcome taste, was the only thing I enjoyed having that night! I could hardly sleep with all the pain and was looking forward to getting back home.

It was an important operation and one that helped prolong my cricket career. It also draws attention to the lack of specialized sports science centres in India at that time. While I could afford to go to Munich and get myself treated by the best experts in the world, for other Indian athletes it might not always have been feasible.

I certainly knew I'd had a serious operation afterwards. I remember leaving the clinic on 16 August in a wheelchair because I felt dizzy every time I tried to stand. I also remember telling Anjali that I was about to faint when standing at the check-in counter at the airport and Anjali rushing to help. After landing in Mumbai, my friend Faisal Momen picked me up and for the first time in my life I asked him to drive as slowly as possible. I was frantically monitoring the road and if I spotted a speed bump I would lift myself a little with my hands to avoid jarring my abdomen.

As soon as I got home Anjali told the kids that for the time being they wouldn't be able to give their father a hug. At that time, Arjun used to like play-fighting with me and I had to show him the bandages to make him understand that I was just too unwell. It was a difficult time for us all. I had already missed days and months of my children's childhood. Now I was finally at home with them all day but was unable to play with them.

Once I'd got over the journey, I started the recovery process under the guidance of Paul Close and Paul Chapman. I did not go out for three weeks during rehab, as I was so tired from all my training, which would start at seven in the morning. I spent the second week of my rehab at the National Cricket Academy, and my training included strengthening exercises, cardio, pool sessions, running – both straight and sideways – specialized exercises with the Thera-Band, and a number of other drills. It would end at around two thirty in the afternoon, following which I would just go home, have lunch and sleep for a few hours, completely exhausted.

The target I had set myself was to recover for the Test series against Australia that was to start in Bangalore at the beginning of October 2008. I knew it would be a race against time and I had a lot of hard work ahead of me. There were days when I would push myself so hard that by the evening I would just collapse on the bed with no strength left at all. Then I would get up very early the next morning and start my exercises all over again. Throughout this period, my group of friends, including Atul Ranade, Sameer Dighe and Jagdish Chavan, were always there to motivate me and would train with me all day. Their presence was a great help and I remain ever indebted to them for their support.

Australia in India, October–November 2008

It was a great relief to be back on the field for the first Test against Australia in Bangalore on 9 October. Australia made 430 in their first innings, with Ponting and Hussey both making hundreds, and we made 360 in reply. I scored only 13 in my first innings, but did better in the second innings before falling to the leg-spin of Cameron White. I scored 49 but, more importantly, I was able to bat for close to three hours and faced more than a hundred balls without feeling discomfort. The match was drawn and we headed to Mohali for the second of the four Tests.

The series had assumed greater significance because Sourav had announced that he would be retiring at the end of the fourth Test at Nagpur. Sourav and I always had a great rapport and we shared a lot of great moments together. As teenagers, we both spent a month at an Under-15 camp and were part of Kailash Gattani's touring team to England. We played together for over a decade in Test cricket and opened the batting for India in countless limited-overs international matches.

One of the habits that we got into was that every time I felt that Sourav was tense or that there was something troubling him, I would say something random to him in Bengali, which is his mother tongue. Often my words made little sense but they were good enough to make him laugh. There was no doubt I was going to miss him. I remember trying to persuade him to carry on, but he was sure it was time to call it a day.

In the second Test at Mohali, starting on 17 October, I scored a fluent 88 in our total of 469 before falling to Peter Siddle, caught at slip. My timing was definitely coming back. In the process I passed Brian Lara's tally and reached the figure of 12,000 Test runs. This achievement was marked by a fantastic fireworks display at the ground. It went on for close to three minutes and I felt privileged and honoured at the affection heaped on me. Mr Inderjit Singh Bindra, one of Indian cricket's most distinguished administrators, who was then president of the Punjab Cricket Association, told me that there were more fireworks than the total number of runs I had scored. I felt overwhelmed. The PCA has always been a great host and is an institution that has made playing in Punjab that much more special.

From the start of Australia's first innings, our bowlers were bowling really good lines and managed to put the Australian batsman under pressure. The ball was reverse-swinging and both Zaheer Khan and Ishant Sharma were making the most of the conditions. In contrast, the Australian bowlers had found it difficult to get their rhythm right and Gambhir, Sehwag and Dhoni had all made big scores against them.

To everyone's delight, Sourav scored a hundred in the first innings. I couldn't have been happier for him and remember how he celebrated what was to be his final Test hundred with a pump of his fist and then raised his arms to acknowledge the well-deserved applause.

The Mohali match is also memorable for me because of the catch I took in the Australian second innings. I was fielding at point when Simon Katich tried to cut Bhajji past me for four. He mistimed the shot and I had to dive forward to reach the ball. I managed to get both hands under it and it was great to feel the leather on my hands. Such a quick reaction put quite a strain on my groin muscles, but I got up unhurt and the relief was evident on my face. My hard work during the recovery had paid off.

It was also an important breakthrough for us in the game and we were able to get into the Australian middle order sooner than expected. Zaheer and Ishant bowled exceptionally well and it was perhaps the best I have seen Zaheer bowl. He was getting the ball to move late and the Australian batsmen struggled against late swing. It's a shame Zaheer suffered so many injuries, otherwise I'm sure we would have seen his match-winning abilities on many more occasions.

We beat the Australians at Mohali by 320 runs and moved to Delhi for the third Test on 29 October leading the four-match contest 1–0. There we managed to keep the momentum going and were happy with a draw, thanks mainly to double hundreds in the first innings by both Gautam Gambhir and Laxman. I scored 68 and felt comfortable enough to believe that a big score wasn't far away; I just had to be patient.

That Delhi Test turned out to be Anil Kumble's last and it was an extremely emotional moment for us all. Anil was one of the biggest match-winners India has produced and we had played together for close to two decades. I was very surprised when he said he was thinking of retiring. He felt he was not bowling close to his best and was not able to give one hundred per cent for the team. My argument was simple. Even eighty per cent of Anil Kumble was good enough for most batsmen and India still needed him.

I almost managed to persuade him to carry on but an injury to his spinning finger on the third day of the Test was the final straw. He had just recovered from a shoulder surgery and with the finger injury, which required eleven stitches, he simply couldn't bowl. We carried him on our shoulders and it was a fitting finale for one of international cricket's true all-time greats.

His final speech was very emotional for all of us and the crowd gave him a standing ovation. I'm glad to say we managed to convince Anil to come to Nagpur for the last Test to be a part of the celebration if India went on to win the series. It was only right that Anil should be there, because he had captained us in two of the first three Tests and had also been the captain when we played in Australia earlier in the year.

We started well at Nagpur on 6 November, with an opening partnership of close to a hundred by Sehwag and Vijay, but then lost two quick wickets. I managed to build decent partnerships with Laxman and Sourav, with a number of lucky breaks going my way. I was dropped in the eighties and nineties and I told Sourav that God wanted me to score a century on the occasion of Sourav's farewell Test match.

In his final Test Sourav scored a valuable 85 for the team. We managed 441 in our first innings but I still felt we were 100 runs short. It was a good batting wicket and the Australians raced on in the last session of day two to finish at 189–2. We knew we could not afford to let them get away the next morning. We had to try something different to make them think and take some risks, because they were the ones under pressure to level the series. I suggested to Dhoni that we needed to slow down the game, and after that we employed an 8–1 field, with eight fielders on the off side and one on the on, something hardly ever tried in Test cricket, to Michael Hussey and Simon Katich, and despite dropping Katich early on we managed to restrict the runs. Zaheer and Ishant bowled well to the field and Australia just could not get away.

They added only 42 runs before lunch and Ishant also dismissed Simon Katich in the process. That wicket changed everything and we took a further three in the session between lunch and tea, conceding just 49 runs. The momentum had shifted and we knew we were back in control. We eventually set Australia a target of 382 in their second innings, and then Amit Mishra, the leg-spinner who had replaced Anil, and Harbhajan Singh finished things off midway through the second session on day five and we won the series 2–0.

The celebrations went on into the night and both Anil and Sourav were asked to give speeches. Gary, who had played a huge role behind the scenes, had organized the farewell at the VCA Club in Jamtha and it was a day everyone who was there will cherish for ever. The whole team stayed on in Nagpur for this very special occasion and I did the same, despite having to miss Anjali's fortieth birthday. I knew that, as always, she would understand and pardon my absence.

India in Sri Lanka 2008

1st Test. Colombo (SSC). 23–26 July 2008
Sri Lanka 600–6 dec (DPMD Jayawardene 136, TT Samaraweera 127, TM Dilshan 125*, SM Warnapura 115; I Sharma 2–124)
India 223 (VVS Laxman 56, **SR Tendulkar 27**; M Muralitharan 5–84, BAW Mendis 4–72) and 138 (f/o) (G Gambhir 43, **SR Tendulkar 12**; M Muralitharan 6–26, BAW Mendis 4–60)
Sri Lanka won by an innings and 239 runs

2nd Test. Galle. 31 July–3 August 2008
India 329 (V Sehwag 201*, G Gambhir 56, **SR Tendulkar 5**; BAW Mendis 6–117) and 269 (G Gambhir 74, V Sehwag 50, **SR Tendulkar 31**; BAW Mendis 4–92, M Muralitharan 3–107)
Sri Lanka 292 (DPMD Jayawardene 86, KC Sangakkara 68, SM Warnapura 66; H Singh 6–102, A Kumble 3–81) and 136 (TT Samaraweera 67*, TM Dilshan 38; H Singh 4–51, I Sharma 3–20, A Kumble 2–41)
India won by 170 runs

3rd Test. Colombo (PSS). 8–11 August 2008
India 249 (G Gambhir 72, SC Ganguly 35, **SR Tendulkar 6**; BAW Mendis 5–56, KTGD Prasad 3–82) and 268 (R Dravid 68, VVS Laxman 61*, **SR Tendulkar 14**; BAW Mendis 3–81, M Muralitharan 3–99)
Sri Lanka 396 (KC Sangakkara 144, HAPW Jayawardene 49, WPUJC Vaas 47; H Singh 3–104, Z Khan 3–105, A Kumble 3–123) and 123–2 (SM Warnapura 54*, DPMD Jayawardene 50*)
Sri Lanka won by 8 wickets

Sri Lanka won the series 2–1

Australia in India 2008

1st Test. Bangalore. 9–13 October 2008
Australia 430 (MEK Hussey 146, RT Ponting 123, SM Katich 66; Z Khan 5–91, I Sharma 4–77) and 228–6 dec (SR Watson 41, BJ Haddin 35*; I Sharma 3–40)
India 360 (Z Khan 57*, H Singh 54, R Dravid 51, **SR Tendulkar 13**; MG Johnson 4–70, SR Watson 3–45) and 177–4 (**SR Tendulkar 49**, VVS Laxman 42*)
Match drawn

2nd Test. Mohali. 17–21 October 2008

India 469 (SC Ganguly 102, MS Dhoni 92, **SR Tendulkar 88**, G Gambhir
  67; MG Johnson 3–85, PM Siddle 3–114) and 314–3 dec (G Gambhir 104,
  V Sehwag 90, MS Dhoni 68*, **SR Tendulkar 10**)
Australia 268 (SR Watson 78, MEK Hussey 54; A Mishra 5–71) and 195
  (MJ Clarke 69; H Singh 3–36, Z Khan 3–71)
India won by 320 runs

3rd Test. Delhi. 29 October–2 November 2008

India 613–7 dec (G Gambhir 206, VVS Laxman 200*, **SR Tendulkar 68**;
  MG Johnson 3–142) and 208–5 dec (VVS Laxman 59*, **SR Tendulkar 47**;
  B Lee 2–48)
Australia 577 (MJ Clarke 112, RT Ponting 87, ML Hayden 83, SM Katich
  64, MEK Hussey 53; V Sehwag 5–104, A Kumble 3–112) and 31–0
Match drawn

4th Test. Nagpur. 6–10 November 2008

India 441 (**SR Tendulkar 109**, SC Ganguly 85, V Sehwag 66, VVS Laxman
  64, MS Dhoni 56; JJ Krejza 8–215) and 295 (V Sehwag 92, MS Dhoni
  55, H Singh 52, **SR Tendulkar 12**; SR Watson 4–42, JJ Krejza 4–143)
Australia 355 (SM Katich 102, MEK Hussey 90, CL White 46; H Singh
  3–94) and 209 (ML Hayden 77; H Singh 4–64, A Mishra 3–27)
India won by 172 runs

India won the series 2–0

20

THE IPL

The Indian Premier League, the franchise-based Twenty20 competition that started in April 2008, has had a revolutionary impact on world cricket. It seems to have captured the imagination of the modern fan and has attracted the best players from around the world. I am convinced that the IPL will continue to be a permanent feature of the global cricket calendar, just as it has already become a part of millions of Indian households every April and May.

Despite sometimes being played in rather adverse weather conditions and on occasions outside of India, most of the games have been played to sell-out crowds. And this is not restricted to the smaller venues. In May 2013, people came out in droves to support quality cricket, despite all the talk of spot- and match-fixing surrounding the tournament. I was disappointed, shocked and angry at the goings-on, and said so in a press release at the time. There has to be a strict zero-tolerance policy against corruption and more should be done to educate the players, but on the other hand the tournament as a whole cannot be blamed for the wrongdoings of a few.

There is little doubt that the IPL has added an entirely new dimension to Indian cricket. Not only has interest grown in domestic competitions, but there is also a spill-over effect that has helped improve general awareness about domestic cricket. It has certainly made domestic performances more significant, with players knowing that playing well on the domestic circuit may earn them an IPL contract.

Early fears

When the IPL was originally launched by the BCCI in late 2007, there was, understandably, a lot of apprehension surrounding the tournament. Indian cricket had to come to terms with the club culture, and the concept of player auctions was alien to the average Indian cricket fan. No one was quite sure what standard the cricket would be or whether fans would come out to support the tournament in the oppressive heat of April and May.

A confession is in order here. While I never had any doubt that the IPL would be popular, I did not expect the tournament to take off quite so quickly. Secondly, I did not expect the standard of cricket to be so high. The matches in the IPL are played with as much intensity as international cricket and the level is very close to the highest international standard. Young players, especially, always try and give their franchise their best, and the fans appreciate their efforts as much as they enjoy seeing the world's best players in action alongside the best of domestic talent.

The IPL and international cricket

There are, however, some fundamental differences between the IPL and international cricket. One is the close involvement of the team owners. Their presence adds to the character of the tournament. For example, some have their own peculiar superstitions, which they impose on the team. For one team, the owner's priest decides when the players should leave their hotel rooms on match days, and the players go along with this, no matter what state they are in at that ordained time.

Another team owner believes in 'vaastu' (which is a little like feng shui) and their dressing room is always organized in a particular manner, with mirrors set at specific angles. Once in a match against us this team even went ahead and changed our dressing room, putting in mirrors just as they did at their home venue. In turn, we changed this arrangement late at night and all the mirrors were covered with towels to unsettle the opposition.

On another occasion we were advised by a particular team management not to use one of the washrooms in our dressing room. It even had an 'OUT OF ORDER' sign on the door. However, one of our players went in, just to take a look, only to discover that it was working perfectly. Eventually, our team made it a point to keep using that particular washroom, and we went on to win the game!

Another key difference between the IPL and international cricket concerns culture. Almost all the players in the Indian team come from a similar background and are well versed in the Indian system of playing the game by the time they make the national team. Within an IPL team there can be a vast difference between the cultural background of a rookie Indian player and that of an Indian stalwart. This means that bonding between team members is absolutely essential. Looking after the youngsters and making sure they are not overawed is added responsibility for the team owners, management and senior players. As part of the Mumbai Indian squad, I have particularly enjoyed mentoring our young Indian talent, acting as a bridge between the international professionals and them,

Impact on Indian cricket

That the IPL has had a profound impact on Indian cricket is beyond doubt. The benefits are obvious, but there are also a few concerns that need to be taken seriously if the tournament is to evolve further in the years to come.

On the plus side, the IPL has contributed to improving international player relations. The best example is the case of Andrew Symonds and Harbhajan Singh. In the fourth season of the IPL in 2011, Symonds and Bhajji played together for the Mumbai Indians. I clearly remember our first meeting with Andrew when he joined the team. I told Andrew that the Sydney controversy of 2008 was in the past and that neither I nor Harbhajan would ever refer to the incident in our dealings with him. Andrew, for his part, reciprocated the camaraderie and we became good friends. We played some really good matches side by side and I am sure when we meet next we will share the same chemistry.

Since the start of the IPL, none of the India–Australia series have featured the kind of acrimony on show during the 2008 tour. In IPL season six in 2013, for example, I had the opportunity to play with Ricky Ponting. Ricky and I had played international cricket against each other for years but the only interaction we had had, before we played together for the Mumbai Indians, was the occasional hello. Now, all of a sudden, we were sharing the same dressing room and opening the batting together. It was an enriching experience for me to get to know Ricky better and to understand his perspective on the game. I also enjoyed opening the batting with Sanath Jayasuriya in IPL season two, Shikhar Dhawan in season three and Dwayne Smith in season five.

The transformation in player relations has also had a knock-on effect on spectator behaviour at IPL matches. For example, when Shane Warne, playing for the Rajasthan Royals, rushed to congratulate the Indian all-rounder Yusuf Pathan after his Super Over heroics against the Kolkata Knight Riders in South Africa in 2009, the large Indian diaspora at the stadium was spontaneous in applauding Warne for his gesture.

Perhaps the biggest benefit of the IPL, however, is that it offers the Indian domestic cricketer an opportunity to play with the best in the world. There are plenty of players in India who are good but have narrowly missed the opportunity to represent their country. Some of them might be on the wrong side of thirty now, and have little hope of playing for their country. The IPL has given a lot of these players recognition and respect they would never have expected a few years earlier, not to mention a good income, too. The IPL is the best platform after international cricket at the moment, with a massive presence of international stars, and the Indian domestic players get a share of the glory associated with the international game by playing in the IPL. IPL performances are covered extensively in the media and the status of the domestic Indian cricketer has vastly improved as a result.

Young rookies cutting their teeth in Twenty20 cricket have also benefited from the competition. To be able to face up to Dale Steyn or Morne Morkel in the nets, share a dressing room with Jacques Kallis, AB de Villiers or Kevin Pietersen, practise and play alongside the likes of Chris Gayle or Michael Hussey is a dream come true for these youngsters. They have a chance to learn from the greats of the contemporary game. In the Mumbai Indians, the youngsters can play in the nets against Lasith Malinga, one of the best Twenty20 bowlers in the world, rub shoulders with the likes of Kieron Pollard and discuss bowling techniques with Anil Kumble, the mentor of the team. I absolutely loved it when Malinga, fielding at mid on, walked up to Dhawal Kulkarni, the Mumbai medium-fast bowler during one of our matches, and offered him tips to improve his bowling. These are advantages that go far beyond the monetary gains provided by the IPL. For established Indian players, there are other benefits to be had. Invaluable knowledge about the strengths and weaknesses of players from other countries can be gained from playing with and against them in the IPL.

Making the national team

The IPL has enabled many an Indian player to get noticed and subsequently make it to the national team and many others to come back into the reckoning. It was by virtue of their standout performances in the first season of the IPL that Yusuf Pathan and Ravindra Jadeja caught the attention of the Indian selectors. Similarly, Irfan Pathan made a comeback to the national side by doing well in the fourth IPL season and there are countless other examples.

While I agree that IPL performances are important enough to open doors to the national team, I am sure that IPL performances should only be used as a reason to pick a player for the Twenty20 format or, in exceptional cases, for ODI cricket. Playing well in the IPL does not make a player good enough for Test cricket, and arguably not fifty-over one-day cricket either, for they require completely different skill sets. For those formats, selectors should continue to look at performances in the Ranji Trophy, the Duleep Trophy, the Irani Trophy and other domestic competitions.

Rewarding our past stars

One of the best legacies of the IPL is that it has allowed the BCCI to reward former cricketers who played for India at a time when there wasn't much money on offer. While every player in the IPL is assured of a decent standard of living, many former Indian greats had to suffer hardship in old age. In a fantastic gesture during the fifth season of the IPL in May 2012, the BCCI decided to use the revenues generated by the competition to reward every player who had ever played for India. Even domestic players who had played a certain number of first-class games were brought within the ambit of this scheme. Such a gesture serves as a huge encouragement for aspiring cricketers, who know that if they make the national team they will never have to worry about the basic necessities of life.

It was a nice touch that these special payments were presented during the play-off stages of the tournament in front of full stadiums, highlighting the achievements of these former servants of Indian cricket. This certainly wouldn't have been possible without the IPL.

Apprehensions

A major apprehension concerning the IPL is that its riches will make playing for India somewhat less significant and consequently less appealing. Many say that a lot of Indian youngsters are content to earn substantial sums of money and lead a good life playing Twenty20. For me personally there is nothing that compares with playing for India, but it depends on the individual: is he prepared to put in the extra work required to play for his country, or is he satisfied with a couple of months of fame a year? Someone who is determined to play for his country will inevitably strive towards his goal, while those who aren't motivated enough to do so don't really deserve to don the Indian team colours.

Another concern is that the IPL may lead to burn-out for some Indian players. I don't quite agree with this contention. While I am not debating the need to control the number of Twenty20 games played each year, putting all the blame for injuries and fatigue on the IPL isn't always right, either. The best players from all countries play the IPL and every country, at the moment, has a similar schedule. Given the amount of cricket being played around the world, injuries are now part of a cricketer's life. Australian players who haven't played the IPL have also been out for months injured, even though Australia has one of the best injury-management programmes in the world. Most international cricketers play with niggles and ultimately players themselves are the best judges of their bodies, and they have to be sensible and responsible when deciding whether to play, and when not to.

Playing for the Mumbai Indians

I thoroughly enjoyed playing for the Mumbai Indians. Just after the IPL was launched in late 2007, Mukesh Ambani, the owner, told me that he would like me to captain the team and I readily agreed. As skipper, I made it very clear to my team-mates that all I wanted from them was total commitment on the field, and that's what we tried to deliver on in the six seasons that I played with them.

It took some time to get used to how the auction system worked. I was in Australia when the first one took place in February 2008 and had provided the management with a list of players I wanted for every position; in fact, I had provided multiple options. But the team we ended up with didn't have quite the balance I'd hoped for and our first season wasn't particularly successful. It also didn't help that I wasn't able to play the first seven games because of injury.

Happily, one of the players we did manage to pick was Lasith Malinga. I was keen to have him at any cost as I was sure he would be a handy option for this format, and he has proved to be an excellent performer in Twenty20. Mind you, no one bowls quite like Malinga. With his low, slingy action, it's almost as if the umpire becomes the sightscreen. I remember an occasion in Sri Lanka when Malinga was bowling to me with a white ball and I had to ask the umpire to remove his white hat, because I was losing the ball against it! Unfortunately for us, Malinga wasn't able to play the entire first season owing to a knee injury.

After the Mumbai Indians failed to make the semi-finals in the first two seasons, we were determined to put in a better performance in 2010. Mrs Nita Ambani was personally involved from the beginning of the season and this time we began our preparations weeks before the season started. We had a two-day bonding camp at the Waterstones Club in Mumbai and enjoyed getting to know each other. Mrs Ambani was present on both days and the players enjoyed interacting with her. The youngsters in the team mingled with the senior players and I remember that Zaheer Khan, Harbhajan and I were asked a series of questions by the other players about our careers and our lives as Indian cricketers. It was interesting to learn that Zaheer found it very difficult to adjust to the Mumbai lifestyle after coming from the relatively smaller town of Ahmednagar and I was particularly fascinated by Harbhajan's stories about his childhood while growing up in Punjab. We played a variety of sports, including table tennis, squash and water polo, but no cricket.

The camp worked brilliantly and that season we finally did the franchise justice, and were the team to beat throughout the competition. Unfortunately, I got injured while catching a ball in the slips in the semi-final, splitting the webbing between my fingers on my right hand. I had to have six stitches and couldn't hold the bat properly and most people who saw the injury felt I wouldn't make the final against the Chennai Super Kings, led by MS Dhoni. I was determined to take part, however.

On the morning of the final I tried having an injection to numb the injured area, which I thought would help me hold the bat. I had also had some special gloves made, with added protection for the injury, but it seemed that the pain was going to be too much. However, the plan did not work as well as I'd hoped and after the area was numbed I found I had no idea where my fingers were. I actually went back to the hotel, disappointed that even after having the excruciatingly painful injection the situation had not improved. In the end, though, I managed to play in the final, despite being in considerable pain. In the gap between the semi-final and the final I had also visited a doctor in Sri Lanka, who said he could get me ready for the final and that I would have to take the medicine he prescribed twice a day. However, as a side effect I would not be able to sleep properly for the first three days, but once the medicine had run its course I would sleep a lot. He was right. The medicine did help and I did eventually play in the final – but, as warned, I wasn't able to sleep for three nights and then slept for the next three days!

In the warm-up before the match, the umpires walked up to me to check that I was aware of what I was getting into: because I was carrying an injury suffered before the game started, I would not be allowed a substitute. But I had considered all the consequences and was ready to pull myself through the pain to try and win the coveted IPL trophy.

Twice in the match the ball hit my injured hand. The first time was when I was fielding at fine leg. On the second occasion I was standing at cover when Suresh Raina, the left-handed middle-order bat, played a full-blooded cover drive that came to me in a flash. I instinctively stopped the ball and realized soon afterwards that my stitches had burst open. At the changeover my hand was bleeding. I ignored it and went out to bat wearing the special gloves, which had no gap between the middle and index fingers. With these gloves on, I could at least get a good grip on the bat, and I managed to make 48. Unfortunately for us, the IPL trophy continued to elude us as we lost too many wickets in a heap and fell 22 runs short of the target.

A lot was written about the decision to bat Kieron Pollard at number seven during the run chase in that 2010 final. It was a decision taken by the management based on my input and the reasoning was clear. As long as the spinners were bowling, we wanted the likes of Ambati Rayudu and Saurabh Tiwary, both of whom were good players of spin, to be out in the middle. Pollard could then come in and take on the faster bowlers. In hindsight, however, I believe that sending Pollard up the order would have been the better option. It was a mistake and I have no hesitation in admitting it.

We had another good competition the following season and made the play-offs again. I got my first and only Twenty20 hundred against the Kochi Tuskers team. In fact, in those two seasons, I was consistent at the top of the order and there was talk about me playing for the Indian team for the World Twenty20 in the Caribbean in April–May 2010. However, the thought never crossed my mind. By early 2010 the Indian Twenty20 team had a settled look to it and it would not have been right to reconsider my decision not to play international Twenty20 cricket for just one tournament.

I thoroughly enjoyed my experiences in Twenty20 with the Mumbai Indians. The overwhelming sense of positivity that surrounds the team made playing for them a real pleasure. I also enjoyed being captain in the first four seasons, but I am glad that I then handed over the captaincy to Harbhajan, a decision that caused a stir in the media at the time. The fact was that 2011–12 was one of my toughest years in cricket and by the time of the fifth season of the IPL, which started on 4 April 2012, I was feeling mentally drained. I was in no position to cope with the stress of captaincy and just wanted to continue as a batsman. It was for this reason that I asked the owners to consider giving the captaincy to Harbhajan. I would be there to help and offer advice to him on and off the field, especially because he and I had always shared great comradeship while playing for India.

I have known Bhajji since 1994, when he first bowled a few doosras to me during practice in Chandigarh, and we became very good friends when he broke into the Indian team against Australia in Bangalore in 1998. Bhajji had already shown his mettle as captain of the Mumbai Indians in the Champions League Twenty20 in October 2011, which I missed through injury, when he did brilliantly to lead the team to the title.

The final season

I knew that 2013 was always going to be my last year in the IPL. Dedicating three more years to the IPL as a player after I turned 40 in April 2013 was never an option. I was desperate to win the title, having come so close in 2010. We had a good unit and all the players were fit going into the tournament. Ricky Ponting was now captain, John Wright was coach, and Anil Kumble had joined us as mentor, making it a very strong support unit.

I started the season with a disappointing run-out but batted well from the middle of the tournament. Ricky, however, was not in the best of form and he decided to drop himself for a few games and hand the captaincy to Rohit, who was batting well. Rohit did a very good job as skipper and the bowling too came together nicely, with Malinga, Mitchell Johnson, Harbhajan and Pragyan Ojha consistently doing well for us. But just when my own form was peaking, I sustained the injury that brought my IPL career to an end.

We were playing the Sunrisers Hyderabad on 13 May 2013 and were in control, having scored 91 off twelve overs, with the loss of just one wicket. The asking rate was slightly over ten runs an over and with nine wickets in hand we had every reason to feel confident. I was starting to accelerate and hit the first ball of the thirteenth over for six over long on. Just as I was completing the shot, I heard a click in my left hand and then felt excruciating pain. I immediately called for the physio, but massage didn't do any good. I was finding it impossible to hold the bat, let alone play a shot. It was a critical time in the match and there was no way I could keep playing on and waste balls in the process. The only option was to retire hurt.

I had a series of scans, which showed inflammation of the tendons and fluid accumulation in the hand. The doctors said it would take a minimum of three weeks to heal and it was clear my campaign was over. Though I wasn't able to play, I decided to travel with the team. I bowled long stints in the nets and did what I could to help the boys with their preparation. It was hard to sit out for the final, though, particularly because I was getting into a good rhythm, but it was an incredible feeling when the Mumbai Indians won the 2013 IPL trophy in front of a packed Eden Gardens crowd in Kolkata. To cap it all, my team-mates very graciously dedicated their victory to me.

It was during the final that I was asked in an interview if I would play the first game of the next IPL season in front of my home crowd at the Wankhede. It was clear to me that I would not be able to and I found myself saying so. I hadn't actually planned to announce my retirement from the IPL and it happened on the spur of the moment. Anjali was at the ground and a number of journalists went on to ask her what she thought of me announcing my retirement from the IPL. She was a little taken aback at what I'd said, though she knew very well that season six was going to be my last.

While I was very sorry not to play for Mumbai in the last five games of IPL season six, I will look back with fondness at my IPL career, which came to a satisfying end with me hitting a six off the last ball I faced!

The Mumbai Indians in the 2013 Indian Premier League

Points table

	M	Won	Lost	Tied	N/R	Pts	Net RR
Chennai Super Kings	16	11	5	0	0	22	+0.530
Mumbai Indians	16	11	5	0	0	22	+0.441
Rajasthan Royals	16	10	6	0	0	20	+0.322
Sunrisers Hyderabad	16	10	6	0	0	20	+0.003
Royal Challengers Bangalore	16	9	7	0	0	18	+0.457
Kings XI Punjab	16	8	8	0	0	16	+0.226
Kolkata Knight Riders	16	6	10	0	0	12	−0.095
Pune Warriors	16	4	12	0	0	8	−1.006
Delhi Daredevils	16	3	13	0	0	6	−0.848

Play-off stage

Qualifier 1. Chennai Super Kings v Mumbai Indians at Delhi. 21 May 2013
Chennai Super Kings 192/1 (20/20 ov); Mumbai Indians 144 (18.4/20 ov)
Chennai Super Kings won by 48 runs

Eliminator. Rajasthan Royals v Sunrisers Hyderabad at Delhi. 22 May 2013
Sunrisers Hyderabad 132/7 (20/20 ov); Rajasthan Royals 135/6 (19.2/20 ov)
Rajasthan Royals won by 4 wickets (with 4 balls remaining)

Qualifier 2. Mumbai Indians v Rajasthan Royals at Kolkata. 24 May 2013
Rajasthan Royals 165/6 (20/20 ov); Mumbai Indians 169/6 (19.5/20 ov)
Mumbai Indians won by 4 wickets (with 1 ball remaining)

Final. Chennai Super Kings v Mumbai Indians at Kolkata. 26 May 2013
Mumbai Indians 148/9 (20/20 ov); Chennai Super Kings 125/9 (20/20 ov)
Mumbai Indians won by 23 runs

21

NUMBER ONE

Having beaten Australia 2–0 at home in October–November 2008, we were optimistic about the home series against England in December. Gary Kirsten, our coach, had instilled a sense of confidence in the players and all we needed to do now was sustain the momentum after the retirements of Anil and Sourav, two of the best players to represent India.

England in India, December 2008

England's tour started with a seven-match series of ODIs. I did not play in the first three because I was suffering from another elbow problem, this time what is known as a 'golfer's elbow'. It troubled me throughout the season, but not enough to miss a Test match, and it actually turned out to be one of the best seasons of my career. My good form extended into the next season, and I was nominated the ICC's Cricketer of the Year for 2009–10.

After making only 11 in my comeback match in Bangalore, I was more satisfied with a fifty in the fifth game at Cuttack on 26 November, which we won comfortably, taking a 5–0 series lead. Shortly after the game we heard that some sort of gang war had started in Mumbai. We were deeply perturbed by what we saw on the news channels in the dressing room. It was obviously much more than a gang war and the live footage left us shocked. Our thoughts and prayers went out to the people who were caught up in the tragedy.

Most of the players watched what was happening on television till late into the night and it became clear to us that India was essentially under attack. It was the most barbaric of acts and what was happening in the streets of Mumbai was shocking. These were places that were part of our daily life. It was devastating to see flames coming out of the Taj Mahal Palace Hotel, one of India's iconic landmarks. I anxiously called Anjali to check that she and all our friends and loved ones were safe.

What made it all even more personal was that, just the day before, Anjali had been in Leopold's restaurant, which was one of the prime targets, and had also visited another target, the Oberoi, for dinner the previous night. She had gone to see a play at the National Centre for the Performing Arts and ended up having dinner with her friends there. She could so easily have been caught up in the mayhem.

The terror attack continued the next morning and the pictures were beamed live all day on 27 November 2008. We had a team meeting and were informed that England had decided to call off the series and had already left for Dubai. It was understandable, because none of us was in a frame of mind to play cricket. I returned to Mumbai that evening and was met by security personnel at the airport, who escorted me home. It was unnerving to think that it was all happening so close to where I lived. I was angry and upset and it was a horrible feeling having to sit back and pray for the ordeal to end.

A week after the terror attacks, it was announced that England were coming back for a two-Test series. This was a terrific gesture and each one of us appreciated the efforts of the English to return to India within two weeks of the carnage. While nothing could compensate for the trauma inflicted by these terror strikes, a resumption of cricket was a welcome sign of positivity for us all.

Cricket for peace

When we assembled in Chennai for the first Test on 11 December we were still finding it difficult to concentrate on cricket. Our thoughts were with the victims of the attacks and everyone was talking about those traumatic three days. But we had a Test match on our hands and we felt it was important for all our fans that we should put in a good peformance in Chennai for all our fans.

England started well, with captain Andrew Strauss becoming the first England player to make a century in both innings on the subcontinent and Paul Collingwood also making a century. Unless we managed to pull things back on the morning of day four, it was going to be difficult to save the match. Zaheer and Ishant bowled very well in the English second innings but it was Zaheer's spell of three wickets in five overs, including the centurion Collingwood, that brought us back into the game. For the first time we sensed we had the opposition on the back foot and it was now up to the batsmen to chase down the target of 387. It would not be easy – in fact it would be the highest ever run chase on Indian soil – but under Gary we had started to believe that anything was possible.

Sehwag set up the match wonderfully by scoring a brilliant counter-attacking 83 on the fourth evening. It was an innings of outstanding ability. I went in to bat on the morning of the final day and for the first hour or so just tried to soak up the pressure. Once we had weathered the early storm we started to look for runs. Every positive stroke put the pressure back on England and slowly but steadily the balance started to tilt in our favour.

Laxman and I had a good partnership and once Laxman fell, Yuvraj joined me in the middle. I was determined to bat till the end of the match. Indians love cricket and if, for just a minute or two, a victory in Chennai could lift their mood after everything that had happened, I would feel humbled.

Yuvraj batted well under pressure, making 85. There was a time in his innings when he attempted to play the reverse sweep to Monty Panesar and I walked up to him to tell him that all he needed to do was remain not out and finish the game. I reminded him of the Pakistan game at Chennai in 1999 and said I had been in a similar position before and remembered well how painful it was to lose from a winning position. Yuvraj reined himself in and we finally reached our target in the last hour of the fifth day. I had scored an unbeaten hundred for the team, but it was the extra significance of the game that made it particularly gratifying. In a first in Indian cricket, even the groundswomen, who hardly ever came to the foreground, celebrated the victory with great vigour. As we were walking back to the changing rooms, I was asked who I planned to dedicate the hundred to. I had not thought about it and was still very much in the moment, but on behalf of the team I dedicated our victory to the victims of the terrorist attack.

India in New Zealand, one-day series, March 2009

We followed up the victory at Chennai with a well-played draw at Mohali and won the series 1–0. Back-to-back series wins at home were an excellent way to cap off the year and we were all looking forward to our next away series in New Zealand.

Beating the Black Caps in New Zealand can be a tricky task, but we knew we had a great opportunity. We were in good form and seemed to have developed the useful ability to pull ourselves out of difficult situations; if one person failed, the second would step up.

In the five-match one-day series, we easily won the rain-affected first match, thanks largely to the batting of Sehwag and Dhoni. The second match was a washout, but in the third match at Christchurch, one of the smaller grounds, I had reached 163 when I was forced to retire hurt with a strained stomach muscle in the forty-fifth over.

It was frustrating to have to go off in that kind of form. I like to think I was in with a chance of scoring a double hundred had I been able to bat on, and I wasn't alone in thinking that. As soon as I entered the dressing room, Sehwag walked up to me, saying, '*Paaji yeh apne kya kar diya. Double hundred ka chance thha.*' (What have you done, brother? You had a realistic chance of scoring a double hundred.) I laughed and said to him, '*Arre main mar hi nahi pa raha hoon, double hundred kaise banaunga. Pitch achha hai aur hame abhi runs chaiye. Double hundred kabhi na kabhi ho jayega.*' (I can't even hit the ball, so how can I score a double hundred? It is a good pitch to bat on and we need big runs at the moment. I will score a double hundred at some point in the future.') Sehwag, however, wouldn't let up and said, '*Arre woh toh doosra double hundred hoga, aaj ka to aaj karna chahiye thha!*' (When you score a double hundred again it might be the *second* double hundred. Today you should have scored the *first ever* ODI double ton!)

The match was a high-scoring one and, despite setting a target of 392, with Yuvraj Singh and Dhoni both making half-centuries, we were not safe. New Zealand played well to get to 334, thanks in no small part to an opening partnership of 166 between Brendon McCullum and Jesse Ryder, and the aggregate score of 726 in the two innings was the second highest in the history of ODI cricket.

I missed the next match at Hamilton, which we also won thanks to an onslaught from Sehwag that brought him 125. To celebrate taking a 3–0 lead in the series, Bhajji, Zaheer, Yuvi and I met up in Bhajji's room for dinner, which was next to the health club in the hotel. There was a wonderful outdoor Jacuzzi and it had started drizzling outside, making it a beautiful setting. While my team-mates wanted to get into the Jacuzzi, I said I was content to stay where I was. Seeing my reluctance, the three of them hatched a plot.

We had ordered food in the room and were chatting while we waited for it when they grabbed me from behind and hurled me into the water. I was screaming at them, saying my watch would get spoilt, but it made no difference, as they were determined to have fun at my expense. They all followed me into the Jacuzzi and we started messing around in the water. By now the food had arrived and within minutes the French fries, sandwiches and ketchup had found their way into the Jacuzzi. It was certainly an unusual way to celebrate!

India v England

(1st Test)

Played at MA Chidambaram Stadium, Chepauk, Chennai, on 11–15 December 2008

Umpires: BF Bowden & DJ Harper (TV: SL Shastri)
Referee: JJ Crowe
Toss: England

ENGLAND

AJ Strauss	c and b Mishra	123		c Laxman b Harbhajan Singh	108
AN Cook	c Khan b Harbhajan Singh	52		c Dhoni b Sharma	9
IR Bell	lbw b Khan	17		c Gambhir b Mishra	7
KP Pietersen*	c and b Khan	4		lbw b Yuvraj Singh	1
PD Collingwood	c Gambhir b Harbhajan Singh	9		lbw b Khan	108
A Flintoff	c Gambhir b Mishra	18		c Dhoni b Sharma	4
JM Anderson	c Yuvraj Singh b Mishra	19	(10)	not out	1
MJ Prior†	not out	53	(7)	c Sehwag b Sharma	33
GP Swann	c Dravid b Harbhajan Singh	1	(8)	b Khan	7
SJ Harmison	c Dhoni b Yuvraj Singh	6	(9)	b Khan	1
MS Panesar	lbw b Sharma	6			
Extras	(lb 7, nb 1)	8		(b 10, lb 13, w 2, nb 7)	32
Total	(128.4 overs)	316		(for 9 wkts dec) (105.5 overs)	311

INDIA

G Gambhir	lbw b Swann	19		c Collingwood b Anderson	66
V Sehwag	b Anderson	9		lbw b Swann	83
RS Dravid	lbw b Swann	3		c Prior b Flintoff	4
SR Tendulkar	c and b Flintoff	37		not out	103
VVS Laxman	c and b Panesar	24		c Bell b Swann	26
Yuvraj Singh	c Flintoff b Harmison	14		not out	85
MS Dhoni*†	c Pietersen b Panesar	53			
Harbhajan Singh	c Bell b Panesar	40			
Z Khan	lbw b Flintoff	1			
A Mishra	b Flintoff	12			
I Sharma	not out	8			
Extras	(b 4, lb 11, nb 6)	21		(b 5, lb 11, nb 4)	20
Total	(69.4 overs)	241		(for 4 wkts) (98.3 overs)	387

INDIA	O	M	R	W		O	M	R	W	Fall of wickets				
											Eng	Ind	Eng	Ind
Khan	21	9	41	2		27	7	40	3	1st	118	16	28	117
Sharma	19.4	4	32	1		22.5	1	57	3	2nd	164	34	42	141
Harbhajan Singh	38	2	96	3	(5)	30	3	91	1	3rd	180	37	43	183
Mishra	34	6	99	3	(3)	17	1	66	1	4th	195	98	257	224
Yuvraj Singh	15	2	33	1	(4)	3	1	12	1	5th	221	102	262	–
Sehwag	1	0	8	0		6	0	22	0	6th	229	137	277	–
ENGLAND	O	M	R	W		O	M	R	W	7th	271	212	297	–
Harmison	11	1	42	1		10	0	48	0	8th	277	217	301	–
Anderson	11	3	28	1		11	1	51	1	9th	304	219	311	–
Flintoff	18.4	2	49	3	(4)	22	1	64	1	10th	316	241	–	–
Swann	10	0	42	2	(5)	28.3	2	103	2					
Panesar	19	4	65	3	(3)	27	4	105	0					

Close of play: Day 1:   Eng (1) 229–5 (Flintoff 18*, Anderson 2*, 90 overs)
    Day 2:   Ind (1) 155–6 (Dhoni 24*, Harbhajan Singh 13*, 45 overs)
    Day 3:   Eng (2) 172–3 (Strauss 73*, Collingwood 60*, 54 overs)
    Day 4:   Ind (2) 131–1 (Gambhir 41*, Dravid 2*, 29 overs)

Man of the Match: V Sehwag
Result: **India won by 6 wickets**

India in New Zealand, Test series, March–April 2009

In the first Test at Hamilton, which started on 18 March, New Zealand batted first and made 279, with Daniel Vettori scoring a hundred. I still jokingly tell our bowlers whenever I see them, '*Arre, usko kaise hundred maarne diya thha tum logne?*' (How could you allow him to score a hundred?) He did play well, though, and took some calculated risks that paid off.

When I went in to bat in the afternoon of day two, I couldn't time the ball to save my life. I just didn't feel comfortable, so I decided to change my stance. This was something I used to try from time to time and it often did the trick. Normally I bat with a side-on stance, but in Hamilton I opened myself up slightly and also increased the gap between my feet a little. The umpire Simon Taufel noticed the difference and mentioned to me that I looked a completely different batsman after the drinks break and asked what I had done to myself. Sometimes such tiny adjustments can make a big difference.

Towards the end of the first day, the light dropped appreciably and Iain O'Brien, New Zealand's best bowler in the series, was bowling from one end. The umpires were reluctant to stop the game, which I thought was unfair because it was a crucial time in the match and there was no chance of the light improving. I somehow managed to survive, though, and was unbeaten on 70 at the end of the second day. The next morning I got off to an aggressive start. My knock of 160 contributed to a sizeable first-innings lead, alongside fifties from Gambhir, Dravid and Zaheer Khan. Our bowlers, led by Bhajji with six wickets, delivered once again to set up a very satisfying win.

Unfortunately, I missed the latter parts of the match because I was injured in the very first over of the New Zealand second innings when I dived forward to take a catch at slip off Zaheer's bowling. The edge from Tim McIntosh had come low and as I tried to get my fingers under the ball I damaged the index finger of my left hand. I had to be taken to hospital to have the injury checked and X-rays revealed I had a fracture.

There wasn't much time before the second Test at Napier but the early end of the first one at least gave me an extra day to recover. To protect the finger, I tried putting three finger caps one on top of the other and also applied a fibre plaster, which I moulded after soaking it in hot water, topped off with a lot of padding. With all that protection, I had little sense of where my finger actually was, but in the end I decided I could last a Test, as long as I stood in a relatively quiet fielding position.

This time it worked out well and I managed to score runs in both innings of the second Test at Napier. New Zealand scored 619 in their first innings, with Jesse Ryder following up his 102 in the first Test with a double century, supported by hundreds from Ross Taylor and Brendon McCullum. We had to bat out a little more than two days to save the match. We had a brief team meeting ahead of the second innings and there was a strong belief that we could do it. Gary had a big role to play in this and exuded a kind of quiet confidence, which in turn had a positive impact on the team.

Gautam Gambhir batted superbly in the second innings and thanks to his magnificent 137 we saved the match comfortably in the end. He batted for ten and a half hours and played 436 balls in an exemplary display of patience and character. Laxman also scored a hundred and the draw was a true reflection of the team's mind-set at the time: we were relishing the challenges set before us.

In the third Test in Wellington, we scored a reasonable 379, batting first, but then Zaheer Khan and Harbhajan Singh combined to bowl out New Zealand for 197, giving us a 182-run lead. In our second innings, a magnificent 167 from Gambhir helped set New Zealand a target of 717.

We picked up four wickets on day four and had the whole of the fifth day to take the remaining six wickets to wrap up the series 2–0. Zaheer, Ishant and Munaf Patel were bowling extremely well for us, as they had right through the series. The plan was to bowl short and attack the shoulder/ribcage area in an attempt to rattle the opposition. It seemed to work and I could sense the discomfort in some of the New Zealand batsmen.

With the wind behind him, Ishant was unplayable at times. Munaf took on the challenging job of bowling into the wind and for those who are not aware of the difficulties involved, the wind at Wellington can reduce your pace by at least 10 kph. Batsmen have to be able to make subtle adjustments to adapt to conditions like these. One problem with looking into strong winds is that you can't keep your eyes open for too long at a stretch. Also, when facing someone bowling with the wind, your bat speed has to be slightly faster than normal because the ball hurries on quicker than expected. On the other hand, a batsman can put pressure on someone bowling into the wind because the bat swing is naturally faster with the wind behind you.

On this occasion, our bowlers made sure the New Zealand batsmen were never at ease and despite another century from Ross Taylor in the second innings, we were always in control. Jesse Ryder, who had been their most successful batsman in the series, failed in both innings at Wellington, which definitely helped our chances. I was given the ball a little before lunch on day five and was pleased to get the crucial wicket of Brendon McCullum, caught at slip for 6. Then I could tell that James Franklin, the last recognized batsman, wasn't picking my googlies and was trying to sweep every ball to negate the overspin. I asked Dhoni to take the fielder away from point and place two fielders at short square leg. This would stop Franklin from playing the sweep shot and would force him to cut. The plan worked and I had Franklin lbw soon after making the field change.

We would have won the match if Ishant had held on to a chance from Iain O'Brien in the deep. The spilled catch allowed New Zealand a lifeline before the heavens opened after lunch, bringing a premature end to the match. Close to two sessions of play were lost to rain and we missed out on a golden opportunity.

An incident from this New Zealand series gives an idea of how much difference local conditions can make to a team's chances. It happened at Christchurch during the ODI series when Zaheer was bowling. He had bowled a good-length ball and the batsman's attempted front-foot slog over midwicket turned into a top edge. Zaheer screamed out 'MINE!' and carefully positioned himself for the catch. To his dismay, the wind got hold of the ball and it landed at least fifteen feet away. Later we all joked with him, saying, 'So the catch was *yours*, was it, Zak?'

Aiming for the top

Our rise up the ICC Test rankings had started in England back in 2007. Now, after the successful series in New Zealand, we had the opportunity to take the number-one position if we beat Sri Lanka at home in November–December 2009.

The series against Sri Lanka was also special for personal reasons, because I notched up twenty years in international cricket in November 2009. I celebrated the occasion by speaking to the media for more than seven hours, giving close to fifty one-on-one interviews. So much for people complaining that I did not talk to the media enough! Looking back at how uncomfortable I was at my first press conference in 1990, I had indeed come a long way.

I remember being confronted with a camera for the first time as an awkward teenager. In my early TV advertisements, I was not what you might call camera-friendly. I was self-conscious about using make-up and insisted on being natural, with nothing on my face and nothing done to my hair. It was only later that I realized that it was just a normal part of working with cameras. Later in my career, I really enjoyed shooting commercials and there were some incidents that I can never forget.

On one occasion I was at a shoot with one of India's greatest cinema icons, Amitabh Bachchan, in the Rajasthan city of Jodhpur. While we were taking a break, I suddenly realized that Arjun, who was only a toddler then, had finished his meal and was happily wiping his hands on Amitabh Bachchan's churidar (the lower garment worn with a kurta). Anjali and I were both mortified, but he kindly kept telling us that it was perfectly all right and that a child of Arjun's age hardly knew what he was doing. While Mr Bachchan was looking at the funnier side of the incident, as parents we were extremely embarrassed by it. I even said to him that '*Arjun jabh bada ho jayega to iss incident ko yaad karke sharminda ho jayega.*' (When Arjun grows up he will remember what he did and feel seriously embarrassed.) His gracious demeanour during that episode heightened my respect for the great man.

Another commercial I have fond memories of involved another Bollywood legend, Shah Rukh Khan. Shah Rukh and I were shooting for Pepsi at Lord's on the eve of the 1999 World Cup and the plan was for Shah Rukh to pose as me and open the refrigerator in the dressing room to take out a chilled Pepsi. That's when I was supposed to confront him for impersonating me. I ended up adding my own ideas to the commercial and said we should not stop there, but I should take the Pepsi bottle from him and force him to go out and bat in my place as well. The director loved the idea and changed the script on the day of the shoot.

Sri Lanka don't make it easy

Before the first Test of the three-match series started in Ahmedabad on 16 November, Anjali had planned something special for me, to mark my twenty years in international cricket. As a surprise, she and a few of my closest friends hired a private jet and flew into Ahmedabad on the morning of the game. I was having breakfast with MS Dhoni and had my back to the restaurant door when I saw in Dhoni's eyes that something was going on behind me. Even before I could turn to see what was happening,

Anjali and the gang had reached me. It was totally unexpected and I was deeply touched by the gesture.

Halfway through the Test, we found ourselves in a spot of bother. Centuries from Dravid and Dhoni had helped us to a decent first-innings total of 426, but Sri Lanka had scored 760 runs in response, thanks to hundreds from Dilshan and Prasanna Jayawardene and a double hundred from Mahela Jayawardene. We now needed to bat for a day and a half to save the game. But our never-say-die spirit came to the fore again and we batted exceptionally well to draw the match, with the opener Gambhir setting the foundation with 114.

I also scored a hundred on the last day and it was not a century free of incidents. Once it was evident to the Sri Lankans that they could no longer win, they set ultra-defensive fields. At one point Kumar Sangakkara, the Sri Lankan skipper, asked if I really wanted to carry on because there was no longer a possibility of a result in the match. I said to him bluntly that a Test hundred was a Test hundred and I would have got there long before if he had set sporting fields. While I had no problem with him trying to make things difficult for me, there was no reason for me to call it off when there was time left in the game.

At this, Sangakkara set a 7–2 off-side field and must have asked his left-arm fast bowler Welegedara to bowl to me a couple of feet outside my off stump with the ball going further away. I felt the need to improvise and on one occasion moved almost two feet outside the off stump and flicked Welegedara to square leg for four to get into the nineties. When I eventually reached my century, I asked Sangakkara if he wanted to continue the game. I was happy to carry on batting, but then we both decided to call off the game.

There was a similar situation in the same series during the third ODI in Cuttack on 21 December 2009. Chasing the Sri Lankan total of 239, I was in the nineties and Dinesh Karthik was giving me very good support at the other end. With only a few runs needed to win, Sangakkara decided to place most of his fielders on the boundary when I was facing, while for Dinesh he would bring the field right in. To counter the ploy, Dinesh played a number of dot-balls before I intervened and asked him just to finish the match. The win, I said, was far more important than my hundred. In the end, I remained unbeaten on 96 as Dinesh hit the winning runs.

I'm also reminded of what the Sri Lankans did against Virender Sehwag on 16 August 2010 during a one-day international in Dambulla. With Viru on 99 and only one run needed, the off-spinner Suraj Randiv bowled a flagrant no-ball and even though Viru hit him for six, the runs did not count because technically the match was over the moment the no-ball was bowled. Viru fell short of the hundred by one run and the incident created quite a storm in the media at the time.

Number one at last

After the hard-fought draw in the first Test, we routed the Sri Lankans in the next Test at Kanpur, which started on 24 November 2009. Our first three batsmen, Gautam Gambhir, Virender Sehwag and Rahul Dravid, all got hundreds and the bowlers backed them up with some disciplined bowling, so that we won by an innings and 144 runs. The series had been set up beautifully for a grand finale at the CCI in Mumbai the following week.

At the CCI, Virender Sehwag produced one of the best Test innings I have seen. He played some breathtaking shots and scored 284 not out in a single day of cricket. He fell the next morning for 293, narrowly missing out on the third triple ton of his career. The pace at which he scored also allowed our bowlers plenty of time to bowl out the opposition. In that sort of form, he could demoralize any bowling attack in the world and in a way he helped change approaches to opening the batting in Test cricket. Zaheer did the rest of the job in style, picking up a five-for in the Sri Lankan second innings, and we won the match by an innings and 24 runs. It was a tremendous victory – and it meant that we were now officially the number-one Test team.

A more personal high point in this match was running out Angelo Mathews for 99 in the Sri Lankan first innings. He played the ball to fine leg and turned for a second run in a bid to get to his century. I managed to get to the ball quickly and sent in a flat powerful throw, which landed right on top of the stumps. All Dhoni had to do was knock off the bails. While celebrating the dismissal I joked with my team-mates that the old man could still field even after playing international cricket for twenty long years!

We had played terrific cricket as a team. Each and every player had chipped in and Gary and the support staff – Paddy Upton, our high-performance and mental-conditioning coach; Ramji Srinivasan, our fitness trainer; Nitin Patel, our physio; Ramesh Mane and Amit Shah, our masseurs; and Dhananjay, our computer analyst – had all played important roles in our rise to the top. For me, Test cricket is the format that matters the most and this was undoubtedly a high point in my career. The fact that it coincided with my twentieth anniversary in international cricket had made it even more special.

England in India 2008

1st Test. Chennai. 11–15 December 2008
England 316 (AJ Strauss 123, MJ Prior 53*, AN Cook 52; H Singh 3–96,
   A Mishra 3–99) and 311–9 dec (AJ Strauss 108, PD Collingwood 108;
   Z Khan 3–40, I Sharma 3–57)
India 241 (MS Dhoni 53, H Singh 40, **SR Tendulkar 37**; A Flintoff 3–49,
   MS Panesar 3–65) and 387–4 (**SR Tendulkar 103***, Y Singh 85, V Sehwag
   83, G Gambhir 66)
India won by 6 wickets

2nd Test. Mohali. 19–23 December 2008
India 453 (G Gambhir 179, R Dravid 136, **SR Tendulkar 11**; A Flintoff
   3–54, GP Swann 3–122) and 251–7 dec (G Gambhir 97, Y Singh 86,
   SR Tendulkar 5)
England 302 (KP Pietersen 144, A Flintoff 62, AN Cook 50; H Singh 4–68,
   Z Khan 3–76) and 64–1
Match drawn

India won the series 1–0

India in New Zealand 2009

1st Test. Hamilton. 18–21 March 2009
New Zealand 279 (DL Vettori 118, JD Ryder 102; I Sharma 4–73,
   MM Patel 3–60) and 279 (BB McCullum 84, DR Flynn 67, MJ Guptill 48;
   H Singh 6–63)
India 520 (**SR Tendulkar 160**, G Gambhir 72, R Dravid 66, Z Khan 51*;
   CS Martin 3–98, IE O'Brien 3–103) and 39–0
India won by 10 wickets

2nd Test. Napier. 26–30 March 2009
New Zealand 619–9 dec (JD Ryder 201, LRPL Taylor 151, BB McCullum
   115, DL Vettori 55, JEC Franklin 52; I Sharma 3–95, Z Khan 3–129)
India 305 (R Dravid 83, VVS Laxman 76, **SR Tendulkar 49**; CS Martin
   3–89) and 476–4 (f/o) (G Gambhir 137, VVS Laxman 124*, **SR Tendulkar 64**,
   R Dravid 62, Y Singh 54*)
Match drawn

3rd Test. Wellington. 3–7 April 2009
India 379 (**SR Tendulkar 62**, H Singh 60, MS Dhoni 52; CS Martin 4–98)
   and 434–7 dec (G Gambhir 167, VVS Laxman 61, R Dravid 60, MS Dhoni
   56*, **SR Tendulkar 9**; CS Martin 3–70)
New Zealand 197 (LRPL Taylor 42; Z Khan 5–65, H Singh 3–43) and 281–8
   (LRPL Taylor 107, MJ Guptil 49, JEC Franklin 49; H Singh 4–59,
   SR Tendulkar 2–45, Z Khan 2–57)
Match drawn

India won the series 1–0

Sri Lanka in India 2009

1st Test. Ahmedabad. 16–20 November 2009
India 426 (R Dravid 177, MS Dhoni 110, Y Singh 68, **SR Tendulkar 4**;
    UWMBCA Welegedara 4–87, M Muralitharan 3–97) and 412–4 (G Gambhir
    114, **SR Tendulkar 100***, V Sehwag 51, VVS Laxman 51*)
Sri Lanka 760–7 dec (DPMD Jayawardene 275, HAPW Jayawardene 154*,
    TM Dilshan 112)
Match drawn

2nd Test. Kanpur. 24–27 November 2009
India 642 (G Gambhir 167, R Dravid 144, V Sehwag 131, Y Singh 67,
    VVS Laxman 63, **SR Tendulkar 40**; HMRKB Herath 5–121)
Sri Lanka 229 (DPMD Jayawardene 47, KC Sangakkara 44; S Sreesanth
    5–75) and 269 (f/o) (TT Samaraweera 78*; H Singh 3–98, PP Ojha 2–36)
India won by an innings and 144 runs

3rd Test. Mumbai (BS). 2–6 December 2009
Sri Lanka 393 (TM Dilshan 109, AD Mathews 99, NT Paranavitana 53;
    H Singh 4–112, PP Ojha 3–101) and 309 (KC Sangakkara 137,
    NT Paranavitana 54; Z Khan 5–72)
India 726–9 dec (V Sehwag 293, MS Dhoni 100*, M Vijay 87, R Dravid 74,
    VVS Laxman 62, **SR Tendulkar 53**; M Muralitharan 4–195)
India won by an innings and 24 runs

India won the series 2–0

22

STAYING AT THE TOP

In 2010, we faced three of the toughest assignments in international cricket and to maintain our number-one position we needed to do well in all of them. We had to play South Africa at home in February–March, Australia at home in October and New Zealand at home in November, before finally travelling to South Africa in December.

Before all these, however, we went to Bangladesh for a two-Test series in January 2010. While many feel Bangladesh are a pushover, they have surprised many a good side in the past and you underestimate them at your peril. This was evident in the first Test at Chittagong, which started on 17 January, where we were reduced to 209–8 in the first innings. The crowd was behind the local team and batting was a serious challenge against an inspired bowling attack, with Shahadat Hossain and Shakib-Al-Hasan both finally taking five wickets. Every wicket was greeted with a loud cheer and every boundary with pin-drop silence.

It was interesting to bat in front of such a partisan crowd. I scored 105 not out and we somehow managed to post a score of 243. Our bowlers did well to restrict Bangladesh in their first innings to one run less than our total, then Gambhir scored a century in our second innings, helping us to 413. Despite a century from Mushfiqur Rahim, the 415-run target proved too much for Bangladesh and we ended up winning by 113 runs.

In the second Test at Dhaka a few days later, where it was hot and sultry after the haze and chill in Chittagong, our fast bowlers again delivered in difficult conditions, with Zaheer bowling at his best in the second innings, getting an incredible amount of reverse swing to take seven wickets. We had batted well in our first and only innings, making 544, and Rahul and I scored centuries, setting the match up for Zaheer.

South Africa in India, February 2010

We reassembled to take on the South Africans in the first of two Tests at Nagpur on 6 February. The points situation meant that whoever won the series would be the number-one Test team.

In the first Test, Dale Steyn bowled brilliantly, ending up with ten wickets, and we were comprehensively beaten. Hashim Amla, with 253, and Jacques Kallis, with 173, batted superbly for South Africa and Amla was in extraordinary batting form right through the series. Kallis has always been a champion performer and is undoubtedly the best all-round cricketer of our generation. It has been a pleasure competing with players like these, who will surely be remembered as all-time greats.

Though we lost the game, I did manage to make a hundred in the second innings and I liked to think that my plan against Dale Steyn had started to work. He is an exceptional fast bowler and we knew we would need to play him well to make a comeback in the second Test, so the second-innings batting effort gave us a little hope in this regard. On the other hand, we had to accept that we had made it difficult for ourselves and were going to have to play out of our skins to retain our number-one Test ranking.

We were surprised to see a green top awaiting us at Eden Gardens. It had all but nullified the concept of home advantage, but there was nothing we could do about the pitch at that stage.

Again South Africa started well, but then we staged a miraculous comeback towards the end of the first day. From a position of strength at 218–1, South Africa collapsed to a modest 296 all out thanks to some terrific bowling from Zaheer and Harbhajan. We sensed we were in with a chance and put together a big first-innings total, with as many as four of us – Sehwag, Laxman, Dhoni and myself – getting hundreds. Sehwag and I had a terrific partnership of 249 after losing two quick wickets and we also scored at a phenomenal pace, unsettling the South Africans. Anything on middle-and-leg was flicked to the on side, while anything outside off stump was cut or driven. It was a dominant partnership and swung the pendulum in our favour.

Laxman and Dhoni built on the platform and we finally declared at a whopping 643–6, leaving the South Africans two whole days to bat to save the game. Unfortunately for us, the weather intervened on day four and a lot of overs were lost. By the end of the day South Africa had lost three wickets and we still needed seven wickets to close out the match.

The final day at Eden Gardens was Test cricket at its very best. Bhajji, who has a phenomenal record in Kolkata, bowled superbly, finishing with eight wickets in the match, and we took the final South African wicket with just a few overs remaining. The Eden Gardens crowd was behind us and the last wicket, Morne Morkel lbw to Bhajji, was greeted with a deafening roar. Bhajji ran almost half the length of the ground in delight and we were thrilled to have pulled off a stunning victory. We had retained our number-one ranking in the process and I felt all the more satisfied to think that, although my first hundred didn't save the first Test, my second one did contribute to our win in the second Test.

In the three-match one-day series that followed I was run out for four in the first game at Jaipur on 21 February. I was disappointed with the dismissal but was pleased that I managed to make a contribution in the last over of the game, when the South Africans needed just ten runs to win. Dale Steyn and Wayne Parnell had staged a fantastic fightback after being reduced to 225–8 chasing 299, and though Praveen Kumar picked up Steyn with the first ball of his final over, the South Africans were within striking distance of the total. The last man, Charl Langeveldt, hit the third ball of the over past short fine leg and at long leg I dived full length to save what was a certain boundary. The umpires consulted the third umpire before finally ruling it a legal save. This made the difference in the end, with India winning the match by one run.

By the time of the second match, in Gwalior on 24 February, I was starting to feel really tired. It had been a long season and my body was beginning to raise some objections. I had aches and pains everywhere; my back was stiff, my ankles felt tight and my knees hurt. The physio Nitin Patel had to treat me for an hour and a half on the morning of the match and I told him that I wanted to finish the series off at Gwalior so that I could ask to be rested for the third and final game of the series.

When I got to the ground, all the pains and aches had just disappeared! I don't know how it happened but it was one of those days when everything seemed to go my way. We batted first and I barely pushed at a ball from Wayne Parnell in the second over and was amazed to see it racing to the boundary. After that the balls consistently hit the middle of my bat and the run rate didn't drop for the entire innings.

I had some good partnerships, first with Dinesh Karthik, then with Yusuf Pathan and finally with MS Dhoni, and they all batted well to take the pressure off me. It was only after I had passed 175 that I started to think about a double hundred. I had lost a bit of strength by then and, unable to play big shots, switched to finding the gaps and running hard. I was still running even when I was in the 190s, while Dhoni was pounding the bowling at the other end.

The moment finally arrived in the fiftieth over of our innings, when I steered the ball behind point for a single, becoming the first in the history of cricket to score an ODI double century. I was particularly glad I had been able to achieve the landmark in front of a home crowd. The team total had reached 400 and the sensation could not have been any better. In the changing room, Sehwag said to me, '*Aakhir aapne 200 bana hi diya!*' (So you finally did score the ODI double ton!)

The job, however, was only half done and we knew South Africa had successfully chased 434 in 2006 – against Australia, no less – so it wasn't a time to relax. History was not repeated in Gwalior, though, and in the end we managed to win the match convincingly by a 153-run margin.

Back in the hotel, I was feeling really tired but, because of all the excitement, was unable to sleep. Lying awake in bed, I decided to check my phone and found that it was flooded with messages congratulating me and I spent two hours responding to them, a task that eventually took me two days to complete. I was up early the next morning, too, but it didn't really matter, as I was heading home for a much-needed break after one of my best ever seasons in international cricket.

I have to admit that there was another reason I could not sleep in Gwalior. The hotel authorities had very kindly given both Dhoni and me a suite each and these were located at a fair distance from the rooms of the rest of the team. My suite was enormous and even had a private swimming pool. The bathroom was gigantic and was separated from the main living room by a glass door. Outside there were huge trees and at night, with the silk curtains fluttering in the breeze, I didn't find it the most comfortable room to sleep in. It was pitch dark outside and the size of the room, together with the unfamiliar sights and sounds around, made me seriously uneasy and I had to keep the bathroom lights on all night!

India v South Africa

(2nd ODI)

Played at Roop Singh Stadium, Gwalior, on 24 February 2010 (D/N)

Umpires: IJ Gould & SK Tarapore (TV: SS Hazare)
Referee: AJ Pycroft
Toss: India

INDIA

		R	M	B	4	6
V Sehwag	c Steyn b Parnell	9	15	11	1	0
SR Tendulkar	not out	200	226	147	25	3
KD Karthik	c Gibbs b Parnell	79	124	85	4	3
YK Pathan	c De Villiers b Van der Merwe	36	47	23	4	2
MS Dhoni*†	not out	68	37	35	7	4
V Kohli						
SK Raina						
RA Jadeja						
P Kumar						
A Nehra						
S Sreesanth						
Extras	(lb 3, w 5, nb 1)	9				
Total	(for 3 wkts)　　　(50 overs)	**401**				

SOUTH AFRICA

		R	M	B	4	6
HM Amla	c Nehra b Sreesanth	34	41	22	7	0
HH Gibbs	b Kumar	7	12	8	1	0
RE van der Merwe	c Raina b Sreesanth	12	16	11	1	1
JH Kallis*	b Nehra	11	28	13	2	0
AB de Villiers	not out	114	154	101	13	2
AN Petersen	b Jadeja	9	18	16	1	0
J-P Duminy	lbw b Pathan	0	2	1	0	0
MV Boucher†	lbw b Pathan	14	29	31	1	0
WD Parnell	b Nehra	18	53	43	1	0
DW Steyn	b Sreesanth	0	6	4	0	0
CK Langeveldt	c Nehra b Jadeja	12	24	11	3	0
Extras	(lb 5, w 8, nb 4)	17				
Total	(42.5 overs)	**248**				

SOUTH AFRICA	O	M	R	W		Fall of wickets:				
							Ind		SA	
Steyn	10	0	89	0	(1 nb)					
Parnell	10	0	95	2	(1 w)	1st	25	(1)	17	(2)
Van der Merwe	10	0	62	1	(1 w)	2nd	219	(3)	47	(3)
Langeveldt	10	0	70	0	(2 w)	3rd	300	(4)	61	(1)
Duminy	5	0	38	0		4th	–		83	(4)
Kallis	5	0	44	0	(1 w)	5th	–		102	(6)
						6th	–		103	(7)
INDIA	O	M	R	W		7th	–		134	(8)
Kumar	5	0	31	1		8th	–		211	(9)
Nehra	8	0	60	2	(4 w)	9th	–		216	(10)
Sreesanth	7	0	49	3	(3 nb)	10th	–		248	(11)
Jadeja	8.5	0	41	2	(1 nb, 2 w)					
Pathan	9	1	37	2						
Sehwag	5	0	25	0	(2 w)					

Man of the Match: SR Tendulkar
Result: **India won by 153 runs**

Australia in India, October 2010

We started the 2010–11 season with a two-Test series against Australia. In the first match in Mohali at the beginning of October, VVS Laxman played one of his best ever innings for the team. Needing 216 to win, we had lost our eighth wicket with 92 runs still to get and Laxman, nursing a sore back, was our only hope. He batted like a man possessed, supported by Ishant Sharma, who showed exemplary grit for his 31. Though Ishant fell with 11 runs still to get, Laxman batted on and took us over the line, to win by one wicket. Laxman tormented the Australians throughout his career and this was another occasion when they threw everything at him but still couldn't dislodge him. Laxman is one of the few batsmen capable of playing two different shots off every ball and his supple wrists made him a joy to watch from the other end.

Having beaten Australia at Mohali, we had already retained the Border-Gavaskar Trophy when we arrived at Bangalore for the second and final Test of the series on 9 October. At the Chinnaswamy Stadium, Australia batted first, scoring a healthy 478, helped by a career-best 128 from Marcus North. I felt in good form from the very start of my innings. Not out on 44 at the end of day two, I batted through the whole of the next day and remained unbeaten on 191. I reached my forty-ninth Test hundred with consecutive sixes off Nathan Hauritz. It was my sixth Test century of the year and I had amassed more than 1000 Test runs in a calendar year for the sixth time in my career.

I eventually fell for 214 and, with the help of Murali Vijay's 139, we managed a slender first-innings lead of seven runs before our bowlers got in on the act and dismissed Australia for just 223 in their second innings. We needed 207 to win the series 2–0 and I had the privilege of taking the team to victory with young Cheteshwar Pujara, who, on debut, scored a valiant 72 not out batting at number three, a position he has now made his own for India. I am convinced he has a great future ahead of him as a Test player.

An unwelcome distraction

Next up was a three-Test home series against New Zealand in November 2010. Though we won the series 1–0, my own form took a dip. Everyone had started talking about my fiftieth Test hundred and it became hard to concentrate. The crowds were trying to get behind me and in Hyderabad, during the second Test, people kept waving at me even when I was batting. My usual routine was to walk away towards the square-leg umpire after playing each ball, but the crowd at square leg went up every time I looked at them, which unsettled me. I know they meant well, but I couldn't help thinking to myself, 'They should let me bat in peace,' and it wasn't long before I was out.

When you are batting well, it's good to have the crowd behind you like that. When you are struggling, it can make things doubly difficult. After the Hyderabad Test I said to Gary and Paddy that I was looking forward to the South Africa series because at least the crowds there wouldn't obsess about it so much.

I actually had a good chance to get the century out of the way in Nagpur in the third Test, which started on 20 November. I was 57 not out overnight in our only innings and went in on the third day feeling pretty confident. It didn't work out, however, as I lost my wicket after adding only four runs to my score, getting an edge off the left-arm seamer Andy McKay to the wicket-keeper. It was a ball that kicked up from short of a good length – the only one to do so all morning.

India in South Africa, December 2010–January 2011

Playing South Africa in South Africa was always a difficult proposition. The nature of the pitches, an excellent fast-bowling attack and a good batting unit combined to make them a formidable opponent at home.

In a poor start to the series, we were bowled out for 136 in our first innings at Centurion Park on 16 December, with Morne Morkel taking five wickets, and it was almost impossible to stage a comeback from that position. I was the top scorer with 36 and I wasn't playing too badly when a Dale Steyn delivery came in more than expected to trap me in front. South Africa put together a huge total in response, with a double century for Jacques Kallis and hundreds for Amla and de Villiers, and we were left to bat for almost two and a half days to save the game.

We at least put up more of a fight in the second innings. Dhoni and I were involved in a very good counter-attacking partnership of 172 and I was relieved to make my fiftieth Test hundred at last. We could see the South Africans getting frustrated and towards the end of the fourth day Dale Steyn and I exchanged a few words. The fading light had prompted Graeme Smith to give Steyn a final burst and he came charging in. At one point he joked to me that he wasn't bowling too fast, for it was a touch above 150 kph. At this I asked him, 'Where was your bravado when the sun was out?' To be honest, all this banter did was strengthen my resolve. It was all in good spirit, though. I have always been opposed to ugly sledging, but a little bit of banter isn't a bad thing on the cricket field and in fact can add something to a high-intensity contest – as long as it remains within reasonable limits, of course.

We had lost eight wickets by the end of day four and on the final day South Africa closed out the match comfortably to win by ten wickets. We went to Durban for the Boxing Day Test knowing that we had a hard task ahead of us. Yet the improved batting effort in the second innings at Centurion had given us a bit of a boost, and we felt we had at least adapted to the conditions by the time we stepped out in Durban.

India v Australia

(2nd Test)

Played at Chinnaswamy Stadium, Bangalore, on 9–13 October 2010

Umpires:	BF Bowden & IJ Gould (TV: AM Saheba)
Referee:	BC Broad
Toss:	Australia

AUSTRALIA

SR Watson	c Dhoni b Ojha	57	lbw b Ojha		32
SM Katich	c Dravid b Harbhajan Singh	43	c Dhoni b Harbhajan Singh		24
RT Ponting*	lbw b Raina	77	lbw b Khan		72
MJ Clarke	c Raina b Harbhajan Singh	14	st Dhoni b Ojha		3
MEK Hussey	c Sehwag b Khan	34	lbw b Ojha		20
MJ North	c Sreesanth b Harbhajan Singh	128	b Harbhajan Singh		3
TD Paine†	st Dhoni b Ojha	59	c Dhoni b Sreesanth		23
MG Johnson	lbw b Ojha	0	b Khan		11
NM Hauritz	run out (Pujara)	17	not out		21
BW Hilfenhaus	not out	16	b Sreesanth		0
PR George	st Dhoni b Harbhajan Singh	2	c Dhoni b Khan		0
Extras	(b 9, lb 12, w 1, nb 9)	31	(b 1, lb 5, w 3, nb 5)		14
Total	(141 overs)	**478**	(75.2 overs)		**233**

INDIA

M Vijay	c Paine b Johnson	139	lbw b Watson		37
V Sehwag	c Johnson b Hilfenhaus	30	c Paine b Hilfenhaus		7
RS Dravid	c North b Johnson	1	(5) not out		21
SR Tendulkar	b George	214	not out		53
CA Pujara	lbw b Johnson	4	(3) b Hauritz		72
SK Raina	c Hilfenhaus b Clarke	32			
MS Dhoni*†	c Clarke b Hauritz	30			
Harbhajan Singh	c Ponting b Watson	4			
Z Khan	c Clarke b George	1			
PP Ojha	not out	0			
S Sreesanth	lbw b Hauritz	0			
Extras	(b 6, lb 26, w 8)	40	(b 8, lb 5, w 4)		17
Total	(144.5 overs)	**495**	(for 3 wkts) (45 overs)		**207**

INDIA	O	M	R	W	O	M	R	W	Fall of wickets:				
Khan	23	5	84	1	11.2	1	41	3		Aus	Ind	Aus	Ind
Sreesanth	21	1	79	0	14	2	48	2	1st	99	37	58	17
Ojha	42	7	120	3	25	5	57	3	2nd	113	38	58	89
Harbhajan Singh	43	3	148	4	21	2	63	2	3rd	132	346	65	146
Sehwag	4	1	7	0	4	0	8	0	4th	198	350	126	–
Raina	8	1	19	1					5th	256	411	131	–
									6th	405	486	181	–
AUSTRALIA	O	M	R	W	O	M	R	W	7th	415	491	185	–
Hilfenhaus	31	6	77	1	7	0	27	1	8th	458	494	217	–
Johnson	28	2	105	3	14	4	42	0	9th	459	495	218	–
George	21	3	48	2	(4) 7	0	29	0	10th	478	495	223	–
Hauritz	39.5	4	153	2	(3) 12	0	76	1					
Clarke	8	0	27	1									
Watson	12	2	35	1	(5) 5	0	20	1					
Katich	5	0	18	0									

Close of play:	Day 1:	Aus (1) 285–5 (North 43*, Paine 8*, 85.5 overs)
	Day 2:	Ind (1) 128–2 (Vijay 42*, Tendulkar 44*, 34.2 overs)
	Day 3:	Ind (1) 435–5 (Tendulkar 191*, Dhoni 11*, 122 overs)
	Day 4:	Aus (2) 202–7 (Johnson 7*, Hauritz 8*, 65 overs)

Man of the Match:	SR Tendulkar
Result:	**India won by 7 wickets**

The start of the Boxing Day Test match was different, to say the least. There was a light drizzle on the first morning and yet the pitch was left uncovered. Even the pitch report was done by the commentators braving the drizzle, a fact that was brought to my attention by one of my team-mates. The more the moisture, the more it was expected to favour the South African fast bowlers. I remember telling my team-mate that such things don't matter and it all evens out in the end.

This reminded me of something that had happened in Melbourne in December 2003. On the last day of the Test match, with Australia needing 97 runs to win, there was a delay to the start of play despite conditions apparently being perfect. The reason was that the pitch had been tampered with by the groundsmen, in clear violation of the rules. At the end of day four, there was a big crack in the pitch as a result of the wear and tear, and balls landing in the crack could have done anything. To our surprise, the groundsmen had filled up the crack before the start of play on day five, incurring the umpires' wrath. The umpires spotted it because the repaired area had not fully dried out and was a different colour from the rest of the wicket. The umpires had to instruct the groundsmen to undo the repair and restore the pitch to its original condition.

Durban was a low-scoring Test match but no less exciting for that. Zaheer came back to lead our attack and both he and Bhajji bowled brilliantly after we had made a modest 205 in our first innings. They combined well to finish South Africa off for just 131 in their first innings and were aided by some brilliant catching behind the wickets. Rahul picked up his 200th catch in this match when he caught Dale Steyn off Bhajji at slip. It was one of Rahul's best catches and he had to dive full length to his left and pick it up almost from behind the wicketkeeper. We celebrated the dismissal in the knowledge that the match was gradually turning in our favour.

In our second innings, it was another VVS Laxman special that got us out of trouble. He showed class in his innings of 96 and gave us a lead of over 300 to defend in the final innings. Laxman batted brilliantly with the tail, which was something he was a master at in the latter stages of his career. He was always unflustered and exuded a sense of calm which rubbed off on the other batsmen.

It was now up to Zaheer, Ishant, Sreesanth and Bhajji to finish the job and level the series. They did it in some style. South Africa were never allowed to get away and our bowlers sent down some unplayable deliveries. Sreesanth's ball to Kallis that jumped from short of a length and left him in no position to do anything was the best of the match. Zaheer had taken six wickets in the match and had again shown his importance as the leader of the attack. It was an amazing victory, one of our best away wins.

Before the final Test, I met up with Anjali and the kids and my friends Vivek and Sonia Palkar in Cape Town on 30 December and we celebrated the Durban win and the penultimate day of 2010 at a fantastic vineyard, the Constantia Uitsig. The place also had a cricket field and an excellent restaurant. It was an experience I was looking forward to, having consciously tried to learn more about red wine after visiting Australia in 1999. The celebrations continued on 31 December, when the team ushered in the New Year at a fabulous hotel in the foothills of Table Mountain.

In the third and deciding Test match at Cape Town on 2 January 2011, South Africa batted first on a pitch that offered reasonable help for the seam bowlers throughout the match. The ball was doing a lot off the pitch and in the air and batting wasn't easy. It was apparent to us all that South African captain Graeme Smith was not at all comfortable against Zaheer's left-arm swing. This was evident to us when he played a ball to midwicket and just jogged a single when he could easily have picked up two runs. I remember Bhajji running beside the ball and urging Smith to go for a second run. His refusal to do so suggested he had lost the mental battle to Zaheer, and we used the opportunity to give him a hard time in the middle. Kallis played brilliantly again, however, and, thanks to his 161, South Africa posted a competitive 362 in their first innings.

I went in to bat towards the end of day two and played a handful of deliveries to settle in. Then I came forward to a ball from Dale Steyn pitched on middle-and-leg and played it to midwicket for four. Everything about that shot – the swing and flow, my body position and foot movement – felt perfect and something told me I was in for a good innings.

The next day I resumed on 49, knowing the morning was going to be tough. Gautam Gambhir and I were up against two of the finest bowlers in the world in Dale Steyn and Morne Morkel – and in helpful bowling conditions. In an attempt to counter the movement, I deliberately stood outside the crease. My thinking was that if I was beaten from there, the ball would most likely go over the stumps. To get bowled I would have to miss an over-pitched delivery, which was unlikely, and if the South Africans decided to dig in short I could play the upper cut over the slips.

For the entire first hour, I played Dale Steyn while Gautam negotiated Morne Morkel and we both scored a number of fours in the first ten overs. It seemed that whenever we connected, the ball raced to the boundary. The South Africans had a lot of fielders in catching positions and it meant we got full value for our shots. I went into lunch unbeaten on 94 and knew it would be one of my best hundreds if I managed to get there. The task wasn't easy, with the second new ball just two overs old.

My tactic of batting outside the crease seemed to work. That day the only delivery for which I stood inside the crease was the fifth ball from Morne Morkel after lunch. I had a premonition that Morkel would bowl short and so moved back inside the crease, ready to play the hook shot. Sure enough, the ball turned out to be a chest-high bouncer and, though I got a top edge, the ball flew over the wicketkeeper's head for six, taking me to the fifty-first, and last, Test hundred of my career.

I know it's bizarre but it seemed to me that five days earlier I had seen Morne's delivery in a dream. In the dream he had bowled a bouncer to me that I hooked to get to my hundred. I mentioned this to my batting partner Dhoni, saying *'Yeh ball mere life mein pehle bhi aaya hai. Mein yeh pehle dekh chuka hoon. Aaj ye dusri bar ho raha hai.'* (This delivery has already come once before in my life. I have seen and faced this delivery before. Today I faced it for a second time.) Who knows, maybe it was the dream that prompted me to stand back inside the crease for that one ball!

When Harbhajan Singh came in, we were still more than a hundred runs behind South Africa and needed one more decent partnership to get close to their total, but Harbhajan was finding it difficult to negotiate Steyn's fast swinging deliveries. Bhajji had scored consecutive hundreds against New Zealand in the series before and was in good batting form, but those conditions were not best suited to him.

I went up to tell him to forget about technique for the time being: *'Batsman ki tahra batting mat kar tu. Technique bhul ja. Agar ball tere range me dikhi tu ghuma. Ghuma tu kyun ki runs chahiye humhe. Kaise bhi ho runs chahiye.'* (Don't try to bat like a batsman. Forget about technique for the time being. If you see the ball in your arc just hit it. We need runs at the moment. It doesn't matter how they come as long as they come.)

Harbhajan listened to the advice and in no time was on his way. He pulled the left-arm seamer Lonwabo Tsotsobe for six and hit Morne Morkel for a four. But his best shot was off Dale Steyn. It was a full delivery and Harbhajan just stood there and hit through the line. Bhajji has power and the shot sailed over the long-on boundary at least ten rows back for a huge six. To add insult to injury, Bhajji offered a wry smile to Steyn, who by now was furious.

Bhajji's assault forced Graeme Smith to push his fielders back and so I walked up to Bhajji again to say that he could stop trying to hit every ball now; he could just tap the ball and run. Our partnership yielded 76 very valuable runs and when Bhajji was finally out for 40 with the score on 323 we were within striking distance of the South African total. Eventually we managed a two-run lead.

Our bowlers started well in the South African second innings and Bhajji was again simply brilliant. He snapped out the first four South African wickets with just 64 on the board and when Zaheer picked up AB de Villiers with the score on 98, we started to believe a series win was possible. Ashwell Prince got out with the score on 130 and we needed just one more wicket to get into the tail. Instead, Kallis and Mark Boucher put together a match-saving partnership. Kallis played a superb innings despite nursing a rib injury and his second hundred of the match took the game and also the series beyond us. We were left to bat out the last day for a draw, which we did fairly comfortably.

Looking back, this was our best chance to win a series in South Africa. With half the side out for 98, all we needed was one final burst to roll over the opposition, but instead we let South Africa off the hook. Bhajji took seven wickets, but unfortunately the fast bowlers weren't quite so successful at the other end. In normal circumstances, a 1–1 series result in South Africa would be considered a really good performance, but this was clearly a contest we should have won.

Weighty matters

The Test series was followed by a one-day series, which in effect would start our preparations for the 2011 World Cup. Annoyingly, I injured my hamstring right at the start of the series and was forced to return to India. Before leaving, I asked every member of the squad to make a pledge. I told my team-mates that with the World Cup in the subcontinent approaching, which was one of the most significant competitions of our lives, it was important for everybody to sacrifice something ahead of the tournament. My suggestion was to lose 3 kilos each and become a fitter side in the process.

I kept my promise and in fact lost 3.8 kilos. Some of my team-mates did so as well. To do this I had to watch my diet and was on salads after returning to Mumbai. I underwent a rigorous rehabilitation programme on my hamstring under the watchful eyes of Patrick Farhat, physio of the Mumbai Indians, and also hit the gym regularly to strengthen my upper body. This World Cup was promising to be the biggest tournament of my life. It was the one title that had eluded me so far, and it looked like this would be my last crack at being part of a world-beating side – and on home soil too.

India in Bangladesh 2010

1st Test. Chittagong. 17–21 January 2010
India 243 (**SR Tendulkar 105***, V Sehwag 52; S Al-Hasan 5–62, S Hossain
    5–71) and 413–8 dec (G Gambhir 116, VVS Laxman 69*, A Mishra 50,
    SR Tendulkar 16; Mahmudullah 2–52)
Bangladesh 242 (Mahmudullah 69, M Rahim 44; Z Khan 3–54, A Mishra
    3–66) and 301 (M Rahim 101, T Iqbal 52; A Mishra 4–92, I Sharma
    3–48)
India won by 113 runs

2nd Test. Dhaka. 24–27 January 2010
Bangladesh 233 (Mahmudullah 96*, M Ashraful 39; I Sharma 4–66,
    Z Khan 3–62) and 312 (T Iqbal 151, J Siddique 55, S Hossain 40;
    Z Khan 7–87)
India 544–8 dec (**SR Tendulkar 143**, R Dravid 111, MS Dhoni 89, G Gambhir
    68, V Sehwag 56; S Islam 3–86) and 2–0
India won by 10 wickets

Indian won the series 2–0

South Africa in India 2010

1st Test. Nagpur. 6–9 February 2010
South Africa 558–6 dec (HM Amla 253*, JH Kallis 173, AB de Villiers 53;
    Z Khan 3–96)
India 233 (V Sehwag 109, S Badrinath 56, **SR Tendulkar 7**; DW Steyn 7–51)
    and 319 (f/o) (**SR Tendulkar 100**, H Singh 39; DW Steyn 3–57, PL Harris 3–76)
South Africa won by an innings and 6 runs

2nd Test. Kolkata. 14–18 February 2010
South Africa 296 (HM Amla 114, AN Petersen 100; Z Khan 4–90, H Singh
    3–64) and 290 (HM Amla 123*; H Singh 5–59, A Mishra 3–78)
India 643–6 dec (V Sehwag 165, VVS Laxman 143*, MS Dhoni 132*,
    SR Tendulkar 106; M Morkel 2–115)
India won by an innings and 57 runs

Series drawn 0–0

Australia in India 2010 – The Border-Gavaskar Trophy

1st Test. Mohali. 1–5 October 2010
Australia 428 (SR Watson 126, TD Paine 92, RT Ponting 71, MG Johnson
    47; Z Khan 5-94, H Singh 3–114) and 192 (SR Watson 56; I Sharma 3–34,
    Z Khan 3–43)
India 405 (**SR Tendulkar 98**, SK Raina 86, R Dravid 77, V Sehwag 59;
    MG Johnson 5–64) and 216–9 (VVS Laxman 73*, **SR Tendulkar 38**;
    BW Hilfenhaus 4–57, DE Bollinger 3–32)
India won by 1 wicket

2nd Test. Bangalore. 9–13 October 2010
Australia 478 (MJ North 128, RT Ponting 77, TD Paine 59, SR Watson 57;
    H Singh 4–148, PP Ojha 3–120) and 223 (RT Ponting 72; Z Khan 3–41,
    PP Ojha 3–57)
India 495 (**SR Tendulkar 214**, M Vijay 139; MG Johnson 3–105) and 207–3
    (CA Pujara 72, **SR Tendulkar 53***)
India won by 7 wickets

India won the series 2–0

New Zealand in India 2010

1st Test. Ahmedabad. 4–8 November 2010
India 487 (V Sehwag 173, R Dravid 104, H Singh 69, **SR Tendulkar 40**;
    DL Vettori 4–118, JS Patel 3–135) and 266 (H Singh 115, VVS Laxman 91,
    SR Tendulkar 12; CS Martin 5–63, LRPL Taylor 2–4)
New Zealand 459 (KS Williamson 131, JD Ryder 103, BB McCullum 65,
    LRPL Taylor 56; PP Ojha 4–107) and 22–1
Match drawn

2nd Test. Hyderabad (Deccan). 12–16 November 2010
New Zealand 350 (TG McIntosh 102, MJ Guptill 85, JD Ryder 70; Z Khan
    4–69, H Singh 4–76) and 448–8 dec (BB McCullum 225, KS Williamson
    69, TG McIntosh 49; S Sreesanth 3–121)
India 472 (H Singh 111*, V Sehwag 96, VVS Laxman 74, G Gambhir 54,
    R Dravid 45, **SR Tendulkar 13**; DL Vettori 5–135, TG Southee 3–119) and
    68–0 (V Sehwag 54*)
Match drawn

3rd Test. Nagpur. 20–23 November 2010

New Zealand 193 (JD Ryder 59, BB McCullum 40; I Sharma 4–43, PP Ojha
  3–57) and 175 (TG Southee 31; I Sharma 3–15, H Singh 3–56)

India 566–8 dec (R Dravid 191, MS Dhoni 98, G Gambhir 78, V Sehwag 74,
  SR Tendulkar 61; DL Vettori 3–178, CS Martin 2–82)

India won by an innings and 198 runs

India won the series 1–0

India in South Africa 2010

1st Test. Centurion. 16–20 December 2010

India 136 (**SR Tendulkar 36**; M Morkel 5–20, DW Steyn 3–34) and 459
  (**SR Tendulkar 111***, MS Dhoni 90, G Gambhir 80, V Sehwag 63; DW Steyn
  4–105)

South Africa 620–4 dec (JH Kallis 201*, HM Amla 140, AB de Villiers 129,
  AN Petersen 77, GC Smith 62; I Sharma 2–120)

South Africa won by an innings and 25 runs

2nd Test. Durban. 26–29 December 2010

India 205 (VVS Laxman 38, **SR Tendulkar 13**; DW Steyn 6–50, LL Tsotsobe
  2–40, M Morkel 2–68) and 228 (VVS Laxman 96, **SR Tendulkar 6**;
  LL Tsotsobe 3–43, M Morkel 3–47, DW Steyn 2–60)

South Africa 131 (HM Amla 33; H Singh 4–10, Z Khan 3–36) and 215
  (AG Prince 39*; S Sreesanth 3–45, Z Khan 3–57, H Singh 2–70)

India won by 87 runs

3rd Test. Cape Town. 2–6 January 2011

South Africa 362 (JH Kallis 161, HM Amla 59, AG Prince 47; S Sreesanth
  5–114, Z Khan 3–89) and 341 (JH Kallis 109*, MV Boucher 55; H Singh
  7–120)

India 364 (**SR Tendulkar 146**, G Gambhir 93; DW Steyn 5–75) and 166–3
  (G Gambhir 64, **SR Tendulkar 14***)

Match drawn

Series drawn 1–1

23

WORLD CUP 2011

The 2011 World Cup was jointly hosted by India, Sri Lanka and Bangladesh and we launched our campaign against Bangladesh in the very first game of the competition on 19 February in Dhaka. As we knew only too well, having lost to them in the 2007 World Cup in the Caribbean, Bangladesh can be a dangerous one-day side and at the Shere Bangla National Stadium in Mirpur they had raucous crowd support.

The general excitement was the first thing that struck us when we arrived in Bangladesh. Every time we went for practice there were close to 30,000 people outside the ground waiting to catch a glimpse of the cricketers. Most of them didn't have tickets for the game, but they were happy just to be there singing, dancing and enjoying the moment. The passionate and enthusiastic Dhaka crowd undoubtedly added a unique dimension to the tournament.

We were feeling confident after winning both of our warm-up games against Australia and New Zealand in Chennai and we all knew this was our best chance to win cricket's ultimate prize. The whole country was behind the team during the competition – in fact, for a month and a half it seemed that all that mattered in India was how we fared in the World Cup. However, we needed to remain calm, and Gary, Paddy Upton, Mike Horn – the well-known explorer who was with us for most of the World Cup and shared stories of his adventures – and the support staff did a wonderful job of keeping our minds on the task at hand.

In Dhaka I invited Yuvraj Singh to my room to have dinner. I have always enjoyed a special friendship with Yuvi and believed that he had a key role to play in the tournament. Yuvi was a little down at the time, as things had not been going well for him, so I encouraged him to set some targets and concentrate on meeting them. We really needed a fully focused Yuvraj and I am delighted to say that's what we got from him all the way through the tournament.

It is a priceless moment in a cricketer's career when he lines up for the national anthem at the start of a multi-nation competition. Right through my career, listening to the anthem while standing alongside my team-mates has given me goose-bumps. As they played the 'Jana Gana Mana' at Mirpur, none of us could hold back our emotions. We knew that for the millions of Indians supporting us, what we were playing was not just a game but a passion.

We won the toss and Virender Sehwag and I stepped out to start our campaign. Viru began in style, hitting the very first ball for a four, and we were off. The early nerves disappeared in no time and we started to enjoy ourselves. We set up a good foundation, scoring at a fair clip, before I was run out for 28 and then Gautam Gambhir for 39. Viru was sublime in his innings of 175 and Virat Kohli contributed a superbly orchestrated century to help take us to 370−4. In the end we won the match comfortably by 87 runs. The 2007 defeat had been avenged and we were off to the start we had hoped for.

An epic encounter

Our next match was against England in Bangalore on 27 February and, as it was our first match at home, the excitement was off the scale.

Something a little odd happened just hours before the England match. In the tournament I was using a favourite bat of mine, the one I had used the previous season, when I was the ICC Cricketer of the Year. Though it was showing its age, I had not discarded it. Rather, I had repaired it time and again and had even sent it to the bat manufacturers for restoration. There was a kind of emotional bond with this bat and every time I couriered it to the manufacturers I felt nervous and prayed that it would not get lost in transit. In the dressing room, with just a few hours left until the match, for some reason I started to knock in a brand-new bat and work on it in my usual way to get the weight exactly right. I even remember telling myself that I was being foolish and wasting my time, because there was no way I would be using a new bat and I would be better off concentrating on the game.

We won the toss at the Chinnaswamy Stadium in Bangalore and opted to bat first. I used my trusted old bat and managed to hit a few boundaries. However, most of them were deflections behind the wicket and it was only when I tried to play a square cut off Ajmal Shahzad that I realized something was wrong. It was a full-blooded stroke but the ball did not travel to the fielder as fast as it should have. It was time to retire the old bat and call for the new one I had been knocking in. While I felt a little sad sending the old bat back to the pavilion, I did score a century with the new one – though I ended up breaking it in the quarter-final against Australia.

I have always enjoyed playing in Bangalore. I began cautiously and with Sehwag in full flow I was content to anchor the innings, but I decided to push the accelerator when Viru was dismissed for 35. Graeme Swann was England's leading spinner and I hit him for consecutive sixes at the start of his second spell, swinging the momentum in our favour. I was finally out for 120 and, with fifties from Gambhir and Yuvi, we made 338 in our fifty overs.

England were brilliant in reply and also benefited from the very heavy dew, which meant our spinners had been rendered ineffective. In conditions of heavy dew the ball just skids on to the bat, something England were to encounter in their match against Ireland at Bangalore. (The Irish, despite losing five wickets cheaply, managed to get home, with Kevin O'Brien scoring a very good hundred.) Against us, Andrew Strauss played one of his best ever one-day innings, making 158, and he almost took England to victory before Zaheer pulled it back for us with a superb second spell, taking three wickets for just 11. The match finally ended in a tie, and it was a terrific advertisement for the game. A total of 676 runs were scored and still the two sides could not be separated. The fans loved the contest and the World Cup had captured the imagination of the cricket-playing world.

It was immediately after this match that talk of us winning the title started in the digital world and slowly the messages started reaching us in the dressing room. These discussions were based not just on our on-field performances. Someone had pointed out that every time Dhoni had been involved in a tie in a multi-nation competition, he had ended up winning the title. This had been the case in the World Twenty20 in 2007 (the India–Pakistan game was tied before India won in a bowl-out), in the IPL and even in the 2010 Champions League Twenty20 that Dhoni had won. This World Cup, it was argued, would be no different.

There's many a slip

We won our next two pool matches against Ireland and the Netherlands fairly comfortably and met South Africa in Nagpur on 12 March 2011. It was this match that in many ways turned our campaign on its head. We began well and were soon firmly in control. Sehwag and I got off to a quick start – I scored my ninety-ninth international century in this match, but it was not much talked about at the time because the focus was squarely on the World Cup – and we set South Africa a target of 297 after a dramatic batting collapse, losing nine wickets in the last ten overs, with Steyn getting a five-for. Eventually we lost the match with two balls of the South African innings remaining and the defeat hurt us badly.

Unsurprisingly, there was stinging criticism in the media. We had slipped once but we all knew we could not afford to slip again. We simply had to get the campaign back on track in the next match, against the West Indies in Chennai on 20 March, and we managed to do just that, thanks to a Yuvraj Singh century and a surprise slower ball from Zaheer Khan to dismiss the in-form Devon Smith for 81. The crucial knockout phase was about to begin and in the quarter-final at Ahmedabad we drew Australia, the defending champions.

Spicing up practice

It was on the eve of that West Indies match that I tried to introduce an element of fun into my batting practice. I was practising to some throw-downs from Gary Kirsten and was just about to wrap up the session when the idea came to me. I decided to close my eyes for six deliveries, just after the bowler released the ball, then I asked Gary if he had noticed anything different. Gary said he hadn't, except that my head was staying up when I was driving. I had to keep my head steady, because with your eyes shut you can easily lose the path of the ball with a very slight movement of the head. When I told him I'd had my eyes closed, he was shocked. I explained that I had watched his wrist position when he released the ball, to see if it was, say, an outswinger, and then closed my eyes and visualized the path the ball would travel. After that I went a step further by keeping my eyes shut and telling the fielders where I had hit the ball, based on how and where I felt the ball on the bat. It was just for fun, and I only did it once, but it did help me focus on the release of the ball, which is so important for a batsman.

In my early days I used to practise in an even more unusual manner. In the monsoon season in Mumbai – in June/July/August – it's not possible to play much normal cricket, but my friends and I would still get together and play in the rain, using rubber balls. Sometimes this would be on a normal pitch without any cover, sometimes on a wet concrete pitch and sometimes on a concrete pitch with a plastic cover. There were times when I actually wore a proper helmet and my full cricket gear in the pouring rain. The rubber ball would come off the surface at quite a pace and it was a good way of sharpening up my reactions. While practising in the rain I would always ask the guys to bowl to me from 18 yards. They were allowed to bowl or chuck, but the object was always to try to hit me!

It was great fun but it also had a serious side. At the time, we didn't have any indoor facilities and I had to practise somewhere. Things have changed, of course, but in some ways I miss all that. I've even thought about doing it again with my son. Young players now grow up with all the best facilities, whereas I had nowhere to go. I had to practise on the roads or on wet outfields, where first the mud would splash onto my face and then the ball would follow! It was tough at times but it all contributed to my enjoyment of cricket, and I would love my son to share that experience.

Taking on the champions

Australia were chasing their fourth consecutive World Cup title and, remarkably, were meeting us for the first time in the competition since beating us in the 2003 final in South Africa. I remember two things about getting ready for the quarter-final. First, I did not eat non-vegetarian or spicy food after setting foot in Ahmedabad, which was boiling hot. I don't really know why not. Something inside just seemed to suggest that I should stay away from that kind of food in the heat. I ate a lot of salad and yoghurt and things that I hoped would keep my system cool.

The other thing I remember is that I did not sleep well. This time it was not the mounting tension but my hotel bed that caused the problem. On the eve of the match I even resorted to sleeping on the floor. It was our masseur Amit Shah who pointed out that the problem was with my bed. When he came to give me a head massage to help me sleep, he immediately noticed that it was raised on one side, but unfortunately it was impossible to replace the bed at that late hour!

Playing against Australia is always a high-pressure contest, and a knockout game even more so. Despite a good start by Australia at Ahmedabad on 24 March, our bowlers did well in the powerplay to keep the run rate close to four an over. Eventually, the Australians put 260 on the board, with Ponting making an impressive 104, and we knew it wouldn't be easy to chase down that total under lights.

Viru and I were aware of the enormity of the occasion as we walked out to deafening applause at the Sardar Patel Stadium. It really was now or never. When Viru got out for 15 trying to pull Shane Watson, caught at midwicket, we had put 44 on the board. Gautam and I added exactly 50 runs before I got out after reaching my half-century. We then lost Gautam and Dhoni in quick succession and Suresh Raina, playing only his second World Cup game, joined Yuvraj in the middle with 74 runs still needed.

At the time, I was lying on the massage table with my eyes closed, with Viru on the other table. I lay there completely still while Amit Shah gave me a neck massage. I was actually praying, asking God to do the best for us. At one point Viru thought I was sleeping and told Amit Shah, '*Tu apna time waste mat kar, woh so gaya hai. Ja ke match dekh le.*' (Don't waste your time. He has gone off to sleep, please go and watch the match.) I could hear his every word, but I didn't want to move or react. Amit was aware that I was awake and said, '*Woh soya nahi hai, mujhe malum hai!*' (He is not sleeping, I know!)

As Yuvraj and Raina gradually pulled things round I remember hearing my team-mates shout, 'One more boundary . . . ah! Two more runs.' We were getting very close to the semi-final and were about to knock the three-time champions out of the World Cup! And when Yuvi hit the final boundary, the Indian dressing room went crazy. It was an unforgettable match.

On our way back to the hotel, it seemed as if the entire city was celebrating – or rather the entire country. When the team bus left the ground at close to midnight, there were still a few thousand fans at the gate waiting to cheer us. People were honking, dancing and waving the tricolour at every roundabout and street corner – and we hadn't even reached the final yet.

I remember standing on the balcony of my hotel room and watching the celebrations till late at night. I also remember telling Anjali that it was an unbelievable sight and she had to see it to believe it. It made me realize, yet again, just how much the World Cup meant to our cricket fans. However, it was only to get bigger with India meeting Pakistan in the semi-final.

Neighbours

Soon after we landed in Mohali and were on our way back to the hotel, I asked my team-mates if any of them had the Amit Kumar song 'Bade achhe Lagte Hain' on their iPods. Finally, it was Mane Kaka, our masseur, who said he did. Mane Kaka has always been an exceptionally affectionate person, constantly doing the best for us without expecting anything in return. I subsequently requested DJ, our computer analyst, to download the song onto my iPod as soon as possible, and it was the only song I listened to for the next seven days.

The match in Mohali on 30 March was always slated to be the most intense of the competition and in fact it turned out to be one of the most high-pressure games of my career. Playing Pakistan in a World Cup semi-final on Indian soil – it just couldn't get any bigger. As the two teams practised side by side we could feel the tension. Both teams badly wanted to win this one. Up till then, India had an impeccable record against Pakistan in World Cups, and we wanted to keep that record intact.

We got off to a dramatic start in what turned out to be a roller-coaster of a game, thanks to Virender Sehwag taking on Umar Gul. He was the form fast bowler for Pakistan in the tournament and Viru's assault set us rolling. Viru raced off the blocks and hit Gul for four fours in his second over. Fortunately the Pakistanis dropped me a few times, the chance to midwicket being a relatively simple one, and my innings of 85 proved vital as we lost a few quick wickets in the middle overs, with Wahab Riaz taking five in the match. Riaz bowled Yuvi first ball and the momentum shifted like a pendulum many times in the course of the match. So much so that I had my heart in my mouth on a number of occasions during this nail-biter of a match. Suresh Raina played well for his 36 not out and helped us to 260, exactly the score we had chased down in the quarter-final against Australia. It was a good total but not a clear winning score on a decent pitch.

In their reply, Pakistan also got off to a good start, but just as the pressure was starting to build on us, Zaheer struck. Munaf also got a wicket in the powerplay and then Yuvraj took two quick wickets to put us in control. In the middle of the innings, Umar Akmal was trying to counter-attack but we knew that all it would take was one good delivery. Harbhajan did the job for us by bowling Akmal with the first ball of his second spell. He had decided to come round the wicket and Akmal misjudged the line.

Pakistan still had a chance while Afridi and Misbah were batting, but then Afridi fell to Harbhajan, trying to hit a full toss out of the ground. He would normally have made that shot nine times out of ten but on that night he spooned a simple catch to cover. It was one of those days when things seemed destined to go our way. After dismissing Afridi, we knew we could close out the match. Soon enough Misbah holed out to Virat at long on and we were in the World Cup final. As if that wasn't enough, I also received the Player of the Match award, the third time I had that honour in a World Cup match against Pakistan.

The celebrations were quite something. We could see thousands of fans waving the tricolour and celebrating in Mohali. Navigating our way back to the hotel was a tricky business, with every corner taken over by delirious fans wanting to relish the moment. My friend Aamir Khan, the actor, came over to my room to offer his congratulations and I remember chatting away into the small hours. It was a night that India could never forget and we, having played a part in it, will never want to forget.

A number of dignitaries had come to Mohali, including our prime minister, Dr Manmohan Singh. The Pakistani premier, Yousaf Raza Gillani, was also present, but frankly we were not really taking in what was going on beyond the boundary because we were so preoccupied with the job at hand. We were soon on our way to Mumbai, convinced that we were peaking at the right time.

A city full of expectations

When we arrived in Mumbai for the final against Sri Lanka, the first thing I noticed was the increased police presence. It didn't feel like the same city. Despite all the extra security, there were fans everywhere waiting to catch a glimpse of the team and wish us well. It was a kind of passion we had not seen before.

On the way from the airport, the police didn't want to take any chances and escorted our bus to the hotel. On the way, I met Anjali on Mumbai's Sea Link, the bridge that is now a landmark and has made commuting in the city much easier. (Before, there were times when I was playing a first-class match in Mumbai and I would choose to stay the night at the CCI rather than go back home, as it could take an hour and thirty minutes to drive there, which is not what you want after a long day in the field!) I had already informed the security personnel on the team bus that Anjali would be waiting for me and that I would be moving from the team bus to my car. Driving my own car didn't make the journey to the hotel any quicker, as I tried to keep the team bus in my sight. There were people everywhere and I don't think I went above 40 kph. In fact I remember saying to Anjali that my car must think someone else is driving it at that speed.

While driving to the hotel I was also trying to take stock of the situation. It was hard to imagine I was going to play the World Cup final in front of my home crowd. I couldn't help thinking back to March 2007 when I had returned to Mumbai after a disastrous World Cup campaign. That year, in hindsight, was a real nightmare. However, the 2011 campaign felt different, as if we were scripting a fairy tale for the whole nation. I told Anjali that this time there was no turning back.

We had played Sri Lanka a number of times in the recent past, in 2010 and 2011, and knew exactly what to expect from them in the final. They were a good side but we were confident of beating them. There was no need for a long team talk. We did meet for a team dinner, but after barely five minutes of cricket discussion, Mike Horn took over. All through the final week, Mike talked to us about his experiences. While for most of us there is always another day, for Mike it was often a matter of life and death. One mistake and it could all be over. The stories of how he coped with extreme pressure during his adventures – such as circumnavigating the globe at the Equator without motorized transport or walking to the North Pole during the dark season – definitely helped us deal with our own concerns on the eve of the World Cup final. They put our situation into perspective, reminding us that we were not the worst off in this world.

Unlike in Ahmedabad or even Mohali, I slept well in Mumbai on the eve of the final. On 2 April, we left the hotel early for the stadium and I was surprised not to see a single soul on the way. Security was so tight that fans were not even permitted to stand along the team bus's route. It was difficult to believe that I had not seen a single cricket fan. However, the Wankhede presented a completely different picture. It was already packed, hours before the match was due to start.

As we did our warm-up exercises on the pitch, I could feel the buzz inside the stadium, which was feeling more like an amphitheatre. All round there were excited faces. India were playing the most important match ever on home soil. No team had won the World Cup as hosts, but one good day and we could call ourselves world champions for the rest of our lives.

The final

We managed to get off to a good start in the match thanks to an excellent early spell from Zaheer and some great fielding at point and cover from Yuvraj and Raina. Zaheer reeled off three maidens on the trot, which said it all. Sri Lanka lost Upul Tharanga for two to an excellent catch in the slips by Viru off Zaheer and we had sprinted off the blocks. While Zaheer was bowling very well, Sreesanth was not quite so effective from the other end. Harbhajan and I, fielding at mid off and mid on, kept telling him not to give up, saying that he just needed to land one ball on the spot and he would get us a wicket. He said he was not feeling well and felt like being sick. To his credit, he forced himself to keep going in the oppressive Mumbai heat. Sometimes you have to endure pain to succeed, especially when you are playing the World Cup final.

Sri Lanka fought back well through Kumar Sangakkara and Mahela Jayawardene, two of the finest batsmen in the world. But as was the case throughout the World Cup, Yuvraj made a vital breakthrough to get us back in the match by having Sangakkara caught behind for 48. Jayawardene, however, was still out there and he played one of the truly great World Cup final innings. His century set the match up for Sri Lanka, with 274 the target that faced us.

It was not insurmountable, but it was important for us to forge partnerships in the early overs, because the wicket was expected to become slightly easier as the match progressed. The outfield was dewy and I thought it was important for us to try to get the ball outside the thirty-yard circle to make it wet. That would mean the ball would stop swinging. Unfortunately for us, we lost Sehwag for a duck in the first over of the chase and it was down to Gambhir and me to build a platform. I hit a couple of crisp boundaries and was timing the ball well, but just when I thought the ball had stopped swinging, I was tempted to play a drive outside the off stump. That ball from Malinga swung and I edged it to the wicketkeeper and was out for 18. It was disappointing, and I won't forget the walk back to the dressing room.

We were in a potentially dangerous situation when Virat Kohli arrived at the crease to join Gambhir. Virat had started the World Cup with a hundred against Bangladesh and now he finished off with a key innings in the final. The importance of his contribution is not always acknowledged, but his 35 was part of a key partnership, as both Gautam and Virat managed to score at a brisk pace and so the asking rate was never out of reach. Once Virat was out, Dhoni promoted himself up the order to negotiate the Sri Lankan off-spinners, Muralitharan, Randiv and Dilshan. It was the Gambhir–Dhoni partnership of 109 that won us the World Cup. Both played exceptionally well under intense pressure.

I have to confess that I did not actually see what millions of Indians watched with ecstasy and delight that night. I did not see my ultimate dream being fulfilled, the moment I had waited to savour since making my international debut in November 1989. The reason was that when Mahendra Singh Dhoni hit the winning six at the Wankhede Stadium, I was with Virender Sehwag in the dressing room praying. I wasn't asking God to help us win. All I wanted was that God should do what was best for us, for Indian cricket and for the Indian cricket team. I had turned superstitious on the night and made Viru sit near me in one position. Neither of us ventured out till Dhoni's shot had crossed the boundary. A little earlier, when it seemed that an Indian win was on the cards, Viru had wanted to go out of the dressing room to celebrate. I advised him not to till the match was finally over. I said to him that he could watch the moment a hundred times on television if he wanted to, but for the time being he should just sit where he was and pray. It was only after Dhoni's shot had finally crossed the boundary that I went out.

Many people have asked me what I felt at that particular moment. Frankly, at first it was difficult to take in the fact that we had won the World Cup. It was almost as if there was still a match left in the tournament. But when I ran onto the ground and embraced an emotional Yuvi, it was impossible to control my emotions. It was one of those life-changing moments and we wanted to live each and every second of it. While some players shouted and some cried, others were keen to go ahead with the victory lap in front of an ecstatic Wankhede crowd.

Virat and Yusuf Pathan lifted me onto their shoulders and someone gave me an Indian flag to wave. Being carried by my team-mates, waving the tricolour at my home ground, having won the World Cup – what more could I ask for? Life, to be honest, seemed complete. It was the greatest moment of my cricketing journey. Amidst all the euphoria, I remember telling Yusuf Pathan not to drop me. At this he said, *'Gir jayenge par aapko niche nahi aane denge.'* (We may fall down but we will not let you go down.)

It felt incredible. It was a kind of satisfaction I had never experienced before. Cricket's greatest prize was finally ours. On our victory lap, I waved to the section of the crowd where I thought my children Sara and Arjun were sitting. I waved to them, hoping they would see me do so and come down. Luckily, they saw me wave and soon joined me in the middle. To be with my family while celebrating the greatest sporting moment of my life was special.

Anjali was not at the ground. She had stuck to her superstition of not coming to the stadium and she left home for the Wankhede only after we had won. She had a funny experience while driving to the ground. It was one of those nights when 'anything goes'. Men and women were jumping on top of cars to celebrate and no one was objecting. The country had never seen anything like it.

Just as Anjali was taking the turn to the Wankhede, a section of the crowd tried to get on top of her car to dance. At this point a couple of boys spotted her inside and said, '*Arre yeh unka gaadi hai, unko jaane do. Unke jaane ke bad humlog naachenge.*' (Hey, it's their [the Tendulkars'] car; let her go. We will dance after the car has dropped her off.) And they did exactly that. After Anjali was dropped at the main gate, they climbed on top of the car to dance, creating a dent, which we were happy to see as they captured for us the fond memories of that day!

Something else that made the World Cup triumph really special was the fact that many of my team-mates dedicated the achievement to me. I felt overwhelmed. Once we had finished with the awards ceremony and the lap of honour, the scene of action moved to our dressing room. I opened the first bottle of champagne and subsequently made a point of getting it signed by all my team-mates. It now has pride of place in the cellar at my house.

We tried to make the most of the moment in as many different ways as possible. We took countless photographs. First it was the players, then we took some with Gary, who had just served out his last match as India coach. Paddy Upton and Mike Horn, both important members of our support unit, soon joined in and it seemed totally acceptable for adults to behave like children.

As my team-mates were posing with the trophy one by one, I remember wandering out of the dressing room to soak up the atmosphere. It seemed that not a single soul had left the ground. People were busy capturing every possible angle on their mobile phones. I saw Sudhir Gautam, now a familiar face in India as the man who paints his body with the tricolour and paints my surname and number '10' on it, blowing his conch at full blast. The noise from his conch and the sound of the firecrackers blended together to create quite an atmosphere. It felt surreal.

I waved at Sudhir Gautam to come and join us inside the dressing room. He was startled to see me do so, to say the least. For him it was totally unexpected. It was already a night to

remember for us; his was about to become even more memorable.
I asked the security personnel to allow him into the dressing
room and passed him the trophy to hold. He was overwhelmed.
I felt a deep sense of satisfaction at being able to make him so
happy. He had travelled with us all the way through the World
Cup and it was our way of showing him and the rest of our fans
that we cared. I only wish I could have let every supporter at the
Wankhede pose with the trophy.

The players' families soon joined in the celebrations and I
remember trying to explain to Arjun and Sara the significance
of the World Cup for a cricketer. I told them it was the pinnacle
and could never be surpassed. Almost two hours after the victory,
we finally left for the hotel. The normally short journey from
the stadium to the hotel was one of the slowest but also one of
the best of my life. While I had not seen a soul on my way
to the ground in the morning, on the way back there was a sea
of humanity and the trip back took almost an hour.

Marine Drive was quite a sight. Although I remembered dancing
and celebrating as a kid after India's first World Cup win in 1983,
the memory was a bit of a blur. This was our moment. It was
sweet liberation. We had finally scaled the Mount Everest of the
game of cricket and each and every soul on the streets of Mumbai
was celebrating. We had brought boundless joy to the faces of
millions of Indians, and as Team India, that was all we could
have asked for.

A night to remember

The entrance to the Taj Mahal Palace hotel had been cordoned
off and the lobby was packed with people. When we entered we
were presented with a bottle of champagne and a special cake,
which I cut before heading up to our rooms on the sixth floor.
The second round of celebrations was about to begin.

India v Sri Lanka

World Cup Final

Played at Wankhede Stadium, Mumbai, on 2 April 2011 (D/N)

Umpires: A Dar & SJA Taufel (TV: IJ Gould)
Referee: JJ Crowe
Toss: Sri Lanka

SRI LANKA

		R	M	B	4	6
WU Tharanga	c Sehwag b Khan	2	30	20	0	0
TM Dilshan	b Harbhajan Singh	33	87	49	3	0
KC Sangakkara*†	c Dhoni b Yuvraj Singh	48	102	67	5	0
DPMD Jayawardene	not out	103	159	88	13	0
TT Samaraweera	lbw b Yuvraj Singh	21	53	34	2	0
CK Kapugedera	c Raina b Khan	1	6	5	0	0
KMDN Kulasekara	run out (Dhoni)	32	41	30	1	1
NLTC Perera	not out	22	10	9	3	1
SL Malinga						
S Randiv						
M Muralitharan						
Extras	(b 1, lb 3, w 6, nb 2)	12				
Total	(for 6 wkts)　　(50 overs)	**274**				

INDIA

		R	M	B	4	6
V Sehwag	lbw b Malinga	0	2	2	0	0
SR Tendulkar	c Sangakkara b Malinga	18	21	14	2	0
G Gambhir	b Perera	97	187	122	9	0
V Kohli	c and b Dilshan	35	69	49	4	0
MS Dhoni*†	not out	91	128	79	8	2
Yuvraj Singh	not out	21	39	24	2	0
SK Raina						
Harbhajan Singh						
Z Khan						
MM Patel						
S Sreesanth						
Extras	(b 1, lb 6, w 8)	15				
Total	(for 4 wkts)　　(48.2 overs)	**277**				

INDIA	O	M	R	W	
Khan	10	3	60	2	(1 w)
Sreesanth	8	0	52	0	(2 nb)
Patel	9	0	41	0	(1 w)
Harbhajan Singh	10	0	50	1	(1 w)
Yuvraj Singh	10	0	49	2	
Tendulkar	2	0	12	0	(3 w)
Kohli	1	0	6	0	

SRI LANKA	O	M	R	W	
Malinga	9	0	42	2	(2 w)
Kulasekara	8.2	0	64	0	
Perera	9	0	55	1	(2 w)
Randiv	9	0	43	0	
Dilshan	5	0	27	1	(1 w)
Muralitharan	8	0	39	0	(1 w)

Fall of wickets:

	SL		Ind	
1st	17	(1)	0	(1)
2nd	60	(2)	31	(2)
3rd	122	(3)	114	(4)
4th	179	(5)	223	(3)
5th	182	(6)	–	
6th	248	(7)	–	
7th	–		–	
8th	–		–	
9th	–		–	
10th	–		–	

Man of the Match: MS Dhoni
Result: **India won by 6 wickets**

In the confines of my room, Anjali and I poured each other a drink and let our hair down. We plucked flowers out of the bouquets that were piled up everywhere and put them behind our ears and danced to the music. This was the night of a World Cup triumph, so why hold back? In an instant, all that time away from my family, missing out on seeing my children grow up, seemed worthwhile. Their father had finally become part of a World Cup-winning team, something he had strived for all his life.

The party went on into the early hours of the morning. With loud music blaring out, the doors to all the players' rooms were wide open. Anyone could come in and have a drink and celebrate. In one memorable moment, Virat, Bhajji and Yuvi went down on their knees and sang *'Tujhme rab dikhta hai, yaara, main kya karoon'* (What to do, my friend, in you we see God himself!) from the film *Rab Ne Bana Di Jodi* and managed to seriously embarrass me.

At around 3 a.m., we were called to go up and join in a special celebration put together by the team management. A couple of hours later, I finally went back to my room to get some sleep. This time I bolted my door, knowing that otherwise some of my team-mates were bound to crash in, as the party was still in full swing.

At 7 a.m. I heard Zaheer Khan and Ashish Nehra banging on my door, wanting to share a drink. I just smiled to myself and went back to sleep.

A happy homecoming

The day after the final went by in a rush. After fulfilling the ICC's requirements of a few photo shoots and meeting our president, Mrs Pratibha Patil, at Raj Bhavan, I finally made it home in the evening. It was a deeply emotional experience, made more memorable by my friends and neighbours, who welcomed me to our building by playing the *dhol* (drums) and letting off firecrackers.

Every time I did something worthwhile in my career my friends and neighbours wanted to celebrate the homecoming, and normally I would ask Anjali to persuade them not to because I felt embarrassed by such celebrations – but the World Cup was an exception!

When my mother was performing *aarti* (a flame ritual for good luck) and putting the *tika* (a vermilion mark representing her blessings) on my forehead (a family ritual in most Maharashtrian families), it seemed that this time I had come back to her having achieved something substantial. I felt as if I had performed my duties as a son and deserved her welcome. My family was delighted with the achievement and I felt a sense of genuine pride at having given them such joy.

There were countless bouquets of flowers waiting for me. Abhishek and Aishwarya Rai Bachchan, two of India's best-known Bollywood stars, dropped by to congratulate me and we happily relived the final all over again.

Looking back on it now, it still feels like a dream. Beating Australia, Pakistan and Sri Lanka in the course of one week to win the World Cup in front of huge Indian crowds just feels unreal. The television audience for our semi-final match against Pakistan, I was told, was the highest ever recorded in India's sporting history. I must confess that I continue to get goose bumps every time I think about that week.

On a personal note, I was pleased to have scored a total of 482 runs, the highest for India and the second highest in the tournament, at an average of 54 with two hundreds. I felt that I had proved to myself that after twenty-two years of gruelling tests, I was still good enough to compete with the very best, and that the hunger and the passion were still very much alive in me.

A number of my friends have asked me why I didn't retire from one-day cricket after winning the World Cup, as the summit had been scaled and there was nothing left for me to achieve. They may well have a point. It could indeed have been a grand exit. Emotions were running high and the timing could not have been better. But to be honest, such a thought never occurred to me. I wanted to remember the World Cup as a happy moment, and announcing my retirement straight after winning the trophy would have shifted the focus from the cup triumph to my retirement.

The Indian cricket team had stuck together through difficult times to make the world stage their own. Each player had made sacrifices and each one deserved to enjoy the moment. Cricket is a team sport and I feel immensely proud to have been part of the World Cup-winning team.

Finally, I had always wanted one memorable send-off from international cricket that I would never forget in my life. Multiple send-offs could end up diluting the significance of the event and that was not something I ever wanted.

India in the 2011 World Cup

1st match, Group B. Bangladesh v India at Dhaka. 19 February 2011
India 370–4 (50/50 ov); Bangladesh 283–9 (50/50 ov)
India won by 87 runs

11th match, Group B. India v England at Bangalore. 27 February 2011
India 338 (49.5/50 ov); England 338–8 (50/50 ov)
Match tied

22nd match, Group B. India v Ireland at Bangalore. 6 March 2011
Ireland 207 (47.5/50 ov); India 210–5 (46/50 ov)
India won by 5 wickets (with 24 balls remaining)

25th match, Group B. India v Netherlands at Delhi. 9 March 2011
Netherlands 189 (46.4/50 ov); India 191–5 (36.3/50 ov)
India won by 5 wickets (with 81 balls remaining)

29th match, Group B. India v South Africa at Nagpur. 12 March 2011
India 296 (48.4/50 ov); South Africa 300–7 (49.4/50 ov)
South Africa won by 3 wickets (with 2 balls remaining)

42nd match, Group B. India v West Indies at Chennai. 20 March 2011
India 268 (49.1/50 ov); West Indies 188 (43/50 ov)
India won by 80 runs

2nd quarter-final. India v Australia at Ahmedabad. 24 March 2011
Australia 260–6 (50/50 ov); India 261–5 (47.4/50 ov)
India won by 5 wickets (with 14 balls remaining)

2nd semi-final. India v Pakistan at Mohali. 30 March 2011
India 260–9 (50/50 ov); Pakistan 231 (49.5/50 ov)
India won by 29 runs

Final. India v Sri Lanka at Mumbai. 2 April 2011
Sri Lanka 274–6 (50/50 ov); India 277–4 (48.2/50 ov)
India won by 6 wickets (with 10 balls remaining)

THE QUEST FOR THE 100TH HUNDRED

India's first international engagement after the World Cup was a tour of the West Indies in June 2011. I was allowed to opt out because India had a busy year ahead and I was desperate to spend some time with my family. I had been playing continuous cricket for eight months and realized that if I travelled to the West Indies it would mean I would not have spent much time with Anjali and the children for close to twenty months. India had a number of assignments coming up and this was the one tour that coincided with the kids' summer holidays. I was on ninety-nine international centuries at the time but it never occurred to me that I should try and get the 100th ton as quickly as possible. Then again, I never imagined that I would have to wait for more than a year.

India in England, July–August 2011

I rejoined the team in July 2011 and was looking forward to playing against a resurgent English side in their home conditions. Under Andrew Strauss they had recently won the Ashes in Australia and were playing some excellent cricket. However, we were still the number-one Test team and it was expected to be a keenly contested series. The fact that our recently appointed coach, Duncan Fletcher, was returning to take on the England team he used to coach with such success also added spice to the series.

For me personally the tour did not start well. My foot started to trouble me on the first day of the tour when we played Somerset in a two-day fixture at Taunton. We fielded first and by lunch the pain in my toe was bad enough to make me stay off the field for treatment. When we got to London before the first Test match at Lord's, I had a few scans done and it was revealed that the problem was again with the sesamoid bone. While there was some inflammation, luckily it wasn't serious enough to keep me off cricket and I played in all four Tests.

At Lord's on 21 July 2011 we started reasonably well after winning the toss, with Zaheer picking up Andrew Strauss early on, but we were thrown off-course when Zaheer pulled a hamstring soon after lunch. In such situations you can't do much but rue your luck. The loss of the leader of our attack undoubtedly affected us for the rest of the series.

I remember that on the very first day I saw Zaheer, way back at the start of his career, I told him he would always have to take care of his body and bowl right through the year to keep himself fit. His physique was such that he needed to do more than others to remain in good shape. Back in 2005 I encouraged him to play county cricket, and when he came back to India after playing his first season in England, there was no doubt he was a more mature performer. Over the years he turned himself into a match-winning premier fast bowler.

To add to our concerns, we lost Yuvraj in the second Test when he fractured his finger, then Bhajji suffered a stomach-muscle tear and Gautam Gambhir fell over and had severe concussion, which prevented him from opening the batting in the fourth Test. What's more, we didn't have Sehwag for the first two Tests, as he was still recovering from a shoulder operation. I don't want to take anything away from England, who played superb cricket throughout the series, but it was a remarkable sequence of disasters on our side, and it wasn't easy to cope with the loss of so many key players.

One unexpected complication at Lord's was that I found I had great difficulty picking up the ball from the new Media Centre

End. England had tall fast bowlers in Chris Tremlett and Stuart Broad and I had serious trouble because the bowler's hand was sometimes lost against the dark-coloured steps above the sight-screen. This meant I had much less time to react than usual and I had to play the ball off the pitch rather than watching the bowler's wrist. From the Pavilion End I had no problem at all.

After the game I spoke about the problem with the late Christopher Martin-Jenkins, who was then President of the MCC, and he promised to do something about it for the ODI at Lord's later in the tour – but in the end I wasn't able to play in that game. More recently, when I captained an MCC XI against Shane Warne's Rest of the World XI at Lord's in the Bicentenary Match in July 2014, I raised the problem again. They couldn't increase the height of the sightscreen, but I asked them to make the staircase above it as white as possible, which they did. In the end, I didn't have any problems because Peter Siddle was bowling and he's not as tall as, say, Broad or Tremlett and that makes a huge difference.

I must also confess that while I love Lord's, I always found it difficult to cope with the slope that runs across the ground, no matter how much I tried to work out its effect. I remember facing Chris Lewis once when he was bowling from the Pavilion End. He tended to bowl inswingers and I thought I'd worked out that the slope would bring the ball in to me even more, so I played inside the line – and the ball went the other way and I was bowled!

In 2011, on the evening of the third day of the Lord's Test, I was laid low by a viral infection. My friend Atul Bedade, the former India international and someone who has always supported me at critical times, had come to visit me for the evening, but I realized something was wrong as soon as we got back to the hotel. I asked for a paracetamol from the physio and took it while ordering an early dinner in the room. By 8 p.m. we had finished our meal and I suggested to Atul that he should take off, but Atul didn't want to leave me in that state and kindly decided to sleep on the sofa, so that he could make sure I was all right.

By the middle of the night my condition had worsened and the next morning I was in no state to get up. Atul called Ashish Kaushik, our physio, and he advised complete rest. This was the only time in my career I was not able to join the team on the morning of a match. I slept in my hotel room till well after lunch and it was only when I checked the score on television that I called our team manager and told him I was coming to the ground. I wanted to try and play a part in the second innings, as I thought I was needed.

Although I wasn't able to contribute much to the team, I forced myself to field towards the end of the England innings, to make sure I would have an opportunity to bat on day five. At the end of the day's play, I was in a really bad state. To make matters worse, when I got back to the hotel I found that the air conditioning in my room had leaked and everything was wet. While I did manage to bat for a while on day five, I was nowhere near my best and found it difficult to maintain my balance in the middle.

England ended up winning the first Test comfortably, thanks to centuries from Pietersen and Prior and five wickets for James Anderson in the second innings. In the second Test at Trent Bridge, starting on 29 July, we came back strongly and Sreesanth and Ishant Sharma helped reduce England to 124–8 at one point in their first innings, but Swann and Broad managed to bail them out, taking their score to 221. It was still not a threatening total, however, and we passed it with six wickets in hand, only to lose them all for just twenty runs, with Broad taking six wickets in the innings, and the match slipped from our grasp.

After failing to win the second Test from a position of strength, things gradually went from bad to worse. The pain in my foot was not going away, and as a team we were outplayed yet again in the Third Test, which did not start in the best of circumstances, with riots in Birmingham creating a very tense atmosphere. The shopping centre next to our hotel was vandalized and there was talk of cancelling the tour. It was only after we were given an assurance that things were under control that the match went ahead.

In fact, this was not the only time that off-the-field events threatened to disrupt the tour. Before the one-day series, a match against Kent in Canterbury caused us all a lot of worry. In the closing stages of the game we noticed a large number of security personnel hovering near the dressing room. We were told that a suspect package had been found on the team bus and the bomb squad were on their way. Then we were asked to go and wait on the field because the dressing room was close to the danger area. We all waited patiently until we were finally told that we could leave by the back entrance of the ground. There was yet another bomb scare at night in the shopping arcade next to our hotel and a number of the players were starting to feel anxious about our security. The following morning we were told that things were fully under control and eventually the tour continued.

In the third Test at Edgbaston, England won the match with their first-innings total of 710, which included a career-best 294 from Alastair Cook and 104 from Eoin Morgan. I was pleased to bat well in the second innings and I don't think anyone would deny I was unlucky to get out for 40. MS Dhoni had played a straight drive off Graeme Swann and the ball hit Swann's hand and ricocheted onto the stumps at the non-striker's end, running me out. With nothing going our way, we headed to The Oval for the fourth and final Test very low on morale. What was worse was that we had also lost our number-one ranking in the process, having lost three Test matches on the trot.

Stuck on ninety-nine

I had scored my ninety-eighth international hundred on 27 February 2011 while playing England in our second World Cup game in Bangalore, but there was no mention of the 100th hundred in the media at that stage. Less than two weeks later, I scored the ninety-ninth against South Africa at Nagpur, but still no one brought up the 100th. The topic did come up on television when I was in the eighties against Pakistan in the World Cup semi-final, but that was no more than a passing mention. It was only after the World Cup win that the media needed a new cause to obsess over and the 100th hundred fitted the bill: it had never been achieved before, it made for good television and newsprint and it was a landmark fans could be proud of. It was a recipe for an unprecedented frenzy, and few members of the media and fans anticipated the adverse impact it might have on me.

I first became aware of all the fuss when I was on a family holiday in England in June 2011 before the Test series. I was asked if I had deliberately skipped the West Indies tour to ensure that the 100th hundred came at Lord's in the first Test. I did not have a Test hundred at Lord's (and now never will) and this, I was informed, was my way of setting the record straight. Only, it was news to me. I would, of course, have been delighted to get the hundred at Lord's, but hundreds simply do not happen as easily as that.

The obsession soon turned into hysteria. Every time I went in to bat, I was supposed to get to the landmark hundred. Believe me, I wanted to get it out of the way. I was spending hours at the nets and felt good about my batting, but gradually the 100th ton was starting to play on my mind.

At The Oval in the fourth and final Test, which started on 18 August, England scored 591 in their first innings, with 235 from Ian Bell and another century from Pietersen. We were bowled out for 300 in reply and asked to follow on. I was dismissed for

23 in our first innings, trying to play a sweep shot to Graeme Swann, and was extremely angry at getting out that way. My mood wasn't helped by the fact that earlier I had been hit on my left shoulder by a ball from Stuart Broad and scans later revealed a tear.

I was keen to make amends in the second innings when I went in at the fall of our second wicket with an hour of play left on day four. There was a patch of rough created by the left-arm seamer RP Singh outside the right-hander's off stump and while batting against Graeme Swann I decided to take an off-stump guard to negate the impact of the rough. The strategy paid off and I was able to negotiate the last hour with relative ease. Resuming on 35 the next day, I focused on the thought of returning to the dressing room after batting all day to save the match.

Amit Mishra, our leg-spin googly bowler, was batting with me and we were both conscious that the first hour on the final day was critical, with the English attack led by James Anderson bowling superbly in home conditions. Amit, the nightwatchman, was resolute in protecting his wicket and I walked up to him at the end of every over to tell him that he should bat as if it was our last wicket.

I managed to hit a few good boundaries and began to feel I was getting a grip on proceedings. We saw off Anderson and the first hour went more or less to plan. Stuart Broad and Swann took over but we continued our resistance and got to lunch without losing a wicket. We had won the session and scored 87 runs in the process. I was on 72 and Amit had played superbly for his 57.

On resumption, I kept telling Amit that he should focus on getting another 50 runs. Every run was getting us closer to the England total. I was on 91 when Amit was finally bowled by Swann for 84. We were just 29 adrift of the English total and the partnership had put on 144 for the fourth wicket. We had almost managed to play out the first hour after lunch and there was a good chance of saving the game if we batted well for three more hours. And that's when I got out for 91. I was standing well outside my crease and the ball from Tim Bresnan came back a long way to hit my pads as I tried to play it to midwicket. While batting, you can usually sense the trajectory of the ball and there was little doubt in my mind that the drift would have taken the ball past the leg stump, so I was surprised to see umpire Rod Tucker raise his finger.

A sense of helplessness descended on me. All the good work of the morning had been undone and it was going to be difficult to save the match with so many overs left in the day. The decision, replays showed, was not the best; luck, a key ingredient in cricket, had once again deserted me. When I met umpire Tucker later in the year he jokingly suggested to me that his friends were not happy with the decision and had given him a lot of grief for it. It was good of him to come and speak to me and we both decided to forget it and move on.

The Test series was followed by a five-match one-day series and I was looking to carry forward the form I had shown at The Oval. Just then, my shoulder injury really started to bother me again. Even when I was resting during the two Twenty20 matches, it showed no signs of settling down and I was forced to have an ultrasound-guided injection in the shoulder joint. It was in Durham on the eve of the first ODI that my toe also started to play up again during training. I did everything possible to settle the pain and took a few anti-inflammatory pills at night, but they didn't help and I woke the next morning feeling worse. I was worried all the way from the hotel to the ground, and as soon as we reached the stadium, I asked Ashish Kaushik to strap my foot. The moment I stepped down from his physio table onto the hard tiles I suspected I was in trouble. When I tried getting into my spikes, I knew I couldn't play. At the end of the second Test match I had not been able to think of missing a game. Now the pain was such that I could not think of playing a game.

We decided to go to London for a fresh set of scans. I was given two injections in the sole of my foot and I must say they were two of the most painful injections I have taken in my life. The doctors then informed me that I needed to rest my foot for five to six weeks. I finally started training again on the eve of the three-Test series against the West Indies at home in November 2011.

As soon as I resumed practice, the clamour for the 100th hundred started again.

West Indies in India, November–December 2011

By November 2011, the pressure had really started to get to me. Every day I was getting a lot of text messages wishing me well for the century and asking me not to worry. They were sent with the best of intentions, but unfortunately they made it impossible for me not to think about the landmark all the time. Everywhere I went people were talking about it – in hotels, restaurants, planes and airport lounges. While it was touching to see the affection, at times it began to get quite unbearable. It was difficult to cope with all the words of sympathy and reassurance and the looks on people's faces day after day.

While recuperating from the toe injury under the supervision of physio Harshada Rajadhyaksha, who has helped me for over a decade, I had started to mentally prepare myself for the visit of the West Indies. It was important for the team to put the England slump behind us, especially as we had another tough tour of Australia lined up for the end of the year. Preparation was important because the West Indies attack, with Fidel Edwards, Ravi Rampaul, Kemar Roach and Darren Sammy, was not the easiest to face, a fact that became all too clear at Delhi in the first Test, which started on 6 November.

Contrary to the general expectation that we would roll the

West Indies over, we were bowled out for 209 in our first innings at Delhi and conceded a lead of 95 to the tourists. Though our bowlers did well to bowl them out for 180 in the second innings, with Ashwin taking six wickets, we were confronted with a tricky chase of 276 to win the game. I went out to bat with our score at 95–2 and was eventually out with just 30 runs needed for victory. I had scored 76 and was delighted to have helped us take a 1–0 lead in the series.

Fans and critics, however, were not quite so pleased. As far as they were concerned, I had fallen twenty-four runs short and the headline was 'Sachin fails again'. The hundred had turned into a fixation and people were starting to calculate my scores backwards from 100. I don't think this had ever happened to a cricketer before and deep down it started to get to me. As the wait continued, a section of the media started making things even more difficult. They suggested that I was only playing to achieve personal milestones. It was a strange paradox. Here I was in Delhi scoring 76 and helping India to victory, yet I was criticized for playing for selfish reasons.

Three Indian batsmen made centuries in our only innings in the second Test at Eden Gardens in Kolkata starting on 14 November, but unfortunately I wasn't one of them. Laxman was unbeaten on 176, while Rahul made 119 and Dhoni 144 in our total of 631. My contribution was only 38. Our bowlers then dismissed the West Indies twice to give us a win by an innings and 15 runs.

The final Test in Mumbai started on 22 November and the West Indies dashed our hopes of a 3–0 whitewash by posting 590 in their first innings, with Darren Bravo making 166 and their first six batsmen all making fifties. At the end of the third day I was not out on 67 in our first innings and playing well. Could I really make that elusive 100th hundred on my home ground?

On our way to the ground on the morning of the fourth day, the number of outside-broadcast vans lined up opposite the stadium was staggering and that's when I realized this was a very different occasion from normal. Darren Sammy, the West Indies captain, took the second new ball and immediately there was some movement for both Fidel Edwards and Ravi Rampaul. I was standing outside the crease to counter the movement and told myself not to chase any balls outside off stump while the ball was swinging. I started the day well by flicking Rampaul for four in the very first over, following it up with a punch off Edwards through cover. I then produced an upper cut over slip for six against Edwards and was just seven short of the hundred.

Just then, I looked at the scoreboard and started to feel distinctly strange. My feet were heavy and it was as if I had no strength left. I had never felt as nervous in my career, not even when I was about to make my first Test hundred in 1990. I walked away towards square leg and took a few deep breaths. I kept telling myself to concentrate hard and not lose focus. It was a sensation I had never experienced before.

My ninety-fourth run was a single to deep point. In the next over from Rampaul, I played the last three balls after Virat had taken a single off the third delivery. The fourth ball was full and I played it to cover, moving well to the pitch of the ball and negating any possible movement. The next ball bounced a little but I managed to play it down with soft hands. Rampaul was trying to get the ball to move away and I needed to be watchful. The last ball of the over came in quicker and bounced a little more than I had anticipated and the shot travelled quickly to Sammy at second slip, who held a good catch. It all happened within a fraction of a second and only when I glanced back did I realize that I was out.

The realization was exceedingly painful. I had come within one shot of the century. But you can never take anything for granted in the game, and that's part of its beauty. I was still dazed as I walked back to the pavilion, trying to take in the applause of a very appreciative crowd. The wait would have to continue and the pressure was bound to become even more intense in the days ahead.

After the Test series, I decided to withdraw from the one-day series. There was speculation that it was because I didn't want to get the hundred in an ODI against the West Indies, but that had nothing to do with it. My big toe had started to trouble me again. I was finding it difficult to change direction while running and simply could not cope with the pressure of one-day cricket. I knew I needed to do something about it before the next Test series in Australia.

India in Australia, December 2011–February 2012

I left for Australia on 8 December to get acclimatized to the conditions and be fully prepared for the Boxing Day Test in Melbourne. The injury hadn't disappeared completely and I went to a podiatrist to get the toe examined again. When I tried out some new insoles, the experiment actually made things worse and I had to go back to my old ones, but that was when I came up with the idea of using corn caps. These were cut in the shape of doughnuts and filled with a gel, and placed right underneath the toe to absorb the pressure of the spikes. They seemed to work to a certain extent. The first time we had to apply the strapping, it took about forty-five minutes, because we were still figuring out exactly how to do it so that the padding stayed in the same place throughout the day. Within a week it was taking twenty minutes and soon I was doing the strapping myself in my own room, so that I didn't have to start every day in the physio's room. Every night during Test matches, I would get the tape ready, cut to the exact size needed. That way I got a few extra minutes in the morning and wasn't so rushed.

In the Boxing Day Test at the MCG we started extremely well, bowling Australia out for 333 in their first innings, In our reply, I came in when the score was 97–2 and found that I was moving as well as I had done in years and I was able to play all my shots. For example, in the first over after tea I was in complete control against Peter Siddle, the leader of their attack. After hitting the first ball for six over third man, I flicked him for three runs the very next ball. In the thirty-fifth over of our innings, I hit him for two consecutive fours, the second of which was a cover drive I particularly remember. The ball was pitched slightly outside off stump and I sent it racing to the boundary.

I was playing aggressively and followed up the Siddle cover drive with another off Ben Hilfenhaus. He tried to compensate and bowled a full delivery to me in the same over and I played a straight drive past mid on for yet another four. I had reached 32 off twenty-nine balls. It was just the kind of start I wanted and it was time for consolidation. I managed to get to my fifty off just fifty-five deliveries and the momentum had swung our way.

When I look back at this innings, I have little doubt that I was batting as well as I could have done. If I had managed to survive the last over of the second day, the entire series might have been different, but I was out for 73 to a Siddle delivery that moved in late after pitching, forcing me to play away from my body. My wicket gave the Australians an opening and they did very well to capitalize on the opportunity on the third morning.

Anjali and the kids were in Melbourne at the time and it would have been fantastic to get the hundred there after batting so well. Rahul was out in the first over the next morning and Laxman and Dhoni followed soon after, handing Australia control of the match. I was so disappointed after getting out that I sought solace in food that night when I went out for dinner with Anjali, the kids and my mother-in-law. Not only did I end up eating two huge main courses in frustration but, to add to my woes, I also lost my credit card.

We struck back in the Australian second innings and reduced them to 27–4, with Umesh Yadav taking three of those wickets. Then Ponting and Michael Hussey came together in what turned out to be a game-changing partnership of 115. We had one final opportunity when Hussey was out on the fourth morning for 89, reducing Australia to 197–9. At that point the lead was less than 250 and we still had a realistic chance of winning the match. But a 43-run last-wicket partnership between Hilfenhaus and Pattinson took it out of our reach and Australia went 1–0 up in the series.

The Sydney Test was even more disappointing. The wicket had a lot of grass and Australia won the toss and decided to bowl, which is unusual for an Australian team at home. They took full advantage of the conditions and bowled us out for only 191 on the first day. I scored 41 before dragging a James Pattinson delivery on to my stumps. We did well at the start of the Australian innings and had them at 37–3, but then we lost our way. Batting in much-improved conditions on days two and three, Australia went on to run up a very big score, with skipper Michael Clarke contributing a triple hundred to their 659, and this left us two whole days to bat to save the match.

Batting for two days was difficult but not impossible. At the end of day three, I was unbeaten on eight, having faced forty deliveries. I was batting to a plan and was determined to leave everything outside off stump. It had got a little cloudy in the evening and with Ben Hilfenhaus and Peter Siddle bowling really well, I was satisfied to survive the last hour so that I could resume the following morning.

Before I walked out to bat on the fourth day, our masseur Amit Shah wished me luck and I said to him that he should get prepared to keep me going for two days. I knew that if I did so I would be able to save the game, and if the 100th ton should come along the way, so much the better. Once again I was batting well and should have gone on, but infuriatingly I got myself out to part-time left-arm spinner Michael Clarke for 80 to a ball which pitched around off stump on a fourth-day pitch with a few cracks and, just as I was trying to play forward, kissed the outside edge of my bat and hit Brad Haddin on his thigh before going to Mike Hussey at slip.

It was a soft dismissal. I had actually told myself to wait an over before starting to attack Clarke, who was bowling with a somewhat defensive field. A very strong wind was blowing and I wanted to wait for it to die down before I risked stepping out and hitting him over mid off. It was just one of those moments in the game that you are not able to control, moments that make cricket one of the most challenging of all sports.

Despite scoring 73, 32, 41 and 80 in the first four innings in Australia, the talk about me 'failing' had resumed and the consensus among the critics was that I was getting out because I was thinking too much about the 100th hundred. Such comments were sometimes hard to take, because for me playing for my country has always come first. The critics were welcome to give their opinions, but none of them had ever been in my predicament and it was impossible for them to understand what I was thinking or feeling.

After Sydney, the series went steadily downhill for us at Perth and Adelaide. We should have played much better and I must say the eight-Test-match losing streak on foreign soil was very difficult to come to terms with. Our team had not lived up to its potential and had been outplayed in all departments. It was a very trying time.

My toe was continuing to pose problems and mentally I was frustrated. It was then that a foot specialist suggested to me that I should have an operation on both my sesamoid bones. In my frustration, I almost agreed and was ready to be on crutches for the next four months, but Anjali dissuaded me from doing so, and in fact spoke to Prof. Cathy Speed in London, who advised that I should avoid surgery. Anjali then came all the way to Australia for just two days to spend some time with me because she was worried that I would go ahead with the surgery out of frustration. I am glad I listened to her and that good sense prevailed.

After the Test series, there was widespread speculation that I had made myself available for the subsequent limited-overs tri-series against Sri Lanka and Australia just so that I could score my 100th century. Such statements were frustrating because they were simply untrue. One of the main reasons I played in

Arjun and Sara: the two little diamonds of my life.

With Anjali at my fortieth birthday celebration in Kolkata on 24 April 2013.

Above: Walking out to bat in the World Cup final at the Wankhede in April 2011. That win will always remain the highest point of my career.

Below: Sangakkara caught Dhoni, bowled Yuvraj – a huge moment in the final.

Right: Gary Kirsten, one of the best coaches I have played under.

My dream fulfilled – relishing victory on the shoulders of Yusuf Pathan and Harbhajan Singh.

With Honourable President Pratibha Patil the day after winning the final.

Finally the trophy is ours – in front of the Gateway of India in Mumbai.

What a champion! With Roger Federer at Wimbledon in 2011.

Later on Yuvi confessed, '*Ki paaji aap toh bahut bhari ho!*' (Oops! Paaji did not know you were that heavy!)

Lata Mangeshkar and Asha Bhosle: two of my all-time favourite singers. It is always a privilege listening to them.

Left: Finally the wait is over. The 100th international hundred in Dhaka in March 2012.

Above: The next day, my friends from the media kindly presented me with this special cake.

Below: My core strengths – with my brothers and sister and their better halves after receiving the Order of Australia in 2012.

Above: My bats adorned with the tricolour before my 200th and last Test. I was so excited I couldn't resist taking this picture and sharing it with Anjali.

Acknowledging the crowd after making 74 in my final innings, at the Wankhede in November 2013. I wasn't sure if I would get another chance to thank everyone.

Below: The final few moments – with Anjali, Arjun and Sara at the presentation ceremony.

'Mama, please control yourself!' – Arjun and Sara consoling Anjali as she struggles to hold back her tears during my farewell speech.

The last goodbye – I hope I have been able to leave some lasting memories.

The notes for my speech that I carried with me on my last day in international cricket.

Paying my respects to the 22 yards – the final namaskar.

Bharat Ratna – the ultimate honour. With Honourable President Pranab Mukherjee in New Delhi on 4 February 2014.

Showing the Bharat Ratna to Achrekar Sir. I hope I have been a good student and made you proud.

the series was that MS Dhoni came and said to me, '*Aap ruk jao. Aap rahoge to achha hoga. Aap agar sab match na bhi khelte ho phir bhi aap ruk jao.*' (Please stay. It will be good if you stay. Even if you don't play all the games, please stay.) Perhaps it's difficult for some to understand the obsessive urge to do well for India, but this is what has given my sporting life a purpose.

Despite playing well in patches, however, we didn't make it to the final of the tri-series. There seemed to be a cloud of negativity surrounding the game and fans were starting to lose faith in the team. We needed to get things moving again and the next opportunity to do so was in the Asia Cup in Bangladesh in March 2012.

Try, try, try again . . .

I scored only six in our first Asia Cup game, a 50-run victory against Sri Lanka in Dhaka on 13 March 2012, and the 'Sachin fails again' cry started up immediately. Fortunately I was not particularly aware of it at the time, as my family and friends did their best to shield me from what appeared in the press.

Our next match was against Bangladesh on 16 March on a track that was slightly slower than the one used against Sri Lanka. The ball did not always come on to the bat and it was going to be important to pace the innings and set a big score for the hosts to chase down. Virat and I rotated the strike well and the scoring rate hovered just above the five-runs-an-over mark for most of the innings. We had set ourselves a target of 280–90 and were on course to achieve it.

As I passed 80, the pressure started to build and I began to feel the burden of the hundred again. I did my best to put it out of my mind, but it was a truly difficult and frustrating period. I remember an over against Mashrafe Mortaza during the batting powerplay in which three shots I played should have gone for four. They were stopped by some really good fielding or they went straight to the fielders. On another day, I could have taken 12 from the over. On that day, I got nothing.

I had to counter the mounting pressure and somehow I played a shot for four when I was on 90 that calmed my nerves a little. Meanwhile Suresh Raina, who had come in to bat after Virat, was finding the boundary consistently, keeping the scoring rate up. I was now on 94 and, with another single in the same over, had come the closest to a hundred for a year.

In the forty-first over I took three more singles and was left needing just two more runs. They were perhaps the two most difficult runs of my career. Despite having scored ninety-nine international hundreds, I had experienced nothing like it. Determination, anxiety, relief – all of these feelings came together. I kept telling myself to stay focused and play each ball on its merit. It was time to go back to basics and rely on skills I had honed all my life.

When I got to 99 by driving Shakib al Hasan to long off, I told myself that the situation demanded patience and it was no time for heroics. Shakib was getting the ball to spin and so when I faced him next I stepped out just a little to smother the turn. As the ball trundled to square leg, I jogged to my 100th international century.

Instantly I felt completely drained. I removed my helmet and pointed to the Indian flag on the front. As I patted the tricolour on my helmet with my bat, I felt a tremendous sense of satisfaction. It gave me a great feeling of fulfilment that the player who was the first to achieve this feat of scoring 100 hundreds was an Indian. Then I looked at my bat and asked God why it had taken so long when my commitment had been steadfast throughout. And then I felt relieved.

Friends often say to me that my celebrations that day seemed rather muted. I remind them that I had been like that for over two decades. I have always preferred restraint and reticence. This is not to say I wasn't proud of my achivements. Of course I was.

When I first played for India against Pakistan in 1989, I had never imagined I would still be playing for the country in 2012, let alone score 100 centuries.

Unfortunately, we went on to lose the match. Bangladesh played really well to chase down a challenging score of 289, with Tamim Iqbal, Jahurul Islam and Nasir Hossain all making fifties and Shakib Al Hasan and Mushfiqur Rahim getting very close. I was amazed to hear some people say we should have got a few more runs to be safe, as 289 wasn't a bad score on that pitch, considering that we had restricted a much better Sri Lankan batting line-up to 254 in their run chase in the previous match on a better batting pitch. Sometimes you have to give the opposition full credit and on this occasion the Bangladeshis truly deserved it.

While we were all disappointed at losing the match, my teammates were extremely happy for me. It was gratifying to see such powerful emotion within the team. This is what one plays for, the respect and affection of one's team-mates, and I was touched to hear the sentiments expressed in the dressing room.

After finishing a rather long press conference, it was time to speak to Anjali and the children. They were holidaying in Goa and were having dinner at Martin's, one of my favourite seafood restaurants, when I first spoke to them. They were extremely happy and relieved at the same time. My family had also been feeling the effects of the pressure and now they felt a sense of liberation. It was only natural that I should dedicate the hundred to my brother Ajit, who has spent a life making me the cricketer I am. My mother was at our house in Mumbai and was extremely thrilled to watch me score the hundred. I could sense the joy in her voice. Though I was not around to see my mother's face, I could picture her and imagine what she must be feeling. Sensing her delight gave me a feeling of contentment that is difficult to describe. Suffice to say I was a very proud son.

When I got back to India, I was overwhelmed at the reception and wish to put on record my deepest gratitude to everyone who had prayed for me. The event organized by Nita and Mukesh Ambani, the owners of the Mumbai Indians, was fantastic, and to listen to the legendary Lata Mangeshkar sing for me was an unbelievable experience. These are moments I will never forget, moments that more than made up for the year of frustration.

Feeling 50 kilos lighter

We were still involved in the Asia Cup and were due to play Pakistan in Dhaka a couple of days later. I was suddenly feeling a lot more relaxed and was looking forward to batting in what is always a special game for an Indian cricketer, wherever it's played.

When I was interviewed by the former Pakistani captain Rameez Raja, I suggested to him that I was feeling 50 kilos lighter. In reality it was a little more. The desperation had vanished and it was time to enjoy batting again. Life, it seemed, was finally back to normal. A number of journalists asked me what I was thinking after scoring the 100th ton. I said to them in jest that I was wondering whether all those who were quick to give me batting advice remembered the ninety-nine hundreds I scored before this one. Then someone asked me, 'What were you thinking when you scored your first Test hundred in 1990?' I said to him that I was thinking of the ninety-nine still to go!

I felt completely different when I went out to open the batting against Pakistan, trying to chase down a formidable score of 329. We lost Gautam Gambhir in the first over, but Virat and I batted freely and put together a 133-run stand at almost seven runs an over. We set up the chase and when I was out for 52, Virat and Rohit finished off the job in style, with Virat ending up with a brilliant 183.

The innings against Pakistan put into perspective how difficult the wait had been and how much pressure I had been under. Despite trying not to think about the 100th hundred, I hadn't been able to escape the tension that had built up. Finally I felt liberated and, more importantly, the media's fiery obsession had been doused. Maybe now I would be allowed to concentrate on my batting. For the time being, there was a rare period of calm, and I was keen to make the most of it.

India in England 2011 – The Pataudi Trophy

1st Test. Lord's. 21–25 July 2011
England 474–8 dec (KP Pietersen 202*, MJ Prior 71, IJL Trott 70; P Kumar 5–106) and 269–6 dec (MJ Prior 103*, SCJ Broad 74; I Sharma 4–59)
India 286 (R Dravid 103, A Mukund 49, **SR Tendulkar 34**; SCJ Broad 4–37, CT Tremlett 3–80) and 261 (SK Raina 78, VVS Laxman 56, **SR Tendulkar 12**; JM Anderson 5–65, SCJ Broad 3–57)
England won by 196 runs

2nd Test. Nottingham. 29 July–1 August 2011
England 221 (SCJ Broad 64; P Kumar 3–45, I Sharma 3–66, S Sreesanth 3–77) and 544 (IR Bell 159, TT Bresnan 90, MJ Prior 73, EJG Morgan 70, KP Pietersen 63; P Kumar 4–124)
India 288 (R Dravid 117, Yuvraj Singh 62, VVS Laxman 54, **SR Tendulkar 16**; SCJ Broad 6–46) and 158 (**SR Tendulkar 56**, H Singh 46; TT Bresnan 5–48, JM Anderson 3–51)
England won by 319 runs

3rd Test. Birmingham. 10–13 August 2011
India 224 (MS Dhoni 77, **SR Tendulkar 1**; SCJ Broad 4–53, TT Bresnan 4–62) and 244 (MS Dhoni 74*, **SR Tendulkar 40**, P Kumar 40; JM Anderson 4–85, SCJ Broad 2–28, GP Swann 2–88)
England 710–7 dec (AN Cook 294, EJG Morgan 104, AJ Strauss 87, KP Pietersen 63, TT Bresnan 53*; A Mishra 3–150, P Kumar 2–98)
England won by an innings and 242 runs

4th Test. The Oval. 18–22 August 2011
England 591–6 dec (IR Bell 235, KP Pietersen 175, RS Bopara 44; S Sreesanth 3–123, SK Raina 2–58)
India 300 (R Dravid 146*, A Mishra 43, **SR Tendulkar 23**; TT Bresnan 3–54, GP Swann 3–102) and 283 (f/o) (**SR Tendulkar 91**, A Mishra 84; GP Swann 6–106, SCJ Broad 2–44)
England won by an innings and 8 runs

England won the series 4–0

West Indies in India 2011

1st Test. Delhi. 6–9 November 2011

West Indies 304 (S Chanderpaul 118, KC Brathwaite 63; PP Ojha 6–72,
R Ashwin 3–81) and 180 (S Chanderpaul 47; R Ashwin 6–47, UT Yadav
2–36)

India 209 (V Sehwag 55, R Dravid 54, **SR Tendulkar 7**; DJG Sammy 3–35,
R Rampaul 2–44, D Bishoo 2–55) and 276–5 (**SR Tendulkar 76**, VVS Laxman
58*, V Sehwag 55; DJG Sammy 2–56)

India won by 5 wickets

2nd Test. Kolkata. 14–17 November 2011

India 631–7 dec (VVS Laxman 176*, MS Dhoni 144, R Dravid 119,
G Gambhir 65, **SR Tendulkar 38**; KAJ Roach 2–106, DJG Sammy
2–132)

West Indies 153 (DM Bravo 30; PP Ojha 4–64, UT Yadav 3–23) and 463 (f/o)
(DM Bravo 136, MN Samuels 84, AB Barath 62, KA Edwards 60,
S Chanderpaul 47; UT Yadav 4–80)

India won by an innings and 15 runs

3rd Test. Mumbai. 22–26 November 2011

West Indies 590 (DM Bravo 166, KA Edwards 86, KOA Powell 81, KC Brathwaite
68, AB Barath 62, MN Samuels 61; R Ashwin 5–156, VR Aaron 3–106) and
134 (DM Bravo 48; PP Ojha 6–47, R Ashwin 4–34)

India 482 (R Ashwin 103, **SR Tendulkar 94**, R Dravid 82, G Gambhir 55,
V Kohli 52; MN Samuels 3–74, R Rampaul 3–95) and 242–9 (V Kohli 63,
V Sehwag 60, **SR Tendulkar 3**; R Rampaul 3–56)

Match drawn

India won the series 2–0

India in Australia 2011–12 – The Border-Gavaskar Trophy

1st Test. Melbourne. 26–29 December 2011

Australia 333 (EJM Cowan 68, RT Ponting 62; Z Khan 4–77 R Ashwin 3–81,
UT Yadav 3–106) and 240 (MEK Hussey 89, RT Ponting 60; UT Yadav 4–70,
Z Khan 3–53)

India 282 (**SR Tendulkar 73**, R Dravid 68, V Sehwag 67; BW Hilfenhaus
5–75, PM Siddle 3–63) and 169 (**SR Tendulkar 32**; JL Pattinson 4–53,
PM Siddle 3–42)

Australia won by 122 runs

2nd Test. Sydney. 3–6 January 2012

India 191 (MS Dhoni 57*, **SR Tendulkar 41**; JL Pattinson 4–43, BW
Hilfenhaus 3–51, PM Siddle 3–55) and 400 (G Gambhir 83, **SR Tendulkar
80**, VVS Laxman 66, R Ashwin 62; BW Hilfenhaus 5–106, PM Siddle 2–88)

Australia 659–4 dec (MJ Clarke 329*, MEK Hussey 150*, RT Ponting 134;
Z Khan 3–122)

Australia won by an innings and 68 runs

3rd Test. Perth. 13–15 January 2012

India 161 (V Kohli 44, **SR Tendulkar 15**; BW Hilfenhaus 4–43, PM Siddle
    3–42) and 171 (V Kohli 75, R Dravid 47, **SR Tendulkar 8**; BW Hilfenhaus
    4–54, PM Siddle 3–43)

Australia 369 (DA Warner 180, EJM Cowan 74; UT Yadav 5–93)

Australia won by an innings and 37 runs

4th Test. Adelaide. 24–28 January 2012

Australia 604–7 dec (RT Ponting 221, MJ Clarke 210, BJ Haddin 42*; R Ashwin
    3–194) and 167–5 dec (RT Ponting 60*; R Ashwin 2–73)

India 272 (V Kohli 116, WP Saha 35, **SR Tendulkar 25**; PM Siddle 5–49,
    BW Hilfenhaus 3–62) and 201 (V Sehwag 62, **SR Tendulkar 13**; NM Lyon
    4–63, RJ Harris 3–41)

Australia won by 298 runs

Australia won the series 4–0

25

MY LAST FULL SEASON

With the 100th hundred finally out of the way, I was looking forward to a busy season of Test cricket at home. For once, we were not touring much and in 2012–13 we were due to host New Zealand, England and Australia. You don't often get to play ten uninterrupted Test matches at home. I had prepared well but must concede things rarely went to plan from a personal point of view. In the lead-up to the season I continued to be bothered by the toe injury, so much so that I visited BKS Iyengar, one of the foremost yoga gurus in the world, together with Zaheer Khan for a day in May 2012, during the fifth edition of the IPL. I had been introduced to Guruji in 1999 by Kiran More when I was suffering from the back injury and had spent a week with him in Pune at the time. In June 2012 I travelled to Germany to the Adidas factory to get some special shoes made and during this visit I was accompanied by Prof. Cathy Speed, who had travelled from London to be with me.

In August 2012, we won both Tests against New Zealand, with Ravichandran Ashwin and Pragyan Ojha bowling well and getting us wickets at regular intervals. In each of my three innings in the series, I got a start before being bowled, which prompted a lot of speculation in the press about my technique – had my reflexes slowed down and was I the batsman I once was? In my mind, however, there was nothing seriously wrong with my technique or my approach. One problem, perhaps, was that in the off season I had trained a lot indoors and had got too used to the high indoor bounce. In Hyderabad in the first Test, for example, I was dismissed for 19 by a delivery from Trent Boult that I expected to bounce more.

I travelled to the second Test match in Bangalore determined to play a big innings. However, this time round I was bowled for 17 by a ball from the right-arm fast bowler Doug Bracewell that didn't swing as much as I expected and went straight on. When I went out to bat in the second innings I tried to play myself in, hoping that spending some time at the crease would help. I managed to hit a few fours before getting out for 27 to a Tim Southee delivery that swung back in to knock me over.

It was not the best start to the season, but I put it behind me and focused my attention on the England series that started in November 2012. As part of the preparation I played for Mumbai in a Ranji Trophy game against the Railways team on 2 November. In my one innings, I had to battle physical exhaustion, as I had had serious food poisoning just before the game and was feeling extremely weak; so much so, in fact, that I asked Rohit Sharma to bat ahead of me. By the time I went in, I had recovered enough to make 137, which was a very satisfying knock considering how I'd felt a few hours earlier. Suddenly I was playing my shots and feeling positive again.

England in India, November–December 2012

I thought I started well against England in the first Test at Ahmedabad on 15 November. My body position and balance were perfect and I was getting into a really good rhythm. From the off, I played some cracking strokes, including a very pleasing lofted shot against Swann over midwicket. I set out to bat aggressively and not hold myself back, because that was how I had scored the Ranji Trophy hundred. Seeing me go over the short midwicket fielder, Swann pushed a man back and I decided to counter him by going over mid on. The ball had drift, however, and instead of playing it over mid on, I hit it straight to the midwicket fielder and I was out for 13. I was very angry with myself for not making the most of my good form.

In the context of the match, my failure in Ahmedabad did not matter in the end, with Sehwag making 117 and Cheteshwar Pujara going on to score an excellent double century. He paced his innings beautifully and has the temperament and the patience to be a top-class Test batsman in the years to come. He has all the shots and is a much-improved player since his debut against Australia in 2010. Pragyan Ojha and Ravi Ashwin then got in on the act and ran through England in both innings.

The second Test started in Mumbai on 23 November and rather unexpectedly England turned things around on the first day. I had always been worried about the Mumbai match and had shared my concerns with coach Duncan Fletcher. I felt that the pace and bounce of the Wankhede wicket would help the England bowlers. England had beaten us at the Wankhede in 2006 and I thought we should have prepared a good batting wicket instead of a turner.

The inclusion of Monty Panesar in the team was an inspired selection and I got out to him on the first morning before lunch for eight, to a ball that spun from leg stump to hit the top of my off stump. Nobody expects the ball to turn square at the Wankhede in the first session of the first day of a Test. Not only that but, when Monty was bowling, I had chatted with Pujara, who was batting at the other end, and he said the ball was not turning at all. I had scored thousands of runs playing the shot I tried against Monty. When there's not much turn you can just smother the spin and turn a ball pitched on leg stump to square leg for a single, but the shot isn't on if there's vicious turn. It was just my luck that it was the first delivery that spun square. I was gutted at having failed in front of my home crowd.

Monty had taken Sehwag's wicket earlier in the innings and triggered a rare batting collapse on home soil, which handed England control of the match. Only Pujara, who scored a brilliant 135, stood up against the English spinners, Panesar and Swann, and we squandered the advantage of winning the toss and batting first.

England then batted excellently, with skipper Alastair Cook

and Kevin Pietersen playing extremely well in difficult batting conditions to set up the game. Cook made 122 and Pietersen an imperious 186. They were instrumental in giving their team a first-innings lead of 86. Cook showed great patience and throughout the series played spin better than most visiting batsmen have done in recent times.

In the second innings, I again got out to Monty Panesar. This time the ball came on with the arm while I played for turn. Gautam Gambhir was batting at the other end and at the end of the day's play, he told me that, as I was walking back to the pavilion, Monty had said to Gautam, '*Ball apne aap seedha nikal gaya!*' (The delivery went straight on its own!) I was out fair and square, but couldn't help feeling unlucky to get out to an arm-ball that wasn't even intended by the bowler! To add to the frustration, we lost the match in under four days. Losing at home was not something we were accustomed to and it came as something of a rude jolt.

I realized that I needed to take my mind off cricket for a while, so I called Yuvi, Zaheer and Bhajji and suggested that we should watch a movie in the hotel room on reaching Kolkata for the third Test. I had already seen *Barfi!* – an award-winning film about a deaf mute – but it was so good that I really wanted to watch it again. Forty-five minutes into the film Bhajji said, '*Paaji yeh log kuch bolenge ki film aise hi chalta rahega?*' (Brother, are they going to say anything or is it going to continue in this silent vein for the whole movie?) Only Harbhajan could have come out with something like that!

After a string of failures, I decided to change my approach in the third Test in Kolkata, starting on 5 December 2012. I would stop being aggressive and instead play within myself, even though it was a really good batting pitch. Because of this defensive mind-set I missed out on a number of balls that in normal circumstances I would have put away for four, but I was mindful that I had done something similar in Australia in 2003–04 when I had scored a double hundred. This time I managed 76 before getting out to a good delivery from James Anderson straight after a drinks break. Anderson bowled beautifully throughout the series and was the central figure in the English attack. He used reverse swing well and picked up wickets at critical moments.

Yet again we had failed to make the most of our opportunities and we were all out for a modest 316. England were brilliant in response and Cook again led from the front with a spectacular 190. A skipper leading from the front is always good for a team and England put us under pressure again with a 207-run lead. Our second innings was nothing to write home about and I got out for five, caught at slip off Graeme Swann. None of the batsmen played to their potential and we lost the Test in four days.

We went to Nagpur for the last Test on 13 December 2012, needing a win to draw the series. Virat Kohli made a hundred and Dhoni was run out on 99, but my poor series continued as I was bowled by James Anderson for two in my only innings. It seemed that things were just not going my way and as I went into bat, I faced two balls from Monty Panesar that spun viciously. Till then the wicket had appeared flat and even the England players were surprised. That's what seems to happen when you're going through a bad patch. Trott made a hundred in England's second innings and the game ended in a draw, meaning that we had lost the series 2–1.

England were easily the better team in the series but I must say I was terribly disappointed with the way I performed in the six innings I played in those four Test matches. Anjali had actually come to Nagpur because my frame of mind was not good and when the press saw that she was there, they assumed that I was going to announce my retirement. Something that helped me regain some perspective at the time was a conversation with Ravi Shastri. Ravi and I have always been good friends and in Nagpur we had dinner in my room and he repeatedly told me that I should not start to doubt myself after a few failures. His confidence in me was reassuring and I greatly appreciated the gesture.

Time for change

I took some time off after the England series to clear my mind after all the scrutiny and speculation and to think carefully about my career. I gave retirement some serious thought, but I concluded that I still had the hunger and runs left in me. I might not have made many runs in the England series, but the way I was batting had given me enough confidence to carry on.

One-day cricket was another matter, and India were due to play three ODIs against Pakistan at the end of 2012. I had not played ODI cricket between March and December and I had to ask myself whether I was realistically going to take part in the World Cup in Australia and New Zealand in 2015. If not, what goals would I have left in ODI cricket? I realized I had to accept that I was not going to be around till then. The next question was whether I wanted to play a farewell ODI series against Pakistan before calling it a day. I decided that it was better to take a break and focus my energies on the Australia Test series in February– March 2013.

Having informed the BCCI, the chairman of selectors and Duncan Fletcher of my decision to retire from ODIs, I boarded a flight for Dehradun on my way to Mussoorie, a quiet hill station in the North Indian state of Uttarakhand that I love to visit. A break in Mussoorie is a great way to escape from city life and unwind, and that's what I needed. The news of my retirement had become public while I was in the air between Mumbai and Delhi and as soon as we landed in Delhi I got a series of messages from friends and well-wishers. As the same aircraft was continuing on to Dehradun, I told Anjali that I was going to sit with the captain in the cockpit while the new passengers boarded, as I didn't feel like speaking to anyone for the time being.

I also asked Anjali if she would gently break the news of my decision to Arjun, as I was concerned about how he would take it. Anjali later told me that she would never forget his reaction.

He said that he was sure I still had a lot of cricket left in me and there was no reason for me to retire, but when Anjali explained to him that the decision was final, he turned his face away and leaned his head on the window and a tear drop rolled down his cheek. Anjali and I both got very emotional when she told me this. Sara, being a little older, said that she would miss seeing me play but had full faith in my decision. My children were growing up fast and it mattered to me that they were both by my side at a time like this. Whenever they are with me, it always makes a huge difference to my well-being.

Mussoorie was a timely break. There was no one there except family and a few very close friends and I had some time to myself and a chance to think about my future. The media and fans allowed me the privacy to do so and while I still followed Mumbai's progress in the Ranji Trophy, I also managed to switch off from cricket for a while. I played table tennis, went for long walks and relaxed in the evenings, and managed to get my sense of optimism back. When I started to feel the urge to resume training, I knew it was time to return to Mumbai.

Australia in India, February–March 2013

I used to reach the Wankhede Stadium for training at around seven every morning, and for a while I would be completely alone in the stadium. On some days trainer Rahul Patwardhan would join me. The early-morning dew coated the lush green outfield and I could feel the dampness on my feet as I ran, leaving a trail behind me. When I looked up at the empty galleries I knew that this was where I belonged. This was my refuge.

I would jog and then run for a while and do my fitness drills before the groundsmen arrived. The Mumbai team would normally turn up around 8.30 a.m., by which time I would be in the dressing room taking a breather. Then I would train with my team-mates, doing my regular net sessions to prepare for the

Ranji Trophy. In all my years of playing international cricket, I never resorted to short cuts and there was no question of changing that at the start of 2013.

In the Ranji Trophy we beat Baroda and Services on the way to the final against Saurashtra, which we won by an innings and 125 runs. Mumbai then took on the Rest of India in the Irani Cup game, in which I got a hundred. It was an innings that gave me a lot of satisfaction and confidence going into the Test series.

We started the first of four Tests against Australia on 22 February at the Chepauk in Chennai, one of my favourite grounds. Australia did well to make 380 in the first innings, with skipper Michael Clarke contributing a hundred. In reply, we didn't start well, losing two quick wickets for 12 runs, and when I walked to the wicket we badly needed a partnership.

James Pattinson was bowling fast and I decided to take the battle to him and play my shots. The first ball was slightly wide of off stump and I presented the full face of the blade and was happy to see the ball race past the fielders to the boundary. I repeated the shot to the second ball and the result, to my delight, was the same. The final ball of the over was short of a length and I moved inside the line to flick it to fine leg for another four. I had hit three boundaries in four balls and the pressure had eased. My comeback had started well.

Cheteshwar Pujara, who batted sensibly for his 44, kept me company and I was unbeaten on 71 at the end of the second day, confident of kicking on and getting a big hundred. However, it didn't turn out that way as I was bowled for 81 by the off-spinner Nathan Lyon on the third morning with a ball that was slightly fuller in length than I expected. I had made up my mind to get to the pitch of the ball and hit it between midwicket and long on with the turn. It was only when I realized that the length was full that I quickly changed my shot and that was my down-fall.

Thankfully, the dismissal did not affect the team's momentum, with Virat getting a hundred and Dhoni a blistering double hundred, one of the best innings I have seen at the Chepauk, to give us a lead of 192. Our spinners, led by Ashwin, then ran through the Australians in the second innings, leaving us needing just 50 to win the match. In my second innings, I played the same shot to Nathan Lyon's first two balls and on both occasions the ball flew between midwicket and long on for six and we soon closed out the match.

In the second Test at Hyderabad, starting on 2 March, we played brilliantly to reach 503, with Murali Vijay scoring 167 and Cheteshwar Pujara making a double century. Australia had managed a disappointing 237 in their first innings and the second-wicket partnership of 370 between Vijay and Pujara meant our bowlers had enough runs on the board to bowl the Australians out in the second innings without us having to bat twice.

I got out to James Pattinson for seven, getting the faintest edge down the leg side. I was cursing my luck for having got bat on ball, prompting the caught-behind appeal, but was also surprised to see the umpire, after he had initially given me not out, deciding to check with the third umpire after a prolonged rethink. In a series in which there was no Decision Review System (DRS) there was no reason for the umpire to reconsider his decision once he had given me not out. If he had not seen or heard the nick, that should have been the end of the decision. I do not know what prompted the rethink and it was strange to see the umpire deciding to check with the TV umpire.

The reason that India has steadfastly refused to use the DRS in bilateral series is because the technology is inconclusive on occasions. We witnessed how random it could be during our tour of England in 2011–12, when the DRS resulted in a number of wrong decisions. We are not against technology per se, but we do think that the DRS needs to be close to 100 per cent correct before we can accept it. We feel it is a perfectly reasonable stance and I am sure we will revisit the situation when the technology has improved. The other point is that we believe that the technology used should be the same across all countries, because only then can we achieve uniformity in decision-making.

At Hyderabad, we won the match comfortably and were gradually starting to establish a stranglehold over the series. We had never beaten Australia 4–0 in a Test series, but such a scoreline was now beginning to seem a distinct possibility.

The third Test started in Mohali on 14 March and the Australians scored a healthy 408 in their first innings, with Mitchell Starc contributing 99 batting at number nine. Our response was emphatic, with a 289-run opening partnership between Shikhar Dhawan, playing superbly on debut for his 187, and Murali Vijay, who got his second consecutive Test hundred. I started my innings well and was feeling confident when Steve Smith, the part-time leg-spinner, came on to bowl. I had never faced Smith before and walked up to Vijay to check if the ball was turning. Vijay said that Smith was giving the ball a rip and I should play for turn. The first ball I faced was the perfect line and length – and it didn't turn an inch. I was out caught bat-pad at forward short leg for 37.

On the last day at Mohali, we needed 133 to win and I went in to bat with the score at 70–2, intent on finishing the game. Australia were keeping things tight and we finally reached a stage when Dhoni and I were at the crease and we needed 24 off twenty-five balls to win. They had bowled a couple of tight overs and we needed to play a few shots to ease the pressure. I did exactly that to a delivery from Mitchell Starc that was angled in to me. I hit it over mid off for a four. In the next over by Peter Siddle, I missed a ball that came in and hit my pad before rolling away on the off side. I thought the ball had gone towards point and started running. The ball had actually gone more towards short cover, but I had committed myself to the single. David Warner came darting in and picked up the ball before flinging himself on the stumps. I had no chance. It was a spectacular effort from him and I was left to rue not checking where the ball had travelled. It was disappointing not to stay till the end and close out the game myself, but Dhoni and Ravindra Jadeja did the job. We were 3–0 up and a whitewash looked distinctly possible as we headed to Delhi for the fourth and final Test of the series.

At Delhi, one look at the wicket was enough to suggest that it would assist the spinners from day one. I remember telling Anjali that the match was not likely to last the distance and I might well be home early. I said the same thing to Ajit, who had come to Delhi to watch the game. Sure enough, the spinners got into the action very early and it promised to be a low-scoring game. Australia batted first and scored 262, a reasonable total in the conditions. In reply we made 272, of which I scored 32.

In the second innings, our spinners ran through Australia, with Ravindra Jadeja again picking up a five-for. Ashwin and Jadeja had bowled well right through the series and Jadeja had even managed to get the Australian captain Michael Clarke out a number of times, which may have started to play on Clarke's mind. Some of the deliveries Jadeja bowled to him in the first three Tests were excellent (Clarke was injured for the fourth), pitching on leg and spinning right across the face of his bat to hit the off stump.

Eventually we cruised to a win, thanks to a courageous knock from Pujara, who batted with a broken finger and remained unbeaten on 82. It was an act of real courage and will do him a lot of good in the rest of his career.

It was the first time in our history that we had achieved a 4–0 series win against Australia and the victory could not have come at a better time for Indian cricket. In one fell swoop we had managed to erase the unpleasant memories of losing to England at home and the team had started to come together again.

From a personal point of view, I had started the series well in Chennai and had looked good in patches, but I lost my wicket after getting a start on at least three occasions. Unfortunately for me, I was not able to get a century in the 2012–13 season and it was something I was definitely looking to change at the start of the following season.

New Zealand in India 2012

1st Test. Hyderabad (Deccan). 23–26 August 2012
India 438 (CA Pujara 159, MS Dhoni 73, V Kohli 58, V Sehwag 47,
    SR Tendulkar 19; JS Patel 4–100, TA Boult 3–93)
New Zealand 159 (JEC Franklin 43*; R Ashwin 6–31, PP Ojha 3–44) and
    164 (f/o) (KS Williamson 52, BB McCullum 42; R Ashwin 6–54, PP Ojha
    3–48)
India won by an innings and 115 runs

2nd Test. Bangalore. 31 August–3 September 2012
New Zealand 365 (LRPL Taylor 113, CFK van Wyk 71, MJ Guptil 53;
    PP Ojha 5–99) and 248 (JEC Franklin 41; R Ashwin 5–69, PP Ojha 2–49,
    UT Yadav 2–68)
India 353 (V Kohli 103, MS Dhoni 62, SK Raina 55, **SR Tendulkar 17**;
    TG Southee 7–64) and 262–5 (V Kohli 51*, CA Pujara 48, **SR Tendulkar 27**;
    JS Patel 3–68)
India won by 5 wickets

India won the series 2–0

England in India 2012

1st Test. Ahmedabad. 15–19 November 2012
India 521–8 dec (CA Pujara 206*, V Sehwag 117, Y Singh 74, **SR Tendulkar 13**;
    GP Swann 5–144) and 80–1 (CA Pujara 41*)
England 191 (MJ Prior 48; PP Ojha 5–45, R Ashwin 3–80) and 406 (f/o)
    (AN Cook 176, MJ Prior 91; PP Ojha 4–120, UT Yadav 3–70, Z Khan
    2–59)
India won by 9 wickets

2nd Test. Mumbai. 23–26 November 2012
India 327 (CA Pujara 135, R Ashwin 68, **SR Tendulkar 8**; MS Panesar 5–129,
    GP Swann 4–70) and 142 (G Gambhir 65, **SR Tendulkar 8**; MS Panesar
    6–81, GP Swann 4–43)
England 413 (KP Pietersen 186, AN Cook 122; PP Ojha 5–143, H Singh 2–74,
    R Ashwin 2–145) and 58–0
England won by 10 wickets

3rd Test. Kolkata. 5-9 December 2012

India 316 (**SR Tendulkar 76**, G Gambhir 60, MS Dhoni 52; MS Panesar
4-90, JM Anderson 3-89) and 247 (R Ashwin 91*, V Sehwag 49,
SR Tendulkar 5; JM Anderson 3-38, ST Finn 3-45)

England 523 (AN Cook 190, IJL Trott 87, NRD Compton 57, KP Pietersen 54;
PP Ohja 4-142, R Ashwin 3-183) and 41-3 (R Ashwin 2-31)

England won by 7 wickets

4th Test. Nagpur. 13-17 December 2012

England 330 (KP Pietersen 73, JE Root 73, MJ Prior 57, GP Swann 56;
PP Chawla 4-69, I Sharma 3-49) and 352-4 dec (IJL Trott 143, IR Bell 116*;
R Ashwin 2-99)

India 326-9 dec (V Kohli 103, MS Dhoni 99, **SR Tendulkar 2**; JM Anderson
4-81, GP Swann 3-76)

Match drawn

England won the series 2-1

Australia in India 2013 - The Border-Gavaskar Trophy

1st Test. Chennai. 22-26 February 2013

Australia 380 (MJ Clarke 130, MC Henriques 68, DA Warner 59; R Ashwin
7-103) and 241 (MC Henriques 81*; R Ashwin 5-95, RA Jadeja 3-72)

India 572 (MS Dhoni 224, V Kohli 107, **SR Tendulkar 81**; JL Pattinson 5-96)
and 50-2 (V Sehwag 19, SR Tendulkar 13)

India won by 8 wickets

2nd Test. Hyderabad (Deccan). 2-5 March 2013

Australia 237-9 dec (MJ Clarke 91, MS Wade 62; RA Jadeja 3-33, B Kumar
3-53) and 131 (EJM Cowan 44; R Ashwin 5-63, RA Jadeja 3-33)

India 503 (CA Pujara 204, M Vijay 167, **SR Tendulkar 7**; GJ Maxwell 4-127,
XJ Doherty 3-131)

India won by an innings and 135 runs

3rd Test. Mohali. 14-18 March 2013

Australia 408 (MA Starc 99, SPD Smith 92, EJM Cowan 86, DA Warner 71;
I Sharma 3-72, RA Jadeja 3-77) and 223 (PJ Hughes 69; B Kumar 3-31,
RA Jadeja 3-35)

India 499 (S Dhawan 187, M Vijay 153, V Kohli 67*, **SR Tendulkar 37**;
PM Siddle 5-71) and 136-4 (V Kohli 34, **SR Tendulkar 21**)

India won by 6 wickets

4th Test. Delhi. 22-24 March 2013

Australia 262 (P Siddle 51, SPD Smith 46, PJ Hughes 45; R Ashwin 5-57)
and 164 (P Siddle 50; RA Jadeja 5-58, PP Ojha 2-19, R Ashwin 2-55)

India 272 (M Vijay 57, CA Pujara 52, **SR Tendulkar 32**; NM Lyon 7-94)
and 158-4 (CA Pujara 82*, V Kohli 41, **SR Tendulkar 1**; GJ Maxwell 2-54)

India won by 6 wickets

India won the series 4-0

26

WINDING DOWN

After surgery on my left hand in London in July 2013, I worked hard on getting back to full fitness. It was painful and time-consuming and it was a great relief to be able to resume practice by the end of August, some weeks ahead of the Champions League Twenty20. However, the period of recuperation was never boring. When I'd got back from England my friends Atul Ranade, Faisal Momen and I decided to start cycling as a part of my cardio exercise. Atul was already cycling on alternate days to stay fit, and Faisal decided to join in, making the whole thing a lot more enjoyable. On the first day, after cycling for nearly forty minutes in the early morning, we decided to attempt the really steep incline that leads to the Mount Mary Church in Bandra. Faisal opted out when he saw the steep slope, but Atul and I embarked on the climb. It was a difficult one, and by the time we reached the top we were both breathing heavily. I suggested repeating it, and Atul and I tried going up again. On the second attempt, I overtook Atul halfway up, but when I got to the top I started feeling seriously giddy. I tried drinking some water and did a few stretching exercises, but that did not help and, by the time Atul had reached the top, I was blanking out and was forced to sit down on a divider on the road with my arms stretched out. In panic, Atul started fanning me with a huge leaf that he plucked from a nearby tree! Things did not improve and I soon realized that what I really needed was to lie down to get the blood circulation back to my brain. When I told Atul, he saw an open-top jeep standing next to the church and, in desperation, suggested I lie down in it. That's when I spotted a rickshaw and asked Atul to request the driver to allow me to lie on the passenger seat for a while. The driver seemed shocked to see me in that state, to say the least. As Atul stood outside explaining to him what had happened, I got onto the seat and lay flat for a good five minutes. Never in my life had I imagined I'd be doing such a thing just a few minutes away from my house, at 6 o'clock in the morning! When I was feeling a little better we thanked the rickshaw driver profusely for his help, paid him a hundred rupees and started slowly cycling back down the hill. By now Faisal, waiting at the foot, was getting impatient, assuming we were having a cup of tea near the top of the hill. He was stunned to hear what had transpired in the time he spent waiting for us. However, none of this deterred me from continuing with my training ahead of what turned out to be my last few months in international cricket.

I had announced my retirement from the IPL in May 2013 and this was to be my last Champions League. To my great satisfaction, the Mumbai Indians won the trophy, beating Rajasthan Royals in the final, and it meant my team had won both the IPL and the Champions League in my last season as a player. We had gelled well as a team and Rohit Sharma did well as captain.

It was during the Champions League campaign that, for the first time in my career, I found I had to force myself to go to the gym. It was also the first time in my career that I didn't feel bad about missing a session. Now, it wasn't as if I hit the gym every day of my career. I have always tended to train in bursts, before taking a break for a few days. But this was the first time that I just did not feel like pushing myself. I was also taking far longer to recover from injuries and was feeling a number of aches and pains.

India's next scheduled Tests were in South Africa in December 2013 and that's where I was expecting to play my 200th Test match. After that, there was an away series in New Zealand in early 2014 and I was looking forward to both tours. A number of my friends had discussed the 200th Test match with me and made plans to travel to South Africa to watch me reach this milestone. In fact, I had to keep reminding Ajit to book his tickets. But then the BCCI announced that there would be a two-Test home series against the West Indies at the beginning of November 2013 and I had to rethink my plans. It was then, and I don't know exactly how and when, that the thought of retirement first came to me. I started to wonder whether those two Tests against the West Indies should be my last.

I remember discussing it with Anjali and Ajit. We were sitting in the first-floor lounge of my house when I told them that I was thinking about retiring after the West Indies series. The second Test would be my 200th and I would not have another opportunity to retire on home soil until the end of 2014, and I wasn't sure if I could battle with injuries for that long. There was no point in dragging things out if my heart wasn't in it.

Anjali and Ajit were both fully supportive and Anjali said that she was behind me in anything that I decided. She just wanted me to be sure that I wouldn't regret the decision a few months down the line. Ajit agreed that the timing was right and that it was a good decision to retire while still in India. Playing my final Test away from home just wouldn't feel the same.

Once I had made up my mind, I decided to ask the BCCI if they would consider allotting the second Test to Mumbai. It would mean that I would play my last series in front of my home crowd and above all I would get my mother to watch me for the first time in my life. My mother had never watched me play live and this was something I really wanted to do for her. I had begun my first-class career in Mumbai in 1987 and playing my last Test at the Wankhede would mean I had completed the circle. It was as if I was being told from above that this was an opportunity to thank cricket. There would be no better occasion to pay my respects to the game than in a farewell Test match in Mumbai.

When I talked through the decision with my friend and manager Vinod Naidu and our close friend Aparna Santhanam, it turned into a memorable and magical evening. I uncorked a bottle of champagne and we toasted the game of cricket and all the years enjoyed playing it. There was no sense of gloom or dejection or talk of anything ending. Instead, there was a sense of joy, of anticipation and fulfilment. We laughed and reminisced about twenty-four years on the cricket field and chatted happily about the upcoming series. It all convinced me that I had taken the right decision. The timing was perfect. It was a call made from the heart. I wasn't prepared to let my mind interfere in the decision because the mind has a habit of asking too many awkward questions. I had not given a thought to what I would do after retirement. I was simply sure that this was the best time to stop.

It was a day later, on the morning of 10 October 2013, that I called BCCI President N Srinivasan to communicate my decision to retire. He said that while the BCCI would always want me to continue for as long as I wanted, they would back me no matter what decision I made. He was clear that retirement was entirely my call. Then I raised the question of allotting my last Test match to Mumbai and he promised to look into the matter. Allotting a Test match to a city based on a request from a player was a rare and touching gesture.

Before speaking to the BCCI president, I had informed my family that I was planning to retire. Sara asked me if I was retiring from all forms of cricket. I realized she was feeling emotional about the decision. It was natural, but she did her best to conceal it. Arjun was in South Africa at the time and I knew that giving him this news wouldn't be easy. I was aware of just how much my cricket meant to him. Arjun and I used to laugh about retirement and I often joked that the next series would have to be my last as I was getting so old. This time it wasn't a joke.

On the morning of 10 October, I called Arjun in South Africa and asked him to go to a room where he would be alone as I wanted to tell him something very important. I rang him back after a few minutes and told him that the two Tests against the West Indies in November would be my last. There was complete silence at the other end, so much so that I had to ask if he was still on the line. He said he was but he wasn't able to say anything else and actually hung up on me. I knew he was crying. There was a lump in my throat. I was suddenly feeling a sense of emptiness and needed a few minutes to regain my composure. He called me back ten minutes later and chatted away about what he was up to in South Africa, but my retirement was not mentioned again. It was his way of coping with the news.

The decision was made public that afternoon and it was an emotional time for my family. I felt remarkably calm, though, because I was convinced I had made the right call at the right time. Soon after the news broke, Anjali suggested to me that she should go and fetch Sara from school. On the way back, Anjali read Sara the kind messages she had received on her phone, telling her they were indicative of what the world thought about her *baba*. When Sara got home, she ran up to me and, without saying a word, just hugged me tight. This time I couldn't help getting emotional too. I was a happy father. My children mean the world to me and it touched me to know that they were proud of what I had achieved. I hoped it also meant that they understood why I had had to go away for such long periods when they were growing up.

By now a crowd had started to build outside the house and I was overwhelmed by the outpouring of emotion. I received a huge number of text messages and calls and made plenty myself. Despite trying my best to speak to every person who played a key role in my life, I missed out on calling many. I am sure they will all understand how much I value their contribution and that the omission was totally unintentional.

I continued sending messages late into the night, but that is not to suggest I was having trouble sleeping again. On the contrary, I slept very well and was very much at peace with myself. On the other hand, I was still an active cricketer. I wasn't prepared to lead a retired cricketer's life just yet and I was looking forward to resuming practice the next day and doing my best for Mumbai and India in the month I had left.

Getting ready for the West Indies

My practice sessions following the announcement were very interesting. The next morning I went to the Mumbai Cricket Association's Bandra facility to practise and the groundsmen came over to see me. They all thanked me for my contribution to cricket, when it should have been me thanking them for all they had done for me. Some became quite emotional and said they would miss me now that I wouldn't be turning up to practise any more. I reminded them that I hadn't retired quite yet, and in any case I would still come and practise after I'd retired – there was no way I was going to leave them in peace!

The evening before my last session at the MCA, I called the supervisor Ajay Desai and asked him to inform all the groundsmen and helpers that I would like to meet them personally the next morning. It was my way of recognizing everything they had done for me and thanking them for their contribution to my career. I carried tokens of appreciation for them and it was deeply touching to see them all waiting patiently for me. As I thanked them for their help and support, some hugged me and a few had tears in their eyes. It was a very moving moment and I felt humbled. The best part, however, was yet to come. When I'd finished, I was expecting the groundsmen to resume their normal duties. However, to my surprise they announced that on this occasion they weren't going to leave me. Instead, they all stood there while I went through my routine. Having spent a lifetime with the groundsmen in Mumbai, I must say I was overwhelmed at the gesture.

It was a similar story with the groundsmen at the Wankhede. I have known these men for years and many watched me grow up as a cricketer. Once again I brought tokens of appreciation for all of them and we took a group photograph to mark the occasion. I will always remember the way they treated me.

It was during my early-morning training sessions at the Wankhede that I met up with the MCA officials and told them about the ramp

I required for my mother. I did not want to leave a single thing to chance and also checked out the box allocated to my family. In fact, it was when I was doing the initial recce that I realized that my mother would find it difficult. She is not in the best of health and it would have been difficult getting her up to the box from the car. That's when we decided that she should sit in the president's box instead, and be safe, I had also booked a room for her at the Garware Pavilion in case she felt tired and wanted to rest.

Having checked the route the wheelchair would have to take from the car to the ramp and finally to the president's box, and being fully convinced that it could all be done, I went ahead with the plan of formally inviting her. Being able to make these arrangements for my mother made my retirement Test match all the more special.

The last Ranji match

When I first met my team-mates from the Mumbai Ranji Trophy team after the announcement, a lot of them came up and asked me why I had decided to retire when I could have carried on for a while. It was an encouraging reaction and it felt good to see the faith they continued to have in me.

The last Ranji Trophy game I played for Mumbai was in Lahli against Haryana, which is a state just north of Delhi, and it turned out to be quite an experience. Before travelling to Lahli, I spoke with Anirudh Chaudhry, who was our manager in England in 2011, and his father Ranbir Singh Mahendra, who was our manager in Australia in 1991–92, at the Haryana Cricket Association. Anirudh had made special arrangements to put some of us up in the Chief Minister's guest house, which he said was a very relaxing place to stay. He had also arranged for extra security in order to make us feel comfortable.

We flew to Delhi on our way to Lahli and when we landed we were told by Anirudh that we should have lunch at the ITC

Maurya hotel while he made the final arrangements. There was a pleasant surprise awaiting me. As soon as we stepped into the lobby the lights were dimmed and I was accorded a red-carpet welcome by the general manager Anil Chadha, with all the employees standing in line and throwing rose petals at me. It was a deeply touching gesture.

After lunch we left for Lahli. It took us approximately two and a half hours to drive to the guest house, but all along the route people were waving banners and posters and all sorts of ornaments, making it a very memorable journey. When we finally reached the guest house, I was surprised to see the butler who had been with me in Delhi already stationed there to take care of us! He informed us that four of them had travelled from Delhi at Anirudh's request and would be looking after us all the way through the match.

At Lahli I felt like trying some local food and asked the manager to recommend some authentic local cuisine. The manager did not say anything in response and left the room, but then he apologized to Zaheer and informed him that Anirudh had left strict instructions about what should be served to us. He had made it clear that every day breakfast, dinner and snacks would come from the ITC Maurya in Delhi and that nothing else should be served, to avoid any risks. I must say it really was a maharaja-style outing. The Haryana Cricket Association had gone out of its way to spoil us.

The stadium was forty minutes away from the guest house but the roads were nearly empty and it was never a problem reaching the ground in the morning. It was a beautiful arena and the conditions were tailor-made for fast bowling. The outfield was a little soft to start with because of the dampness and it would be a good test of my fitness ahead of the West Indies series. Soft outfields can put pressure on calves and hamstrings and if I had no trouble on this outfield, I would be fine at Eden Gardens or the Wankhede, the venues for my 199th and 200th Test matches.

Mumbai's first Ranji match of the season, which was also my last, turned out to be fascinating. A large crowd had come along and the build-up to the four-day game was unprecedented. Media from India and the rest of the cricket-playing world had descended on the small town of Lahli and while the police tried their best to keep them at a distance, I knew that my every move was being followed and every practice session filmed.

In the first innings I was out bowled for five to a ball that jumped a little and ricocheted off my elbow onto the stumps. It was a rather disappointing dismissal after all the build-up. At Lahli, most matches are low-scoring and, sure enough, our reply to their first-innings total of 134 was only two runs more. It was a keenly contested match and in our second innings we were set 240 to win, which in a way was more like 280 because of the slow outfield.

I had a brief chat with my team-mates in the innings break and emphasized to them the need to be aggressive after the opposition had bowled close to fifty overs, which would be approximately around teatime. On a pitch offering assistance to the fast bowlers, that was the best time for batsmen to cash in and score quickly, because that was when the ball would be older and the opposition bowlers tired. Better to take a few chances then than wait for the morning, when the bowlers would be fresh again and the new ball would also be due.

Dhawal Kulkarni, the fast-medium bowler, and I had a really good partnership towards the end of the day's play and I kept telling him that he needed to hang in there at any cost. There wasn't much batting left after him and a new batsman would find it difficult on the greenish pitch. Dhawal batted extremely well and showed great courage. He was hit on the helmet a couple of times but never got rattled or gave up. By the end of the day we needed 39 runs to win, with four wickets left.

It was a 9 a.m. start on the last day and it was important to make the right call with the roller. Having seen the wicket, I told Zaheer, our captain, that the grass was dry at the top but at the bottom it was still wet. It still needed some sun to dry out completely. If we took the heavy roller the wetness would seep up to the top and the pitch would turn damp. I suggested that we should not use a roller, but just leave the surface as it was, because all that was required was 39 runs, which wouldn't take more than an hour or so to get.

Again Dhawal batted well and showed great resilience and we managed to knock off the runs in an hour or so. His contribution of 16 was critical because on that surface we could easily have lost the last four wickets for ten runs. I was pleased to remain unbeaten on 79 in my final Ranji outing. It was a satisfying victory and a good way for Mumbai to start their Ranji Trophy campaign.

At the end of the game, the Haryana team gave me a guard of honour and my own team-mates chaired me off the ground on their shoulders. While the gesture was touching, it's always slightly concerning being carried on the shoulders of team-mates. There's a good chance of being dropped and with two Test matches still to play, it wouldn't have been a great way to get injured. The Mumbai team had also arranged for a send-off in the room adjoining our dressing room, which was particularly touching. The Mumbai Cricket Association secretary Nitin Dalal was also there and a cake was cut in my honour and all the players said a few words. A number of them turned emotional as they spoke, and some had tears in their eyes. It was all very moving.

That wasn't the only surprise at Lahli. Unbeknown to me, Anirudh had invited a few of my closest friends – Sameer Dighe, Faisal Momen and Jagdish Chavan – to watch the game. He had sent them tickets himself and also arranged for their accommodation. On the evening of the first day of the game, the local manager came up to me and said there was someone waiting to take a picture and it wouldn't take more than a minute. I stepped outside, ready to pose, only to see my friends grinning at me. It was a great feeling to see them in Lahli. They have all been by my side through good and bad and it was a pleasant surprise to have them around me for my last domestic game.

Winning that Ranji Trophy match meant I had won all my final matches in every format of the game so far. It was a record I was extremely proud of and I hoped I would be able to keep it intact in my final series for India. Lahli had served as good preparation. Now I was looking forward to my penultimate Test match in Kolkata.

Farewell to Eden Gardens

Having relaxed for a couple of days at home in Mumbai, and having visited the temples in Mumbai and Goa that I always visit to seek the blessings of God, I arrived in Kolkata on the evening of 3 November 2013. As always, Dwarkanath and Kalpa Sanzgiri had sent me *laddoos* (a type of Indian sweet) on the eve of the series to wish me luck. There was a mini welcome ceremony arranged by the Cricket Association of Bengal at the airport and there were a lot of people inside the terminal to receive me. In fact, the police were finding it very difficult to control the crowd and I had to hurry into the lounge to give them time to calm things down.

The situation showed no signs of improving over the next half an hour and I realized that the longer I waited, the more difficult it would be for us to leave the airport. I called the police and informed them I had to leave for the hotel as soon as possible. A large number of security personnel accompanied me to the car while the crowd showered me with rose petals. The affection was overwhelming. Kolkata has always been a city that loves its cricket and the people there have always embraced me with warmth. I was delighted that the 199th Test match was being played at Eden Gardens, one of the best cricket grounds in the world when it comes to atmosphere.

During my first two days in Kolkata, Pintu (Raghunath Basak) gave me a massage for almost two hours each day to help me relax and my friend Samar Paul brought us some sumptuous home-cooked food which we all enjoyed for dinner along with Virat, Rohit, Ajinkya and Pragyan. I have known Samar-da since 1991 and was first introduced to him by Dilip Vengsarkar. Every visit to

Kolkata has been made special by the meals that Samar-da has graciously brought for us. Pintu too, has been a constant in Kolkata from 1994, and it has been a routine that he would give me a massage and we would then end up having dinner in my room. Also, Joydeep Mukherjee would always take me to the Kali temple whenever I went to Kolkata, visits I have always looked forward to.

When I arrived at the ground on the morning of 4 November, I was very surprised by what was there to greet me. A wax statue of me was standing right outside the dressing room and the walls were covered with pictures of me from different stages of my career.

I tried to follow my normal pre-match routines as far as that was possible. I batted for a while in the nets, but I was fairly cautious while playing football with the rest of the boys, because the last thing I wanted to do was get injured. Afterwards we went back to the hotel and I went to the gym and later relaxed in my room watching movies and listening to music. It was all very normal. I ate dinner with my team-mates and was in a very good frame of mind.

Since the retirement announcement, every news channel had been talking about my career and I tried to cocoon myself from it all as much as possible. I did see some of the coverage, however, and couldn't help thinking about how many years had gone by since my debut. It was pleasing to be reminded of everything I had been able to achieve in my career, but I still had a job to do and I didn't want to let myself get distracted. I did not want to retire mentally before I finally called it a day at the end of the second Test in Mumbai.

The 199th Test

On 6 November 2013, the West Indies won the toss and decided to bat first. There was a sizeable crowd at Eden Gardens on the first morning. Making a rare exception to her routine of praying at home, Anjali had come to see the match and it was a real surprise for me to see her and Arjun in the stands. When I had spoken to her the night before, I had sensed that something was cooking but didn't know exactly what. It turned out she had spoken with my friend and co-writer Boria Majumdar and planned the visit as a surprise. I became aware of her presence only when an announcement was made that she was in the stands. I must say it was a delight to see them both when we met up at the end of the day's play.

This is what Anjali told me about making that special trip to Kolkata. It was a ritual with us that she would wish me well on the eve of a Test series. Before leaving for Kolkata, I had said to Anjali that it would be the last time she would have to do so. Anjali told me later that as I left for the airport with Ajit, who always dropped me off whenever I travelled, she could not control her tears. She had to go to meet Arjun's cricket coaches, who had come from England, at the Waterstones Club, which was close to the airport, and so she was in a car behind me for most of the way, with tears rolling down her cheeks. Even when she reached the club, she just could not control her emotions and burst into tears when she met up with Arjun's coaches. The poor chaps did not understand why coming to see them had made her cry! That's when she told them the real reason and then they insisted on accompanying her to Kolkata to watch me play.

We had bowled the West Indies out for 234 on the first day and I was keen to do well when I went out to bat on the morning of day two. I had played a couple of good shots when I fell to an lbw decision I wasn't very happy with. These things are part of the game, of course, but it seemed to me that the ball from the off-spinner Shane Shillingford was going over the stumps. It was frustrating, but there was nothing I could do about it. Replays suggested the ball would have gone at least six inches over the stumps.

Having lost a few quick wickets, we were under pressure when Rohit Sharma and Ashwin got down to rebuilding the innings.

Rohit played spectacularly on debut and Ashwin was the perfect foil. Both got hundreds, and their partnership of 280 was instrumental in winning us the Test. It had taken the wind out of the West Indies' sails. Mohammed Shami, another debutant, finished the job in the second innings with an excellent spell of reverse-swing bowling, taking five wickets to add to his four in the first innings. He was getting the ball to move appreciably, and I believe has a bright career ahead.

We won the match by an innings and 51 runs in under three days. The awards ceremony turned into a special occasion, with tricolour balloons released to commemorate my 199th Test match, and I left Eden Gardens with some really pleasing memories.

Time to gather my thoughts

I decided to go back to Mumbai on the evening of 8 November to give myself more time at home before my 200th Test match. At Kolkata airport on the way back, a huge crowd started to walk with me everywhere I went. Luckily for me, there were eight armed commandos with me at the airport, otherwise things might have got a little out of hand. It was slightly disconcerting because there was no way I could oblige the entire crowd with pictures and autographs and I asked the airport manager to take me to the lounge as quickly as possible. We walked to the far end of the terminal past the security check and it was only then that I saw it was a public lounge.

The crowd was continuing to follow me around and I asked the manager if we could go and sit in another lounge instead. He said this was the only available option after the security checkpoint and he would cordon off the area where I would be sitting. I wasn't prepared to do this because I didn't want to give people the wrong message. It was not as if I wasn't willing to meet them or sign autographs. I have never refused to sign autographs, because I consider it my duty towards my fans, who have stood by me throughout my careeer. However, if I did start to sign or pose for pictures, there was a risk that it would become a serious security issue inside the lounge.

It was then that I advised the duty manager to check if the aircraft was ready, hoping that I could go and sit in it. I was informed it was being cleaned but I thought it was still better to board it than to keep the crowd at a distance. I went in and sat all by myself. Once inside, I posed for pictures with all the cleaners and the crew that had brought the aircraft to Kolkata, who were still on board. I waited patiently as the crew changed. The old crew was replaced and new crew took up their positions. I requested them to screen off one side so that the incoming passengers wouldn't start taking pictures, which might end up delaying the flight. I was happy to sign autographs once we were airborne rather than inconveniencing other passengers and delaying the journey. The crew agreed and I settled down in my seat.

Soon after take-off it hit me that I was travelling to play the last Test match of my career. It had all come to an end very quickly. In no time I would have a microphone in my hand and would be expected to speak to the world, to say something to all my fans and supporters about what I was feeling. It would also be my last opportunity to thank the people who had stood by me over the years. And yet I had not planned what I would say or exactly who I needed to thank. I knew I had to be careful, because on a previous occasion I had had to make a similar speech and thought I had thanked everybody – until the commentator Harsha Bhogle came to the rescue and whispered in my ear that I hadn't mentioned Anjali! Sitting on that plane from Kolkata, I realized that I had two hours when no one would call me or speak to me and it was the ideal time to think about my speech. I took out my iPad and started to make a list of all the people I needed to thank, going right back to the very beginning.

While I was doing so, I had to keep reminding myself that I

still had ten days left in my career and that I was going to enjoy every moment on the field. I had two innings left and wanted to leave my fans with memories they would cherish. As the flight started its descent into Mumbai, all my years as a cricketer flashed through my mind. It had been quite a journey.

27

THE FINAL TEST

Thanks to the early finish at Kolkata, I was able to spend two days at home before rejoining my team-mates. I made the most of that quiet time ahead of all the frenzy. The only cricket I played was with my son in our backyard, when he tried to test me out with some short-pitched stuff – with a tennis ball. It was great just to have some fun with him.

On 11 November, I met up with the rest of the team on the Mumbai Sea Link on our way to Kandivali Gymkhana, which was being renamed after me in a function organized by the Mumbai Cricket Association. It was a great honour. It is an excellent facility and I hope it will serve as a breeding ground for young talent in the region.

When we eventually got to the Taj Mahal Palace hotel, I couldn't believe the lengths they had gone to. My pictures were in all the lifts and on the nineteenth floor, where the team was staying, there were photographs on every wall. In my own room every little thing you could think of was personalized. From the soaps and shampoos to the pillow covers, everything had my name on it, and every day the Taj management sent me a personalized sweet of some kind, such as a cake or chocolate.

I was busy sorting things out in my room when I got a call from our coach, Duncan Fletcher. He said the team wanted to honour me by wearing special shirts that said 'Sachin Ramesh Tendulkar – 200th Test match', and he asked if I had any problems with that. I was overwhelmed and said it was an absolute privilege.

There was no doubt that this would be a Test match like no other. There was a huge media presence everywhere, bigger than ever before. They were outside the hotel at all hours, waiting to catch us getting on and off the bus on our way to and from practice. I did my best not to be affected by it all. It helped that the practice sessions were just the same as they'd always been and I batted in the nets and played football with the boys just as I had always done.

Sporting the tricolour

One thing I was looking forward to was playing with some special new bat stickers and grips. The design featured the tricolour and I had worked closely on it with my sponsors Adidas and my manager Vinod Naidu. The stickers had been specially designed for my last game and they were never going to go on any other bat in the market. I looked forward to revealing them when I batted in my 200th and final Test match.

The stickers and grips arrived the day before the game and I didn't want to let anyone see them till the morning of the match. I borrowed Rohit Sharma's bag to take all my bats to my room, where I spent hours changing the stickers and putting on the new grips. I have always worked on my bats myself and have spent many happy hours doing repairs over the years. I enjoyed that close connection with the tools of my trade, and the rest of the team often took advantage of this. If anyone wanted sandpaper, glue or bat tape, bat coat, grip or gripper, it was me they would come to.

I couldn't resist taking a picture of the new-look bats to send to Anjali. I was very happy with the way they had turned out. The tricolour has always meant the world to me and this was my way of showing respect to my country. I was looking forward to using them the next morning. As I was packing my clothes and other things to take to the ground the following day, my sense of excitement was also tinged with sadness at the thought that I only had a few days left.

14 November 2013, day one of the final Test

After a good night's sleep, I got up at my usual time on the morning of the first day. I made my own tea in the room, which I have always done, and went through my routine of taking a shower and doing my prayers before putting on my headphones and going down to board the team bus, which was surrounded by at least a thousand people.

When we got to the ground, I carefully brought out my bats from Rohit's bag with their new livery and walked out to practise with them. They were looking superb and my team-mates all commented on them as they could see the thought that had gone into the design. There's no doubt they added to the occasion.

One way and another, it was a morning like no other. First the Mumbai Cricket Association congratulated me on notching up 200 Test matches and then the Government of India launched a special stamp to celebrate the achievement. I was told that I was only the second living person to be honoured with a stamp in that way, the first being Mother Teresa. What could I say to an honour like that? I was speechless!

Cricket at last

Most of the crowd wanted to see me bat, so a loud cheer went up when it was announced that India had won the toss. But they were quickly disappointed when MS Dhoni opted to field because the wicket was expected to offer some assistance to the fast bowlers in the morning. There was some bounce and even the spinners might come into play on the first day.

As we left the dressing room, the captain gave me the honour of leading the team out, which I did throughout the match. Gestures like that are memories I will always cherish. As we stepped onto the field the team also presented me with a special commemorative cap, and I spoke to them briefly during the team huddle. I reminded them of our duty towards the sport and the need to uphold the spirit of cricket at all times. I consider it the duty of every generation of cricketers to set an example for the next generation and inspire the youth to embrace the sport. It is the least we can do for the sport that has given us our identity.

As I looked around the stadium I was feeling really happy that, for the first time, my mother was there to watch me. In fact, my entire family, my wife and children, brothers, sister and her husband, uncle and aunt, were all in the stadium and I felt blessed by the affection and support the crowd was showering on me. There was nothing more a sportsman could have asked for. All I needed to top it off was to perform well with the bat and leave my final mark on the sport I love so dearly.

We bowled brilliantly to get the West Indies out for 182 on the stroke of tea, at two, with Pragyan Ojha taking five wickets and Ashwin three. My mother, I was later told, had been planning to leave the ground at tea when a friend told Anjali that there was a chance I might bat after all if India lost a couple of wickets. Anjali asked my mother if she felt up to it and luckily she agreed to stay on, hoping to see me bat from the stands for the first time.

The gods must have been listening and it was a little past 3.30 p.m. when, with the score at 77–2, I walked out to the middle. The crowd was chanting 'Sachin, Sachin' and the West Indians and the on-field umpires assembled to give me a guard of honour as I walked to the pitch to take strike. I tried to soak in every moment. I was relieved to score the first run quickly. After that, I started to enjoy myself, my confidence growing with every boundary.

It was during the last over of the first day's play that my mother was shown on the stadium's giant screen for the first time. The moment she appeared the crowd gave her a standing ovation. As soon as I saw her face I got very emotional. I now had to deal with two very difficult challenges – protecting my wicket and controlling my emotions. I took my time to settle down before taking guard again.

In hindsight, I'm not sure it was such a good idea to show my mother on the screen with just one over to go for the day. The broadcasters could have shown her on television but to show her in the stadium when I was doing my best to survive the day was perhaps inappropriate. While I understand they were trying their best to make the occasion memorable, and I much appreciate them for doing so, this one thing could perhaps have been done differently. It did not stop with my mother. One after the other, they kept showing my family members on the screen, much to the delight of the huge crowd.

It all made it very difficult to concentrate and I had to keep telling myself that I needed to shut out everything that was happening around me. On this day of all days I wanted to give it my absolute best. Happily, I managed to survive the day and was unbeaten on 38. I was delighted to have stayed out there for close to an hour and a half. As I was about to leave the park, I raised my bat towards my family.

When I look back at these moments they feel surreal, to say the least. My mother's reaction when she first saw herself on the giant screen, her tongue coming out in embarrassment because she wasn't used to the limelight, was so natural that I had tears in my eyes. The crowd standing up to acknowledge her was more than I could have asked for as a son and I am deeply thankful to everyone for showing her that affection and respect.

Amidst all the emotion, I was actually rather surprised to see Arjun there. Before I left home for the Test match we had had a lengthy discussion about whether he should watch me or play his own Under-14 match. It was eventually decided that he should go to his match. Yuvraj Singh then kindly dropped Arjun off at his game to try and make up for his disappointment at missing my 200th Test match. All of Arjun's friends were delighted to see Yuvi and Arjun was proud to be dropped off by him. Arjun's day then got even better when his team got a walkover and he jumped into a taxi and found his way to the Wankhede. He managed to convince the police about who he was and the next thing I see is on the giant screen, doing his bit as a ball boy.

Back in the hotel that evening, I tried to relax and enjoy the moment. I was exhausted but happy that I was still batting. I had my dinner and retired early, knowing that I had important business to attend to in the morning.

15 November 2013, day two of the final Test

The next day I got up at my usual time and, having finished my morning routine, put my headphones on and listened to some music. As I was walking down to the lobby and then to the bus, people wished me luck. There were happy and excited crowds on both sides of the road. I just tried to concentrate on the music and stay removed from what was happening around me. Clearly, it was not business as usual, but I did not want the scale and significance of the occasion to get to me.

After reaching the ground, I took out my bats and went out to the middle. It was our batting day and on such days players are allowed to follow their own routine. On fielding days, we are expected to take a few catches and do some fielding practice. Duncan said that we just needed to do a few stretching exercises and then we were on our own. I went to the nets to bat to a few throw-downs and then came back to the dressing room to get ready.

When we went out to bat I was feeling surprisingly good. Every time I took guard and saw the new bat sticker I felt a strange feeling of elation. I had always played cricket for the tricolour. Now I could see it on my bat every time I looked down. It was a terrific feeling. My mother's presence in the stands only added to my determination.

Tino Best produced an inspired spell of fast bowling, testing me on quite a few occasions. It was only later that I learned that it was his son's birthday and he had promised him he would get my wicket as a birthday present. On one occasion when I was beaten, he appealed and I laughed and asked what was wrong with him, because the ball was miles away from my bat! In the next over I could sense that he was about to bowl me a bouncer and I was ready for it. I had all the time in the world to play the upper cut – but I missed it by a few inches. I don't know why I wasn't able to connect with any of the short balls. I finally managed to play a cover drive and as the ball was being retrieved from the boundary, I mock-punched Tino Best and said it was his lucky day because I had missed out on at least four boundaries against him. We are good friends off the field and fierce competitors on it.

I brought up my half-century with a straight drive and raised my bat to my mother. The delighted crowd kept shouting 'Sachinnn, Sachinnn' and it was tremendous to be out there. Even when I was not facing the ball, the crowd kept chanting.

About five minutes after the first drinks break, Narsingh Deonarine was given the ball. I was aware that he was an occasional off-spinner who would probably bowl only three or four overs. I told myself that I should do nothing foolish against him but just take a few singles. Only if there was a loose ball should I put it away for a boundary.

The ball I got out to bounced slightly more than I expected. It was a fuller delivery and faster than his normal one. I thought I could cut it to backward point for four. I had played a similar shot against Shillingford a little earlier. It all happened in a flash. Before I knew it, I had played the shot and the ball was on its way to Darren Sammy at slip. It hit his chest and he caught it on the rebound. I was out, for 74, with the score at 221–3.

As I turned to walk to the pavilion, my mind was flooded with thoughts. Why did I have to play that stroke? Why cut the ball when I could have played it to cover for a single or even left it for the keeper? What prompted me to go for the cut shot at all?

Throughout my career I have always questioned my shot selection after getting out and it was no different in that innings.

That's when the thought came to me that there might not be another innings. It dawned on me that this could well be the last time I walked off the field as an India batsman. The way the match was going, there was a good chance we wouldn't have to bat again. It was this thought that prompted me to stop for a moment and take in the crowd and raise my bat to them for all their support and encouragement. But the disappointment was still very much with me as I walked up the steps to the dressing room. I knew I had missed out on a big one.

As he had in Kolkata, Rohit Sharma batted exceptionally well and his second consecutive ton, as well as 113 from Pujara, helped us to a total of 495 and a lead of 313. In their second innings, the West Indies top order fell without offering much resistance. At one point the crowd was actually cheering for Chris Gayle. They wanted the game to go on so that I could bat one more time! It was funny and unreal at the same time.

By the end of the second day it was fairly clear that we would win by an innings and that 16 November 2013 would be my last day as an Indian cricketer.

16 November 2013, day three of the final Test

The West Indies started the day at 43–3 and were soon 89–6. It was at the fall of the seventh wicket that I started to feel that there wasn't long to go. Each wicket was bringing the final moment nearer. A quest of twenty-four years was about to come to an end.

When the ninth wicket fell and I ran in to congratulate the bowler, Dhoni asked me to stay away because the team was planning something. I went and stood next to the square-leg umpire while the rest stood in a huddle in the middle. I could not stop myself from getting emotional. It was all ending so quickly.

Within a few overs the final moment arrived. Mohammed

Shami took the final wicket with a full delivery that knocked out Shannon Gabriel's middle stump. I rushed in again from my fielding position and picked up a stump, saying to one of my team-mates 'Yeh stump to mujhe chahiye hi chahiye.' (I want this stump at any cost.) But again Dhoni asked if I could stand apart for a while because they had planned something special.

I stood at the other end of the pitch while the rest of the team went over their plan. Then Ravi Shastri walked across the ground to do his television broadcast. He congratulated me on my career and said some very kind things about my contribution to the game. I was still just about holding myself together. Then the team started another guard of honour, only this time it was different. They stood in two lines on both sides of the wicket with me in the middle, but as I started walking, players from the end of the lines kept running to the front in order to extend the guard of honour all the way to the boundary.

I could no longer hold back my tears. It was just too much. Such respect and affection was overwhelming and I will always remember the way my team-mates gave me my final send-off. By the time I walked off the ground I was openly crying. I could not look people in the eye and had to shake hands with the opposition players with my face turned to the ground. I did not want them to see me cry like a child. I did the same with our support staff and then just ran up the stairs to the dressing room and went straight to the bathroom.

That's where I broke down completely. I cried for about ten minutes until I finally told myself that enough was enough. I washed my face and came back to the dressing room with a towel over my head and sat in my seat completely alone. My team-mates had given me space and there was no one in the dressing room to disturb me. I looked at my kitbag and thanked my gear for being with me all my life.

I was gradually starting to come to terms with the moment when someone came in to say that Brian Lara and the West Indian team were waiting for me and that Brian had planned something special. It was rather unusual for an opposition team to do anything like that and it was very touching. My 200th Test was also Shivnarine Chanderpaul's 150th and Brian congratulated us on our achievements. Brian and I have been great friends and his words meant a lot to me. I then spoke briefly about Chanderpaul and the West Indian way of cricket before all the players took pictures with me.

I went back to the dressing room to get ready to walk out with the team for the presentations. Someone from Star Sports, the host broadcasters, came up to me and said that Ravi Shastri would ask me a few questions at the presentation, but I said I would rather speak by myself. I also said I would like to go on for a bit longer than usual, if they were agreeable, and suggested that it might be better if I was given the microphone after the players had collected their awards. They readily agreed and said I could go on for as long as I wanted, as they had all the time in the world for me!

A speech from the heart

I was finally given the microphone at the end of the presentation, but before I could speak, the crowd started chanting 'Sachinnn, Sachinnn' and they just would not stop. As I have said many times before, these chants will reverberate in my ears for as long as I live. I asked the crowd to calm down and not make me more emotional than I already was. I had also brought a bottle of water in case my throat went dry in the middle of it all.

I took from my pocket the list of people I wanted to thank, the list I had put together on the plane back from Kolkata after the first Test match. The challenge now was to say different things about each one. They all meant the world to me and I wanted to thank them individually for their contribution. Somehow, the words just came to me. I spoke my heart out.

When they showed my team-mates Sourav, Rahul and Laxman

on the big screen I spoke about them. When I was speaking about my wife I could see her break down in front of me and Sara trying to console her. Arjun also comforted his mother as I went on to thank the best partner I have ever had. I can never say enough about her.

I thanked my fans and the supporters of Indian cricket, who have always stood by me. It did not matter to them if I scored a zero or a hundred. They were always there with me and their support has been my biggest source of strength.

It is pertinent to recount here an incident I will remember forever, one that demonstrates what my fans mean to me. I was once in Chennai when I had the opportunity to meet a number of special children. Their teacher pointed to one child in a wheel-chair and said that he was my biggest fan and his ultimate ambition was to hold my bat. I put my arm around him and told him, 'Okay, done. Let's play cricket together.' Immediately, I sent someone to fetch my bat and a couple of tennis balls from the dressing room. To my complete amazement and utter delight, the boy stood up and played three balls on his own. For him to be able to do so was incredible. We all gave him an ovation and I have often spoken about this child, who has left a lasting impression.

After a while I told the crowd I'd finish soon, only for them to scream 'Noooooooooo!' It seemed they wanted me to carry on. In the end, I spoke for twenty minutes, the longest I have ever spoken at a stretch in my life. I genuinely do not know how I did so at such a difficult time; it was as if someone from above had blessed me. Other than that, I can't explain how I managed to navigate the speech without a hiccup.

Once it was over, we went on a victory lap and my team-mates decided to carry me around the Wankhede. No one had left the stadium, and I waved to the crowd from the shoulders of my team-mates and thanked them for being with me all through my career. I had always hoped that this final lap of honour would be one in victory, because that would mean so much more to me as a cricketer. In defeat it would not have had even 10 per cent of the significance it had in victory. We had won the match and the series in style and it also meant I had won all of my final matches in all formats of the game.

That was when Virat Kohli reminded me about going out to pay my respects to the pitch and I walked out to the middle by myself. It was a very personal moment and something I had always meant to do at the end of my innings in cricket. I would be no one without the 22-yard strip and it had taken care of me all my life. It was only right to thank the pitch for everything and do *namaskar*, to offer my gratitude and respect.

One final goodbye

As I was sitting by myself back in the dressing room, Virat walked up to me again. I could see tears in his eyes. He held out his hands and said his dad had given him these threads, the kind that Indians wear around their wrists for good luck, and he had always wondered who he would give them to. It had to be someone very special. Then he handed them to me before touching my feet as a younger brother would. I was speechless. I held him tight and said, '*Arre tu yeh kya kar raha hai? Tujhe yahan nahi, yahan hona chahiye.*' (Why are you touching my feet? You should be giving me a hug instead.) I couldn't say another word as I choked with emotion. A lump had formed in my throat and finally I had to ask Virat to leave, knowing I would burst into tears if I tried to say anything else. It was a gesture I can never forget and I wished Virat all the success he so richly deserves in his career ahead.

A little later, I called Ajinkya Rahane, my Mumbai team-mate who was our twelfth man in this match, to a room adjoining our dressing room. I had known Rahane for years and had seen how much he loved the game. He had served cricket with complete dedication and commitment over the last few years. I said to him that he might feel hard done by what had happened in his career so far, but he should continue to be the way he is, for I was sure Ajinkya would get another chance. For the moment he might feel it is a cruel game, but I was certain the game would take care of him in the future if he continued to serve it the way he had always done.

Finally it was time to leave the stadium. It had been hours since the match had ended and I had not eaten a morsel since breakfast. The Taj management had sent me some *haleem* (a kind of stew with lentils and meat) and I handed it to Anjali so that we could take it back to the hotel and do justice to it there. As we boarded the bus, Sourav Ganguly, one of my closest friends over the years, came to congratulate me one final time. I got off the bus to give him a hug. Dada and I have shared some great moments over the years and have known each other since we were both thirteen.

Once the bus was on its way to the hotel, Anjali asked me to go and stand next to the driver to wave one final goodbye to the supporters. They were waiting on both sides of Marine Drive and were celebrating and shouting 'Sachinnn, Sachinnn'. We had to pinch ourselves to believe what we were seeing. This was my final send-off and these people, each and every one of them, were making it a fairy tale. I don't really know what I had done to deserve all this, but it made me feel really blessed to witness these scenes. I was leaving the cricket field with no regrets whatsoever.

An unexpected honour

There was a special reception in the hotel lobby and it was not until 3 p.m. that Anjali and I finally managed some privacy in my room. I took out the *haleem* that we had brought back and we were both enjoying it and sipping champagne when I received a phone call from the prime minister's office. I was told that

Prime Minister Manmohan Singh wanted to speak to me and after a couple of moments the PM came on the line. He congratulated me on my career and thanked me for serving Indian cricket for twenty-four years. Then he told me that in recognition of my contribution to Indian sport I had been awarded the Bharat Ratna, India's highest civilian honour.

After I put down the phone, I asked Anjali to stop eating and took her to the table where I had placed all the idols of the gods and goddesses that I worship. We both placed our hands on the table and I told her that she was now looking at a Bharat Ratna. Anjali screamed in delight and gave me a warm hug. We did not say a thing to each other for a while as the news sank in. Every dream of mine was being fulfilled and I thanked God for all the blessings and kindness bestowed upon me. Then we opened a bottle of champagne to celebrate and, to be honest, the champagne just flowed from then on.

We watched television for a while as we tried to come to terms with the momentous significance of the award. Every channel was showing it as Breaking News. I was the first sportsperson in the history of India to be awarded the Bharat Ratna. It was certainly the biggest honour of my life and coming on the day I had bid my final goodbye to cricket made it all the more special. I had already been appointed to the Rajya Sabha, the upper house of the Indian Parliament, in 2012, and now to be given the highest civilian honour by the Government of India meant a lot to me. As a Member of Parliament, my plan is to work towards making sports a much more viable option as a vocation as well as an avocation in India (Sport for All), and also to integrate sports within the educational framework of schools and colleges in the country.

The honour was formally conferred on me at the Rashtrapati Bhavan in Delhi on 4 February 2014 in an extraordinary ceremony at the Ashok Hall. As we entered the hall, a military band started to play and when my name was announced, it was one of the most unbelievable moments of my life. To receive the Bharat Ratna in front of my wife and daughter (Arjun could not make it because he had a game in Mumbai), and to be told by the President that the whole country was proud of me, gave me an incredible sense of fulfilment. It was a day when I felt well and truly overwhelmed.

When I started out as a sixteen-year-old against Pakistan in 1989, I could never have imagined how it would all end. I always tried to work as hard as I could and give my best for the team. While I may have failed on occasions, I never gave up. It was my country I was playing for since the time I signed up and that was all I had wanted to do to play under the strict vigil and guidance of Achrekar Sir in Shivaji Park.

In all those years, I never compromised on hard work and discipline and always tried to push the bar higher. To achieve something worthwhile for India was a dream I chased all my life.

Full circle

In my farewell speech at the Wankhede Stadium, I mentioned that during my career Achrekar Sir had never said 'Well done', but the truth is that that was never something I expected from him. The smile on his face was enough to understand he was pleased with my performance. The day after my speech, however, I went to visit Achrekar Sir, to thank him for all he had done for me, to mark the fact that we had come full circle. It was very important for me to pay my respects in this way.

Sir doesn't speak much these days, but I think that he was happy.

The other thing I did on the day of my retirement was attend a farewell party at the Waterstones Club in Mumbai organized by Anjali and my friends Sanjay and Rachna Narang. I have fond memories of the club because it was where Anjali and the Narangs had organized our World Cup celebration party as well. On that occasion, the party was organized overnight and invites sent entirely by text message. This time, however, it was far more elaborate – something I found out later. Friends and well-wishers from around the world had turned up to celebrate my career and we spent a lovely evening together. Some of my closest friends stayed till ten the following morning and we enjoyed reminiscing about the best moments from a twenty-four-year-long career.

West Indies in India 2013

1st Test. Kolkata. 6–8 November 2013

West Indies 234 (MN Samuels 65; M Shami 4–71, R Ashwin 2–52, **SR Tendulkar 1–5**) and 168 (DM Bravo 37, KOA Powell 36; M Shami 5–47, R Ashwin 3–46)

India 453 (RG Sharma 177, R Ashwin 124, **SR Tendulkar 10**; S Shillingford 6–167, V Permaul 2–67)

India won by an innings and 51 runs

2nd Test. Mumbai. 14–16 November 2013

West Indies 182 (KOA Powell 48; PP Ojha 5–40, R Ashwin 3–45) and 187 (D Ramdin 53*, S Chanderpaul 41; PP Ojha 5–49, R Ashwin 4–89)

India 495 (CA Pujara 113, RG Sharma 111*, **SR Tendulkar 74**, V Kohli 57; S Shillingford 5–179, N Deonarine 2–45)

India won by an innings and 126 runs

India won the series 2–0

28

LAST WORD

I leave Indian cricket in safe hands. I have played with the current generation of cricketers who now constitute the core of the Indian team. Batting, I feel, will continue to be our strength and the current crop, which is a good mix of experience and youth, will surely play together for many years and serve the country with distinction. On the bowling side, while some of our bowlers are doing well, we need to find a few more talented fast bowlers. In the past we have had some really good bowling pairs, but what we need now is a bowling unit that will play for the team at the same time. This is a tough challenge, but with the depth of talent available in the country, I am sure we are up to it.

Finally, the game of cricket itself is extremely vibrant. Cricket is the only sport that has three distinctive formats and each format has a constituency of its own. While Test cricket will always remain the pinnacle, one-day international cricket too is in good shape, with the Champions Trophy and the fifty-over World Cup seeing tremendous support the world over. Also, Twenty20 continues to attract the youth, as shown by the popularity of the IPL.

A lot of people have asked me what I will be doing in the future. Frankly, I don't know. When I started out playing cricket at eleven years of age I had no idea I would go on to play for India let alone play in 200 Test matches. All I knew was that I wanted to play the game well and enjoy every second of it. I have always tried to stay in the moment, and live each situation as it unfolded for me.

I had never thought there would come a time when I would not be able to go out for walks with my children, or take them shopping, that going out to watch a film or taking my family out for dinner would require meticulous planning. However, I don't regret any of it, for all of that is a small price to pay for the affection and warmth the people of my country have showered on me all the way through my career.

I am in a very similar state at the start of my second innings. All I am doing now is trying to spend a lot of time with my family and sometimes not doing anything at all! This was impossible when I was an active cricketer but now I am learning to take time off, and I must say I am enjoying myself at home. Cricket allowed us to have a place of our own, our current bungalow in Bandra West, and Anjali and I have taken care to ensure every little thing has been handpicked by us. From growing up as a child in a one-room place next to Shivaji Park, to sleeping in our living room with Ajit till 1994, to finally owning a bungalow in Bandra – by being true to cricket I have been able to fulfil a lifelong dream of owning my own house.

Something else I always wanted was to have my parents stay with me, and while my dream of having my father to stay at my own place was not fulfilled – he passed away in 1999, and we moved into our apartment in La Mer in 2000 – my mother now stays with me, giving me immense fulfilment and pride. In fact, on 28 September 2011, the day we moved into our bungalow in Bandra West, I took my mother to the bungalow at six in the morning and showed her around the whole house in her wheelchair. I had driven her in a small car to avoid attention and wheeled her in her chair myself for the entire time. She was actually the first person to enter the house, which made the occasion all the more joyous.

As I start my second innings, I will do exactly what I did when I was eleven, live and enjoy each moment. I don't know where my life is heading, nor do I want to predict anything. I will just take things as they come, as I did when I played my first innings. There is one difference, however. As I move on in life I will always live with the satisfaction that I managed to play the first innings my way, and have been able to leave behind a legacy I can now look back on with pride.

Appendix
FAREWELL SPEECH

All my friends . . . settle down, let me talk, I will get more and more emotional . . . my life, between 22 yards for twenty-four years, it's hard to believe that that wonderful journey is coming to an end, but I would like to take this opportunity to thank people who've played an important role in my life. Also, for the first time in my life I am carrying this list, to remember all the names, in case I forget someone. I hope you understand . . . it's getting a little difficult to talk, but I'll manage.

The most, the most important person in my life, and I have missed him a lot since 1999 when he passed away, my father. Without . . . without his guidance, I don't think I would have been standing here in front of you. He gave me freedom at the age of eleven and told me 'Chase your dreams, but make sure you don't find short cuts. The path might be difficult, but don't give up.' And I have simply followed his instructions. Above all, he told me to be a nice human being, which I will continue to do so, I have tried my best. Every time, every time I have done something special, whenever I've showed my bat, it was for my father, so I miss him today.

My mother, I don't know how she dealt with such a naughty child like me. I was not easy to manage. She must be extremely patient. For a mother, the most important thing is that her child remains safe and healthy and fit, and that's what she was most bothered about and worried about. She, she took care of me . . . for the last twenty-four years that I have played for India, but even before that, she started praying for me the day I started playing cricket. She just prayed and prayed and prayed, and I think her prayers and blessings have given me the strength to go out and perform, so a big thank you to my mother for all the sacrifices.

In my schooldays, for four years I stayed with my uncle and my aunt, because my school was quite far from my home, and they treated me like their son. My aunt – after having had a hard day's play, I would be half asleep and she would be feeding me food so that I could go and play again tomorrow. I can't forget these moments. I am like their son and I am glad that it has continued to be the same way.

My eldest brother, Nitin, and his family have always encouraged me. My eldest brother doesn't like to talk much, but the one thing he always told me is, 'Whatever you do, I know you will give a hundred per cent, and I have full confidence and faith in you.' His encouragement meant a lot to me. My sister, Savita, and her family, was no different. The first cricket bat of my life was presented to me by my sister, it was a Kashmir willow bat . . . but that is where the journey began. She is one of those many who still continue to fast when I bat, so thank you very much.

Ajit, my brother, now what do I talk about him? I don't know, really. We've, we've lived this dream together. He was the one who sacrificed his career for my cricket. He spotted the spark in me. And it all started from the age of eleven when he took me to Achrekar Sir, my coach, and from there on my life changed. You will find this hard to believe that even last night he called me and we were discussing my dismissal, knowing that there was a remote chance of batting again, but just that, the habit which we have developed and the rapport that we have developed, since my birth, it has continued and it will continue. Maybe even when I'm not playing cricket we will still be discussing technique. Various things, various things we agreed upon, my technique, and so many technical things which I didn't agree with him, we have had arguments and disagreements, but in the end when I look back at all those things, if that hadn't happened in my life, I would have been a lesser cricketer.

The most beautiful thing happened to me in 1990 when I met my wife, Anjali. Those were, those were special years and it has continued and it will always continue that way. I know, I know Anjali, being a doctor, there was a wonderful career in front of her. When we decided to have a family, Anjali took the initiative to step back and say that, 'You continue with your cricket and I'll take the responsibility of the family.' Without, without that, I don't think I would have been able to play cricket freely and without any stress. Thanks for bearing up, bearing with all my fuss, all my frustrations and all sorts of rubbish that I have spoken – I normally do. Thanks for bearing with me and always staying by my side through the ups and downs. You are the best partnership I've had in my life.

Then, then the two precious diamonds of my life, Sara and Arjun. They have already grown up. You know, my daughter is sixteen, my son is fourteen. Time has flown by. I wanted to spend so much time with them on special occasions like their birthdays, their annual days, sports day, going on holidays, whatever. I have missed out on all those things. Thanks for your understanding. Both of you . . . have been so, so special to me . . . you cannot imagine. I promise you, I promise you, for fourteen years and sixteen years I have not spent enough time with both of you, but the next, the next sixteen years or even beyond that, everything is for you.

My, my in-laws, Anand Mehta and Annabel, both have been so, so supportive, loving, caring . . . I have discussed on various, various things in life, generally with them, and taken their advice. You know, it's so important to have a strong family who is always with you and guiding you. Before you start clapping, the most important thing they did was allowing me to marry Anjali, so thank you very much.

In the last, in the last twenty-four years that I have played for India I have made new friends, and before that I have had friends from my childhood. They all have had a terrific contribution.

Right from, you know, as and when I have called them to come and bowl to me in the nets, they have left all their work aside and come and helped me. Be it joining me on holidays and having discussions on cricket, when I was a little stressed and wanting to find a solution so that I could perform better – all those moments, my friends were with me. Even for whenever I was injured, I would wake up in the morning because I could not sleep, I thought my career was over because of injuries, that's when my friends have woken up at three o'clock in the morning to drive with me and just make me believe that 'Your career is not over.' Life . . . would be incomplete without all those friends. Thanks for being there for me.

My cricket career started when I was eleven. The turning point of my career was when my brother took me to Achrekar Sir, my coach. I was extremely delighted to see him up in the stands. Normally he sits in front of the television and he watches all the games that I play. When I was . . . when I was eleven, twelve, those, those were the days where I used to hop back on his scooter and play a couple of practice matches a day. You know, first half of the innings I would be batting on Shivaji Park, the second half some other match at Azad Maidan. Sir would be taking me all over Mumbai to make sure that I got match practice.

On a lighter note, in the last twenty-nine years Sir has never ever said 'well played' to me because he thought I would get complacent and I would stop working hard. Maybe he can, he can push his luck and wish me now 'well done' on my career, and because there are no more matches, Sir, in my life. I will be witnessing cricket, and cricket will always stay in my heart, but you had an immense contribution in my life, so thank you very much.

My cricket for Mumbai started right here on this ground, the Mumbai Cricket Association, which is so dear to me. I remember landing from New Zealand at four o'clock in the morning and turning up for a game at eight o'clock here, just because I wanted to be part of Mumbai cricket, not that anyone forced me or Mumbai Cricket Association pressurized me to be here, but that was for the love of Mumbai cricket. And thank you very much – the president is here – thank you very much, along with your team, for taking care of me and looking after my cricket.

The dream was obviously to, to play for India, and that's where my association with BCCI started. BCCI was fantastic, right from the, from my debut. Believing in my ability, selecting me in the squad at the age of sixteen was, was a big step. So thanks to all the selectors for having, having faith in me and the BCCI for giving me the freedom to express myself out in the middle. Things would have been different if you had not been behind me, and I really appreciate your support. Especially when I was injured, you were right with me and making sure that all the treatments were taken care of and I got fit and fine, playing back for India.

The journey has been special, the last twenty-four years. I have played with many, many senior cricketers, and even before that there were many senior cricketers whom I watched on television – they inspired me to play cricket and play it the right way. Thanks so much to all those senior cricketers. Unfortunately I have not been able to play with them, but I have high regards for all their achievements and all their contributions.

We see it on the mega-screen, Rahul, Laxman, Sourav – Anil is not here – and my team-mates right here in front of me. You are, you are like my family away from home. I have had some wonderful times with you . . . it's going to be difficult not to be part of the dressing room, sharing those special moments. All the coaches, for, for their guidance, it has been special for me. I know when MS Dhoni presented me the 200th Test match cap on day one morning, I had a brief message for the team. I would like to repeat that: I just feel that all of us are so, so fortunate and proud to be part of the Indian cricket team, serving the nation. Knowing all of you guys, I know you will continue to serve the nation in the right spirit and the right values. I believe, I believe we have been the lucky ones to have been chosen by the Almighty to serve this wonderful sport. Each generation gets this opportunity to merely take care of this sport and serve it to the best of our ability. I have full faith in you that you'll continue to serve the nation in the right spirit, to the best of your ability, and bring all the laurels to our country. All the very best.

I would be failing in my duties if I didn't thank all the doctors, the physios, the trainers, who've put this difficult body together to go back on the field and to be able to play. The amount of injuries that I've had in my career, I don't know how you've managed to keep me fit, but without your special efforts, it would never have happened. I mean, the doctors have met me at weird hours. I mean, I have called them from Mumbai to Chennai, Mumbai to Delhi, wherever, and then they have just taken the next flight and they've left their work and they've come, they've treated me, which has allowed me to play. So a big thank you to all three of you for keeping me in good shape.

My dear friend, late Mark Mascarenhas, my first manager – we unfortunately lost him in a car accident in 2002, but he was such a well-wisher of cricket, my cricket, especially Indian cricket. He was so passionate. He understood what it takes to represent a nation and gave me all the space to go out and express myself, and never pressurized me to do this ad or promotion, whatever the sponsors demanded. He took care of that and today I miss him, so thank you, Mark, for all your contribution.

My current, my current management team, WSG, for, for repeating what Mark has done, because when we signed the contract I exactly told them what I want from them and what it requires to be representing India. They have understood that and respected that, so thank you very much, WSG.

Someone who has worked closely with me for fourteen years is my manager, Vinod Naidu. He is more like my family and all the sacrifices, spending time away from his family for my work, has been special, so a big thank you to your family as well, for giving so much time for my work with Vinod.

In my schooldays, when I performed well, the media backed me a lot. You continue to do that till this morning. Thank you so much to all the media, for supporting me and appreciating my performances. It surely had a positive effect on me. Thank you so much to all the photographers as well, for those wonderful captured moments will stay with me for the rest of my life, so to all the photographers a big thank you.

I know my speech is getting a bit too long, but this is the last thing I want to say . . . I want to . . . I want to thank all the people here who've flown in from various parts of the world and supported me endlessly, whether I scored a zero or I scored a hundred-plus, whatever. Your support was so dear to me and it meant a lot to me.

Whatever you've done for me – I know I've met so many guys who've fasted for me, prayed for me, done all sorts of things for me – you know, without all that, life wouldn't have been like this for me. I want to thank you from the bottom of my heart, and also say that time has flown by rather quickly, but the memories that you have left with me will always be with me for ever and ever, especially 'Sachin, Sachin'. That will reverberate in my ears . . . till I stop breathing.

Thank you very much. If I've, if I've missed out on saying something, missed out on a few names, I hope you understand. Goodbye.

Wankhede Stadium, Mumbai
16 November 2013

CAREER STATISTICS

Compiled by Benedict Bermange

TEST CAREER

Tests – BATTING

	M	Inns	NO	Runs	HS	Avge	100	50	0
Overall record	200	329	33	15921	248*	53.78	51	68	14

Tests – series by series

	M	Inns	NO	Runs	HS	Avge	100	50	Ct
India in Pakistan 1989–90	4	6	0	215	59	35.83	0	2	1
India in New Zealand 1989–90	3	4	0	117	88	29.25	0	1	1
India in England 1990	3	5	1	245	119*	61.25	1	1	3
Sri Lanka in India 1990–91	1	1	0	11	11	11.00	0	0	0
India in Australia 1991–92	5	9	1	368	148*	46.00	2	0	5
India in Zimbabwe 1992–93	1	1	0	0	0	0.00	0	0	0
India in South Africa 1992–93	4	6	0	202	111	33.66	1	1	4
England in India 1992–93	3	4	1	302	165	100.66	1	2	4
Zimbabwe in India 1992–93	1	1	0	62	62	62.00	0	1	0
India in Sri Lanka 1993–94	3	3	1	203	104*	101.50	1	1	3
Sri Lanka in India 1993–94	3	3	0	244	142	81.33	1	1	2
India in New Zealand 1993–94	1	2	1	54	43	54.00	0	0	0
West Indies in India 1994–95	3	6	0	402	179	67.00	1	2	5
New Zealand in India 1995–96	3	4	2	58	52*	29.00	0	1	3
India in England 1996	3	5	0	428	177	85.60	2	1	2
Australia in India 1996–97	1	2	0	10	10	5.00	0	0	0
South Africa in India 1996–97	3	6	0	166	61	27.66	0	1	1
India in South Africa 1996–97	3	6	0	241	169	40.16	1	0	3
India in West Indies 1996–97	5	6	1	289	92	57.80	0	3	5
India in Sri Lanka 1997–98	2	3	0	290	143	96.66	2	0	1
Sri Lanka in India 1997–98	3	4	0	199	148	49.75	1	0	2
Australia in India 1997–98	3	5	1	446	177	111.50	2	1	2
India in Zimbabwe 1998–99	1	2	0	41	34	20.50	0	0	0
India in New Zealand 1998–99	2	3	0	227	113	75.66	1	1	1
Pakistan in India 1998–99	2	4	0	171	136	42.75	1	0	0
Asian Test Championship 1998–99	2	4	1	186	124*	62.00	1	1	0
New Zealand in India 1999–00	3	6	2	435	217	108.75	2	0	2

India in Australia 1999–00	3	6	0	278	116	46.33	1	2	0
South Africa in India 1999–00	2	4	0	146	97	36.50	0	1	2
India in Bangladesh 2000–01	1	1	0	18	18	18.00	0	0	0
Zimbabwe in India 2000–01	2	3	1	362	201*	181.00	2	0	3
Australia in India 2000–01	3	6	0	304	126	50.66	1	2	1
India in Zimbabwe 2001	2	4	1	199	74	66.33	0	2	0
India in South Africa 2001–02	2	4	1	193	155	64.33	1	0	0
England in India 2001–02	3	4	0	307	103	76.75	1	2	4
Zimbabwe in India 2001–02	2	3	0	254	176	84.66	1	0	2
India in West Indies 2001–02	5	8	0	331	117	41.37	1	2	2
India in England 2002	4	6	0	401	193	66.83	1	2	1
West Indies in India 2002–03	3	5	1	306	176	76.50	1	0	2
India in New Zealand 2002–03	2	4	0	100	51	25.00	0	1	1
New Zealand in India 2003–04	2	4	0	71	55	17.75	0	1	0
India in Australia 2003–04	4	7	2	383	241*	76.60	1	1	3
India in Pakistan 2003–04	3	4	1	205	194*	68.33	1	0	1
Australia in India 2004–05	2	4	0	70	55	17.50	0	1	1
South Africa in India 2004–05	2	3	1	55	32*	27.50	0	0	0
India in Bangladesh 2004–05	2	2	1	284	248*	284.00	1	0	2
Pakistan in India 2004–05	3	5	0	255	94	51.00	0	3	2
Sri Lanka in India 2005–06	3	5	0	189	109	37.80	1	0	0
India in Pakistan 2005–06	3	3	0	63	26	21.00	0	0	4
England in India 2005–06	3	5	1	83	34	20.75	0	0	1
India in South Africa 2006–07	3	6	0	199	64	33.16	0	2	3
India in Bangladesh 2006–07	2	3	1	254	122*	127.00	2	0	4
India in England 2007	3	6	0	228	91	38.00	0	2	4
Pakistan in India 2007–08	2	3	1	139	82	69.50	0	2	0
India in Australia 2007–08	4	8	1	493	154*	70.42	2	2	5
South Africa in India 2007–08	1	1	0	0	0	0.00	0	0	0
India in Sri Lanka 2008	3	6	0	95	31	15.83	0	0	0
Australia in India 2008–09	4	8	1	396	109	56.57	1	2	2
England in India 2008–09	2	4	1	156	103*	52.00	1	0	0
India in New Zealand 2008–09	3	5	0	344	160	68.80	1	2	2
Sri Lanka in India 2009–10	3	4	1	197	100*	65.66	1	1	2
India in Bangladesh 2009–10	2	3	1	264	143	132.00	2	0	0
South Africa in India 2009–10	2	3	0	213	106	71.00	2	0	0
India in Sri Lanka 2010	3	5	0	390	203	78.00	1	2	2
Australia in India 2010–11	2	4	1	403	214	134.33	1	2	0
New Zealand in India 2010–11	3	4	0	126	61	31.50	0	1	0
India in South Africa 2010–11	3	6	2	326	146	81.50	2	0	0
India in England 2011	4	8	0	273	91	34.12	0	2	2
West Indies in India 2011–12	3	5	0	218	94	43.60	0	2	2
India in Australia 2011–12	4	8	0	287	80	35.87	0	2	3
New Zealand in India 2012	2	3	0	63	27	21.00	0	0	0

England in India 2012-13	4	6	0	112	76	18.66	0	1	1
Australia in India 2012-13	4	7	1	192	81	32.00	0	1	1
West Indies in India 2013-14	2	2	0	84	74	42.00	0	1	0

Tests – batting by opponent

	M	Inns	NO	Runs	HS	Avge	100	50	0
Australia	39	74	8	3630	241*	55.00	11	16	4
Bangladesh	7	9	3	820	248*	136.66	5	0	0
England	32	53	4	2535	193	51.73	7	13	0
New Zealand	24	39	5	1595	217	46.91	4	8	1
Pakistan	18	27	2	1057	194*	42.28	2	7	2
South Africa	25	45	4	1741	169	42.46	7	5	3
Sri Lanka	25	36	3	1995	203	60.45	9	6	0
West Indies	21	32	2	1630	179	54.33	3	10	3
Zimbabwe	9	14	2	918	201*	76.50	3	3	1

Tests – batting by country

	M	Inns	NO	Runs	HS	Avge	100	50	0
Australia	20	38	4	1809	241*	53.20	6	7	3
Bangladesh	7	9	3	820	248*	136.66	5	0	0
England	17	30	1	1575	193	54.31	4	8	0
India	94	153	16	7216	217	52.67	22	32	4
New Zealand	11	18	1	842	160	49.52	2	5	1
Pakistan	10	13	1	483	194*	40.25	1	2	0
South Africa	15	28	3	1161	169	46.44	5	3	2
Sri Lanka	12	19	2	1155	203	67.94	5	4	0
West Indies	10	14	1	620	117	47.69	1	5	3
Zimbabwe	4	7	1	240	74	40.00	0	2	1

Tests – batting by continent

	M	Inns	NO	Runs	HS	Avge	100	50	0
Africa	19	35	4	1401	169	45.19	5	5	3
Americas	10	14	1	620	117	47.69	1	5	3
Asia	123	194	22	9674	248*	56.24	33	38	4
Europe	17	30	1	1575	193	54.31	4	8	0
Oceania	31	56	5	2651	241*	51.98	8	12	4

Tests – batting home and away

	M	Inns	NO	Runs	HS	Avge	100	50	0
Home	94	153	16	7216	217	52.67	22	32	4
Away	106	176	17	8705	248*	54.74	29	36	10

Tests – batting by year

	M	Inns	NO	Runs	HS	Avge	100	50	0
1989	4	6	0	215	59	35.83	0	2	0
1990	7	10	1	373	119*	41.44	1	2	1
1991	2	4	0	78	40	19.50	0	0	0
1992	7	11	1	419	148*	41.90	3	0	2
1993	8	9	2	640	165	91.42	2	5	0
1994	7	11	1	700	179	70.00	2	3	0
1995	3	4	2	58	52*	29.00	0	1	0
1996	8	15	0	623	177	41.53	2	2	1
1997	12	17	1	1000	169	62.50	4	3	0
1998	5	9	1	647	177	80.87	3	1	0
1999	10	19	3	1088	217	68.00	5	4	3
2000	6	10	1	575	201*	63.88	2	1	0
2001	10	18	2	1003	155	62.68	3	6	0
2002	16	26	1	1392	193	55.68	4	5	3
2003	5	9	0	153	55	17.00	0	1	2
2004	10	15	5	915	248*	91.50	3	2	0
2005	6	10	0	444	109	44.40	1	3	0
2006	8	12	1	267	63	24.27	0	1	1
2007	9	16	2	776	122*	55.42	2	6	0
2008	13	25	3	1063	154*	48.31	4	3	1
2009	6	9	1	541	160	67.62	2	3	0
2010	14	23	3	1562	214	78.10	7	5	0
2011	9	17	1	756	146	47.25	1	5	0
2012	9	15	0	357	80	23.80	0	2	0
2013	6	9	1	276	81	34.50	0	2	0

Tests – batting by batting position

	M	Inns	NO	Runs	HS	Avge	100	50	0
Number 2	1	1	0	15	15	15.00	0	0	0
Number 4	177	275	27	13492	248*	54.40	44	58	11
Number 5	26	29	3	1552	169	59.69	5	6	2
Number 6	14	20	3	745	148*	43.82	2	4	1
Number 7	3	4	0	117	41	29.25	0	0	0

Tests – batting by team innings

	M	Inns	NO	Runs	HS	Avge	100	50	0
1st team innings	199	197	9	11300	248*	60.10	38	46	9
2nd team innings	147	132	24	4621	176	42.78	13	22	5

Tests – batting by match innings

	M	Inns	NO	Runs	HS	Avge	100	50	0
1st match innings	91	91	6	5608	241*	65.97	20	20	3
2nd match innings	108	106	3	5692	248*	55.26	18	26	6
3rd match innings	73	72	8	2996	176	46.81	10	15	2
4th match innings	74	60	16	1625	136	36.93	3	7	3

Tests – batting by result

	M	Inns	NO	Runs	HS	Avge	100	50	0
Won match	72	113	17	5946	248*	61.93	20	24	2
Lost match	56	112	2	4088	177	37.16	11	18	8
Drawn match	72	104	14	5887	241*	65.41	20	26	4

Tests – batting by series stage

	M	Inns	NO	Runs	HS	Avge	100	50	0
Only match in series	7	10	1	196	62	21.77	0	1	2
1st match in series	64	104	15	5015	248*	56.34	18	18	5
2nd match in series	64	106	12	5481	214	58.30	19	23	2
3rd match in series	46	78	2	3637	217	47.85	9	17	3
4th match in series	14	22	2	1077	241*	53.85	3	6	1
5th match in series	3	5	0	329	114	65.80	1	2	0

Tests – batting by captain

	M	Inns	NO	Runs	HS	Avge	100	50	0
M Azharuddin	47	72	9	3767	179	59.79	15	15	5
MS Dhoni	45	75	7	3595	214	52.86	11	17	0
R Dravid	21	35	3	1304	194*	40.75	4	6	1
SC Ganguly	42	68	8	3768	248*	62.80	11	15	5
A Kumble	12	22	2	904	154*	45.20	2	5	1
V Sehwag	4	8	1	314	105*	44.85	1	1	0
K Srikkanth	4	6	0	215	59	35.83	0	2	0
SR Tendulkar	25	43	3	2054	217	51.35	7	7	2

Tests – batting as captain/as player

	M	Inns	NO	Runs	HS	Avge	100	50	0
As captain	25	43	3	2054	217	51.35	7	7	2
As player	175	286	30	13867	248*	54.16	44	61	12

Tests – centuries

	Opponent	Venue	Season
248*	Bangladesh	Dhaka	2004–05
241*	Australia	Sydney	2003–04

217	New Zealand	Ahmedabad	1999–00
214	Australia	Bangalore	2010–11
203	Sri Lanka	Colombo-SSC	2010
201*	Zimbabwe	Nagpur	2000–01
194*	Pakistan	Multan	2003–04
193	England	Leeds	2002
179	West Indies	Nagpur	1994–95
177	England	Nottingham	1996
177	Australia	Bangalore	1997–98
176	Zimbabwe	Nagpur	2001–02
176	West Indies	Kolkata	2002–03
169	South Africa	Cape Town	1996–97
165	England	Chennai	1992–93
160	New Zealand	Hamilton	2008–09
155*	Australia	Chennai	1997–98
155	South Africa	Bloemfontein	2001–02
154*	Australia	Sydney	2007–08
153	Australia	Adelaide	2007–08
148*	Australia	Sydney	1991–92
148	Sri Lanka	Mumbai	1997–98
146	South Africa	Cape Town	2010–11
143	Sri Lanka	Colombo-RPS	1997–98
143	Bangladesh	Mirpur	2009–10
142	Sri Lanka	Lucknow	1993–94
139	Sri Lanka	Colombo-SSC	1997–98
136	Pakistan	Chennai	1998–99
126*	New Zealand	Mohali	1999–00
126	Australia	Chennai	2000–01
124*	Sri Lanka	Colombo-SSC	1998–99
122*	Bangladesh	Mirpur	2006–07
122	England	Birmingham	1996
122	Zimbabwe	Delhi	2000–01
119*	England	Manchester	1990
117	West Indies	Port-of-Spain	2001–02
116	Australia	Melbourne	1999–00
114	Australia	Perth	1991–92
113	New Zealand	Wellington	1998–99
111*	South Africa	Centurion	2010–11
111	South Africa	Johannesburg	1992–93
109	Sri Lanka	Delhi	2005–06
109	Australia	Nagpur-J	2008–09
106	South Africa	Kolkata	2009–10
105*	Bangladesh	Chittagong-D	2009–10
104*	Sri Lanka	Colombo-SSC	1993–94

103*	England	Chennai	2008–09
103	England	Ahmedabad	2001–02
101	Bangladesh	Chittagong-D	2006–07
100*	Sri Lanka	Ahmedabad	2009–10
100	South Africa	Nagpur-J	2009–10

Tests – bowlers dismissing him most often

	Times	Matches
JM Anderson	9	14
M Muralitharan	8	19
JN Gillespie	6	8
GD McGrath	6	9
AA Donald	5	11
WJ Cronje	5	11
B Lee	5	12
DL Vettori	5	15
NM Lyon	4	6
CC Lewis	4	8
M Ntini	4	8
PM Siddle	4	9
GP Swann	4	10
MS Panesar	4	11
SM Pollock	4	12
RW Price	3	2
KR Pushpakumara	3	4
DR Tuffey	3	4
Saqlain Mushtaq	3	4
IR Bishop	3	4
PT Collins	3	5
SCJ Broad	3	7
DK Morrison	3	7
CS Martin	3	7
PL Harris	3	7
DW Steyn	3	8
Shahid Afridi	3	8
DJ Nash	3	9
Shoaib Akhtar	3	9
CE Cuffy	3	9
BM McMillan	3	10
MJ Hoggard	3	10
WPUJC Vaas	3	11
MG Johnson	3	11
SK Warne	3	12
JH Kallis	3	14

Tests – how he was dismissed

	Times	Dis	%
Bowled	54	296	18.24
Caught wicketkeeper	42	296	14.19
Caught fielder	127	296	42.91
LBW	63	296	21.28
Run out	9	296	3.04
Stumped	1	296	0.34

Tests – batting partners

	Inns	Unb	Runs	Best	Avge	100	50
RS Dravid	143	6	6905	249	50.40	20	29
SC Ganguly	71	3	4173	281	61.36	12	16
VVS Laxman	72	4	3516	353	51.70	9	19
M Azharuddin	42	1	2385	222	58.17	9	5
V Sehwag	23	0	1560	336	67.82	4	5
NS Sidhu	16	0	1239	177	77.43	6	3
MS Dhoni	24	2	969	172	44.04	2	6
G Gambhir	23	0	958	176	41.65	2	4
VG Kambli	5	1	581	194	145.25	3	1
M Vijay	6	0	581	308	96.83	1	3
Yuvraj Singh	11	1	539	163*	53.90	2	2
SK Raina	10	0	530	256	53.00	2	1
M Prabhakar	12	2	526	160*	52.60	1	4
SS Das	10	1	518	118	57.55	1	5
SV Manjrekar	16	2	509	143	36.35	1	3
CA Pujara	13	1	497	144	41.41	1	3
NR Mongia	11	0	395	135	35.90	1	2
A Kumble	16	0	332	58	20.75	0	1
W Jaffer	6	0	331	175	55.16	1	1
Harbhajan Singh	8	0	313	129	39.12	1	2
RJ Shastri	8	0	308	196	38.50	1	0
KS More	7	0	301	128	43.00	1	1
Kapil Dev	14	0	281	75	20.07	0	2
KD Karthik	8	0	262	85	32.75	0	2
SB Bangar	3	0	261	171	87.00	1	0
V Kohli	10	0	247	91	24.70	0	1
Z Khan	5	0	231	133	46.20	1	0
PK Amre	3	1	208	118	104.00	1	0
A Mishra	2	0	176	144	88.00	1	0
S Ramesh	5	0	172	80	34.40	0	2
PA Patel	2	0	141	101	70.50	1	0
AD Jadeja	4	0	124	51	31.00	0	1

IK Pathan	4	1	114	44	38.00	0	0
SB Joshi	5	0	111	37	22.20	0	0
DJ Gandhi	2	1	80	76*	80.00	0	1
HH Kanitkar	3	0	79	30	26.33	0	0
DB Vengsarkar	3	0	71	62	23.66	0	1
MSK Prasad	4	0	68	29	17.00	0	0
SLV Raju	5	0	66	47	13.20	0	0
I Sharma	3	0	65	31	21.66	0	0
AB Agarkar	5	0	54	29	10.80	0	0
WV Raman	2	0	51	46	25.50	0	0
J Srinath	6	0	46	25	7.66	0	0
M Kaif	2	0	35	27	17.50	0	0
ND Hirwani	1	0	31	31	31.00	0	0
RP Singh	1	0	27	27	27.00	0	0
S Badrinath	1	0	26	26	26.00	0	0
CS Pandit	1	0	24	24	24.00	0	0
BKV Prasad	1	1	23	23*		0	0
M Kartik	1	0	20	20	20.00	0	0
D Ganesh	1	0	19	19	19.00	0	0
S Sreesanth	2	0	19	13	9.50	0	0
A Mukund	1	0	18	18	18.00	0	0
AM Rahane	1	0	17	17	17.00	0	0
ST Banerjee	1	0	16	16	16.00	0	0
DB Dasgupta	2	0	15	13	7.50	0	0
SS Dighe	1	0	15	15	15.00	0	0
PL Mhambrey	1	0	15	15	15.00	0	0
R Vijay Bharadwaj	1	0	12	12	12.00	0	0
AR Kapoor	1	0	10	10	10.00	0	0
V Dahiya	1	1	8	8*		0	0
AS Chopra	2	0	6	6	3.00	0	0
JD Unadkat	1	0	3	3	3.00	0	0
V Rathour	1	0	1	1	1.00	0	0
A Nehra	1	0	0	0	0.00	0	0

Tests – BOWLING

	M	Inns	Overs	Mdns	Runs	Wkts	BBI	Avge	Econ	SR	5	10
Overall record	200	145	706.4	83	2492	46	3/10	54.17	3.52	92.1	0	0

Tests – best bowling figures

	Opponent	Venue	Season
3–10	South Africa	Mumbai	1999–00
3–31	Australia	Kolkata	2000–01
2–7	New Zealand	Wellington	1998–99

2–10	Australia	Adelaide	1991–92
2–30	New Zealand	Hamilton	1998–99
2–35	Pakistan	Chennai	1998–99
2–35	Bangladesh	Mirpur	2006–07
2–36	Australia	Adelaide	2003–04
2–36	Pakistan	Multan	2003–04
2–45	New Zealand	Wellington	2008–09
2–107	West Indies	St John's	2001–02

Tests – how he took his wickets

	Times	Wkts	%
Bowled	11	46	23.91
Caught wicketkeeper	2	46	4.35
Caught fielder	21	46	45.66
LBW	10	46	21.74
Stumped	1	46	2.17
Hit wicket	1	46	2.17

Tests – CAPTAINCY

	M	W	L	D	Toss won	Toss lost	TW bat	TW bowl	TL bat	TL bowl
Overall record	25	4	9	12	15	10	10	5	8	2

Tests – results as captain

Start date	Opponent	Venue	Toss	Decision	Result
10/10/1996	Australia	Delhi	Lost	Bat	Won
20/11/1996	South Africa	Ahmedabad	Won	Bat	Won
27/11/1996	South Africa	Calcutta	Lost	Bat	Lost
8/12/1996	South Africa	Kanpur	Won	Bat	Won
26/12/1996	South Africa	Durban	Won	Bowl	Lost
2/1/1997	South Africa	Cape Town	Lost	Bat	Lost
16/1/1997	South Africa	Johannesburg	Won	Bat	Drawn
06/3/1997	West Indies	Kingston	Lost	Bat	Drawn
14/3/1997	West Indies	Port-of-Spain	Lost	Bat	Drawn
27/3/1997	West Indies	Bridgetown	Won	Bowl	Lost
4/4/1997	West Indies	St John's	Lost	Bat	Drawn
17/4/1997	West Indies	Georgetown	Won	Bat	Drawn
2/8/1997	Sri Lanka	Colombo-RPS	Won	Bat	Drawn
9/8/1997	Sri Lanka	Colombo-SSC	Won	Bowl	Drawn
19/11/1997	Sri Lanka	Mohali	Won	Bowl	Drawn
26/11/1997	Sri Lanka	Nagpur	Won	Bat	Drawn
3/12/1997	Sri Lanka	Mumbai	Lost	Bowl	Drawn
10/10/1999	New Zealand	Mohali	Lost	Bowl	Drawn

22/10/1999	New Zealand	Kanpur	Lost	Bat	Won
29/10/1999	New Zealand	Ahmedabad	Won	Bat	Drawn
10/12/1999	Australia	Adelaide	Lost	Bat	Lost
26/12/1999	Australia	Melbourne	Won	Bowl	Lost
2/1/2000	Australia	Sydney	Won	Bat	Lost
24/2/2000	South Africa	Mumbai	Won	Bat	Lost
2/3/2000	South Africa	Bangalore	Won	Bat	Lost

ONE-DAY INTERNATIONAL CAREER

ODIs – BATTING

	M	Inns	NO	Runs	HS	Avge	SR	100	50	0	Ct
Overall record	463	452	41	18426	200*	44.83	86.23	49	96	20	

ODIs – series by series

	M	Inns	NO	Runs	HS	Avge	SR	100	50	0	Ct
India in Pakistan 1989–90	1	1	0	0	0	0.00	0.00	0	0	0	0
Rothmans Cup in New Zealand 1989–90	2	2	0	36	36	18.00	87.80	0	0	0	0
Austral-Asia Cup in U.A.E. 1990	2	2	0	30	20	15.00	81.08	0	0	1	1
India in England 1990	2	2	0	50	31	25.00	81.96	0	0	0	0
Sri Lanka in India 1990–91	3	3	0	119	53	39.66	129.34	0	1	2	2
Asia Cup in India 1990–91	3	2	0	57	53	28.50	70.37	0	1	0	0
Wills Trophy in U.A.E. 1991–92	5	5	2	134	52*	44.66	100.75	0	1	1	1
South Africa in India 1991–92	3	3	0	67	62	22.33	79.76	0	1	0	1
Benson & Hedges World Series in Australia 1991–92	10	10	1	401	77	44.55	62.46	0	4	0	4
World Cup in Australia/New Zealand 1991–92	8	7	1	283	84	47.16	84.73	0	3	0	2
India in Zimbabwe 1992–93	1	1	0	39	39	39.00	69.64	0	0	0	0
India in South Africa 1992–93	7	7	0	144	32	20.57	55.38	0	0	2	2
England in India 1992–93	6	6	1	149	82*	29.80	93.12	0	1	2	2
Zimbabwe in India 1992–93	3	2	1	11	8*	11.00	73.33	0	0	0	0
India in Sri Lanka 1993	3	3	0	61	25	20.33	56.48	0	0	1	1
Hero Cup in India 1993–94	6	6	2	98	28*	24.50	64.05	0	0	1	1
Sri Lanka in India 1993–94	3	3	1	64	52	32.00	74.41	0	1	2	2
India in New Zealand 1993–94	4	4	0	200	82	50.00	118.34	0	2	0	0
Austral-Asia Cup in U.A.E. 1993–94	4	4	0	166	73	41.50	95.40	0	2	2	2
Singer World Series in Sri Lanka 1994	4	4	1	127	110	42.33	83.00	1	0	0	0
West Indies in India 1994–95	5	5	0	247	105	49.40	77.67	1	2	1	1

	M	Inns	NO	Runs	HS	Avge	SR	100	50	Ct
Wills World Series in India 1994–95	5	5	0	285	115	57.00	86.62	1	2	3
New Zealand Centenary Tournament 1994–95	3	3	0	97	47	32.33	91.50	0	0	1
Pepsi Asia Cup in U.A.E 1994–95	4	4	1	205	112*	68.33	109.62	1	0	3
New Zealand in India 1995–96	5	5	0	142	65	28.40	97.93	0	1	2
World Cup in India/Pakistan/Sri Lanka 1995–96	7	7	1	523	137	87.16	85.87	2	3	2
Singer Cup in Singapore 1995–96	2	2	0	128	100	64.00	90.14	1	0	0
Pepsi Sharjah Cup in U.A.E. 1995–96	5	5	0	195	118	39.00	75.87	1	1	1
India in England 1996	3	3	0	37	30	12.33	75.51	0	0	2
Singer World Series in Sri Lanka 1996	3	3	0	157	110	52.33	80.51	1	0	2
Sahara 'Friendship' Cup in Canada 1996	5	5	1	137	89*	34.25	76.96	0	1	3
Titan Cup in India 1996–97	6	6	0	320	88	53.33	80.40	0	4	3
South Africa in India 1996–97	1	1	0	114	114	114.00	90.47	1	0	0
Standard Bank International Series in South Africa 1996–97	8	8	0	243	104	30.37	92.39	1	0	1
India in Zimbabwe 1996–97	1	1	0	13	13	13.00	86.66	0	0	0
India in West Indies 1996–97	4	4	1	119	65*	39.66	85.61	0	1	0
Pepsi Independence Cup in India 1997	3	3	0	123	117	41.00	83.10	1	0	1
Pepsi Asia Cup in Sri Lanka 1997	4	3	0	102	53	34.00	87.93	0	1	0
India in Sri Lanka 1997	4	4	0	99	39	24.75	102.06	0	0	3
Sahara 'Friendship' Cup in Canada 1997	6	5	1	99	51	24.75	55.00	0	0	5
India in Pakistan 1997–98	3	3	0	30	21	10.00	75.00	0	0	3
Akai-Singer Champions Trophy in U.A.E. 1997–98	3	3	0	95	91	31.66	102.15	0	1	1
Sri Lanka in India 1997–98	3	2	1	88	82*	88.00	88.88	0	1	0
Silver Jubilee Independence Cup in Bangladesh 1997–98	5	5	0	258	95	51.60	112.17	0	3	6
Pepsi Triangular Series in India 1997–98	5	5	0	129	100	25.80	90.20	1	0	2
Coca-Cola Cup in U.A.E. 1997–98	5	5	0	435	143	87.00	100.46	2	1	0
Coca-Cola Triangular Series 1998	3	3	1	151	100*	75.50	96.17	1	0	0
Singer-Akai Nidahas Trophy in Sri Lanka 1998	5	4	0	263	128	65.75	112.87	1	2	2
Sahara 'Friendship' Cup in Canada 1998	1	1	0	77	77	77.00	70.64	0	1	0
India in Zimbabwe 1998–99	3	3	1	158	127*	79.00	100.63	1	0	1

	M	Inns	NO	Runs	HS	Avge	SR	100	50	Ct
Wills International Cup in Bangladesh 1998–99	2	2	0	149	141	74.50	104.92	1	0	2
Coca-Cola Champions Trophy in U.A.E. 1998–99	5	5	2	274	124*	91.33	109.60	2	0	1
India in New Zealand 1998–99	4	4	0	73	45	18.25	93.58	0	0	0
World Cup in England/Ireland/Netherlands/Scotland 1999	7	7	1	253	140*	42.16	90.03	1	0	2
Aiwa Cup in Sri Lanka 1999	3	3	0	171	120	57.00	73.70	1	0	0
Coca-Cola Singapore Challenge in Singapore 1999	3	3	0	125	85	41.66	87.41	0	1	0
New Zealand in India 1999–00	5	5	1	221	186*	55.25	101.84	1	0	2
Carlton & United Series in Australia 1999–00	8	8	0	198	93	24.75	76.15	0	1	7
South Africa in India 1999–00	5	5	0	274	122	54.80	88.10	1	1	1
Coca-Cola Cup in U.A.E. 1999–00	4	4	0	65	39	16.25	53.27	0	0	0
Asia Cup in Bangladesh 2000	3	3	0	154	93	51.33	102.66	0	1	1
ICC KnockOut in Kenya 2000–01	4	4	0	171	69	42.75	83.41	0	1	1
Coca-Cola Champions Trophy in U.A.E. 2000–01	5	5	0	179	101	35.80	77.82	1	1	0
Zimbabwe in India 2000–01	5	5	0	287	146	57.40	82.94	1	1	1
Australia in India 2000–01	5	5	0	280	139	56.00	120.17	1	1	2
Coca-Cola Cup in Zimbabwe 2001	5	5	3	282	122*	141.00	82.45	1	2	0
Standard Bank Tournament in South Africa 2001–02	7	6	0	342	146	57.00	82.40	2	0	1
England in India 2001–02	6	6	1	266	87*	53.20	93.99	0	2	3
India in West Indies 2002	2	2	1	99	65	99.00	86.08	0	0	0
NatWest Series in England 2002	7	7	1	337	113	56.16	93.09	2	0	0
ICC Champions Trophy in Sri Lanka 2002–03	5	4	2	39	16	19.50	44.82	0	0	1
India in New Zealand 2002–03	3	3	0	2	1	0.66	6.89	0	0	0
World Cup in Kenya/South Africa/Zimbabwe 2002–03	11	11	0	673	152	61.18	89.25	1	6	4
TVS Cup in India 2003–04	7	7	1	466	102	77.66	89.10	2	2	0
VB Series in Australia 2003–04	7	7	0	236	86	33.71	78.92	0	2	2
India in Pakistan 2003–04	5	5	0	213	141	42.60	90.25	1	0	2
Asia Cup in Sri Lanka 2004	6	6	1	281	82*	56.20	72.42	0	3	1
BCCI Platinum Jubilee Match in India 2004–05	1	1	0	16	16	16.00	94.11	0	0	0
India in Bangladesh 2004–05	2	2	0	66	47	33.00	89.18	0	0	0

	M	Inns	NO	Runs	HS	Avge	SR	100	50	Ct
Pakistan in India 2004–05	6	6	0	145	123	24.16	81.46	1	0	3
Sri Lanka in India 2005–06	6	6	1	231	93	46.20	87.16	0	2	3
South Africa in India 2005–06	4	4	0	36	30	9.00	40.00	0	0	0
India in Pakistan 2005–06	4	4	0	237	100	59.25	90.11	1	1	0
India in Sri Lanka 2006	1	1	1	2	2*	-	66.66	0	0	-
DLF Cup in Malaysia 2006–07	4	4	1	222	141*	74.00	80.14	1	1	1
ICC Champions Trophy in India 2006–07	3	3	0	74	35	24.66	66.07	0	0	2
India in South Africa 2006–07	4	4	0	93	55	23.25	58.12	0	1	3
West Indies in India 2006–07	4	4	1	191	100*	63.66	102.68	1	1	0
Sri Lanka in India 2006–07	3	2	0	55	54	27.50	79.71	0	1	2
ICC World Cup in West Indies 2006–07	3	3	1	64	57*	32.00	110.34	0	1	0
India in Ireland ODI Match, 2007	1	1	0	4	4	4.00	133.33	0	0	0
Future Cup in Ireland 2007	3	3	0	200	99	66.66	77.82	0	2	1
India in England 2007	7	7	0	374	99	53.42	85.77	0	4	0
Australia in India 2007–08	7	7	0	278	79	39.71	69.15	0	2	4
Pakistan in India 2007–08	5	5	0	259	99	51.80	101.96	0	2	0
Commonwealth Bank Series in Australia 2007–08	10	10	1	399	117*	44.33	85.25	1	2	2
England in India 2008–09	2	2	0	61	50	30.50	78.20	0	1	4
India in Sri Lanka 2008–09	3	3	0	18	7	6.00	48.64	0	0	2
India in New Zealand 2008–09	3	3	1	244	163*	122.00	108.44	1	1	0
Compaq Cup in Sri Lanka 2009	3	3	0	211	138	70.33	95.47	1	1	0
ICC Champions Trophy in South Africa 2009–10	2	1	0	8	8	8.00	57.14	0	0	1
Australia in India 2009–10	6	6	0	275	175	45.83	88.70	1	0	2
Sri Lanka in India 2009–10	4	4	1	216	96*	72.00	95.15	0	2	2
South Africa in India 2009–10	2	2	1	204	200*	204.00	134.21	1	0	0
India in South Africa 2010–11	2	2	0	31	24	15.50	56.36	0	0	0
World Cup in Bangladesh/India/Sri Lanka 2010–11	9	9	0	482	120	53.55	91.98	2	2	2
Commonwealth Bank Series in Australia 2011–12	7	7	0	143	48	20.42	82.65	0	0	3
Asia Cup in Bangladesh 2011–12	3	3	0	172	114	57.33	80.37	1	1	1

ODIs – batting by opponent

	M	Inns	NO	Runs	HS	Avge	SR	100	50	0
Australia	71	70	1	3077	175	44.59	84.74	9	15	2
Bangladesh	12	11	1	496	114	49.60	85.07	1	2	0
Bermuda	1	1	1	57	57*	–	196.55	0	1	0
England	37	37	4	1455	120	44.09	89.20	2	10	0
Ireland	2	2	0	42	38	21.00	71.18	0	0	0
Kenya	10	9	3	647	146	107.83	97.00	4	1	0
Namibia	1	1	0	152	152	152.00	100.66	1	0	0
Netherlands	2	2	0	79	52	39.50	84.04	0	1	0
New Zealand	42	41	3	1750	186*	46.05	95.36	5	8	4
Pakistan	69	67	4	2526	141	40.09	87.49	5	16	5
South Africa	57	57	1	2001	200*	35.73	76.31	5	8	1
Sri Lanka	84	80	9	3113	138	43.84	87.54	8	17	3
U.A.E.	2	2	0	81	63	40.50	79.41	0	1	0
West Indies	39	39	9	1573	141*	52.43	78.02	4	11	5
Zimbabwe	34	33	5	1377	146	49.17	91.55	5	5	0

ODIs – batting by country

	M	Inns	NO	Runs	HS	Avge	SR	100	50	0
Australia	47	46	3	1491	117*	34.67	75.26	1	10	1
Bangladesh	16	16	0	827	141	51.68	98.56	2	5	0
Canada	12	11	2	313	89*	34.77	67.02	0	3	1
England	26	26	2	1051	140*	43.79	88.39	3	4	1
India	164	160	15	6976	200*	48.11	88.40	20	38	5
Ireland	4	4	0	204	99	51.00	78.46	0	2	0
Kenya	4	4	0	171	69	42.75	83.41	0	1	0
Malaysia	4	4	1	222	141*	74.00	80.14	1	1	0
New Zealand	22	22	1	821	163*	39.09	97.39	1	5	3
Pakistan	13	13	0	480	141	36.92	88.72	2	1	3
Singapore	5	5	0	253	100	50.60	88.77	1	1	1
South Africa	40	38	0	1453	152	38.23	79.39	4	6	1
Sri Lanka	44	41	5	1531	138	42.52	81.87	5	6	1
U.A.E.	42	42	5	1778	143	48.05	92.79	7	7	1
West Indies	9	9	3	282	65*	47.00	90.38	0	3	1
Zimbabwe	11	11	4	573	127*	81.85	86.68	2	3	1

ODIs – batting by continent

	M	Inns	NO	Runs	HS	Avge	SR	100	50	0
Africa	55	53	4	2197	152	44.83	81.49	6	10	2
Americas	21	20	5	595	89*	39.66	76.37	0	6	2
Asia	288	281	26	12067	200*	47.32	88.60	38	59	11

Europe	30	30	2	1255	140*	44.82	86.61	3	6	1
Oceania	69	68	4	2312	163*	36.12	81.86	2	15	4

ODIs – batting home and away

	M	Inns	NO	Runs	HS	Avge	SR	100	50	0
home	164	160	15	6976	200*	48.11	88.40	20	38	5
away	147	146	10	5065	163*	37.24	81.73	12	24	8
neutral	152	146	16	6385	152	49.11	87.71	17	34	7

ODIs – batting by year

	M	Inns	NO	Runs	HS	Avge	SR	100	50	0
1989	1	1	0	0	0	0.00	0.00	0	0	1
1990	11	10	0	239	53	23.90	98.76	0	1	1
1991	14	14	2	417	62	34.75	74.46	0	4	1
1992	21	20	2	704	84	39.11	69.08	0	6	0
1993	18	17	4	319	82*	24.53	73.16	0	1	0
1994	25	25	2	1089	115	47.34	88.60	3	9	3
1995	12	12	1	444	112*	40.36	101.36	1	1	0
1996	32	32	2	1611	137	53.70	82.44	6	9	0
1997	39	36	3	1011	117	30.63	84.95	2	5	2
1998	34	33	4	1894	143	65.31	102.15	9	7	0
1999	22	22	2	843	186*	42.15	88.64	3	1	4
2000	34	34	0	1328	146	39.05	81.77	3	6	0
2001	17	16	3	904	146	69.53	91.31	4	3	1
2002	20	19	5	741	113	52.92	87.48	2	3	0
2003	21	21	1	1141	152	57.05	87.36	3	8	1
2004	21	21	1	812	141	40.60	80.07	1	5	1
2005	16	16	1	412	123	27.46	77.29	1	2	0
2006	16	16	2	628	141*	44.85	77.05	2	3	1
2007	33	32	2	1425	100*	47.50	85.58	1	13	3
2008	12	12	1	460	117*	41.81	84.24	1	3	1
2009	21	20	2	972	175	54.00	94.00	3	3	0
2010	2	2	1	204	200*	204.00	134.21	1	0	0
2011	11	11	0	513	120	46.63	88.60	2	2	0
2012	10	10	0	315	114	31.50	81.39	1	1	0

ODIs – batting by batting position

	M	Inns	NO	Runs	HS	Avge	SR	100	50	0
Number 1	47	47	2	1625	120	36.11	82.82	2	9	1
Number 2	293	293	21	13685	200*	50.31	88.71	43	66	11
Number 3	10	10	1	92	31	10.22	48.16	0	0	0
Number 4	61	61	8	2059	140*	38.84	77.08	4	15	5

Number 5	36	36	8	797	82*	28.46	81.07	0	5	3
Number 6	4	4	1	148	57*	49.33	134.54	0	1	0
Number 7	1	1	0	20	20	20.00	80.00	0	0	0

ODIs – batting by match innings

	M	Inns	NO	Runs	HS	Avge	SR	100	50	0
Batting first	221	220	15	9706	200*	47.34	84.34	32	44	5
Batting second	242	232	26	8720	175	42.33	88.44	17	52	15

ODIs – batting by result

	M	Inns	NO	Runs	HS	Avge	SR	100	50	0
Won match	234	231	34	11157	200*	56.63	90.31	33	59	8
Lost match	200	200	2	6585	175	33.25	79.86	14	35	11
Tied match	5	5	0	166	120	33.20	96.51	1	0	0
No result	24	16	5	518	105*	47.09	86.91	1	2	1

ODIs – batting by tournament

	M	Inns	NO	Runs	HS	Avge	SR	100	50	0
World Cup	45	44	4	2278	152	56.95	88.98	6	15	2
Asia Cup	23	21	2	971	114	51.10	85.47	2	7	0
Aus Tri Series (CB)	42	42	2	1377	117*	34.42	74.75	1	9	1
ICC Champions Trophy	16	14	2	441	141	36.75	78.75	1	1	0

ODIs – batting by tournament stage

	M	Inns	NO	Runs	HS	Avge	SR	100	50	0
Finals	40	39	5	1851	138	54.44	87.68	6	10	4
Semi-finals	8	8	0	317	85	39.62	72.87	0	3	0
Quarter-finals	4	4	0	263	141	65.75	90.06	1	1	0

ODIs – batting by number of teams in tournament

	M	Inns	NO	Runs	HS	Avge	SR	100	50	0
2 teams	200	196	17	7215	200*	40.30	86.57	14	40	11
3–4 teams	184	180	15	7917	146	47.98	86.42	28	35	7
5+ teams	79	76	9	3294	152	49.16	85.07	7	21	2

ODIs – batting by series stage

	M	Inns	NO	Runs	HS	Avge	SR	100	50	0
Only match in series	4	4	0	173	114	43.25	85.64	1	0	0
1st match in series	44	43	4	1324	127*	33.94	84.17	2	6	3

2nd match in series	44	43	8	1810	200*	51.71	94.22	3	10	3
3rd match in series	42	40	3	1385	163*	37.43	86.13	3	7	2
4th match in series	27	27	2	1043	123	41.72	84.11	3	7	1
5th match in series	23	23	0	1088	175	47.30	84.27	2	8	2
6th match in series	10	10	0	246	94	24.60	83.38	0	2	0
7th match in series	6	6	0	146	39	24.33	71.56	0	0	0

ODIs – batting by day/day-night match

	M	Inns	NO	Runs	HS	Avge	SR	100	50	0
Day match	255	248	24	9593	186*	42.82	86.31	21	56	13
Day-night match	208	204	17	8833	200*	47.23	86.15	28	40	7

ODIs – batting by captain

	M	Inns	NO	Runs	HS	Avge	SR	100	50	0
M Azharuddin	160	156	17	6270	143	45.10	87.69	18	33	7
MS Dhoni	65	64	3	2875	200*	47.13	89.31	8	12	2
R Dravid	53	52	6	2023	141*	43.97	82.20	4	14	3
SC Ganguly	101	99	9	4490	152	49.88	86.21	13	22	3
A Jadeja	2	2	0	44	33	22.00	107.31	0	0	0
A Kumble	1	1	0	68	68	68.00	86.07	0	1	0
V Sehwag	6	6	1	201	96*	40.20	75.84	0	2	0
RJ Shastri	1	1	0	1	1	1.00	33.33	0	0	0
K Srikkanth	1	1	0	0	0	0.00	0.00	0	0	1
SR Tendulkar	73	70	5	2454	186*	37.75	83.49	6	12	4

ODIs – batting as captain/as player

	M	Inns	NO	Runs	HS	Avge	SR	100	50	0
As captain	73	70	5	2454	186*	37.75	83.49	6	12	4
As player	390	382	36	15972	200*	46.16	86.67	43	84	16

ODIs – centuries

	Opponent	Venue	Season
200*	South Africa	Gwalior	2009–10
186*	New Zealand	Hyderabad	1999–00
175	Australia	Hyderabad-RG	2009–10
163*	New Zealand	Christchurch	2008–09
152	Namibia	Pietermaritzburg	2002–03
146	Zimbabwe	Jodhpur	2000–01
146	Kenya	Paarl	2001–02
143	Australia	Sharjah	1997–98
141*	West Indies	Kuala Lumpur	2006–07
141	Australia	Dhaka	1998–99

141	Pakistan	Rawalpindi	2003–04
140*	Kenya	Bristol	1999
139	Australia	Indore	2000–01
138	Sri Lanka	Colombo-RPS	2009–10
137	Sri Lanka	Delhi	1995–96
134	Australia	Sharjah	1997–98
128	Sri Lanka	Colombo-RPS	1997–98
127*	Kenya	Cuttack	1995–96
127*	Zimbabwe	Bulawayo	1998–99
124*	Zimbabwe	Sharjah	1998–99
123	Pakistan	Ahmedabad	2004–05
122*	West Indies	Harare	2001
122	South Africa	Vadodara	1999–00
120	Sri Lanka	Colombo-SSC	1999–00
120	England	Bangalore	2010–11
118*	Zimbabwe	Sharjah	1998–99
118	Pakistan	Sharjah	1995–96
117*	Australia	Sydney	2007–08
117	New Zealand	Bangalore	1996–97
115	New Zealand	Vadodara	1994–95
114	South Africa	Mumbai	1996–97
114	Bangladesh	Mirpur	2011–12
113	Sri Lanka	Bristol	2002
112*	Sri Lanka	Sharjah	1994–95
111	South Africa	Nagpur-J	2010–11
110	Australia	Colombo-RPS	1994–95
110	Sri Lanka	Colombo-RPS	1996–97
105*	England	Chester-le-Street	2002
105	West Indies	Jaipur	1994–95
104	Zimbabwe	Benoni	1996–97
102	New Zealand	Hyderabad	2003–04
101	Sri Lanka	Sharjah	2000–01
101	South Africa	Johannesburg	2001–02
100*	Kenya	Kolkata	1997–98
100*	West Indies	Vadodara	2006–07
100	Pakistan	Singapore-P	1995–96
100	Australia	Kanpur	1997–98
100	Australia	Gwalior	2003–04
100	Pakistan	Peshawar	2005–06

ODIs – bowlers dismissing him most often

	Times	M
SM Pollock	9	28
B Lee	9	30
WPUJC Vaas	9	49
GD McGrath	7	23
HH Streak	7	26
CA Walsh	6	16
Azhar Mahmood	6	23
Abdul Razzaq	6	26
KMDN Kulasekara	5	16
DNT Zoysa	5	17
CRD Fernando	5	17
Shoaib Akhtar	5	19
DW Fleming	5	20
AA Donald	5	26
Aaqib Javed	5	30
M Muralitharan	5	47
ST Jayasuriya	5	71
DK Morrison	4	12
AC Cummins	4	14
TM Moody	4	15
NW Bracken	4	17
PS de Villiers	4	17
SL Malinga	4	18
A Flintoff	4	19
Waqar Younis	4	23
CZ Harris	4	30
JH Kallis	4	32
DR Tuffey	3	7
TJ Friend	3	9
JM Anderson	3	11
Mohammad Sami	3	12
CR Matthews	3	12
SA Thomson	3	14
GP Wickramasinghe	3	18
DJ Nash	3	18
GR Larsen	3	19
DL Vettori	3	20
MG Johnson	3	21
L Klusener	3	21
Shoaib Malik	3	24

Wasim Akram	3	24
WJ Cronje	3	32
SR Waugh	3	33

ODIs – how he was dismissed

	Times	Dis	%
Bowled	68	411	16.54
Caught wicketkeeper	72	411	17.52
Caught fielder	186	411	45.26
LBW	39	411	9.49
Run out	34	411	8.27
Stumped	11	411	2.68
Hit wicket	1	411	0.24

ODIs – batting partners

	Inns	Unb	Runs	Best	Avge	100	50
SC Ganguly	176	3	8228	258	47.56	26	29
V Sehwag	114	2	4386	182	39.16	13	18
RS Dravid	98	5	4117	331	44.26	11	14
M Azharuddin	78	6	3514	175	48.80	8	19
AD Jadeja	41	4	2111	176	57.05	9	8
Yuvraj Singh	46	2	1558	138	35.40	3	9
G Gambhir	51	0	1511	173	29.62	4	5
SV Manjrekar	25	0	1109	102	44.36	1	8
NS Sidhu	36	0	1100	231	30.55	1	6
VVS Laxman	23	1	1056	199	48.00	4	0
M Prabhakar	25	2	942	161	40.95	2	4
MS Dhoni	19	4	928	135*	61.86	5	1
VG Kambli	19	2	704	164*	41.41	2	1
IK Pathan	12	0	647	164	53.91	2	4
V Kohli	10	0	603	148	60.30	2	3
D Mongia	12	1	556	99	50.54	0	5
SK Raina	5	0	354	137	70.80	1	2
NR Mongia	13	1	331	89	27.58	0	2
KD Karthik	6	1	326	194	65.20	1	1
Kapil Dev	12	2	325	76	32.50	0	2
M Kaif	11	1	318	102	31.80	1	1
HK Badani	6	1	280	135*	56.00	1	1
RV Uthappa	7	0	242	94	34.57	0	2
RR Singh	7	0	234	100	33.42	1	1
V Rathour	7	0	195	59	27.85	0	2
RJ Shastri	5	0	195	76	39.00	0	2
S Ramesh	4	0	154	75	38.50	0	1

PK Amre	6	0	152	56	25.33	0	2
WV Raman	4	0	143	90	35.75	0	1
J Srinath	6	1	129	41	25.80	0	0
RG Sharma	1	0	123	123	123.00	1	0
K Srikkanth	4	0	120	62	30.00	0	1
SB Joshi	4	0	94	57	23.50	0	1
YK Pathan	2	0	92	81	46.00	0	1
Harbhajan Singh	2	0	79	78	39.50	0	1
HH Kanitkar	1	0	67	67	67.00	0	1
RK Chauhan	2	0	59	48	29.50	0	0
A Kumble	7	1	54	19	9.00	0	0
SB Somasunder	2	0	49	30	24.50	0	0
RS Sodhi	2	1	37	23*	37.00	0	0
JP Yadav	1	0	35	35	35.00	0	0
RA Jadeja	1	0	32	32	32.00	0	0
S Sriram	2	0	32	22	16.00	0	0
KS More	3	0	24	17	8.00	0	0
M Vijay	2	0	24	21	12.00	0	0
AB Agarkar	4	0	23	9	5.75	0	0
JJ Martin	1	0	21	21	21.00	0	0
PA Patel	1	0	16	16	16.00	0	0
V Yadav	2	0	12	11	6.00	0	0
SS Das	1	0	8	8	8.00	0	0
V Dahiya	1	0	7	7	7.00	0	0
A Ratra	1	0	4	4	4.00	0	0
SS Karim	1	0	3	3	3.00	0	0
RP Singh	1	0	1	1	1.00	0	0
W Jaffer	1	0	0	0	0.00	0	0

ODIs - BOWLING

	M	Overs	Mdns	Runs	Wkts	Avge	Econ	SR	5
Overall record	463	1342.2	24	6850	154	44.48	5.10	52.20	2

ODIs - best bowling

	Opponent	Venue	Season
5-32	Australia	Kochi	1997-98
5-50	Pakistan	Kochi	2004-05
4-34	West Indies	Sharjah	1991-92
4-38	Australia	Dhaka	1998-99
4-54	Bangladesh	Dhaka	2004-05
4-56	South Africa	Faridabad	1999-00
3-21	U.A.E	Dambulla	2004
3-28	Pakistan	Colombo-RPS	2004

3–34	New Zealand	Napier	1998–99
3–35	Australia	Margao	2000–01
3–35	Bangladesh	Colombo-SSC	2004
3–36	West Indies	Chennai	1994–95
3–43	Sri Lanka	Rajkot	1993–94
3–45	Pakistan	Dhaka	1997–98
2–8	Bangladesh	Mumbai	1997–98
2–10	South Africa	Belfast	2007
2–24	Bangladesh	Dhaka	1999–00
2–25	West Indies	Cuttack	2006–07
2–27	South Africa	Durban	2001–02
2–28	Kenya	Durban	2002–03
2–29	New Zealand	Delhi	1994–95
2–29	West Indies	Dhaka	1998–99
2–31	West Indies	Kanpur	1994–95
2–32	South Africa	Nairobi	2000–01
2–32	Pakistan	Guwahati	2007–08
2–34	Sri Lanka	Kolkata	1995–96
2–39	Sri Lanka	Pune	1990–91
2–40	Pakistan	Sharjah	1995–96
2–40	Sri Lanka	Colombo-RPS	2004
2–41	Zimbabwe	Colombo-RPS	2002–03
2–44	Sri Lanka	Dhaka	1999–00
2–49	New Zealand	Pune	1995–96
2–61	Pakistan	Chennai	1996–97

ODIs – how he took his wickets

	Times	Wkts	%
Bowled	31	154	20.13
Caught wicketkeeper	15	154	9.74
Caught fielder	69	154	44.80
LBW	17	154	11.04
Stumped	22	154	14.29
Hit wicket	0	154	0.00

ODIs – CAPTAINCY

	M	W	L	Tied	NR	Toss won	Toss lost	TW bat	TW bowl	TL bat	TL bowl
Overall record	73	23	43	1	6	44	29	25	19	15	14

ODIs – results as captain

Start date	Opponent	Venue	Toss	Decision	Result
28/8/1996	Sri Lanka	Colombo-RPS	Won	Bat	Lost

1/9/1996	Zimbabwe	Colombo-SSC	Won	Bowl	Won
6/9/1996	Australia	Colombo-SSC	Lost	Bowl	Lost
16/9/1996	Pakistan	Toronto	Won	Bowl	Won
17/9/1996	Pakistan	Toronto	Lost	Bowl	Lost
18/9/1996	Pakistan	Toronto	Won	Bat	Won
21/9/1996	Pakistan	Toronto	Won	Bowl	Lost
23/9/1996	Pakistan	Toronto	Lost	Bat	Lost
17/10/1996	South Africa	Hyderabad	Lost	Bat	Lost
21/10/1996	Australia	Bangalore	Lost	Bat	Won
23/10/1996	South Africa	Jaipur	Won	Bowl	Lost
29/10/1996	South Africa	Rajkot	Won	Bat	Lost
3/11/1996	Australia	Mohali	Lost	Bowl	Won
6/11/1996	South Africa	Mumbai	Won	Bat	Won
14/12/1996	South Africa	Mumbai	Won	Bat	Won
23/1/1997	South Africa	Bloemfontein	Lost	Bat	Lost
27/1/1997	Zimbabwe	Paarl	Lost	Bat	Tied
2/2/1997	South Africa	Port Elizabeth	Won	Bat	Lost
4/2/1997	South Africa	East London	Won	Bat	Lost
7/2/1997	Zimbabwe	Centurion	Won	Bat	Lost
9/2/1997	Zimbabwe	Benoni	Won	Bowl	Won
12/2/1997	South Africa	Durban	Won	Bat	No Res
13/2/1997	South Africa	Durban	Lost	Bat	Lost
15/2/1997	Zimbabwe	Bulawayo	Lost	Bowl	Lost
26/4/1997	West Indies	Port-of-Spain	Won	Bat	Lost
27/4/1997	West Indies	Port-of-Spain	Won	Bowl	Won
30/4/1997	West Indies	Arnos Vale	Won	Bowl	Lost
3/5/1997	West Indies	Bridgetown	Lost	Bowl	Lost
14/5/1997	New Zealand	Bangalore	Lost	Bat	Won
17/5/1997	Sri Lanka	Mumbai	Won	Bat	Lost
21/5/1997	Pakistan	Chennai	Lost	Bat	Lost
18/7/1997	Sri Lanka	Colombo-RPS	Lost	Bowl	Lost
20/7/1997	Pakistan	Colombo-SSC	Won	Bowl	No Res
24/7/1997	Bangladesh	Colombo-SSC	Won	Bowl	Won
26/7/1997	Sri Lanka	Colombo-RPS	Won	Bat	Lost
17/8/1997	Sri Lanka	Colombo-RPS	Won	Bowl	Lost
20/8/1997	Sri Lanka	Colombo-RPS	Lost	Bowl	Lost
23/8/1997	Sri Lanka	Colombo-SSC	Lost	Bowl	No Res
24/8/1997	Sri Lanka	Colombo-SSC	Won	Bowl	Lost
13/9/1997	Pakistan	Toronto	Lost	Bowl	Won
14/9/1997	Pakistan	Toronto	Lost	Bat	Won
17/9/1997	Pakistan	Toronto	Won	Bowl	No Res
18/9/1997	Pakistan	Toronto	Lost	Bowl	Won
20/9/1997	Pakistan	Toronto	Won	Bowl	Won
21/9/1997	Pakistan	Toronto	Lost	Bowl	Lost

28/9/1997	Pakistan	Hyderabad	Won	Bat	Lost
30/9/1997	Pakistan	Karachi	Lost	Bat	Won
2/10/1997	Pakistan	Lahore	Lost	Bowl	Lost
11/12/1997	England	Sharjah	Won	Bowl	Lost
14/12/1997	Pakistan	. Sharjah	Won	Bat	Lost
16/12/1997	West Indies	Sharjah	Won	Bowl	Lost
22/12/1997	Sri Lanka	Guwahati	Won	Bowl	Won
25/12/1997	Sri Lanka	Indore	Lost	Bat	No Res
28/12/1997	Sri Lanka	Margao	Won	Bat	Lost
23/8/1999	Australia	Galle	Won	Bat	Lost
25/8/1999	Sri Lanka	Colombo-RPS	Won	Bat	Lost
29/8/1999	Sri Lanka	Colombo-SSC	Won	Bat	Won
4/9/1999	Zimbabwe	Singapore	Lost	Bowl	Won
7/9/1999	West Indies	Singapore	Won	Bat	No Res
8/9/1999	West Indies	Singapore	Lost	Bowl	Lost
5/11/1999	New Zealand	Rajkot	Won	Bowl	Lost
8/11/1999	New Zealand	Hyderabad	Won	Bat	Won
11/11/1999	New Zealand	Gwalior	Won	Bat	Won
14/11/1999	New Zealand	Guwahati	Won	Bowl	Lost
17/11/1999	New Zealand	Delhi	Lost	Bat	Won
10/1/2000	Pakistan	Brisbane	Won	Bat	Lost
12/1/2000	Australia	Melbourne	Lost	Bat	Lost
14/1/2000	Australia	Sydney	Won	Bat	Lost
21/1/2000	Pakistan	Hobart	Won	Bowl	Lost
25/1/2000	Pakistan	Adelaide	Won	Bat	Won
26/1/2000	Australia	Adelaide	Lost	Bat	Lost
28/1/2000	Pakistan	Perth	Lost	Bat	Lost
30/1/2000	Australia	Perth	Won	Bat	Lost

INDEX